FEMINIST
INTERPRETATIONS
OF
FRIEDRICH NIETZSCHE

D1521855

RE-READING THE CANON

NANCY TUANA, GENERAL EDITOR

This series consists of edited collections of essays, some original and some previously published, offering feminist re-interpretations of the writings of major figures in the Western philosophical tradition. Devoted to the work of a single philosopher, each volume contains essays covering the full range of the philosopher's thought and representing the diversity of approaches now being used by feminist critics.

Already published:

Nancy Tuana, ed., *Feminist Interpretations of Plato* (1994)

Margaret A. Simons, ed., *Feminist Interpretations of Simone de Beauvoir* (1995)

Bonnie Honig, ed., *Feminist Interpretations of Hannah Arendt* (1995)

Patricia Jagentowicz Mills, ed., *Feminist Interpretations of G. W. F. Hegel* (1996)

Maria J. Falco, ed., *Feminist Interpretations of Mary Wollstonecraft* (1996)

Susan J. Hekman, ed., *Feminist Interpretations of Michel Foucault* (1996)

Nancy J. Holland, ed., *Feminist Interpretations of Jacques Derrida* (1997)

Robin May Schott, ed., *Feminist Interpretations of Immanuel Kant* (1997)

Céline Léon and Sylvia Walsh, eds., *Feminist Interpretations of Søren Kierkegaard* (1997)

Cynthia Freeland, ed., *Feminist Interpretations of Aristotle* (1998)

Kelly Oliver and Marilyn Pearsall, eds., *Feminist Interpretations of Friedrich Nietzsche* (1998)

FEMINIST INTERPRETATIONS OF FRIEDRICH NIETZSCHE

EDITED BY
KELLY OLIVER
AND
MARILYN PEARSALL

THE PENNSYLVANIA STATE UNIVERSITY PRESS
UNIVERSITY PARK, PENNSYLVANIA

Library of Congress Cataloging-in-Publication Data

Feminist interpretations of Friedrich Nietzsche / edited by Kelly
   Oliver and Marilyn Pearsall.

      p.   cm. — (Re-reading the canon)
      Includes bibliographical references and index.
      ISBN 0-271-01763-5 (cloth : alk. paper)
      ISBN 0-271-01764-3 (pbk. : alk. paper)
      1. Nietzsche, Friedrich Wilhelm, 1844–1900.   2. Woman (Philosophy).
   3. Feminist Theory.   I. Oliver, Kelly, 1958–   .   II. Pearsall, Marilyn.
   III. Series.
   B3317.F45   1998
   193—dc21   97-33640
                                                                  CIP

It is the policy of The Pennsylvania State University Press to use acid-free paper for the
first printing of all clothbound books. Publications on uncoated stock satisfy the mini-
mum requirements of American National Standard for Information Sciences—
Permanence of Paper for Printed Library Materials, ANSI Z39.48-1992.

Contents

Preface

Take into your hands any history of philosophy text. You will find compiled therein the "classics" of modern philosophy. Since these texts are often designed for use in undergraduate classes, the editor is likely to offer an introduction in which the reader is informed that these selections represent the perennial questions of philosophy. The student is to assume that she or he is about to explore the timeless wisdom of the greatest minds of Western philosophy. No one calls attention to the fact that the philosophers are all men.

Though women are omitted from the canons of philosophy, these texts inscribe the nature of woman. Sometimes the philosopher speaks directly about woman, delineating her proper role, her abilities and inabilities, her desires. Other times the message is indirect—a passing remark hinting at women's emotionality, irrationality, unreliability.

This process of definition occurs in far more subtle ways when the central concepts of philosophy—reason and justice, those characteristics that are taken to define us as human—are associated with traits historically identified with masculinity. If the "man" of reason must learn to control or overcome traits identified as feminine—the body, the emotions, the passions—then the realm of rationality will be one reserved primarily for men,[1] with grudging entrance to those few women who are capable of transcending their femininity.

Feminist philosophers have begun to look critically at the canonized texts of philosophy and have concluded that the discourses of philosophy are not gender-neutral. Philosophical narratives do not offer a universal perspective, but rather privilege some experiences and beliefs over others. These experiences and beliefs permeate all philosophical theories whether they be aesthetic or epistemological, moral or metaphysical. Yet this fact has often been neglected by those studying the traditions of philosophy. Given the history of canon formation in Western philosophy, the perspective most likely to be privileged is that of upper-class, white males. Thus, to be fully aware of the impact of gender biases, it is imperative that we re-read the canon with attention to the ways in which philosophers' assumptions concerning gender are embedded within their theories.

This new series, *Re-Reading the Canon*, is designed to foster this process of reevaluation. Each volume will offer feminist analyses of the theories of a selected philosopher. Since feminist philosophy is not monolithic in method or content, the essays are also selected to illustrate the variety of perspectives within feminist criticism and highlight some of the controversies within feminist scholarship.

In this series, feminist lenses will be focused on the canonical texts of Western philosophy, both those authors who have been part of the traditional canon, as well as those philosophers whose writings have more recently gained attention within the philosophical community. A glance at the lists of volumes in the series will reveal an immediate gender bias of the canon: Arendt, Aristotle, de Beauvoir, Derrida, Descartes, Foucault, Hegel, Hume, Kant, Locke, Marx, Mill, Nietzsche, Plato, Rousseau, Wittgenstein, Wollstonecraft. There are all too few women included, and those few who do appear have been added only recently. In creating this series, it is not my intention to reify the current canon of philosophical thought. What is and is not included within the canon during a particular historical period is a result of many factors. Although no canonization of texts will include all philosophers, no canonization of texts that exclude all but a few women can offer an accurate representation of the history of the discipline as women have been philosophers since the ancient period.[2]

I share with many feminist philosophers and other philosophers writing from the margins of philosophy the concern that the current canonization of philosophy be transformed. Although I do not accept the position that the current canon has been formed exclusively by power relations, I do believe that this canon represents only a selective history of the tradition. I share the view of Michael Bérubé that "canons are at once the location, the index, and the record of the struggle for cultural representation; like any other hegemonic formation, they must be continually reproduced anew and are continually contested."[3]

The process of canon transformation will require the recovery of "lost" texts and a careful examination of the reasons such voices have been silenced. Along with the process of uncovering women's philosophical history, we must also begin to analyze the impact of gender ideologies upon the process of canonization. This process of recovery and examination must occur in conjunction with careful attention to the concept of a canon of authorized texts. Are we to dispense with the notion of a tradition of excellence embodied in a canon of authorized texts? Or, rather than abandon the whole idea of a canon, do we instead encourage a reconstruction of a canon of those texts that inform a common culture?

This series is designed to contribute to this process of canon transformation by offering a re-reading of the current philosophical canon. Such a re-reading shifts our attention to the ways in which woman and the role of the feminine is constructed within the texts of philosophy. A question we must keep in front of us during this process of re-reading is whether a philosopher's socially inherited prejudices concerning woman's nature and role are independent of her or his larger philosophical framework. In asking this question attention must be paid to the ways in which the definitions of central philosophical concepts implicitly include or exclude gendered traits.

This type of reading strategy is not limited to the canon, but can be applied to all texts. It is my desire that this series reveal the importance of this type of critical reading. Paying attention to the workings of gender within the texts of philosophy will make visible the complexities of the inscription of gender ideologies.

Notes

1. More properly, it is a realm reserved for a group of privileged males, since the texts also inscribe race and class biases that thereby omit certain males from participation.

2. Mary Ellen Waithe's multivolume series, *A History of Women Philosophers* (Boston: M. Nijhoff, 1987), attests to this presence of women.

3. Michael Bérubé, *Marginal Forces/Cultural Centers: Tolson, Pynchon, and the Politics of the Canon* (Ithaca: Cornell University Press, 1992), 4–5.

Acknowledgments

Sarah Kofman, "Baubô: Theological Perversion and Fetishism," trans. Tracy B. Strong, is reprinted by permission of the translator and The University of Chicago Press from Michael A. Gillespie and Tracy B. Strong, eds., *Nietzsche's New Seas: Explorations in Philosophy, Aesthetics, and Politics*. Copyright © 1988 by The University of Chicago.

Jacques Derrida, "The Question of Style," altered selection and retranslation of the essay by this title originally published with the permission of the author in David B. Allison, ed., *The New Nietzsche* (MIT Press, 1985), done in gratitude to Jacques Derrida by the translator, Ruben Berezdivin, who holds the copyright.

Kelly Oliver, "Woman as Truth in Nietzsche's Writing," is reprinted by permission of the author and publisher from *Social Theory and Practice*, Vol. 10, No. 2 (Summer 1984), 185–89.

Luce Irigary, "Veiled Lips," trans. Sara Speidel, is reprinted by permission of Editions de Minuit from *Mississippi Review*, Vol. 11, No. 3 (1983): 98–119.

Tamsin Lorraine, "Nietzsche and Feminism: Transvaluing Women in *Thus Spake Zarathustra*," is reprinted by permission of the author and Scholars Press from *International Studies in Philosophy*, Vol. 26, No. 3 (1994), 13–22. Copyright © 1994 by Scholars Press.

Kathleen Marie Higgins, "Gender in *The Gay Science*," is reprinted by permission of the author and The Johns Hopkins University Press from *Philosophy and Literature*, Vol. 19, No. 2 (1995), 227–47. Copyright © 1995 by The Johns Hopkins University Press.

Jean Graybeal, "*Ecco Homo:* Abjection and 'the Feminine,' " is reprinted by permission of Indiana University Press from *Language and "the Feminine" in Nietzsche and Heidegger*. Copyright © 1990 by Indiana University Press.

Linda Singer, "Nietzschean Mythologies: The Inversion of Value and the War against Women," is reprinted by permission of the publisher from *Soundings*, Vol. 66, No. 3 (1983), 281–95.

Maudemarie Clark, "Nietzsche's Misogyny," is reprinted by permission of the author and Scholars Press from *International Studies in Philosophy*, Vol. 26, No. 3 (1994), 3–12. Copyright © 1994 by Scholars Press.

Lynne Tirrell, "Sexual Dualism and Women's Self-Creation: On the Advantages and Disadvantages of Reading Nietzsche for Feminists," is reprinted by permission of the University Press of Virginia from Peter J. Burgard, ed., *Nietzsche and the Feminine*. Copyright © 1994 by University Press of Virginia.

Debra B. Bergoffen, "Nietzsche Was No Feminist . . . ," is reprinted by permission of the author and Scholars Press from *International Studies in Philosophy*, Vol. 265, No. 3 (1994), 23–32. Copyright © 1994 by Scholars Press.

Daniel W. Conway, "The Slave Revolt in Epistemology," is reprinted by permission of the author and Routledge from Paul Patton, ed., *Nietzsche, Feminism and Political Theory*, pp. 110–29. Copyright © 1993 by Routledge. And "*Circulus Vitiosus Deus?* The Dialectical Logic of Feminist Standpoint Theory," in *Journal of Social Philosophy* 28, no. 1 (Spring 1997): 62–76.

Ofelia Schutte, "Nietzsche's Politics," is reprinted by permission of the publisher from the *Journal of the British Society for Phenomenology*, Vol. 14, No. 2 (May 1983), 139–57.

David Owen, "Nietzsche's Squandered Seductions: Feminism, the Body, and the Politics of Genealogy," is reprinted by permission of Avebury Publishing Limited from Keith Ansell-Pearson and Howard Caygill, eds., *The Fate of the New Nietzsche*. Copyright © 1993 by Avebury Publishing Limited.

Introduction:
Why Feminists Read Nietzsche

Kelly Oliver and Marilyn Pearsall

Feminists have a varied relationship to the philosophy of Friedrich Nietzsche. His sharp, dramatic, and often ironic style make it difficult for women reading his texts to ignore his frequent polemical references to women and femininity. Yet, until relatively recently, Nietzsche scholars did ignore his comments about women. Most Nietzsche scholars followed one of Nietzsche's most famous commentators, Walter Kaufmann, in dismissing his comments on women as unfortunate products of his time and irrelevant to his philosophy. Within the last twenty years, however, philosophers are no longer ignoring Nietzsche's remarks on women and femininity. Debates about the figure of women in Nietzsche's texts have become central to Nietzsche scholarship as well as feminist philosophy. Today it takes an act of willed ignorance to analyze any one of Nietzsche's texts without confronting the question of the role of woman or femininity therein. Some philosophers have even suggested that Nietzsche's philosophy cannot be understood or analyzed apart from his remarks on women.

Nietzsche has the reputation of being a virulent misogynist—so why are feminists interested in his philosophy? The essays in this collection represent some of the most important work done to date on this question. These essays represent different positions on whether Nietzsche's reputation of misogyny is deserved, how to diagnose his remarks about women, and whether his philosophy can be useful to feminist theories.

In general, feminists take two approaches to the question of Nietzsche and woman. First, many debates have focused on how to interpret Nietzsche's remarks about women and femininity. Are all of Nietzsche's comments about women to be read literally, or is he being ironic, perhaps even parodying and challenging derogatory stereotypes about women? Second, is his philosophy useful to feminist theory? Can we separate his philosophy from his seemingly derogatory remarks about women? Can feminists use his criticisms of truth, objectivity, reason, and the autonomous subject, to challenge the exclusion of women from the history of philosophy? What can feminists gain from reading Nietzsche?

In this introduction, we shall discuss some of the elements of Nietzsche's philosophy that attract feminists, thereby suggesting some of the ways that feminist philosophy has gained from reading Nietzsche. In addition to the question, What does Nietzsche offer to feminist philosophers? we shall take up the question, What does feminist criticism offer to Nietzsche scholarship? Next, we shall detail the ways in which the various articles in this collection engage with the issues of woman, feminism, and Nietzsche's writing,

As some of the essays in this collection indicate, feminists' criticisms of the history of philosophy share important elements with Nietzsche's criticisms of philosophy. Many feminist philosophers have pointed out that philosophy has traditionally been written by men who promote specific values over others in the name of objectivity and truth. Traditionally, philosophers have valued mind over body, culture over nature, reason over irrationality, truth over illusion, and good over evil. Women, femininity, and maternity have been associated with body, nature, irrationality, illusion, and even evil. Because of the associations among women, femininity, maternity, and nature or irrationality, discussions of women and femininity have been topics traditionally excluded from serious consideration by philosophers. Many feminists have challenged the traditional associations among women and irrationality and evil by questioning the supposed objectivity of philosophy. They point out that philosophy has been written by men about men and that it can only pretend to be objective. In other words, what philosophers have described as human experience really only represents the experience of men, more specifically a subset of men who have certain privileges accorded by their positions in society.

Feminists have taken various approaches to challenge the male bias in philsophy. Some feminists have argued that what has passed for objectivity and truth must be reexamined and that only when different people are involved in philosophy can it hope to become objective or speak the truth about human experience. Other feminists have maintained that all objectivity or truth result from certain perspectives and that it is deceptive to discuss the truth apart from particular contexts. In his writings, Nietzsche makes similar criticisms of objectivity and truth. He argues that all truth is perspectival; every truth comes from a particular perspective. He maintains that objectivity in the sense of a detached observation or a perspectiveless truth is impossible. He even suggests that perhaps the most objective truth would include all different perspectives.

In addition, Nietzsche discusses the ways in which some truths and values develop out of particular situations to benefit certain groups of people. In *On the Genealogy of Morals*, for example, he describes values that give priority to mind over body as the result of resentment and cruelty. There, he also suggests that these values cause us to be weak and accept suffering and guilt. In this work, and in others, Nietzsche inverts the priority given to mind over body. Since women have been identified with the body, and since it is the erasure of differences between bodies that make the illusions of objectivity possible, Nietzsche's emphasis on the importance of the body seems promising for feminist philosophy. Also, the methods that Nietzsche employs in order to diagnose why some things are valued over others could be useful to feminist philosophers trying to analyze why women, femininity, and maternity have been devalued by, or excluded from, traditional philosophy.

Nietzsche challenges the hierarchy of reason over irrationality by claiming that our preference for reason, or specifically the logic of associating cause and effect, is a product of the grammar of language. He calls reason in language a "deceptive old witch." The way that we talk about the world is not just a reflection of the world, but actually creates our sense of the reality of the world. In his early essay, "On Truth and Lie in the Ultramoral Sense," Nietzsche argues that words are not just reflections of things; rather they pick out, even create, some things at the expense of others. The notion that language creates rather than merely reflects reality holds out the promise to feminists that we can not only diagnose sexism, patriarchy, and women's "inferiority" as creations rather than natural facts but also use language differently in order to create a new nonsexist reality.

In addition to his criticism of reason, Nietzsche brings irrational elements back into philosophy. He is famous for his praise of the Greek god Dionysus and his attempts to envision a more Dionysian philosophy. Dionysus was the god of fertility and wine, associated with passion and intoxication. Insofar as the body and irrational passions have been associated with women, Nietzsche's revaluation of bodily passions could also revalue women. One question for Nietzsche's feminist readers, a question raised in this collection, is whether or not Nietzsche's attempt to return the body and passions to philosophy continues to exclude women. Are all of the bodies that he brings back into the focus of philosophers the bodies of men? What is the place of women's bodies in Nietzsche's writings? While Nietzsche challenges traditional hierarchies between mind and body, reason and irrationality, nature and culture, truth and fiction—hierarchies that have been used to degraade and exclude women—his remarks about women and his use of feminine and maternal metaphors throughout his writings confound attempts simply to proclaim Nietzsche a champion of feminism or women.

Although we can read Nietzsche, as he has been read for decades, without attending to his remarks about women and his use of metaphors of femininity and maternity, a reader on the lookout for such metaphors and remarks will soon notice that they are everywhere in Nietzsche's writings. He uses gendered metaphors and categories in all of his texts, metaphors of pregnancy, castration, effeminancy, emasculation, gestation, birth, sexual potency, impotence, and so forth. Once we realize this gendering in Nietzsche's texts, it is difficult to interpret his philosophy without attending to these remarks and metaphors. If Nietzsche often criticizes certain types for being emasculated or effeminate and he often praises others for being pregnant or virile, don't we have to interpret what he means by masculine and feminine, maternal and paternal?

Finally, even one of his contemporaries, Lou Andreas-Salomé, identifies Nietzsche's own writing as feminine. Salomé says that there is something feminine in Nietzsche's "spiritual nature" and that he considered genius to be feminine genius.[1] Today, Nietzsche's most famous critic, Jacques Derrida, takes a similar approach to Nietzsche's writings when he suggests that Nietzsche performs the "feminine operation." The feminine quality of Nietzsche's philosophy is a highly contested yet critical issue in Nietzsche scholarship and feminist philosophy.

Nietzsche's philosophy and its feminist engagements pose some of the most difficult and central problems for contemporary feminist philosophers: What is truth? Is objectivity possible? What are the political and cultural motivations for certain identifications of truth and objectivity? Why do we value masculine and devalue feminine? What is the relationship between feminist criticisms and the history of philosophy? What is the role of the body and sexual difference in philosophy? What is feminine philosophy? What is feminist philosophy? If there is a feminine philosophy, can men write in feminine ways? To whom does the category *woman* refer? Is there a homogeneous group that we can call women? Does feminism require identity politics, identifying a particular group called women? These are among the questions addressed in this volume through an engagement with Nietzsche's philosophy.

Nietzsche's Use of Woman

A tenet of contemporary feminist philosophy is that women and the feminine have been excluded from traditional philosophy, which is characterized as masculinist or phallocentric. It is with respect to this canonical exclusion of femininity, and maternity, that Nietzsche's texts have elicited much recent philosophical interest. How do feminists reconcile his apparent woman-hating aphorisms with the plethora of female figurations that "haunt" his writings? Far from evading and ignoring femininity and maternity, as other canonical philosophers do, Nietzsche seems compelled to speak of them. His texts abound with references to women, the feminine, and specifically to feminists themselves. He continually deploys woman as trope—for life, for art, and for truth.

His texts are replete with maternal metaphors and with scenarios of female figurations, such as Ariadne and Baubô. Jacques Derrida comments on: "the manifold typology in his work, its horde of mothers, daughters, sisters, old maids, wives, governesses, prostitutes, virgins, grandmothers, big and little girls."[2] Nietzsche not only acknowledges a manifold typology of women and the feminine, but frequently poses the riddle of femininity, or the enigma of woman. Instead of imposing on feminist readers a single philosophical construction, his work continually problematizes the question of women and the feminne. From a feminist perspective, therefore, Nietzsche's writings are of particular interest.

Sarah Kofman's landmark essay, "Baubô: Theological Perversion and Fetishism," refers to the multiplicity of women in Nietzsche's texts to claim that there is not an essentializing woman (*das Weib an sich*) in his discourse. Kofman's project is to save Nietzsche's texts for feminists. She does this by referring to the rhetorical strategies in them, especially his metaphors. She finds an affirmation of women and the feminine in his apparent misogyny. For example, she reads his metaphors of higher/lower as perspectival rather than hierarchical since they apply to women as well as men. She contrasts the Circe of philosophers "who has reasons to show herself" with the affirmative woman, Baubô.

Kofman refers to the ascetic ideal as the theological perversion of nature and life. By contrast, Baubô is the signifier for life and fecundity in Nietzsche's writings. The mythological figure to whom he refers, Baubô, by raising her skirts makes Demeter laugh even while the goddess is mourning the loss of her daughter, Persephone. Baubô is associated with the god of life and fecundity, Dionysus. As a Dionysian figure, she becomes, according to Kofman, Nietzsche's "affirmative woman."

Responding to Nietzsche's apparent misogyny, Kofman asks: "What is it in Nietzsche that leads him to judge women as he does?" She notes the severity of his well-known "maxims and arrows" on women, which appear to contrast with his positive figuration of Baubô. Kofman attributes this structuring ambivalence to the ambivalence Nietzsche displays toward the maternal body. This self-conscious restraint on his perspectivism, she claims, limits the pretense of his speaking the "truth" about women. Yet Kofman leaves us with another question: "Does it still make sense to speak of misogyny in Nietzsche?"

Jacques Derrida's "The Question of Style" was first published in *Nietzsche aujourd'hui* in 1973, the same year that Kofman first delivered her lecture on Baubô. Derrida, like Kofman, identifies various types of women in Nietzsche's texts. In this selection, Derrida suggests that woman is a metaphor for truth in Nietzsche's writings; more specifically, woman is a metaphor for the untruth of truth. This puts woman/truth in a paradoxical position of both telling the truth and lying.

Derrida identifies three possible positions assigned to woman in Nietzsche's work: (1) Woman is a lie; she is castrated. (2) Woman plays with the truth; she is a castrator. (3) Woman is Dionysian self-affirmation; she is affirmative. Yet, as Derrida points out, Nietzsche's styles and metaphors cannot be reduced even to these three categories. The reduction to categories in this way necessarily identifies things according to principles of clear-cut opposites, principles that Nietzsche undermines in his work. For Nietzsche, things are never simply good or evil, true or false, woman or man, and so forth. Rather, Derrida argues that ultimately within Nietzsche's writings we cannot simply decide between two opposing poles. Things can be both and neither.

Derrida associates a logic that breaks everything into opposing poles with an economy of castration. In Freudian psychoanalysis, for example, persons are divided into two types: those who have a penis and those who do not (the castrated). Seeing the world in this way defines everything in having or not having something, in Freud's case, the penis. Derrida suggests that Nietzsche's texts with their multiple styles and various types of women cannot be categorized according to the logic of castration. Rather, he proposes what he calls the "graphics of the hymen" that cannot be reduced to having or not having. Within the graphics of the hymen there is always something in excess of any attempts to create a neat system of categories. Hymen signifies marriage (fusion) and the membrane that stretches across the opening of the vagina (in-between inside and outside). Within Derrida's essay, hymen signifies fusion and what is in-between. Derrida suggests that Nietzsche's texts set up a graphics of the hymen, of the in-between. The exact meaning of any of his texts, like the meaning of woman, remains question, or undecidable.

In "Woman as Truth in Nietzsche's Writings," Kelly Oliver, in contrast with Kofman, proposes that woman as metaphor or trope may serve to reappropriate the feminine for the (masculinist) philosopher. Oliver accepts and radicalizes the Nietzschean woman/truth nexus of Derrida, reading as follows:

> He was, he dreaded this castrated woman.
>
> He was, he dreaded this castrating woman.
>
> He was, he loved this affirming woman.

Oliver responds to the Derridean triad with the claim that it is exemplary of the correspondence between the three value-positions of woman and

truth. In her own reading of the passage in Nietzsche's texts, she identifies
the castrated woman as will-to-truth, the castrating woman as will-to-
illusion, and the affirming woman as will-to-power.

Oliver's tripartite grid of Nietzsche's woman/truth is rendered as follows:

1. castrated woman   will-to-truth   dogmatic, metaphysical/
                                         scientific; feminists
2. castrating woman   will-to-illusion   metaphor, seduction, masks;
                                         Apollonian
3. affirming woman   will-to-power   truth as perspectival; life;
                                         Dionysiac.

The value-position of the affirming woman who has no need for (dogmatic) truth corresponds to Baubô, the Dionysian figuration that Kofman
foregrounds. According to Oliver, each level of woman/truth in the formulation may be ascending (life-affirming) or descending (life-denying);
the Dionysiac (affirming) woman may create or destroy. Oliver surmises
that, for Nietzsche, there is no one woman, or one truth: there are only
"interpretations." She endorses the claim that woman and truth are im-
bricated and perspectival in Nietzsche's writing; to unpack his concept of
woman is to unpack his concept of truth. Her essay encourages feminists
to problematize the undecidability of women and the feminine.

In "Veiled Lips," the central section of *Marine Lover of Friedrich Nietzsche*, Luce Irigaray interrogates Nietzsche's "feminine style." She responds to him because Nietzsche (and Derrida) find a linkage of woman
with style. She views his writings as supportive of "women's writing": "In
a way, Nietzsche made me take off and go soaring; I had the feeling that
I was in the midst of poetry, which made me perfectly happy. One could
say that there is a philosophical thought in this." Her address to Nietzsche as her marine lover may be foregrounded against the feminist critical
project "to dismantle phallogocentric Western tradition which relegates
the feminine to the other." Irigaray, however, has made a special contribution to the critique of the philosophical tradition. She proposes to
uncover silenced femininity by "romancing the philosophers." Instead of
placing herself in the position of the proper wife or the dutiful daughter
to the philosophers, Irigaray chooses to seduce them. She "initiates dialogue with her philosopher-lover by weaving herself in and out of their
arguments, thus insinuating the feminine into their systems."[3]

The sexual difference that Irigaray calls for would be for the feminine to be "the other of the other." Now masculinity creates femininity in its own image or sameness, indifferent to women's specificities. Irigaray proposes to uncover the silenced feminine in the canonical texts by, as she says, "the deliberate assumption of the feminine posture assigned to her within the realm of discourse in order to uncover the mechanisms by which it represses her." Irigaray's "feminine operation" takes the form of mimesis or repeating the philosophers' "back to themselves" through their own texts, rather than challenging them from the "outside." As she comments, "the option left to me was to have a fling with the philosophers." Through the strategic mimicry of their texts, she explores a way for women to enter the philosophical canon and to retrieve the repressed women and the feminine.

In "Veiled Lips," Irigaray mirrors Nietzsche's styles back to him in order to make his texts productive for the (female) imaginary. Her amorous exchange with the (male) philosopher seeks the femininity in his writings. She focuses on his set of female mythological figures: Athena, Ariadne, and Demeter's Persephone. Nietzsche's deployment of the "feminine operation" in these female figurations does not mean, according to Irigaray, that his writings avoid complicity with the phallogocentric tradition.

In her summary, the goddess Athena, not born of a mother but from the head of her father, Zeus, is in the service of the patriarchal order. She famously denies the mother and maternity and consigns women to the domestic sphere. The nymph, Ariadne, is woman contained and silenced in patriarchy; she is averted from herself, continually spinning webs, remaining in the labyrinth. Only Persephone is partially redeemed; she returns at intervals to her mother, the goddess Demeter. According to Irigaray, Persephone is "the goods" or merchandise that men exchange as wives in the patriarchal order.

While Kofman finds the affirmation of woman in the figure of Baubô, and the feminine in Nietzsche's misogyny, Irigaray finds the reappropriation by the paternal or patriarchy, in Nietzsche's "feminine." Her philosopher-partner, she cautions, does not come to terms with sexual difference in his texts. She invites us to view his ambivalence toward maternity and the maternal body. Although she uncovers the feminine in Nietzsche's writing by her strategic mimicry, Irigaray proposes that his deployment of (female) figurations remains under the (male) imaginary and in the tradition of the sexual difference ("sameness") of phallocentrism.

Tamsin Lorraine proposes that we neither ignore nor fixate on Nietzsche's misogyny. In the essay, "Nietzsche and Feminism: Transvauing Woman in *Thus Spoke Zarathustra*," she takes up the question, "If Nietzsche is not a feminist, can the feminist reader find inspiration in his texts?" Specifically, what can she learn from Zarathustra about her own future? Lorraine presents a subversive reading, a feminist reading "against the grain." Lorraine develops four identity-positiions on woman that she sees as possible for the female reader in relation to Zarathustra:

1. the woman who is the object of Zarathustra's speech;
2. the male disciple, or subject, to whom Zarathustra speaks;
3. the woman who serves as Zarathustra's trope or metaphor for life;
4. with Zarathustra himself, as ideal or role-model.

As Lorraine cautions us, however, these identity-positions privilege Zarathustra and not woman; therefore, they are not options for female subjectivity. For example, the aphorism that refers to woman and the "whip" shows that woman is to obey man; the trope of woman-as-life is for men only. Can she be Zarathustra's disciple? No, she must affirm her own body. How can I find Nietzsche affirmative for woman, asks Lorraine, and use Zarathustra's "truths?" Lorraine advises us to sort out and deploy these "truths" for ourselves. She concludes that her Zarathustra is a strong woman who breaks boundaries.

Kathleen Higgins, in "Gender in *The Gay Science*," reads Nietzsche's text in ways that advance her thesis that Nietzsche's figure of woman is enabling for feminists. She holds that his assessment of relations between men and women in passages of this work opens new thinking on gender. Higgins criticizes some feminist attacks on Nietzsche as sexist; it is oversimplistic to take Nietzsche's woman as fixed or essentialist. Higgins supports feminist readings by Kofman, Clark, and Bergoffen (all in this volume) that see Nietzsche as useful for women in spite of his reputation as misogynist.

Higgins presents a close reading of *The Gay Science*, especially sections 59 to 68, which deal with woman and femininity. She interprets apparently sexist references as Nietzsche's comments on male fantasies, dream construction, and—more specifically—women's reveries. According to Higgins, these key passages exhibit women's psychological motivations from within. Nietzsche offers the (male) reader an array of women in order to show gender complexity. Most important, (male) readers are stimulated to examine and assess their own views of women. In this way, there may be a breakthrough of what she terms the "barrier of gendered consciousness." The outcome, she holds, is that sex roles are problematized and the possibility of change is suggested. Higgins concludes that Nietzsche's text is enabling for feminism. His sexist "jokes" may undercut complacencies and provoke readers to see gender as questionable.

In *"Ecce Homo:* Abjection and 'the Feminine,' " Jean Graybeal reads the opening line of the first chapter of *Ecce Homo*—"The happiness of my existence, its uniqueness perhaps, lies in its fate: I am, to express it in the form of a riddle, as my father already dead, while as my mother I still live and grow old"—as Nietzsche's failed attempt to articulate his relation to the feminine, specifically his relation to his mother. Graybeal points out that there are two versions of this section of *Ecce Homo*. There is a revised version that was discovered only relatively recently because it had been suppressed by Nietzsche's friend Peter Gast after Nietzsche's collapse in January 1889. As she explains, Nietzsche collapsed very shortly after sending the revised version to his publisher. After his collapse, Peter Gast edited the manuscript and omitted the revised version. Graybeal proposes that there could be a correlation between the later version of the chapter of *Ecce Homo* and Nietzsche's collapse.

Graybeal describes the significant differences between the earlier and later versions of the first chapter of *Ecce Homo*. She maintains that both versions are Nietzsche's attempt to come to terms with the influence of his mother on his life. She argues that his first attempt to look directly at his mother paralyzes him whereas the second attempt plunges him into rhetorical excess and frenzy. In the first version, after his riddle, Nietzsche says only that his mother is "very German." The rest of that version describes his father. In the later version, however, Nietzsche launches into a miniature diatribe against his mother and sister, calling them "rabble" and "hell-machine." Graybeal suggests that had Nietzsche been able to articulate the sublime and the horror he experienced in relation to his mother, he might have retained his sanity longer.

Feminists' Use of Nietzsche

It falls to feminist philosophers to explore the complex legacy that Nietzsche bequeathed to feminists. There are two main approaches to the emphasis on sexual dualism in Nietzsche's writings. The first camp sees his sexual dualism as incompatible with feminist principles. Those holding this view point to Nietzsche's apparent privileging of masculinity and denigrating of femininity and his paradigms of domination such as the master/slave morality. They find that the Overman is masculine; woman can only be mate or mother. They cite his attack on the feminist demand for sexual equality.

The second approach, while recognizing the insistence on sexual dualism in Nietzsche's tests, find his distinction of masculinity and femininity compatible with feminism. They view his sexual dualism within the context of Nietzsche's anti-essentialism and anti-dualism. They cite his ironic treatment of an "eternal feminine" or essential woman. They see his perspectivism as questioning the fixity of sexual difference in favor of a social constructionism. In his critique of the will to truth or the ascetic ideal, some find affinities with feminist emphasis on the bodily and "playfulness." Others hold that Nietzsche's perspectivism supports the transvaluation of value for women and the feminine.

Linda Singer, in "Nietzschean Mythologies: The Inversion of Values and the War Against Women," delineates how Nietzsche's argumentative strategies are highly charged as sexist and misogynist for women readers. For example, in contrast to some readings of his aphorisms on pregnancy as metaphors for creativity, Singer views them as the not particularly complex, and highly conventional, association of women with maternity. While Kofman deconstructs his aphorisms as exhibiting ambivalence toward the maternal, Singer claims that they express Nietzsche's unserious and uncritical treatment of women.

Singer outlines a systematic antiwoman positionality in Nietzsche's writings that relies on three strategies (or "mythologies"), as follows:

1. the "eternal feminine" or biological essentialism; in this scenario, woman is the mother of the Overman, naturally inferior and morally devious;
2. the image of woman as the negation of man's ideal; she is the bearer of lower (slave) values in contrast to higher (master) values, and she has an aversion to truth;
3. woman as the embodiment of resentment and the source of the inversion of higher/lower values; feminists are cited as aggressive and therefore as "unwomanly."

Singer holds that in an otherwise radical critique of Western thought, Nietzsche continually prioritizes masculinity and devalues femininity. The philosopher-warrior is male. She concludes that Nietzsche betrays his best insights, especially his anti-essentialism. Singer addresses Nietzsche's views on women without resentment; however, she cautions feminists to seek a transvaluation of Nietzsche's values if they are to overcome his misogyny.

In "Nietzsche's Misogyny," Maudemarie Clark asks why there are no Nietzschean feminists in the American tradition comparable to the French Nietzschean approaches of Derrida and Kofman. She hypothesizes that Nietzsche is an immoralist and feminists are moralists. However, she sees his reputation as a misogynist as the real obstacle. Clark notes that "Nietzsche's misogyny" has been less harmful for women than Freud's and that it reflects the construction of masculinity of his age.

Clark presents an analysis of the worst scenario: "The Seven Little Sayings on Women" (in *Beyond Good and Evil*). In a close reading, she assesses what appear to be highly charged antiwomen statements. She outlines the following claims:

1. Nietzsche uses these apparently misogynistic aphorisms to indicate his views about philosophers and the will to truth;
2. they are on the level of sentiment and not belief;
3. they challenge feminists to exhibit his virtues, especially honesty. His "truths" are "my truths," and not truths about women.

If this is puzzling, Clark notes that it is partially because in these "truths" Nietzsche expresses his feelings of resentment toward women. His writings about the "eternal feminine" (*das Weib an sich*) is only a construction, since he does not believe in Kant's *Ding-an-sich*. The turn that Clark's argument takes is to announce that actual women do not need to be property (as in the Sayings); Nietzsche does not claim that his comments are true, since he refuses the ascetic ideal or the will to truth. In Clark's complex analysis, Nietzsche's misogyny reflects the contrast between his beliefs about women, and his sentiments (what he would like to believe) about women. By stating his own feelings of resentment, Nietzsche shows how feminists too might reclaim honesty from the will to truth.

Clark submits that, by this means, feminists might reconcile Nietzsche's overt antifeminism with what she terms a Nietzschean feminism.

She holds that feminism that espouses truth-seeking as will to truth is life-denying. Nietzsche's playfulness in these aphorisms supports truthfulness and sublimates resentment with laughter. She suggests that without the ascetic ideal we can promote feminism that is "beyond good and evil."

Debra B. Bergoffen, in "Nietzsche Was No Feminist," augments Oliver's view of the centrality of Nietzsche's woman/truth nexus for feminist critique. However, Bergoffen takes the discussion in another direction from Oliver's Derridean reading. Bergoffen notes affinities between women and philosophy as well as women and rhetoric in Nietzsche's writings. She seeks the outcome that would "make philosophy a matter between man and woman." Bergoffen focuses on the question of man's desire for truth. She shifts the question from "what is woman/truth?" to "what is man's desire for woman/truth?" Or, genealogically, "why does man want truth?"

Bergoffen claims that woman as truth destablizes metaphysical and epistemological certainty. Woman is an enigma in Nietzsche's texts. She follows Nietzsche in disclaiming the ascetic ideal or the (dogmatic) will to truth. She endorses the self-speaking woman who can return man's desire for truth to him. In her reading, Bergoffen points out that there are "no anchors" for man in either woman or truth. Her self-spoken woman is offered as the counterpart to the Overman. She refuses to be the same as man; she prefers the "flirtation," or free-play, of her self-choosing, as well as the reciprocity of desire between man and woman.

In "Sexual Dualism and Woman's Self-Creation: On the Advantages and Disadvantages of Reading Nietzsche for Feminists," Lynne Tirrell considers other aspects of men and women, or sexual dualism. She considers the troubling (for feminists) relationship of the feminine and ontological difference in Nietzsche's texts. Tirrell focuses on what she accepts as Nietzsche's anti-dualistic ontology. She believes that Nietzsche's writings are useful for feminist theory because of his rejection of the dualism of traditional (masculinist) philosophy. However, she cautions feminists that his normative sexual dualism limits his texts as resource, in that he affirms masculinity and devalues femininity.

Tirrell argues that Nietzsche's sexual dualism is mitigated since it does not rest on essentialism; men and women, in his writings, are formed by "interpretations." Tirrell suggests that in this social constructionist position, Nietzsche anticipates Simone de Beauvoir's existential formulation. Nietzsche maintains that sexual dualism is a cultural "arrangment between the sexes." He destabilizes his own sexual dualism in his rejection of ontological dualism, and in his perspectivalism.

Tirrell concludes that there are affinities between Nietzsche's views and some feminist theory, especially in his emphasis on self-creation and the power of naming. Nevertheless, Nietzsche does not see his options, and remains fixated on hierarchical arrangements between the sexes.

The complex relationship between women and Nietzsche is the focus of Kathleen Wininger's "Nietzsche's Women and Women's Nietzsche." Although Nietzsche inveighed against feminism, Wininger maintains, nineteenth-century feminists favored his critical interrogation of Western (patriarchal) culture. His critique of asceticism, for example, was supportive of their attitude toward the body and sensuality. Yet there is a tension between the "feminine" Nietzsche and the apparently misogynist Nietzsche; Wininger claims that the latter expresses a nineteenth-century construction of masculinity. She notes that contemporary feminism is incompatible with both master-morality and slave-morality. However, Nietzsche's philosophy of power is useful for feminists; his genealogical method is connected for women with models of moral change.

In *"Das Weib an Sich:* The Slave Revolt in Epistemology," Daniel Conway shifts our attention to the application of Nietzschean themes to feminist epistemology. He cites Nietzsche's warning in regard to science expressing the will to truth or the ascetic ideal. Conway proposes that Nietzsche's perspectivism serve as epistemic framework of the radically situated experiences of women. He articulates some linkages betwen Nietzsche's perspectivism and feminist epistemology: the contextual nature of knowledge; affective investments in knowledge; and the politicized, stratgic access to knowledge.

Conway critically appraises two positions: feminist standpoint theory and the feminist episteme of "situated knowledges." He considers the affinities of each with elements of Nietzsche's perspectivism. In the feminist episteme of "situated knowledges," Conway finds a reconstituted notion of objectivity that incorporates "subjugated standpoints." He sees this viewpoint as accomodating perspectivism, since it calls for situated (i.e., politicized) knowledges and not epistemic purity. In this way, nonsubjugated perspectives, as part of the aggregation, are not eliminated.

In feminist standpoint theory, by contrast, Conway finds a less supportable version of feminist epistemology, in Nietzschean terms. He argues that, like the episteme of "situated knowledge," feminist standpoint theory does permit the aggregation of partial perspectives in radically constituted knowledges. However, it privileges a cluster within the aggregation that is distinguished by victimage, or as being oppressed. According to Conway, these subjugated standpoints are viewed as more accurate, or less distorted, than the master viewpoint. Therefore, "slave" is the epistemically privileged standpoint. Conway finds the view from below, as *Weib an Sich*, to be totalizing. He suggests that epistemic purity is not necessary for political agendas. Therefore, he argues that the "slave revolt" in epistemology, like the slave revolt in morality, valorizes slave/woman as privileged standpoint. Conway sees the feminist episteme of "situated knowledges" as more compatible with Nietzschean perspectivism.

In "Nietzsche's Politics," Ofelia Schutte maintains (in contrast to Tirrell) that his sexual dualism is incompatible with feminist principles. She outlines Nietzsche's defense of elitism and his hierarchical dichotomy of aristocracy/slavery. She charges him with a dualism of master/slave that represents the domination of women by men, in marriage and the family structure. Like Singer, she focuses on the contrast between his advocacy of the transvaluation of values, and his espousal of gender difference that incorporates sexual inequality. Schutte argues that while Nietzsche's writings may be anti-dualistic and anti-authoritarian, patriarchal thinking surfaces in his texts, in regard to women and the feminine.

Nietzsche's political theory, according to Schutte, is based on the exploitation of the lower (slave and female) by the higher (master and male). She does not see the higher/lower opposition as metaphorical, as does Kofman. His order-of-rank, according to Schutte, is not life-affirming, since Nietzsche's woman is lower/slave and life-denying. Therefore, she can never be the Overman. (For Singer, she can only be the mother of the Overman.) Schutte believes that Nietzsche suspends an otherwise critical project (philosophy of becoming; genealogical method; beyond good and evil) in the service of men's domination of women. According to Schutte and other feminists, Nietzsche does not posit the master-race; however, he does promote the master-sex.

In "Nietzsche's Squandered Seductions: Feminism, the Body and the Politics of Genealogy," David Owen further interrogates the question of Nietzsche's anti-essentialism in relation to ontological politics. Owen particularly examines' Nietzsche's perspectivism and his doctrines of will to power, eternal recurrence, and genealogy as they impact on feminism. He cites the linkage in Nietzsche's texts of reason and affect/body, or affective reason, as compatible with feminist theory.

Summarizing Nietzsche's position as "strategic essentialism," Owen articulates some of the implications for gender theorists. While Nietzsche espouses biological foundationalism or essential difference between men and women, he does not support biological determinism, or fixed difference between the sexes. The figure of woman in his writings is contingent or changeable; there is no woman-as-such but women are constituted through "practical interests." In emphasizing perspectivism as associated with the concept of woman, Owen judges Nietzsche as useful for feminist theory.

Owen outlines two main strategies that Nietzsche employs in regard to an essentialist view of woman. First, Nietzsche rejects metaphysical essentialism in regard to "woman-as-such" as well as the general notion of sex equality espoused by feminists. He reevaluates the value of women by equating the figure of woman with truth perspectivally, thus opening new possibilities. Owen holds that we can accept Nietzsche's critique of essentialism without accepting his attack on the demand for sex equality of feminism.

The essays in this collection offer the reader a sense of the variety of feminist approaches to Nietzsche's texts. In addition, these essays represent some of the most important contributions to feminist Nietzsche scholarship to date. As the issues of woman, femininity, and gender in Nietzsche's texts move toward the center of Nietzsche scholarship, feminist readings of Nietzsche become crucial to understanding his work. This collection should provide the reader with a sense of what is compelling about Nietzsche for feminists and what is essential about feminist readings of Nietzsche for Nietzscheans.

Notes

1. Biddy Martin, *Women and Modernity: The (Life)Styles of Lou Andreas-Salomé* (Ithaca: Cornell University Press, 1991), 98.

2. Jacques Derrida, *Spurs/Eperons: Nietzsche's Styles/Les Styles de Nietzsche*, trans. Barbara Harlow (Chicago: University of Chicago Press, 1979), 7.

3. Carolyn Burke, "Romancing the Philosophers: Luce Irigary," *Minnesota Review* 29 (1987): 105.

Part One

Nietzsche's Use of Women

1

Baubô: Theological Perversion and Fetishism

Sarah Kofman
Translated by Tracy B. Strong

> As my father I am already dead, while as my mother I live on and grow older.
> —*Ecce Homo*

An Old Woman

In a frequently cited passage from *Twilight of the Idol*, Nietzsche uses the term *fetishist* to describe a primitive psychology found at the origins of language, reason, and metaphysics (VI 3, 71). In these cases, Humans

Translated by permission of Editions Galilée from Sarah Kofman, *Nietzsche et la scène philosophique* (Paris: Union Générale d'Editions, 1979; Editions Galilée, 1986). This essay was written at the invitation of Jean Gillibert of the Institute of Psychoanalysis on rue Saint-Jacques, Paris, in May 1973 and was published in its first version in *Nuova Corrente* 69–69 (1975–76). The postscript was written for the American edition.

I should like to express my gratitude to Sarah Kofman for her persistent help with this translation. TRANS.

think of the self as a substance and as the cause of their actions. The will is seen also as a cause, and when one projects this conception onto the world, one believes the world to be made up of things, substances, beings, and will. These beliefs constitute fetishism.

Is Nietzsche here the inheritor of August Comte, for whom "fetishism" was the first stage of the "theological" era and a kind of childhood period in which the human spirit was least developed and in which people were incapable of explaining natural phenomena to themselves except by projecting fictions onto the world?[1]

It is true that Nietzsche does think that language activates a genetic psychology; nevertheless, fetishism is not for him, as it was for Comte,[2] a necessary and spontaneous solution discovered early by the human spirit as a result of the torment over the need to explain phenomena. Contrary to Comte, Nietzsche does not derive the notion of causality from a speculative need, but from a feeling of *fear:* "The causal instinct is thus conditional upon, and excited by, the feeling of fear" (VI 3, 87). Humans do not invent "the idea of causality" out of a need for causality: they do not invent *causality* per se, but a *particular kind* of cause, "a cause that is comforting, liberating, and relieving . . . [that] searches . . . for a particularly selected and preferred kind of explanation. . . . One kind of positing of causes predominates more and more, is concentrated into a system, and finally emerges as *dominant,* that is, simply precluding other causes and explanations" (VI 3, 87). For Nietzsche, "causality" is thus not strictly a simple error, another "one of the four great errors," but rather an illusion or yet again a lie. "By lie I mean wishing *not* to see something that one does see; wishing not to see something *as* one does see it. . . . The most common lie is that with which one lies to oneself. . . . Now this wishing *not*-to-see what one does see, this wishing-not-to-see *as* one sees, is almost a first condition for those who are of a *party* in any sense" (VI 3, 236).

If fetishism should not be considered as an error necessary and particular to certain periods of human development and thus destined to disappear over time, but corresponds instead to a *refusal* to see, then one can ask oneself if Nietzsche's notion of fetishism is not close to that of Freud. For Freud, abnegation is the particular process of fetishism whereby castration is at once recognized and denied, and where the absence of a penis in women, more particularly in the mother, is both grasped and disregarded.[3]

Castration? Penis? Nietzsche does use Comte's expression of "coarse fetishism," but he seems very far from thinking of Freud's referents. It is, of course, true that Freud notes that a feeling of fear is attached to these concepts; nevertheless, nothing here allows us to say that Nietzsche is afraid of women, still less of his mother. And yet . . .

And yet: woman, a woman, an old woman, accomplice to the belief in the existence of God, continuously haunts Nietzsche's text.

And yet: Nietzsche designates as *perverse* that system of theological judgments that ends up by dominating to the point of excluding anything that is not itself.

And yet: well before Freud, many passages in Nietzsche do invoke the notion of castration.

With what stitches might one knit a cloth from castration and the perversion of the ascetic priests, from women, and from the concept of causality? Should we distinguish young women from old? Does Nietzsche not himself repeat the ancient theological misogyny that woman is the locus and source of all evil? (IV 3, 224–25). Or should this famous misogyny not itself be rethought and reevaluated from a standpoint that would differentiate it into types?

Perversion

"Fetishism" occurs rarely in Nietzsche, whereas "perversion" plays a major and varied role. Perversion appears with multiple connotations and referents and is associated with the inversion or the transposition of values. Perversion is the diagnosis by the philosopher-physician of the reversal or the transposition of values. it is decoded as a symptom of sickness and as a state of degeneration. As a corruption of nature or life, perversion consists in preferring those values that are in opposition to natural "finality," to the affirmation of life, to the will to increasing power, to aggression. Perversion denies the immanent finality to life understood as will to power.

Thus, perversion is the "choice" of values other than those that affirm life. It is a will to death, to nothingness. It is a typical disease of the ascetic priest, but also of all those who are animated by the theological instinct. There are thus as many forms of perversion as there are forces that make use of and take form as (*s'emparent*) the ascetic ideal, which, by itself, has no definition (cf. VI 2, 367). All that which wills (*veut*) death may be called perverse. The term is even more accurately applied to that which *cannot* will anything other than death and which therefore always takes the side of that which is feeble, low, misbegotten, the side of all that is opposed to a life of strength and to that which permits a life to grow. Perverse values are nihilistic values hiding themselves under sacred names. It was the work of the priest to falsify the meaning of names and nouns; this was the condition of survival and of the triumph of the weakest.

I can an animal, a species, or an individual corrupt when it loses its instincts, when it chooses and prefers that which is disadvantageous for it. . . . Life itself is for me the instinct for growth, for durability, for an accumulation of forces, for *power*. . . . All the supreme values of mankind *lack* this will. The values symptomatic of decline, *nihilistic* values, are lording it under the holiest names. (VI 3, 170)

The Christian conception of God—God as God of the sick, God as a spider, God as spirit—is one of the most corrupt conception. . . . God degenerated into the *contradiction* of life instead of being its transfiguration and eternal "Yes." (VI 3, 183)

The history of Israel is invaluable as the typical history of all *denaturing* [*Entnatürlichung*] of natural values. (VI 3, 191)

A parasitical type of man, thriving only at the expense of all healthy forms of life, the priest . . . at all natural occurrences in life, at birth, marriage, sickness, death, . . . meals—the holy parasite appears in order to denature them—in his language, to "consecrate." (VI 3, 194)

Everything that contains its value *in itself* is made altogether valueless, *anti*valuable by the parasitism of the priest. . . . The priest devalues, *desecrates* nature: this is the price of his existence. (VI 3, 193–94)

I call Christianity the one great curse, the one great innermost corruption [*Verdorbenheit*]. (VI 3, 251)

Perversion is thus antinature. Drives change goals, turn back against themselves, become denatured and in turn denature all that is living.

This is a reflexive movement, no longer a direct discharge. It correlates with the invention of a fictitious, abstract world that one has placed beyond nature, made *super*natural, and set down as the origin of the world here below. Such a world inverts the relations of cause and effect, perverts reasons, and is a symptom of the corruption of nature (VI 3, 82).

How should one understand the ideas of "denaturing," of "antinature," and of perversion? There is not an obvious answer. Many passages in Nietzsche denounce the idea of a nature in itself, as they do that of a finality, indeed of the whole idea of nature. Like most of the other "old words," "nature" (as well as denaturation and thus also perversion) needs to be revalued, read as if crossed-out. This is because the abstract, "dena-tured," "antinatural" world is still a "natural" world: it too is the expres-sion of a certain form of life. In this sense, all "culture" is natural. These forms of life are, however, "denatured," in that their will to power has "degenerated," which means they are not strong enough to rejoice in (*jouir*) and affirm themselves in the very activity of their strength. Their affirmation and rejoicing is rather shadowy, oblique, cunning. A "dena-tured" world is nonetheless "natural" as it is still a means—the only means—by which the weak can affirm their power and win out over the strong. That which is perverse and against nature is the will to impose one's own nature on another, the will to impose the perspective of illness on all, the will to project the "evil eye" on everything, the will to corrupt that which is healthy. It is to designate as "supernatural" the fictitious world and not to will to recognize its natural, too natural character. It is, in short, the refusal to acknowledge perspective as such. Denaturation resides in the transformation of names, in the counterfeiting that sancti-fies. The changing of a name creates the belief that nature has changed and imposes on life the ideal of a higher, supernatural, origin.

When through reward and punishment, one has done away with natural causality, an *antinatural* causality is required. . . . *Moral-ity*—no longer the expression of the conditions for the life and growth of a people, no longer its most basic instinct of life, but become abstract, become the antithesis of life—morality as the systematic degeneration [*Verschlechterung*] of the imagination, as the "evil eye" for everything. What is . . . Christian morality? Chance done out of its innocence, misfortune besmirched with the concept of "sin"; well-being as a danger, a "temptation." It is

a physiological disposition poisoned by the worm of conscience.
(VI 3, 192)

How has this counterfeiting succeeded? How have the weak managed
to win out over the strong and thus generalize decadence? The triumph
of the weak is so "antinature" that it may be understood only as the result
of a magical enchantment and a cunning seduction. The general process
of denaturalization works by blocking the way (le détournement) of the
strong, a detour that leads to death along a path embellished with the
tawdry tinsel of morality and religion. What is important here is that the
weak act like women: they try to seduce, they charm, by misrepresenting
and disguising nihilistic values under gilded trim.

First of all, then, woman is a picture of weakness and magical seduction: she is the figure of the magical Circe who knew how to seduce
Ulysses' companions in order to transform them into pigs. Circe? She is
a scorpion, a Medusa, or yet again a she-devil.

> [Morality], often with no more than single glance, succeeds in
> paralyzing the critical will and even enticing it over to its own
> side; there are even cases in which morality has been able to turn
> the critical will against itself, so that like a scorpion it drives the
> sting into its own body. It [sie] is expert in every diabolical nuance
> of the art of persuasion. . . . For as long as there has been speech
> and persuasion on earth, morality has shown itself to be the great-
> est of all mistresses of seduction [Verführung] . . . the actual Circe
> of philosophers. . . . All philosophers were building under the se-
> duction [Verführung] of morality, . . . they were apparently aiming
> at certainty, at "truth," but in reality at "majestic moral structures"
> (V 1, 5)

So: Circe is the appearance of woman, known for and knowing disguise
and adornment, with reason to pervert reason, with reason to have nothingness taken for being, with reasons not to show herself naked. Does
not Nietzsche take up here the old theological motif of the female seduction? It would seem that, on the one hand, he "deconstructs" metaphysics
and theology and denounces the ascetic ideal, but, on the other, remains
caught in the net of the theologians.

Yet: Is Circe "woman"? Or simply a certain woman? Is there for Nietzsche woman in herself? Does only woman escape differentiation and ty-

pology? Even more, is it really true that the art of seduction is thus scorned by Nietzsche? Is it not, rather, the special art of Dionysus?

Let us not then rush headlong to "decide" this question and pronounce Nietzsche "misogynist." Rather, we must weave a cloth from both theological perversion and the veils whose reality one cannot or will not see, a reality which one has a reason to hide. Freud, himself, taught that women invented cloth, by which this dissimulation operates. And Freud, again, called attention to the importance of clothes for fetishism, especially the undergarments of a beloved woman.

The Reversal

A counterfeit is a perverse invention of a fictional metaphysical realm; its goal is to pass off the "real" world as a world of "appearances." Nature is devalued and held, as it were, in suspension in order to establish a supernatural world which alone would be true, consistent, and eternal. Nevertheless, the value of perverse judgments appears only in opposition to natural judgments; they are thus secondary to the judgments of the strong. An instinct of hatred tends to devalue all this as natural and affirmative; new values are not shaped by a positive instinct of preservation. *Ressentiment* toward life and its affirmative force is the basis of the construction of a perverse and phantasmagoric neoreality. It is a need to struggle against pain and to malign life, not a desire for satisfaction by using one's ability (*pouvoir*). The ascetic ideal is negative and destructive; perversion is always also *inversion* and *reversion* (*renversement*). The fictional perverse world is defined purely negatively. It is distinguished from that of dreams in that dreams are positive accomplishments of desire and reflect the real world; it is especially different from the worlds of play and art—of true art—in which appearance is willed and the world repeated not in order to devalue it but to enhance the creative capacity (*pouvoir*) of life. Thus art wills for life yet again its eternal return in difference, a dionysian mimetic power at one with creation and affirmation. Dreams and art are the doubles of reality: they imply positive relations. Fictions born from *ressentiment* are inverted and evanescent shadows, able only to depreciate it.

So that it could say No to everything on earth that represents the ascending tendency of life, to that which has turned out well, to power, to beauty, to self-affirmation, the instinct of *ressentiment*, which had here become genius, had to invent *another* world from whose point of view this affirmation of life appeared as evil, as the reprehensible as such. . . . [The Jewish people] have a life interest in making mankind *sick* and in so twisting [*umzudrehen*] the concepts of good and evil, true and false, as to imperil life and slander the world. (VI 3, 190–91)

I have dug up the theologians' instinct everywhere: it is the most widespread, really *subterranean*, form of falsehood found on earth. Whatever a theologian feels to be true *must* be false: this is almost a criterion of truth. His most basic instinct of self-preservation forbids him to respect reality at any point or even to let it get a word in. Wherever the theologian's instinct extends, *value judgments* have been stood on their heads and the concepts of "true" and "false" are of necessity reversed [*umgekehrt*]: whatever is most harmful to life is called "true,"; whatever elevates it, enhances, affirms, justifies it, and makes it triumphant, is called "false." (VI 3, 173–74)

The *world of pure fiction* is vastly inferior to the world of dreams insofar as the latter *mirrors* [*widerspiegelt*] reality, whereas the former falsifies, devalues, and negates reality . . . : This whole world of fiction is rooted in *hatred* of the natural (of reality!); it is the expression of a profound vexation at the sight of reality. *But this explains everything.* Who alone has good reason to lie his way out of reality? He who suffers from it. But to suffer from reality is to be a piece of reality that has come to grief. The preponderance of feelings of displeasure over feelings of pleasure is the cause of this fictitious morality and religion; but such a preponderance provides the very formula for decadence. (VI 3, 179–80).

If the phantasmagorical world is born out of *ressentiment* and the reversal of noble values, how can it deny its origins and cut itself off from its living roots so as to appear as an autonomous world and a reality in *itself*? How can the world of "appearances" and that of "reality" seem to be in opposition to each other when the latter derives all its "reality" from the realm of "appearance"? If the fictitious world is born out of a simple reversal of the natural world, it loses all autonomy: from whence then the illusion of autonomy? How is the rift [*coupure*] between it and the real world possible? The aim of the weak is to struggle against pain; to do this, they invent a ruse whose aim is *not* to grasp the real—it would be difficult to imagine such a general and generalized negative hallucination—but no longer to be *affected* by it. Reality is, properly speaking, not denied but held in suspension by the disqualification which afflicts it. Thereafter, all that touches us belongs to the other world, the divine world, the internal, immaterial world with which contact is never a wound:

> *The instinctive hatred of reality:* a consequence of an extreme capacity for suffering and excitement which no longer wants any contact at all because it feels every contact too deeply. . . .

> The fear of pain, even of infinitely minute pain—that can end in no other way than in a *religion of love*. (VI 3, 198–99).

> We know a state in which the *sense of touch* is pathologically excitable and shrinks from any contact, from grasping a solid object. One should translate such a physiological *habitus* into its ultimate consequence—an instinctive hatred of every reality, a flight into "what cannot be grasped," "the incomprehensible," an aversion to every formula, to every concept of time and space, to all that is solid, custom, institution, church; a being at home in a world which is no longer in contact with any kind of reality, a merely "inner" world, a "true" world, an "eternal" world. . . . (VI 3, 198)

If weakness thus "spontaneously" cuts itself off from the real world (*le réel*) and becomes the means of avoiding all sensuous contact with the world (*tout contact solide*), religion is the only means of elaborating this into a system and of radicalizing the rift between the two worlds. Only religion permits the movement from the reversal of values to the edification of an autonomous and absolute metaphysical world. Religion operates by interiorization, isolation, and symbolization. Concepts are progressively purified and spiritualized; they become increasingly bloodless, ghastly, and fleshless as they are reduced to the state of a symbol.

Here the priest plays the central role. As a noble in whom the *pathos of distance* works to pathological excess, he is responsible for the chasm that has been dug between "reality" and "appearance." Because of the priest, purity—in the symbolic sense—becomes the fundamental value. The ideal is to have a pure heart, to reach a world of pure ideas (VI 2, 261ff). Thus "reality testing" in the fictitious world cannot be a matter of being "in touch" (se faire par le toucher): the ideal is pure unadulterated being, disqualified, neither touching nor touched by the lower world, nor by the higher one. At most, the intelligible heavens may be contemplated, a privilege perversely awarded by the eye, that most speculative organ at the top of the face.

The reversal of values effected by the priests always goes in one direction, from low to high. Here one has to take into account the fact that the metaphor of reversal is spatial as well as perverse, even though Nietzsche's reversal is not in fact spatial. Nietzsche's "deconstruction" implies that one passes through a phase of reversal of hierarchy where that which traditionally has been depreciated and placed in the lowest rank is placed at the top and generalized. Spatial reversal is the metaphor of the hierarchical reversal. For, if Nietzsche places "at the top" that which metaphysics judged to be low and vile, he retains "the top" as the metaphor for true value. Affirmative, noble evaluations are those that go from "top to bottom." Their point of view is that of the heights, of the summit, of mountains. Evaluations of the slaves are rather from "bottom to top," the point of view of the quagmire, the mud, of the swamp in which frogs delight. A gulf separates these perspectives and points of view; no communication is possible between them. The weak, however, understand this radical difference to be one of opposition, and, in fact, the spatial metaphor seems to make such a misunderstanding inevitable. Why then does Nietzsche keep this old metaphor with its opposition of high and low? Why does he keep the companion metaphor of "perspective"? Is it his usual practice of keeping an "old" noun in order to reevaluate it? Or is it rather that difference cannot be described other than as distance, a metaphor necessarily of spatial opposition? Difference is always described by Nietzsche as between points of view: that of health and sickness; of the aristocrat and the plebian; the esoteric point of view of the few which has no need of ratification and the exoteric and vulgar one that wants to generalize its perspective.

> Our highest insights must—and should—sound like follies and sometimes like crimes when they are heard without permission by those who are not predisposed and predestined for them. The difference between the exoteric and the esoteric, formerly known

to philosophers—among the Indians as among the Greeks, Per-
sians, and Muslims, in short, wherever one believed in an order
and rank and *not* in equality and equal rights—does not so much
consist in this, that the exoteric approach comes from the outside
and sees, estimates, measures, and judges from the outside, not
the inside: what is much more essential is that the exoteric approaches sees things from below, the esoteric looks *down from
above*. There are heights of the soul from which even tragedy
ceases to look tragic. . . . There are books that have opposite
values for soul and health, depending on whether the lower soul,
the lower vitality, or the higher and more vigorous ones turn to
them: in the former case, these books are dangerous and lead to
crumbling and disintegration; in the latter, they are heralds' cries
that call the bravest to *their* courage. Books for all the world are
always foul-smelling books: the smell of small people clings to
them. Where the people eat and drink, even where they venerate,
it usually stinks. One should not go to church if one wants to
breathe *pure* air. (VI 2, 44–45).

The first draft of this passage added: "But there are few men who are
entitled to pure air and who would not die were they to breathe pure air.
This by way of answer to those who suspect me of wanting to invite free
thinkers into my garden."

Does not the necessity of retaining the metaphor of high and low and
the ongoing valuation of high over low derive from the necessity of marking the difference as hierarchical, does it not come from the belief in
hierarchy, that is, in a situation where "top" has always served to describe
the first rank of society? If, however, "noble" and "aristocratic" are for
Nietzsche metaphors for the point of view of health, for affirmation, then
the determination of health is inseparable from a sociopolitical connotation, at least to the degree that it implies relations of mastery and subordination or power relations between different drives [*pulsions*—French for
Freud's *Triebe*, "instincts"—TRANS.]: The *problem of hierarchy* is Nietzsche's problem; difference is difference in the will to power; and the spatial metaphor is necessary to give expression to difference even though it
risks confusing difference with opposition (cf. IV 2, 15–16).

More important, even if Nietzsche keeps the old metaphor and the
privilege of "top" over the bottom, he still achieves a hierarchical reversal
by generalizing the most devalued term. In one sense, there is for Nietz-

sche nothing except that which the tradition called the "base": drives and the will to power. By holding on to the ancient metaphor, even while he reevaluates it, Nietzsche is able to take hold of it and effectuate a reversal of the reversal. The perverse, theological point of view denies perspective by its reference to God and to the world above us; it finds itself entitled to look down from the heights to the world here below. Nietzsche reverses these terms: the so-called absolute world "above" us is only the result of an evaluation from a lower perspective, one which goes from the bottom to the top. The theological point of view finds its roots in the will to power, in the very instinctive nature that the priests see as base and vile. To borrow the language of morality: since all evaluations are instinctive, they have a "low" origin. From this common origin, one can distinguish those evaluations that go from "bottom to top" and those that go from "top to bottom."

> I have found the theologians' instinctive arrogance . . . wherever a right is assumed, on the basis of some higher origin, to look at reality from a superior and foreign vantage point. . . . As long as the priest is considered a *higher* type of man—this *professional* negator, slanderer, and poisoner of life—there is no answer to the question, What *is* truth? For truth has been stood on its head when the conscious advocate of nothingness and negation is accepted as the representative of "truth." (VI 3, 172–73)

Precisely that which priests and metaphysicians refuse is to admit a common origin for the base and the sublime, to good and evil; they refuse to admit that the sublime, the "high," could have had a beginning.

> They place that which comes at the end . . . namely, the "highest concepts," which means the most general, the emptiest concepts, the last smoke of evaporating reality, in the beginning, *as* the beginning. . . . The higher *may not* grow out of the lower, may not have grown at all. Moral: whatever is of the first rank must be *causa sui.* . . . Thus they arrive at their stupendous concept, "God." That which is last, thinnest, and emptiest is put first, as *the* cause, as *ens realissimum.* (VI 3, 70)

The reevaluation of the metaphor of height and baseness thus permits a denunciation of the metaphysicians' fundamental prejudice for the autonomy and the opposition of values. As the sublimation of "low," height is the provisional point of view of a certain form of life—a "perspective from a certain angle, from low to high, a 'frog perspective' to use an expression proper to painters" (VI 2, 10).

In "frog perspective," images are flattened and persons appear foreshortened and crushed. The world is flattened, devalued, and made ugly; the weak are unable to start action from a noble and "elevated" point of view. Everything is seen by an evil eye. Thus the English psychologists, who start by ignoring hierarchy and distance, give to moral sentiments a perverse, inverted genealogy: "But I am told that they are simply old, cold, and tedious frogs, creeping around men and into men as if in their own proper element, that is, in a *swamp*" (VI 2, 272).

Nietzsche persists in privileging the "high," but he associates "high" with the earth and not with "heaven," even if he still prefers the pure air of heights and the summit of mountains to the swamp and the confined air of churches. He does not hesitate to sink his gaze into the abyss, even at the risk of being thrown there, even at the risk of death.

> [We others], we daredevils of the spirit who have climbed the highest and most dangerous peak of present thought and looked around from up there—we who have looked *down* from there. (VI 2, 20)

> Those who can breathe the air of my writings know that it is an air of heights, a *strong* air. One must be made for it. Otherwise there is no small danger that one may catch cold in it. . . . How freely one breathes! How much one feels *beneath* oneself! (VI 3, 256)

Whether the perspective be that of the frog or of the eagle, no perspective—by definition—can be true, but only that of a particular form of life, a certain species. As there is no absolute "high" or "low," Nietzsche's reversal is not a simple reversal of Platonism. What is called truth is the result of an evaluation that proceeds from bottom to top, which stands "truth" on its head by seeing it as absolute and denying the plurality of perspectives. Considered as perspectives of a certain form or life, truth is irrefutable. The mistake is the will to impose truth on other points of view, to think of truth as "the" truth. If a perspective corresponds to determinate dynamic (*pulsionnelles*) conditions, then it cannot be changed at will. But how then is it possible to do what Nietzsche has done and transmute values? Nietzsche thought himself particularly well qualified for this enterprise in that he had a double set of judgments that allowed him to remain neutral and easily to change perspectives. Having inherited from his father and mother opposing evaluations—he is always his own double—he always has a second gaze for everything, and, perhaps, even a third:

> This duel descent, as it were, both from the highest and the lowest rung on the ladder of life, at the same time a *decadent* and a *beginning*—this, if anything explains that neutrality, that freedom from all partiality in relation to the problem of life, that perhaps distinguishes me. (VI 3, 262)

> Looking down from the perspective of the sick toward *healthier* concepts and values and, conversely, looking again from the fullness and self-assurance of a *rich* life down into the secret work of the instinct of decadence—in this I have the longest training, my truest experience; if in anything I am master it is in *this*. Now I know how, have the know-how, to *reverse perspectives:* the first reason why a "revaluation of values" is perhaps possible for me alone. (VI 3, 264)

The ease with which one moves from high to low and back again is a lightness and absence of weight, a dance, or rather *flight*. The privilege of being able to transmute values is linked to the privilege and happiness of *flight*. It corresponds to a frequently repeated oneiric experience.

> Suppose someone has flown often in his dreams, and finally, as soon as he dreams, he is conscious of his power and art of flight as if it were his privilege, also his characteristic and enduring happiness. He believes himself capable of realizing every kind of arc and angle simply with the lightest impulse: he knows the feeling of a certain divine frivolity, an "upward" without tension and constraints, a "downward" without condescension and humiliation—without *gravity!* How could a human being who had had such dream experiences and dream habits fail to find that the word "happiness" had a different color and definition in his waking life, too? How could he fail to desire happiness differently? "Rising" as

described by poets must seem to him, as compared with this "fly-ing," too earthbound, muscle-bound, forced, too "grave." (VI 2, 116–17)

To what desires does such a dream correspond? In relation to the father? To the mother? According to Freud, such a dream is *typical* and is a symbolic representation of coitus.[4] Such a general explanation, how-ever, does not take account of the particular shadings in this dream, nor of the impression of lightness. Nor, as Bachelard remarks, does it take into account its aesthetic character, unless it be by the invocation of the general need for camouflage to avoid censorship.[5] Bachelard, like Nietz-sche, insists on the deep mark that such oneiric experiences leave on waking life and their importance for the development of the psyche. They are even more important than love itself.[6]

Such a dream must thus be understood in relation to the dynamism of the body, with what Bachelard calls an "ascensional psychology" rather than with psychoanalysis. One sees then that the spatial metaphor of the hierarchial transmutation of values is more than a simple metaphor, for affirmative values are precisely those that make one "light," whereas ni-hilistic values are those that weight one down psychologically speaking and are choking and oppressive. The spatial metaphor is more than a simple metaphor because, in the last analysis, the body evaluates and thus serves as the guiding thread.[7] The values of height and depth are an-chored in the body. The dream of flight indicates that the Nietzschean "reversal" refers us to a fundamental oneiric experience; this experience is in turn tied to the body's sense of itself as light or heavy. The dream of flight is, however, also a forbidden experience. If, in Nietzsche, the double system of evaluations takes us back to the double heritage from father and mother, one can ask if such a dream might not effect an equilibrium between these double tendencies. It would permit the simultaneous se-duction of the father and the mother, without *touching* either. It would allow one to "journey" freely and "fly" from one to the other without assistance. Such a being would be in contrast to Faust's son, Euphorion (one knows what importance he had to Nietzsche), who had only the right to jump wildly about (*bondir*), and all of whose strength came from the earth-mother.

Naked, a genius without wings, faunlike but without bestiality,
He springs on the solid ground; but the ground, counteracting,

Hurries him to the airy heights, with the second, third spring
He rests on the vault of heaven.
Anxiously, the mother cries: "Spring again and at your pleasure,
But guard yourself against flying. Free flight is denied you."
And the faithful father warns you: "In the earth lies the elastic
force
That propels you upward. If you touch earth only with your toe,
Straightaway like the son of earth, Antaeus, your strength is re-
newed.[8]

Camera Obscura

Nietzsche's concept of reversal cannot be completely understood except
by placing it in relation to the metaphor of the camera obscura, Nietzsche's image (*figure*) for universal perspectivism.[9] The camera obscura was
invented in order to give the most perfect imitation possible of nature.
There is, however, no imitation without selection, without the work of
filtering reality. The imitation of nature consists in selecting as model
not *natura naturata* but *natura naturans:* it is a repetition of its creative
power. Art repeats nature by idealizing it, by placing certain forms in
relief, by hiding others, and closing up gaps. In herself, nature is not
beautiful but the play of chance: "She exaggerates, deforms, leaves gaps."
The affirmative artist corrects nature, not in order to devalue it but to
make beautiful the "necessity of things" and to permit *amor fati*. The
artist prefers appearance to reality, but "appearance means reality repeated *once again,* as selection, redoubling, correction."

The camera obscura of painters is immanent in the eye of each viewer
and does not give a preexisting reality. Rather, it constitutes for each his
or her own "reality" which is in fact one with "appearance." The claim
to see reality "as it is" is the symptom of an "anti-artistic spirit," a bad
sign of fatalism and weakness (VI 3, 109–10). We are thus all artists,
whether we would be or not. However, the "artist" is characterized by the
fact that he wills himself to be one, just as he wills appearance, whereas
the scientist, for example, refuses to admit that he works in an artistic
mode and believes that the world is upright (*droit*) and real. In fact, he
sees it reversed like the rest of us.

World of phantoms in which we live! Inverted, upside-down, empty world, yet dreamed of as *full and upright!* (V 1, 109)

For us important relationships are those that are reflected in the mirror, not the true ones. . . . No matter how precise our relationships may be, they are descriptions of men, not of the world: these are the laws of that supreme perspective beyond which it is impossible for us to go. . . . It is not an appearance or an illusion but a coded writing where an unknown thing is expressed for us very readably, as if made for us: it is our human position in relation to things. It is thus that things are hidden from us. (V 1, 638; cf. V 1, 635)[10]

A camera obscura, all-too-human, encloses humanity in an unsurpassable perspective and imprisons it as if in a spider's net: nature has thrown away the key.

My eyes, however strong or weak they may be, can see only a certain distance, and it is within the space encompassed by this distance that I live and move, the lines of this horizon constitutes my immediate fate, in great things and small, from which I cannot escape. Around every being there is described a similar concentric circle, which has a center and which is particular to him. . . . Now it is by these horizons, within which each of us encloses his sense as if behind prison walls, that we *measure* the world. . . . There is absolutely no escape, no backway, no by-path that leads to the real world. We sit within our net, we spiders, and, whatever we may catch in it, we can catch nothing at all except precisely that which allows itself to be caught precisely in *our* net. (V 1, 108)

This general reversal derives from the ineluctable "error" that characterizes humanity. This is not, however, to say that every camera obscura is equal. *Particular* errors, illusions, or lies are inscribed on the general background of error inside this unsurpassable dream—unsurpassable even to him who knows he dreams. Each camera obscura is distant and different from the other; those of the perverse, alone, give us, in a more restrained sense, the world inverted from bottom to top. Theirs is an indecent and dangerous perspective because the "perspective" pretends to emerge from the dark prison and to see the world as it is; it claims,

that is, to deny the perspective that is part of the vital condition of all
that lives. This perspective is dangerous because it is that of a living being
that *wills* death. It seeks to look indecently through a keyhole and see all
without discrimination, to see nature unveiled, like a woman. It is dangerous to lift the veil of nature, for she is fierce like a woman, like a
tiger. Those who claim to look outside the dark room of consciousness
(*la conscience*) forget that "Man rests in the indifference of his ignorance
on that which is pitiless, voracious and murderous; he is attached to
dreams as if to the back of a tiger."[11]

The tiger and the panther, all felines and animals of Dionysus,[12] are
related to woman, the most feline and natural animal of all.[13] She is
beautiful, graceful, and fierce. To will to look through the keyhole is to
outrage feminine modesty.

Of Women

By the indecent glance that he directs toward "truth," the perverted individual shows not only that he treats truth like a woman but also that he
does not know how to approach women. He misunderstands both "truth"
and woman and sees them with their "head to the ground" (VI 3,
140–42; IV 2, 139–40). He misapprehends truth as the absence of truth,
as an abyss without a bottom, and fails to understand that life is feline,
fierce, lying, and protean. He does not see that the most characteristic
virtue of woman is modesty (*pudeur*) and that for women the loss of
modesty is the symbol of degeneration.[14] The will to strip woman naked
is a sign of a lack of virility and of instincts insufficiently strong and
insufficiently beautiful to love appearance and the veil. Such a will misunderstands that behind the veil is another veil and behind the cave is
another cave.[15] Who but a fetishist thus seeks the perverse from bottom
to top?[16] "Among women: 'Truth? Oh! you don't know truth! Is it not an
attempt to assassinate all our *pudeurs*?' " (VI 3, 55).

Woman is a surface that mimes depth (VI 3, 57). She is mistress of the
veil and of the simulacrum, both artifices by which she makes men believe that she is "deep," both ruses through which she holds immense
influence over them. The example of Napoleon's mother bears witness to
this point. Modesty appears as a beguilement that permits the male to
desire a woman without being petrified (*médusé*); it is a veil which avoids

male homosexuality, a spontaneous defense against the horrific sight of female genitalia, and the opportunity for life to perpetuate itself. Nevertheless, certain women also seek "truth" and show themselves as immodest as the theologians. These "degenerate" women, who seek knowledge and assert equality of rights, engage in politics, or write books. Instead of bearing children, they seek to gain a penis. These women believe themselves to be "castrated," and, thus delegitimized, conclude that "woman as woman" is castrated. This is *ressentiment* of sterile women against life, and it is symptomatic of a degeneration of femininity: "woman" is neither castrated nor not castrated, any more than man retains control (*détient*) over the penis. The whole idea of castration and its opposite is part of the syndrome of weakness and keeps one from speaking of a truly living and affirmative life, be this masculine or feminine. The immodest woman is the accomplice of the theologians and of their conception of woman. By dropping her veils and exhibiting a fawning baseness, she makes man fall into pessimism and nihilism. He becomes a disappointed (*déçu*) dogmatist and a skeptic. The belief in castration is the other side of fetishism. Sterile women and old women thus join the perverse theological point of view. Such women are the worst enemies of women, for their *ressentiment* annihilates the fertility that is one with life and with its power of creative affirmation.

> Woman wants to become self-reliant—and for that reason she is beginning to enlighten men about "woman as such": *this* is one of the worst developments of the general *uglification* of Europe. For what must these clumsy attempts of women at scientific self-exposure bring to light! Woman has so much reason for shame. . . . Woe when . . . woman . . . begins to unlearn thoroughly and on principle her prudence and her art—of grace, of play, of chasing away worries, of lightening burdens and taking things lightly. . . . Is it not in the worst taste when woman sets about becoming scientific that way. Before, luckily, explanation of this sort was man's affair. . . . Whatever women write about "woman" we may in the end reserve a healthy suspicion whether woman really *wants* enlightenment about herself—whether she *can* want it. . . . Unless woman seeks a new adornment [*Putz*] for herself this way—I do think adorning herself is part of the eternal feminine?—she surely wants to inspire fear of herself—perhaps she seeks mastery. But she does not *will* truth: what does truth have

to do with woman! From the beginning nothing has been more alien, repugnant, and hostile to woman than truth—her great art is the lie, her highest concern is appearance and beauty. Let us men confess it: we honor and love precisely *this* art and *this* instinct in women. . . .We men wish that woman would not go on compromising herself through explaining herself, just as it was man's thoughtfulness and consideration for women that found expression in the church decree: *mulier taceat in ecclesia!* It was for woman's use that Napoleon gave the all-too-eloquent Madame de Staël to understand that *mulier taceat in politicis.* And I think that it is a real friend of women [*une authentique féministe*] that counsels women today: *mulier taceat de muliere* (VI 2, 176–78)

In the first draft of this passage, Nietzsche wrote, "Is not the desire to 'explain' woman a denial of the feminine instinct, a degeneration? Is it not the will to disillusion men?" (cf. VI 2, 88, 95, 181–84, 98).

Is this another case of Nietzsche's well-known misogyny? It seems that woman herself does not like woman: this seems at least so for the botched and sterile women, who have the will to emancipate themselves and hate the affirmative well-shaped (*bien conformée*) woman. Such a woman differs not at all from the man of *ressentiment* and like him erects her perspective as an absolute. "The abortive woman . . . wants to lower the level of the general rank of woman. . . . At bottom, the emancipated are anarchists in the world of the 'eternally feminine,' the underprivileged whose most fundamental instinct is revenge" (VI 3, 304).[17]

Even though Nietzsche takes up the notion of the "eternal feminine" again here, he still distinguishes different types of women, just as he distinguishes different types of men. From a genealogical point of view, an affirmative woman is closer to an affirmative man than a degenerate woman. And some women are more affirmative than are some men.

Is it correct then to refer that which Nietzsche says of women to truth, when a certain woman is the image (*figure*) of truth? Can one legitimately speak of castration and noncastration? In *whose* picture is truth a woman (*Qui se figure la vérité comme une femme*)?

To speak of truth as a woman derives from a theological perspective and is an image that appears at a precise moment in the long story of error that is the history of truth. "*How the true world became a fable:* The true world—unattainable for now, but promised for the sage, the pious, the virtuous man ('for the sinner who repents'). . . . (Progress of the idea:

it becomes more subtle, insidious, incomprehensible—*it becomes female;
it becomes Christian*)" (VI 3, 74).

The idea of truth presented here as an unveiling leads to a self-castration. *Aletheia,* placed in a comprehensible firmament, is barely perceiv-
able, and woman/truth remains inaccessible even to those who subject
themselves to the most severe tests. Skepticism is both the necessary
consequence and the reverse side of dogmatism. "As an outline: the last
philosopher—modified position of philosophy since Kant. Metaphysics
has become impossible—Self-castration. Tragic resignation. The end of
philosophy. Only art can save us."[18]

One may ask if placing truth/woman in an inaccessible location is not
a way to protect oneself against her. It would be as if it were better not to
be able to see that there is nothing to see, and better not to dive into the
abysses of truth as an absence of truth. Self-castration appears to be a
preventative defense against the castration provoked by the "sight" of the
"truth." Oedipus, "the most daring and the most unhappy of men," dared
to cast his glance on the abyss and blinded himself. "And if thine eye
offend thee, pluck it out: it is better for thee to enter into the kingdom
of God with one eye, than having two eyes to be cast into hell fire: Where
their worm dieth not, and the fire is not quenched' (Mark 9:47f). It is
not exactly the eye which is meant" (VI 3, 219; cf. VI 3, 209–11).[19]

Truth cannot be unveiled without provoking horror. Were she to show
herself naked, the metaphysicians would create a scandal and quickly run
away. Rendering truth inaccessible first makes the fetish that suspends
the real world and nature/woman; then it disqualifies both as vain appearances. The theologians are seduced by the tawdry brilliance of Circe, by
emptiness and by nothingness understood as the fullness of being. They
refuse to recognize women and life as fecundity and disclaim the eternal
return that is beyond suffering and death.

Life is neither appearance nor reality, neither surface nor depth, neither castrated nor not. Its charger cannot be expressed metaphysically,
for castration and fetishism are the perverse invention of instincts that
are not virile enough to "penetrate" woman.

> Supposing that truth is a woman. . . . Would there not then be
> grounds for the suspicion that all philosophers, insofar as they are
> dogmatists, have been very inexpert about women? That gruesome
> seriousness, that clumsy obstrusiveness with which they have usu-
> ally approached truth so far have been very awkward and improper

attempts at winning a woman's heart? What is certain is that she has not allowed herself to be won. (VI 2, 3)

We no longer believe that truth remains truth when the veils are withdrawn; we have lived too much to believe this. Today we consider it a matter of decency not to wish to see everything naked, or to be present at everything and "know" everything. "Is it true that God is present everywhere?" a little girl asked her mother: "I think that's indecent"—a hint for philosophers! One should have more respect for the bashfulness with which nature has hidden behind riddles and iridescent uncertainties. Perhaps truth is a woman who has reasons for not letting us see her reasons? Perhaps her name is, to speak Greek, *Baubo?* Ah, these Greeks! They knew how to live! What is demanded is to stop courageously at the surface, at the fold, the skin, to adore appearance, to believe in forms, tones, words in the whole Olympus of appearance. These Greeks were superficial—*out of profundity.* (V 2, 20; cf. V 2, 248–49)

To respect female modesty is thus to be able to hold oneself to appearance, to interrogate oneself indefinitely on the infinite riddles of nature/ Sphinx, without seeking—perhaps it is only prudence—to "unveil" truth (cf. VI 1, 193–94). "Who has the courage to see these 'truths' without veils? Perhaps there is a legitimate modesty in the face of these problems and postulates, perhaps we are mistaken on their value, perhaps we too are obedient to their will?" (VI 2, 10).

Nietzsche worked this passage over particularly carefully. In the second draft, he wrote: "But who needs to preoccupy himself with such maybes? It is against good taste, especially against virtue, for truth to become so scandalous and deny all modesty: some caution is needed before this lady." Then a third draft: "When truth becomes to this point scandalous, when the woman without scruples strips herself at this point of her veils and renounces all modesty: Back! back! may this seductress go away and follow hereafter her own path. One can never be prudent enough with a woman like this. It would be better, you tell me with a wink of the eye, to commit oneself with a modest and chaste mistake, a small gentle lie."

The attitude of metaphysicians is ambivalent. They wish to see and strip away all veils, but they also fear to see. What is the case with the person of a true philosophical disposition? Does he look truth in the face and risk blindness or death? Does he remain with appearance, with lies and art? Oedipus is the last of the philosophers and the greatest of the unhappy; he is a tragic philosopher, a man petrified by nature who still dares to confront truth but requires forgetfulness and transfiguration by tragic art. "Formidable solitude of the last philosopher, nature petrifies him [umstarrt], vultures plane about him. And he cries to nature: give us forgetfulness! to forget! It is not that he supports suffering as did Titan, until a pardon is granted him in the supreme tragic art."[20]

Ebb and flow are necessary for the philosopher. One must love "truth" enough to dare to die, love life enough to forget, adore appearance as such, as art. With the movement of coming and going, from understanding to life and from life to understanding, the voyager, after having seen the depths of the abyss, calls for still one more mask: "Wanderer, who are you? I see you walking on your way without scorn, without love, with unfathomable eyes; moist and sad like a sounding lead that has returned to the light, impatient for new depths—what did it seek down there— with a breast that does not sigh, with a lip that conceals its disgust, with a hand that now reaches only slowly: Who are you? What have you done?" [And the voyager answers] "Another mask! a second mask!" (VI 2, 239).

On the third draft, Nietzsche adds: "Who are you? I don't know— perhaps Oedipus, perhaps the Sphinx?"

When the name of Oedipus comes up, Hamlet is never far away: "What must a man have suffered to have a need of being such a buffoon? Is Hamlet understood? Not doubt, certainty is what drives one insane. But one must be profound . . . to feel that way. . . . We are all afraid of truth" (VI 3, 285; cf. III 1, 44–48).

So as not to become blind like Oedipus or mad like Hamlet, one must know how to keep oneself on the surface. One must know how to love life like a woman who has deceived you but remains beautiful, to know how to bless life while leaving it, as Ulysses bade farewell to Nausicaa.[21] The true philosopher is a tragic philosopher, for he must will illusion as illusion, knowing that woman has a reason to hide her reasons. Mastery means to know how to keep oneself at a distance, to know how to close doors and windows and keep the shutters closed. To hold oneself in the camera obscura, not to refuse appearance but to affirm it and to laugh, for if life is ferocious and cruel, she is also fecundity and eternal return: her name is Baubô.

The name of a woman: What is her link with the more insistent figure of Dionysus in Nietzsche?

Baubô

Baubô appears in the mysteries of Eleusis consecrated to Demeter. Under the pain of the loss from the disappearance of Persephone, Demeter, goddess of fecundity, had been comporting herself like a sterile woman. For nine days and nine nights, she did not drink, eat, bathe, or adorn herself. Baubô made her laugh.

She made her laugh by pulling up her skirts and showing her belly on which a figure had been drawn (it is thought to be that of Iaachos, the child of Demeter, an obscure deity sometimes identified with Dionysus). This episode is known from six lines of a much-censured orphic verse that the church fathers designated as obscure. Reinach interprets it as a magic scene whose aim is to restore to earth the fecundity that it had lost during the sorrow of Demeter.[22] Comparison with Greek legends such as those of Bellerophon, and with Irish and Japanese ones, allows us to assert that wherever a woman raises her skirts, she provokes laughter or flight, such that this gesture can be used as an apotropaic means.[23] The belly of the woman plays the role of the head of Medusa.[24] By lifting her skirts, was not Baubô suggesting that she go and frighten Hades, or that which comes to the same, recall fecundity to herself? By displaying the figure of Dionysus on her belly, she recalls the eternal return of life: "Demeter recovers joy in the thought that Dionysus will be reborn. This joy, which announces the birth of the genius, is Greek serenity."[25]

The figure of Baubô indicates that a simple logic could never understand that life is neither depth nor surface, that behind the veil, there is another veil, behind a layer of paint, another layer. It signifies also that appearance should cause us neither pessimism nor skepticism, but rather the affirming laugh of a living being who knows that despite death life can come back indefinitely and that "the individual is nothing and the species all."

By calling life "Baubô," one identifies it not only with woman but also with her reproductive organs: *Baubô* is the equivalent of *koilia*, another of the "improper" words used in Greek to designate the female sex.[26] Baubôn, the symbol of the male sex, derives from Baubô. Through the intermediary of Baubôn, the story of Baubô crosses that of Dionysus. On the one hand, Dionysus is born in Nysa, at the spot where Hades carried off Persephone; on the other, when Dionysus was looking for the road to Hades, he encountered Proshymnos with whom he had unspeakable relationships.[27] After Proshymnos's death, Dionysus replaced him with a figwood phallus as a sort of consolation: such an instrument seems to have been called *baubôn*.[28] Baubôn and Baubô, as personifications of the two sexes, appeared under this aspect of the Eleusian rites where Baubô is an animated *koilia*. In the Eleusian mysteries, the female sexual organ is exalted as the symbol of fertility and a guarantee of the regeneration and eternal return of all things.

From this, Baubô can appear as a female double of Dionysus—in fact Otto and Jeanmaire insist on the feminine character of Dionysus himself, or at least on his equivocal sexuality. One can say that like life he is beyond the "metaphysical" distinctions of male and female. There is also a tie between Dionysus and the myths of death and rebirth: according to Nietzsche the Dionysiac cult ensured eternal life, a triumphant affirmation of life beyond death and change.

> I know no higher symbolism that this *Greek* symbolism of the Dionysian festivals. Here the most profound instinct of life, that directed toward the future of life, the eternity of life, is experienced religiously—and the way to life, procreation, as the *holy* way. It was Christianity, with its *ressentiment* against life at the bottom of its heart, which first made something unclean of sexuality: . . . Saying Yes to life even in its strangest and hardest problems, the will to life rejoicing over its own inexhaustibility even in the very sacrifice of its highest types—*that* is what I called Dionysian, . . . the eternal joy of becoming, beyond all terror and pity—that joy which included even joy in destroying.
>
> And herewith I again touch that point from which I once went forth: *The Birth of Tragedy* was my first revaluation of all values. Herewith I again stand on the soil out of which my intention, my *ability*, grows—I, the last disciple of the philosopher Dionysus—I, the teacher of the eternal recurrence. (VI 3, 153-54)

Baubô and Dionysus would thus be both multiple names for protean life. Contrary to Baubô, however, Dionysus is naked. His nakedness does not signify the revelation of a truth but the unveiled affirmation of appearance: it is the nakedness of the strong who is beautiful enough, virile enough, not to need to veil himself. On the other hand, Dionysus is the god of masks; as with women, "to know how to appear is part of his mastery." "He says nothing, nor risks a glance behind which there is not the thought of seduction." Dionysus, a Greek god anterior to the system of theological oppositions, crosses himself out (se rature) of the distinction between the veiled and unveiled, masculine and feminine, fetishism and castration.

Does it still make sense, then, to speak of misogyny in Nietzsche?

One might rather ask oneself: What is it in Nietzsche that leads him to judge woman as he does? What instinct speaks out and or interprets here? For Nietzsche does not pretend to speak the "truth" about "woman in herself," but rather gives an understanding derived from a constraining perspective that limits such a pretense. More than anything else, judgments on "woman" are symptoms.

> Whenever a cardinal problem is at stake, there speaks an unchangeable "This I am." About man and woman, for example, a thinker cannot relearn but only finish learning—only discover ultimately that which is settled [gesteht] in him on this matter. . . . After this abundant civility that I have just assumed in relation to myself, I shall perhaps be permitted more readily to state a few truths about "woman as such," given that from here on one knows how very much these are only—my truths. (IV 2, 176)

That which is "arrested" in him about women is arrested most particularly on the image of his mother that he carries in him. "Every man carries within him an image of woman that he gets from his mother; that determines whether he will honor women in general, or despise them, or be generally indifferent to them" (IV 2, 273).

If one is to believe Nietzsche's many heterogenous texts on woman, one may conclude that this image must have been at least ambivalent. It is an ambivalence that is transposed, in and by its desire, its fear of "looking into the abyss," into the depths of nature. And it requires, after one has dared so to gaze, the cure from luminous images of which the Birth of Tragedy speaks. The camera obscura is perhaps a mechanism that can ward off evil (une machine à valeur apotropaïque). This ambivalence is displaced from the mother to his sister Elizabeth, his lama, the only being except Wagner he says he ever loved.

I am not always able to be "just." Malwida once wrote me that there were two people to whom I was unjust: Wagner, and you, my sister. Why so? Perhaps because I have loved you two the most and am not able to still the resentment that you abandoned me. Read then in my unhappy thoughts and in the severity of my language the sorrow of having lost you and of seeing your name linked with a party [anti-Semitism] with which you have no common thought and with which you have nothing to do. (Letter to Elizabeth, 26 December 1887).

The maxims and arrows Nietzsche directs toward women: Is not their very severity the mark of this ambivalence? Are they not symptomatic of a deep love for women, all of whom had abandoned him, when they might have served him as a lightning rod . . . or even an umbrella? (IV 2, 289).[29]

In the letter of 23 March 1887, he gives five conditions which he indicates might make life livable; none, he indicates, seems realizable.

I would need (1) someone to oversee my stomach; (2) someone gay to laugh with me; (3) someone proud of my company who would hold the others in front of me at a respectful distance; (4) someone who might read to me without making it dull and stupid. There is fifth but I do not even want to mention it.

To marry now would be asinine and would lead to the loss of the independence that I have won at a bloody price. . . . Besides, parenthetically, I have not yet found a woman whose company agrees with my character, who didn't bore and bother me. The lama was a good companion, I can't find a replacement for her, but she really wanted to sacrifice herself and to unleash all her energy. And for whom? For a pitiful humanity completely strange to her, and not for me. Yet I would have been such a thankful beast, always ready to laugh joyfully. Are you still able to laugh?[30]

Postscript

One should recall here the joke by Christian Ehrenfels, analyzed by Freud in *Jokes and Their Relation to the Unconscious* (New York: Norton, 1960,

48   Nietzsche's Use of Women

110–11): "A woman is like an umbrella: sooner or later one takes a cab." For a commentary, see S. Kofman, *Pourquoi rit-on?* (Parish: Galilée, 1986). In addition, it seems very important to refer to Nietzsche's letter to his grandparents (2 November 1857), where we learn that Nietzsche received an umbrella from his mother for his birthday. In another letter (*Kritische Gesammmelte Briefe* I 1, 321–23), his mother reminds him especially not to forget his umbrella when it rains . . .

Notes

1. For Comte, "coarse fetishism" is the necessary starting point for all intelligence, human as well as animal. "Its fundamental principle consists in transporting the human type everywhere. We always come back to thinking the beings that concern us to be alive, in that we explain what properly pertains to them in terms of corresponding phenomena." Auguste Comte, *Cours de philosophie positive*, bk. 3 (Paris: Ballière, 1864).

2. The matter is not so simple, even for Comte; there, even the theoretical impulse required a "practical impulse," even if it was not derived from it.

3. Cf. "Fetishism" in Sigmund Freud, *Collected Papers* (London: Hogarth, 1950), 5:198–204.

4. Sigmund Freud, *The Interpretation of Dreams* (New York: Avon, 1968), 428–31.

5. Gaston Bachelard, *L'Air et les songes* (Paris: Corti, 1943, 28.

6. Bachelard: "The dynamic trace of lightness or heaviness is much more profound. It marks being more deeply that a passing desire, . . . Oneiric levitation is a deeper, more essential, simpler psychic reality than love itself."

7. Cf. Sarah Kofman, *Nietzsche et la métaphore* (Paris: Payot, 1983; Galilée, 1986).

8. Goethe, *Faust*, II, lines 9603–11.

9. Cf. Sarah Kofman, *Camera obscura de l'idéologie* (Parish: Galilée 1973).

10. Friedrich Nietzsche, *Le Livre du philosophe* III 114, 475.

11. *Le Livre du philosophe* III, 175.

12. The panther and the tiger are generally the animals attached to Dionysus's chariot. In the notes for *Zarathustra*, we read: "Dionysus on a tiger, the skull of a goat—a panther: the dreaming Ariadne abandoned by the hero, dream of the overman."

13. Cf. VI 2, 32–33. In "On Narcissism: An Introduction," *Collected Papers* 4:30–59 at 46, Freud, probably by the intermediary of Lou Salomé, seems to have drawn upon this conception of the woman-panther. It permits him to introduce a differential typology, to admit that there is another kind of woman than the penis-envy woman. This is a new type, the narcissistic woman, affirmative, envied by men and feared for her enigmatic character. Any comparison between Nietzsche and Freud must go through this essential text. Cf. S. Kofman, *L'Enigme de la femme* (Paris: Galilée, 1980); English translation by Cathy Porter, *The Enigma of Woman* (Ithaca: Cornell University Press, 1985).

14. Nietzsche's text stands joined here to those of Hume and Rousseau.

15. Cf. VI 2, 243–44. In a recent particularly Nietzschean film by Roman Polanski, *What!* the heroine is progressively stripped of her "veils" but is never completely naked: a coat of blue paint covers one of her legs when at last one might think her completely undressed.

16. "Thus the foot or the shoe owes its attraction as a fetish, or part of it, to the circumstance that the inquisitive boy used to peer up the women's legs toward her genitals" (Sigmund Freud, "Fetishism," *Collected Papers* 5:201).

17. Freud, who in general sees "penis envy" as the bedrock of the female structure and not as the

product of *ressentiment*, also links literary aspirations in women with hostility toward men and penis envy: "Behind this penis envy there comes to light the woman's hostile bitterness against the man, which never completely disappears in the relations between the sexes, and which is clearly indicated in the strivings and in the literary productions of 'emancipated women' " (Sigmund Freud, "The Taboo of Virginity," *Standard Edition* [London: Hogarth, 1975], 2:205).

18. *Le Livre du philosophe*, 85.

19. From a completely different approach and in a completely different style, Jacques Derrida, in *Eperons/Spurs* (Chicago: University of Chicago Press, 1979) has decisively shown what is going on for Nietzsche with women and castration. More particularly, he shows that one cannot find any theses that are for castration or against it. He tries to formalize the different points of view which castration gives us into a code which cannot be exhaustive. The "drawing of the hymen" (*le graphique de l'hymen*), a logic of the space between and the threshold, substitutes itself for the opposition of castration and fetishism in order to inscribe that which might well be the nature of life or of Dionysus, neither veiled nor unveiled, neither masculine nor feminine. As to the "misogyny" of Nietzsche, Derrida shows that there is an enigmatic but necessary congruence between "feminist" and "antifeminist" claims.

20. *Le Livre du philosophe*, 85.

21. Refer again here to Roman Polanski's film *What!* in which the old father blesses life as he dies between the legs of the heroine.

22. Salomon Reinach, *Cultes, mythes, religion*, vol. 4 (Paris: Leroux, 1912). Freud, in his "A Mythological Parallel to a Visual Obsession," also links this episode with the fantasy of one of his patients, who represented his father "as the naked lower part of a body, provided with arms and legs, but without the head or upper part. The genitals were not indicated, and the facial features were drawn on the abdomen." The terra-cottas of Priene "represent Baubô [and] show the body of a woman without a head or chest, with a face drawn on the abdomen: the lifted dress frames this like a crown of hair" (*Standard Edition* 14:337–38).

23. *Apotropaïque* is a neologism from the Greek *apo-tropos:* to displace in space. TRANS.

24. One of the figures drawn on the belly of the statuettes of Priene is considered by Picard to be the analog of the Gorgon.

25. *Fragments posthumes*, 9:261, 269.

26. This relationship is already found in Empedocles.

27. Sexual initiation and opening to the beyond go hand in hand. Proshymnos is to be related to the lyrical muse Polymnie, who Plato says in the *Symposium* represents certain turpitudes of fleshly love.

28. In several of his plays, Aristophanes describes substitute phalluses (*Baubôn*), which women used while their men were away at war.

29. In a letter to his sister, he says that Madame Wagner was a lighting rod for her husband. See also IV 2, 289, where he says that certain women are useful to their husbands (who are egoistic enough to accept it) as "lighting rod, storm-protector [*paratonnerre*] and voluntary umbrella." Wagner, it seems, was the inventor of an umbrella with two handles, apparently on exhibit at Bayreuth. We are grafting all these remarks about the "umbrella," which has been brilliantly "commented" upon by Derrida in *Eperons/Spurs*. He shows that there is no reading that can take away from this aphorism its undecidability; it is a paradigm for any text. This is even the case for an analytic reading, which nevertheless must be undertaken but could never be decisive. Derrida's umbrella thus protects us from all dogmatism.

30. Friedrich Nietzsche, *Briefe an Mutter und Schwester*, ed. E. F. Nietzsche (Leipsig: Insel, 1926), 457.

2

The Question of Style

Jacques Derrida

Translated by Ruben Berezdivin

The title kept for this conference shall have been *the question of style*.

But—it will be woman who shall be my subject.

It would remain to ask whether that amounts to the same—or to something other.

The question of style is always the question of a pointed object; often only a pen, but also a stylet, or even a dagger. With whose help one can certainly cruelly attack what philosophy calls by the name of matter or the matrix, in order to pierce a mark upon it, leave an imprint or a form, but also to repel a menacing force, keep it at a distance, repress it, protect oneself from it—folding oneself or refolding, in flight, behind veils.

As to veils/sails—there we are: Nietzsche will have practiced all the genres.

The style would advance, then, like a spur, for instance that of a sailboat: the *rostrum*, that jut that goes ahead to break up the attack and fend off the adverse surface.

Or else, still in a Nautical sense, that edge of a rock called a spur that "breaks up the waves at the entrance to a harbor."

Hence style can *also* protect by its spur against the terrifying, blinding and mortal menace that *presents* itself, of what is obstinately given to the view: the presence, therefore, content, the thing itself, sense, truth—unless that is *already* the deflowered abyss in all that unveiling of difference. *Already* [*déjà*], name of what is effaced, in advance subtracted, leaving nonetheless the mark, a signature subtracted into where it retires, the here present, to be taken note, which we shall do—although that is an operation neither simple nor to be made in one stroke. [. . .]

To insist then on what impresses the mark of the styled spur on the question of woman—I do not say the figure of woman, clichéd locution—, because it'll be a matter here of seeing the figure of woman be *raised,* the question of the figure being at once opened and shut by what is called woman; to announce henceforth what regulates the play of veils/sails (for example of a boat) around apotropaic anxiety; and finally, to allow to appear some exchange between Nietzsche's style and Nietzsche's woman, here are some lines from the *Gay Science:*

> Women and their action at a distance.
> Do I still have ears? Am I all ears and nothing but?

(All Nietzsche's questions, specifically that on woman, are rolled up in the labyrinth of an ear [. . .].)

> Am I all ears and nothing but? In the midst of the ardent surf [. . .], whose foamy return of white flames splashes against my feet [. . .], there are the howling, threats, strident screams that assail me while from his deep cave the ancient shaker of the earth deafeningly sings his aria, like a bellowing bull: doing which, with his shaking foot he beats a measure such that the heart of the demons of these weather-beaten rocks trembles. When suddenly, as if emerging out of nothing, at the doors of this infernal labyrinth

appears, at merely a few arms' length, a big sailboat that passes by in a silent ghostly gliding. O ghostly beauty! How magically it affects me! Has all the calm and silence of the world embarked upon it? Does even my happiness sit in this quiet place, my happier self, second immortalized ego? Not to be dead and yet no longer alive—a spirit-like intermediate being, quietly observing, gliding, floating. Like the boat with white sails gliding like an immense butterfly over the dark sea. Yes!—to move *over* existence, that's it! That would be something!

It seems as if the noise here led me into fantasying. All great bustle leads us to transfer happiness into some calm distance. When a man stands in the midst of his own noise, his own surf of plans and projects, he is also apt to notice quiet, magical beings glide past him and to long for their happiness and seclusion: *women!* He would also believe his better self dwelling there among them, and that in these calm regions even the loudest surf turns into deadly quiet, life itself into a dream of life.

The preceding fragment, *Wir Kunstler!* (Us Artists!), that began with "When we love a woman," describes the notion marking simultaneously the somnambulistic risk of death, its dream, the sublimation and the dissimulation of nature. The trait of dissimulation remains tied to art and to woman:

And right away the spirit and power of the dream overcomes us, and with our eyes open, coldly contemptuous of all danger, we climb onto the most hazardous paths and scale the roofs and spires of fantasy, without any dizziness, as if born to climb, we somnambulists of the day! We artists! We dissimulators of nature! We moon-struck and god-struck ones! We wander still as death, unwearied, on heights we do not perceive as heights but as our plains, as our safety!

Yet, yet, noble enthusiast! Even on the most calm sailboat there is a lot of noise, and unfortunately even small and petty noise. The magic and most powerful effect of women is, philosophically spoken, action at a distance, *actio in distans;* but this requires first of all and above all else—distance!

Below what step does this *Dis-tanz* open?
Nietzsche's writing mimics it already, with a stylistic effect separated

between the Latin citation (*actio in distans*) parodying the language of philosophers *and* the exclamation point, the dash suspending the word *Distanz:* which invites us to a pirouette or play of silhouettes to hold ourselves far from the multiple veils/sails that make us dream of death.

Woman's seduction operates at a distance, distance is the element of its power. But one must keep away from this chant, this charm, one must keep distance at a distance, not only, as one might believe, to keep guard against this fascination, but just as much to experience it. There's want of distance (wanted), there is a want of keeping distance (*Distanz*), which we are in want of, which we want doing, all this resembling the advice from a man to a man: To seduce while not getting seduced.

If we want to keep a distance from the feminine operation (from the *actio in distans*), which is not the same a simply getting close to it, save to risk death *herself,* it's because "woman" perhaps is not just anything, determinable identity of a figure that she announces at a distance, distant from something else, from whom one would have to get farther or nearer. Perhaps she is, as nonidentity, nonfigure, simulacrum, the very *abyss* of distance, the distancing of distance, the stroke of spacing, distance itself; if one could still say this, which is impossible: distance *her-self.* One would need to have recourse to the Heideggerian use of the word *Entfernung,* at once separation, removing afar, drawing further of the far, the drawing-far [*l'e-loignement*], the destruction (*Ent-*) constitutive of the far as such, veiled enigma of proximity.

The separated opening of this *Entfernung* yields place to truth, and woman is there separated from herself.

There is no essence to woman because woman separates and separates from and of herself. She submerges, veils through the depths, without end, without ground, all essentiality, all identity, all propriety. Blinded here, philosophical discourse plummets, left to plunge to its ruin.

There is no truth to woman but its because this abyssal separation of truth, this nontruth is the "truth." Woman is a name for this nontruth of truth.

I sustain this proposition with a few texts among many.

On the one hand, Nietzsche makes his own in a fashion we shall qualify, this barely allegorical figure, truth as woman or as the motion of the veil of feminine modesty. And in a fragment rarely quoted he develops the complicity rather than the unity of woman, life, seduction, modesty and all the effects of veils (*Schleier, Enthülung, Verhüllung*). The redoubtable problem being what is unveiled but once [. . .]. Here merely the last lines:

> . . . for nondivine reality either never grants us at all the beautiful or just once! I mean that the world thrives with beautiful things, but is no less poor, very poor, in beautiful instants and revelations [. . .] of such. But perhaps that is the most powerful charm [*Zauber*] of life: it is covered with a gold-wrought veil [. . .] of beautiful possibilities that grant it a promising, reticent, modest, ironical allure, sympathetic, seductive. Yes, life is a woman!

But on the other hand, to that truth that is woman, the philosopher who *believes* it, credulous and dogmatic, in truth as in woman, has understood nothing. For if woman is truth, *she* knows that there is no truth, that truth has not taken place and that one does not have hold of truth. And she is woman to the extent that she doesn't believe, she, in truth, hence in that which she is, in what is believed to be her, which therefore she is not.

Distance operates thus when it hides the proper identity of woman and unsaddles the cavalier philosopher, unless he receive from woman herself two spurs, strokes of style or strokes of dagger whose exchange then erases sexual identity:

> If someone cannot guard himself and hence wishes not to, we do not consider this disgraceful; but for anyone who both lacks the capacity and the goodwill for revenge, regardless of whether its a man or a woman, we have little respect. Would a woman be able to hold us in thrall ("enthrall" us) if we didn't consider she could, under given circumstance, quite possibly wield a dagger (any kind) *against* us? Or against herself—which in certain cases would be an even crueller revenge (Chinese revenge).

[. . .]

How can woman, being truth, not believe in it? But also, how could she be truth while still believing in it?

Overture to *Beyond Good and Evil*: "Supposing truth were a woman . . ."

But at this moment Nietzsche turns the truth of woman or the truth of truth:

> What is certain is that she has not allowed herself to be laid a hold of—, and that today every kind of dogmatism is left standing dispirited and discouraged, *if* it is left standing at all!

Woman (truth) doesn't let herself be laid hold of.

Of truth woman the truth in truth cannot lay a hold.

What does not in truth [*à la vérité*] allow laying a hold of is—*feminine*, which one must not hasten to translate as femininity, the femininity of woman, the feminine sexuality and other fetishes which are precisely what one aims to lay hold of when one remains at the level of idiocy of the dogmatic philosopher, the impotent artist, or the inexperienced seducer.

This separation of truth that detaches from itself, raises in quotation marks (machination, cry, flight and pincers of a crane) everything that will constrain Nietzsche's writing to a setting in parenthesis of "truth" and by rigorous consequence, all the rest, what will *inscribe* truth, and by rigorous consequence inscribe in general, *is*, no, let's not say, the feminine, but: the feminine "operation."

She writes. To her style belongs. Rather: If style were (As in Freud the penis would be, "the normal prototype of the fetish") man, writing would be woman.

All these weapons circulate from one hand to another, passing through each contrary, the question remaining as to just what I am doing here at this moment.

Should we reconcile these propositions, in appearance feminist, with the enormous corpus of the voracious antifeminism of Nietzsche? The congruence, here opposed by convention to coherence, would be enigmatic but rigorously necessary. At least that would be the thesis of the present communication.

Truth, woman, is skepticism and veiling dissimulation: there is what one would want to think. The *skepsis* of "truth" in the era of woman:

> I fear old women are more skeptical in their heart's most secret recesses than men; they consider the shallowness of existence as its essence, and all virtue and depth is to them merely a veil over this "truth," a very welcome veil over a *pudendum;* in other words, a matter of modesty and shame, but no more than that!

Truth would therefore be but a surface, would not become profound truth, raw [*crue:* "cruel, crude, crane"], desirable except through the effect of a veil: that befalls her. A truth not suspended by quotation marks that would cover the surface in a motion of modesty. It would suffice to suspend the veil or allow it to fall otherwise so there would no longer be truth or only "truth"—thus written.

Why then the terror, fear, "modesty"?

Feminine distance abstracts from itself truth in *suspending* the tie to castration. Suspend as one may hand out or extend a piece of cloth, a relation, etc., that at the same time one holds—suspended, in indecision.

Suspended relation to castration: not to its truth, in which woman does not believe, nor to truth as castration, nor to truth-castration. Truth-castration is precisely man's thing, man's business, never skeptical dissimulated or old enough, and which in its credulity, its imbecility (always sexual and on occasion assuming the likeness of expert mastery) castrates itself thereby producing the lure of truth-castration.

[. . .]

"Woman"—the term marks an epoch—does not even believe in the straight inverse of castration, anticastration. She is too wily for that and knows, about her, at least about her operation, what us, but which us, should learn, that such a reversal would take away every possibility of a simulacrum, would in truth amount to the same, and would install her all the more assuredly in the old machine, in a phallogocentrism assisted by its accomplice, inverse image of its pupil, rowdy student, disciple of the master.

Now "woman" has need of the effect of castration without which she couldn't seduce nor arouse desire, but evidently she doesn't believe in it. That is "woman," whatever does not believe in castration and plays at it. Plays with it: with a new concept or a new structure of belief about to laugh. About man—she knows, with a knowledge no dogmatic or credulous philosophy will have been able to measure, that castration *has not taken place.*

Formula to be prudently displaced. It marks first that the place of castration is not determinable, undecidable mark or nonmark, discrete margin with incalculable consequences, among which, as I observed elsewhere, what amounts to the strict equivalence between affirming and denying castration, between castration and anti-castration, between its assumption and its denial. [. . .]

If it had taken place castration would be that syntax of the undecidable assuring, in annulling and equating them, all the discourses *pro et contra*. The stroke of nothing [*le coup pour rien*], that is besides never attempted without interest.

Whence the extreme *Skepsis des Weibes*. From the moment she tears the veil of modesty or truth where one has tried to envelop her, "holding her in the greatest possible ignorance *in eroticis*," her skepticism is without bounds. Merely read "On Feminine Chastity" (*Gay Science*, par. 7): in the "contradiction between love and modesty," in the "proximity of god and beast," between "the enigma of the solution" and the "solution of the enigma," how "the ultimate philosophy and skepticism of woman casts anchor there." It is in that void that she casts her anchor.

"Woman" is then so little interested in truth, she believes it so little, that truth regarding her own subject doesn't even concern her. It is "man" who thinks his discourse on woman or in truth *concerns*; such was the topographic question I was sketching, that was being avoided, also, as always, just now, as to the undecidable contour of castration—woman. Circumvented. And truly the feminist women against whom Nietzsche multiples his sarcasm are men. Feminism is the operation by means of which woman wishes to resemble man, the dogmatic philosopher, reclaiming truth, science, objectivity, that is, the whole virile illusion, and the effect of castration, attached to it. Feminism wants castration—even that of woman. To lose style.

Nietzsche well denounces, in feminism, the lack of style:

> Is it not in the worst taste when women sets about becoming scientific that way? So far, enlightment of this kind was fortunately man's affair, man's lot. We kept "among ourselves" in this.

The whole process of the feminine operation is spaced within that appearance of contradiction. Woman is twice the model, in contradictory fashion, she is praised and condemned at once. Like writing does it regularly and not by chance, woman folds the argument of the procurer to the *cauldron's logic*. Model of truth, she enjoys a seductive power that

rules the dogmatism and disorients, making credulous men, the philosophers, flee. But insofar as she does not believe in truth, finding nevertheless her interest in that truth, which fails to interest her, she is again the
model: this time the good model, or rather the bad model as good model:
she plays at dissimulation, cosmetics, lying, art, she the philosopher artist,
she is a power of affirmation. Were one to condemn her yet, it would be
to the degree that she would deny her affirmative power from man's point
of view, that she would come to lie believing still in truth, reflecting in a
mirror the idiotic dogmatism she arouses. [. . .]

The questions of art, style, truth can therefore not be dissociated from
woman. But the simple formation of that common problematic suspends
the question "What is woman?" Woman is no longer to be sought, or the
femininity of woman, or female sexuality. At least one can't find them
according to a familiar mode of the concept or of knowledge, even if one
can't restrain oneself from seeking them.

In the place where it traverses, toward woman's body, the veil of truth
and the simulacrum of castration, the question of style can and must be
measured against the great question of the interpretation of Nietzsche's
text, of the interpretation of interpretation [. . .] in order to disqualify it
in its statement.

To take such measure, how to abbreviate the Heideggerian
reading . . . ? [. . .]

To announce that other no longer coupled within an oppositional reversal, Heidegger refers to a since famous story of a unique fable, "*The
story of an error*," in *Twilight of the Idols* (1888): "How the true world
finally became a fable." [. . .] Heidegger follows therefore Nietzsche's
operation [. . .] but not to ask, here, if Nietzsche has *succeeded* in doing
what he aimed at, and "to what degree' he has effectively surmounted
Platonism. Heidegger calls that a "critical question" [. . .].

It is the horizon of this Heideggerian question, at the moment that it
orients the most rigorous reading, that one will, later perhaps, have to
burst open [. . .]

Which will not be done, undoubtedly, except by the intervention of
some styletic practice.

Styled practice, but of what sort?

It cannot be written except by way of the conjoint fable of woman and
truth. Woman enters the scene [. . .]

The history of an error. In each of its six sequences of six epochs, with the exception of the third, some words are italicized. In the second, the only words italicized by Nietzsche are *sie wird Weib*, "it [the Idea] becomes female."

In looking closer at "*sie wird Weib*" we shall indeed not go *counter* to Heidegger, which would be still to follow his gesture [. . .].

Rather, let us try to decipher *woman's inscription:* its necessity is un-doubtedly neither a metaphorical illustration nor an allegory without concept, nor a pure concept without imaginal schematism.

The context indicates it clearly, what becomes female is the idea. Be-coming female is a "progress of the idea" [. . .]. The idea is a form of the self-presentation of truth. Truth has therefore not always been female. Both have a history, form a story, history itself perhaps, if the strict value of history has always been presented as such within the motion of truth, which philosophy alone cannot decrypt, herself included within it.

Before this progress in the story of the true world, the idea was Pla-tonic. And the *Umschreibung*, the transcription periphrase or paraphrase of the Platonic utterance of truth, in that inaugural moment of the idea, is "*Ich, Plato, bin die Wahrheit*," "I, Plato, I *am* the truth."

The second phase of the becoming female of the idea as presence or setting the scene of truth is therefore the moment when Plato can no longer say "I am the truth," when the philosopher is no longer the truth, separates himself from it as well as from himself, no longer tracks it down save by its trace, exiles himself or lets the idea go into exile. Then begins the story, begin the (hi)stories. Then distance—woman—separates [quarters: *écarte*] truth—philosophy, and grants the idea. Which draws afar, becomes transcendent, inaccessible, seductive, acts and shows the path at a distance, *in die Ferne*. Its sails float afar, the dream of death begins: here's woman.

> The true world out of reach in the present but promised to the sage, the pious, the virtuous ("to the sinner who renders peni-tence").
>
> "Progress of the idea: it becomes more refined, more captious, more unreachable—*it becomes female* . . .).

All the attributes, characteristic traits, attractions that Nietzsche had recognized in woman, seductive distance, captivating inaccessibility, in-finitely veiled promise, transcendence producing desire, the *Entfernung*—all belong indeed to the story of truth as (hi)story of an error.

Then, as if in apposition, as if to render explicit and analyze "it becomes female," Nietzsche adds "*sie wird christlich . . .*" ["she becomes Christian"] and closes the parenthesis.

It's in the epoch of that parenthesis that one could try to lead that fable toward the motif of castration, *within* the Nietzschean text, that is, toward the enigma of a non-presence of truth.

What is indicated in red letters in "it becomes female, it becomes Christian . . ." I shall try to show consists in "she castrates [herself]," she castrates because she is castrated, she plays off her castration within the epoch of a parenthesis, she feigns castration, suffered and inflicted, to master the master from afar, to produce the desire and by the same stroke, here "the same thing," to kill him.

Phase and necessary periphrase within the (hi)story of woman-truth, woman as truth, of verification and of feminization.

Let us turn the page. Let us pass, in *Twilight of the Idols*, to the page that follows "*Story of an error.*" "*Moral als Widernatur,*" (Morals as unnatural) is then opened, Christianity is there interpreted as *castratism* (*Kastratismus*). The extraction of teeth, plucking out of the eye, Nietzsche says, are Christian operations. They are the violence of the Christian idea, of the idea become female:

> All the old moral monsters agree that *il faut tuer les passions* ["one must kill the passions"]. Its most famous formulation is found in the New Testament, in that Sermon on the Mount where, incidentally, things are by no means regarded from a *lofty* standpoint. There for instance it is said, with special reference to sexuality: "If the eye offend thee, pluck it out." Fortunately no Christian follows the prescription. To *exterminate* the passions and desires, merely as a preventive measure against their folly and the consequences of that folly—, today, this itself strikes us as merely another acute form of folly. We no longer admire dentists who *pluck out* the teeth so that they will no longer hurt.

To Christian extirpation or castration, at least that of the "first Church" [. . .], Nietzsche opposes the spiritualization of passion (*Vergeistigung der Passion*). He seems to imply that no castration is at work in such spiritualization, which is not obvious. I leave this problem open.

Hence the Church, the first, truth of the woman-idea, proceeds by ablation, extirpation, excision:

The Church fights passion with *excision* in every sense [*Ausschei-dung:* cutting off, castration]: its practice, its "cure," is *castratism*. It never asks: "How can we spiritualize, beautify, deify a desire?" It has always laid the stress of its discipline on the extirpation (of sexuality, pride, of the lust to rule, avarice, of vengeance). But an attack on the roots of passion means an attack on the roots of life: the practice of the Church is *hostile to life*.

Hence hostile to woman who is life (*femina vita*): castration is an operation of woman against woman, no less than each sex against itself and against the other sex.

The same means in the fight against a craving—castration, extirpation—is instinctively chosen by those too weak-willed, too degenerate, to impose moderation on themselves. One should survey the whole history of priests and philosophers, including the artists: the most poisonous things against the senses have been said *not* by the impotent, nor by ascetics, but by the impossible ascetics, those who were really in dire need of being such. The spiritualization of sensuality is called *love:* it represents a great triumph over Christianity. [. . .] The saint in whom God delights is the ideal eunuch.

The heterogeneity of the text shows it well; Nietzsche did not suffer the illusion, on the contrary analyzed it, of knowing what the effects named woman, truth, castration were about, or the *ontological* effects of presence or absence. He guarded himself well of the precipitate denial that would consist in erecting a simple discourse against castration and its system. Without discrete parody, without writing strategy, without difference or separation [divergence] of pens, without style, therefore, the grand one, the reversal would amount to the same in the noisy declaration of the antithesis.

Whence the heterogeneity of the text.

Renouncing the treatment of the enormous number of propositions on woman by Nietzsche, I shall try to formalize their rule, gather them into a finite number of typed and matrical propositions. Then I shall mark out the essential limits of such a codification and the reading problem it determines.

Three types of statements, three fundamental propositions that are also three value-positions, aroused from three different locations. The value-positions could also take on the sense, after some elaborations I can only indicate here, of what psychoanalysis (for example) gives to the term "position."

1. Woman is condemned, debased, scorned as figure or power of lying. The category of accusation is then made in the name of truth, of the dogmatic philosophy of the credulous male who advances truth and the phallus as his own attributes. The texts—phallogocentric—written from this reactive and negative instance, are quite numerous.

2. Woman is condemned, debased, scorned as figure or power of truth, as a philosophical or Christian being, either identified with truth or, at a distance still enjoying it and using it as a fetish for her advantage without believing in it, dwelling by ruse and naïveté [. . .] within the system and economy of truth, within the phallogocentric space. The trial is then conducted from the point of view of the masked artist. But he still believes in woman's castration and remains at the inversion of the reactive and negative instance.

3. Woman is recognized, beyond this double negation, and affirmed, as affirmative power, dissimulating, artist, Dionysian. She is not affirmed by man but herself affirms herself, in herself and in man. In the sense in which I said just now that castration has not taken place. Antifeminism is in its turn reversed, he didn't condemn woman but to the extent that she was responding to the man of the two reactive positions.

For these three statements to form an exhaustive code so that one could try to reconstitute in them a systematic unity, the parodying stylistic heterogeneity, of styles, would have to be capable of being mastered and reduced to the content of a thesis. On the other hand, but these two conditions are co-implicated, each value implied in the three schemes would have to be *decidable* into a couple of oppositions as if there were a contrary to each term: for instance, for woman, truth, castration.

But the graphics of the hymen or the pharmakon, that inscribes in her the effect of castration without being reducible to it, effect at work everywhere and specifically in Nietzsche's text, limits without appeal the pertinence of these hermeneutic or systematic questions. It subtracts always a margin from the control of the sense or the code.

Not that one would side passively with the heterogeneous or with parody (that would still reduce it), or that one should conclude that the master sense, unique and without grafts, unfindable, belongs to Nietzsche's infinite mastery or his ungraspable power, the impeccable manipulation of a trap, a sort of infinite calculation like that of Leibniz's God, only this time infinite calculation of the undecidable, in order to unhinge the hermeneutic attitude. That would, in trying to evade it, be only a way by a sure stroke to fall back as surely into the trap. It would be a parodying or simulation of an instrument of mastery at the service of truth or of castration, reconstituting religion, for example the cult of Nietzsche, finding there one's interest, priestess of the interpreter of parodies, interpretess.

One must tell oneself brutally that if the aphorisms on woman and the rest can't be assimilated, first of all among themselves, it's because Nietzsche himself couldn't see very clearly nor with one blink of the eyes, in an instant, and that such regular blindness, in beat, with which one shall never finish, has taken place in the text. There Nietzsche is a bit lost. There is loss, that can be affirmed, from the point on where there is hymen.

In the weave of the text Nietzsche is a bit lost like a spider unequal to what is produced through her, I say indeed like a spider, or like many spiders, that of Nietzsche, that of Lautréaumont, that of Mallarmé, that of Freud and of Nicolas Abraham.

> He was and dreaded such a castrated woman.
>
> He was and dreaded such a castrating woman.
>
> He was and loved such affirming women.

All that at once, simultaneously or successively, according to the places of his body and the positions of his history. He had to do in himself and outside himself with so many women.

There is not *a* woman, a truth in itself of woman in itself, that at least he has stated, and [through] the varied typology, the crowd of mothers, daughters, sisters, old maids, wives, governesses, prostitutes, virgins, grandmothers and granddaughters, of his work.

For that very reason there is no one truth of Nietzsche or of Nietzsche's text. When one reads in *Beyond Good and Evil,* "These are *my* truths," in italicizing *"meine Warheiten sind,"* it is precisely in a paragraph on women.

My truths, that undoubtedly implies that they are not *truth* since they are multiple, multicolored, contradictory. There is therefore no one truth in itself, but additionally, even for me, of me, truth is plural.

[. . .]

There is therefore no truth in itself of sexual difference in itself, of woman or of man, which on the contrary all of ontology presupposes, covering that undecidability of which she is the effect of inspection [*arraisonnement*, arreasoning], appropriation, identification: of verification of identity.

Here beyond the mythology of the signature, of the theology of the author, the biographical desire is inscribed in the text and leaves there an irreducible mark which is just as irreducibly plural. [. . .]

And in *Ecce Homo* ("Why I write such good books"), two paragraphs follow (IV and V) in which Nietzsche successively asserts that there are "a great number of possible styles," or that there is no "style in itself," because he "well knows women" [. . .]: "That is part of my Dionysian patrimony. Who knows? Perhaps I am the first psychologist of the eternal feminine. They all love me, its an old story, excepting the accidental females (*verunglückten Weiblein*), the 'emancipated ones,' lacking the stuff to make children. Luckily I am not disposed to be torn to pieces: accomplished woman tears to pieces what she loves . . ."

From the moment the question of woman suspends the decidable opposition of the true and nontrue, founds the epochal regime of parentheses for all concepts belonging to the system of this philosophical decidability, disqualifies the hermeneutic project postulating the true sense of a text, liberates reading from the horizon of the sense of being or from the truth of being, from the values of production of the produced or of the presence of the present, what is unchained is the question of *style* as a question of *writing*: the question of a spurring operation more powerful than all content, any thesis, all sense. The styled spur traverses the veil, not only tears it to view or produce the thing itself, but undoes the opposition to itself, the opposition folded over itself of the veiled/unveiled, truth as production, unveiling/dissimulation of the produced within presence. It neither lifts nor sets down the veil/sail, it de-limits its suspense—its epoch. To delimit, undo, be undone, when it's a matter of veils/sails, does that amount still to unveil? Indeed to destroy a fetish? That question *as question* (between *logos* and *theoria*, saying and seeing) interminably remains.

The Heideggerian reading was off-course [*en rade*]—but we took it as our point of departure—from the moment when it lacked woman in the fable of truth: it didn't pose the sexual question or at least did not submit it to the general question of the truth of being. But has one not just noticed that the question of sexual difference was not a regional question under the authority of a general ontology [. . .]? Indeed, that it was no longer merely a *question?*

Perhaps things are not so simple. The significations or conceptual values that seem to constitute the stakes or the springs of all the Nietzschean analyses on sexual difference, on the "incessant war of the sexes," on "love," eroticism, etc., all have as vector what could be called the trial of *propriation* (appropriation, expropriation, hold, possessive hold, gift and exchange, mastery, servitude, etc.). Through numerous analyses that I cannot follow here, it appeared, according to an already formalized rule, that woman is woman as much in giving, yielding, *in yielding herself*, while man holds and takes, possesses, takes possession, but on the contrary, in giving herself woman *yields-as* [gives-herself-for] to dissimulate and assure herself of possessive mastery.

The "yielding-as" [giving-for], the *as* [*for*], whatever be its value, whether it deceives in yielding an illusion or whether it introduces some destination, finality, or wily calculation, some return, some amortizement or benefit into the loss of the proper, the *as* [*for*] retains the gift of a reserve and changes from that point on all the signs of the sexual opposition. Man and woman trade places, exchange their masks to infinity.

Therefore it cannot be asked any longer "What *is* the proper, appropriation, expropriation, mastery, servility, etc.?" As sexual operation, and *before* it we do not know sexuality, propriation is more powerful, because undecidable, than the question *ti esti* [What is it?], than the question of the veil of truth or of the sense of being. All the more so, neither secondary nor supplementary argument, in that the trial of propriation organizes the totality of the trial of language and of symbolic exchange in general, including, therefore, all ontological *statements*. The (hi)story of truth (is) a trial of propriation. The proper does not stem therefore from an onto-phenomenological or semantic-hermeneutic interrogation. The question of the sense or of the truth of being is not *capable* of the question of the proper, of the undecidable exchange of the more in the less, of yielding-[giving-]taking, of giving-holding [guarding], of giving-to-hurt, of the *stroke of nothing*. It is not capable of her because in her it is inscribed. [. . .]

3

Woman as Truth in Nietzsche's Writing

Kelly Oliver

Nietzsche is as notorious for his struggle with woman as he is for his battle with truth: his writings are a mixture of awe and disdain for both. The infamy of Nietzsche's discussions of both woman and truth is not their only relationship, for in several passages, Nietzsche himself connects truth and woman. "Suppose truth is a woman . . . What is certain is that she has not allowed herself to be won—today every kind of dogmatist is left standing dispirited and discouraged."[1] Both truth and woman are elusive—distance is their power. The connection between truth and woman does not simplify the task of formulating Nietzsche's relationship to woman. Truth is as ambiguous in Nietzsche's writings as woman. This joint ambiguity is no coincidence: for while developing a theory of truth we are unpacking the symbol of woman. Inversely, while developing a theory of Nietzsche's philosophy of woman, we are unpacking a metaphor for truth. Our investigation will take this ambiguity as its axis: at one pole the ambiguity of truth, at the other, the parallel ambiguity of woman. This ambiguity need not be read as an amorphous bewilderment; rather, a dialectic triad can serve us well in order to demonstrate one way this philosophical ambiguity can be coherently articulated. A triad borrowed from Derrida's *Spurs*, which describes Nietzsche's relationship to woman, will set up a grid for interpreting Nietzsche:

> He was, He dreaded this castrated woman.
>
> He was, He dreaded this castrating woman.
>
> He was, He loved this affirming woman.[2]

Nietzsche both identifies with and reacts against the three positions of woman suggested by Derrida: the castrated woman, the castrating woman, the affirming woman. This tri-positioning of woman corresponds neatly to the tri-positioning of truth which we can extract from Nietzsche's works—truth as a manifestation of the will to truth, the will to illusion, and the will to power. Nietzsche has the same love-hate relationship to woman which he has to truth. The castrated woman embodies truth which results from the will to truth, the castrating woman corresponds to truth as a manifestation of the will to illusion, and the affirming woman is truth as the will to power. Each of these positions is a deception employed by the "avidious will" in order to "detain its creatures in life and compel them to live on."[3] Any deception, according to Nietzsche, can serve either ascending or descending life.

That which serves descending life impoverishes life, and gives a one-sided prominence to some things at the expense of others. The coward who serves declining life sacrifices creative multiplicity for a false security. Those weak wills, claims Nietzsche, who need to discover value rather than create it, are degenerate. Rather than create their own value out of the flux of their experience, they try to go "beyond" the changing manifold of senuous experience into a secure world "as-it-is-in-itself." They postulate a preexisting reality, opposed to the variety of our senuous experience, which needs only to be discovered.

Degenerate life worships this postulated reality which overrides the senses: this transcendent reality demands that we suppress our instincts in favor of its stability. "To be obliged to fight the instincts—this formula of degeneration: as long as life is in the ascending line, happiness is the same as instinct."[4] That which is in the ascending line serves our instincts and thereby enhances life; it accommodates a great and multifarious variety with playful ease. Ascending life "reflects its plentitude upon things—it transfigures, it embellishes, it rationalises the world"; declining life "impoverishes, bleaches, mars the value of things; it suppresses the world."[5]

Each of the three positions of truth and woman can serve either ascending or declining life. Nietzsche identifies with each deception, each position of woman and truth, insofar as it serves ascending life, while he rejects any deception when it serves descending life. "I know both sides," says Nietzsche, "for I am both sides."[6]

The woman who serves ascending life revels in the superabundance of life; while she who serves declining life suppresses it. The castrated woman is the feminist who uses the will to truth either to enhance survival or dominate life. The castrating woman is the artist who uses the will to illusion either to playfully affirm the multiplicity of life or cunningly deceive us in order to gain advantage. The affirming woman is the will to power which either creates or destroys life.

1. The Castrated Woman

The castrated woman imitates the will to truth. Just as the will to truth in the service of descending life can be the most tyrannical manifestation of the will to power, so the castrated woman can be the most tyrannical woman. For both betray themselves by identifying with their opposite: truth as the manifestation of the will to truth believes that it is apodictic and necessary when according to Nietzsche it is the opposite, that is, perspectival and contingent. The castrated or de-sexed woman assumes a position as a second type of man. She is the feminist who negates woman in order to affirm herself as man. "There is stupidity in this movement, (the feminist movement)," writes Nietzsche, "an almost masculine stupidity." He continues, "Certainly there are enough of idiotic friends and corrupters of woman amongst the learned asses of the masculine sex, who advise woman to defeminize herself in this manner, and to imitate all the stupidities from which 'man' in European 'manliness,' suffers."[7] The "feminist," in Nietzsche's (unjustified)[8] opinion, denies her sexuality, castrates herself, in order to imitate man. In the castrated position woman suffers from the will to truth; that is, she lays claim to objective truth. She wants to create a science of woman. In this way she resembles the dogmatic philosopher: here the castrated woman stands in the same ty-rannical relation to truth as the metaphysician. The tyranny of the meta-physician's will to truth manifests itself throughout the history of philosophy from Plato's theory of the Forms to Kant's unknowable *ding an sich*. Knowledge of reality/truth, according to Plato, demands a denial of the changing images presented to the senses in favor of pure reflection which penetrates the multiplicity of sense perception in order to confront reality "as it is" rather than "as it appears." We create a tyrannical truth and then put it beyond our grasp; this is the thing-in-itself. "The true world which is unattainable for the moment, is promised to the sage, to the pious man and to the man of virtue. . . . Progress of the idea: it becomes more subtle, more insidious, more evasive,—*it becomes a woman* . . . "[9]

The "feminist," like the metaphysician, worships the "in-itself," or the "as-it-is." She attempts to pierce the veil forced on women by the male dominated society in order to reveal woman as she is. "Woman wishes to be independent, and therefore she begins to enlighten men about 'woman as she is'—this is one of the worst developments of the general uglifying of Europe."[10]

Both the feminist and the metaphysician are hypnotized by the will to truth. Both seek the in-itself, an objective reality. This position of truth or woman, says Nietzsche, is hostile to life.[11] Objective truth is hostile to the flux and passions of sensuous life which surrounds us; it is hostile to the multiplicity of interpretations whose flux is the will to power, the very source of life.

> . . . castration and extirpation, are instinctively chosen for waging war against a passion, by those who are too weak of will, too degenerate, to impose some sort of moderation upon it,—by those natures who need *la Trappe*, or some kind of ultimatum of war, a gulf set between themselves and a passion.[12]

The castrated woman is hostile to the passions of woman as a senuous being. She not only de-sexes herself in order to imitate man, but she also attempts to develop a science of woman, thereby destroying the power of woman which originates, as we shall see, from her multiple meanings, her ambiguity. The will to truth postulates a reality, a woman, which needs only discovery and no interpretation. We hide truth behind a bush, claims Nietzsche, then praise ourselves when we find it.[13] Just as Nietzsche calls this position of truth "the will to truth as the impotence of the will to create,"[14] he calls emancipated women "abortions who lack the wherewithal to have children."[15]

The castrated position of truth/woman is impotent because it is cut off from the source of its power: illusion. This castrated truth/woman mistakes the means to life for the end of life.

> Man has repeated the same mistake over and over again: he has made a means to life into a standard of life; instead of discovering the standard in the highest enhancement of life itself, in the problem of growth and exhaustion, he has employed the means to a quite distinct kind of life to exclude all other forms of life, in short to criticize and select life. I.e., man finally loves the means for their own sake and forgets that they are means: so that they enter his consciousness as aims, as standards for aims—i.e., a certain species of man treats the conditions of its existence as conditions which ought to be imposed as a law, as "Truth," "good," "perfection": it tyrannizes—[16]

In the case of the castrated woman, the "feminist," what she began as a movement—a means—to improve the socioeconomic position of women has become, among some feminists, an end in itself. Feminism has become a type of moral obligation, a truth, rather than a means to improve life. If what began as an instinct to preserve life or a means to life turns against life and begins to tyrannize life by holding itself up as a standard for life, then it serves declining life. According to Nietzsche, a standard is impotent if it does not improve life. In the case of feminism, when it becomes an end in itself, it becomes impotent to further social change. While the will to truth as it manifests itself in feminism is useful to survival, when it presents its fruits as more than the means to survival—as apodictic truths—then it no longer serves life: it no longer helps our survival. Rather, it turns against life and denies life. The will to truth in its dogmatic certitude serves descending life. It sets up a fixed standard, a science of feminism, to which life in its changing physicality, cannot measure up; it is therefore eternally frustrated and unhealthy.

When we apply Nietzsche's theory to contemporary feminism, we see that feminists, like metaphysicians, divided the world into true and apparent in order to enhance life. The apparent world is the world women are living in, a world dominated by men, in which even wages reflect the inferior value of women. Since women occupy inferior socioeconomic positions in this world of submission, it appears that they are inferior beings. The feminist's truth about woman "as she is" rather than "as she appears" was intended to change woman's socioeconomic position: what was intended to change appearance in order to create the world (where women occupy equal socioeconomic positions as men), became the criterion of reality, a science of woman.

At the parallel pole, the metaphysician's intention of dividing the world into true and apparent, as Nietzsche tells us the parable in *The Will to Power*,

> was to deceive oneself in a useful way: the means, the invention of formulas and signs by means of which one could reduce the confusing multiplicity to a purposive and manageable schema. But alas! now a moral category was brought into play: (namely) no creature wants to deceive itself, . . . consequently there is only a will to truth. . . . This is the greatest error that has ever been committed, the essential fatality of error on earth, one believed one possessed a criterion of reality in the forms of reason—while in fact one possessed them in order to become master of reality, in order to misunderstand reality in a shrewd manner.[17]

Both truth and woman, as a manifestation of the will to truth, began in the service of ascending life. Both were castrated and became impotent to serve life when they turned the means to life into the end of life. The will to truth, whether played out through the feminist's science or the metaphysician's truth, only serves ascending life when it recognizes itself as a means to life, a fiction which enhances life. When it takes itself for *the* privileged perspective it serves degenerate life. Fiction is life-enhancing but only when it playfully serves the multifarious openness of life. It is, then, only when the will to truth becomes the will to illusion, and recognizes itself as illusion, that it is in the service of ascending life.

Truth is more primary than illusion; however, in this impotent and castrated position we forget that "truth does not count as the supreme value. . . . The will to appearance, to illusion, to deception, to becoming and change (to objectified deception) here counts as more profound, primeval, metaphysics than the will to truth, to reality, to mere appearance; the last is itself merely a form of the will to illusion."[18]

At times Nietzsche seems to forget that illusion is more powerful than truth. When he attempts to enlighten us about "woman as she is" he falls back into the impotent, castrated truth. Before he begins his discussion of woman in *Beyond Good and Evil*, he asks permission to "utter some truths about 'woman as she is,' provided that it is known at the outset how literally they are merely," he says, "—my truths."[19]

Nietzsche identifies with woman in order to describe the nature of woman. Here Nietzsche seems to invoke some reality, the nature of woman "as she is," which is independent of interpretation. This, of course, is also Nietzsche's paradox when he tries, in a sense, to assert that the truth is "there is no truth." In order to enlighten us about the real nature of the world about which the will to truth deceives us, Nietzsche himself falls prey to the will to truth. In these passages he seems to rely on some form of the correspondence theory of truth which he rejects: true descriptions correspond to the world. Metaphysicians' descriptions do not correspond to the world "as it is," therefore they are deceptions, while Nietzsche's descriptions are more accurate. When Nietzsche identifies with woman, he must identify with the castrated woman as well as the affirming woman. Recall Derrida's statement: "He *was*. He dreaded this castrated woman." Nietzsche is in the castrated position when he talks of woman "as she is"; he attempts to formulate a science of feminism.

2. The Castrating Woman

Although she remains within the discourse of truth, the castrating woman uses illusion craftily in order to cut the power of the metaphysic of truth. She is the actor or the artist who plays with truth; undermining the metaphysician's authority, she will persuade us of one truth only to abandon that one for another:

> If we consider the whole history of women, are they not obliged first of all, and above all to be actresses? If we listen to doctors who have hypnotised women, or finally if we love them—and let ourselves be "hypnotised" by them—what is divulged thereby?

That they "give themselves airs," even when they—"give themselves" . . . Woman is so artistic. . . .[20]

As the actor the castrating woman assumes a role which she knows is only an illusion yet she convinces the metaphysician and his truth-centered culture that she is for real. She is the woman who uses all of the ideas about woman "as she is," those of the feminists as well as the phallocentric society, never believing them, in order to get what she wants. She is the woman who can play the role of the submissive secretary in order to get a job (she uses the beliefs of the phallocentric society to her own advantage); and then she can play the role of the social-activist in order to demand equal pay (she uses the beliefs of the feminist to her own advantage). Through her illusions and role playing she manipulates the dogmatist's castrated truth. She castrates the metaphysic of truth, cuts its power, by playing it against itself. Like a chameleon, she changes to protect herself from threats in the environment, which undermines the fixity of the metaphysician's reality.

Derrida suggests that "in the *guise* of the christian, philosophical being she either identifies with truth, or else she continues to play with it at a distance as if it were a fetish, manipulating it, even as she refuses to believe in it, to her own advantage."[21] If the castrating woman is a christian, she is a heretic. She may pose as a christian or philosopher, but only in order to undermine their authority through her illusion. She poses playfully to her own advantage. In a sense, as Derrida argues, the christian/philosopher/feminist castrates herself for the sake of a castrated truth; the act of castration, however, is not self-conscious—the dogmatist does not realize that her power comes from multiplicity, that variety which she cuts off by identifying with the castrated truth. In contrast, the castrating woman, the artist, intentionally castrates the dogmatist's truth by identifying with illusion: she cuts off the authority of the dogmatic truth by asserting equally believable illusions—she poses as the truth, but never takes herself seriously.

As the artist the castrating woman cuts the power of the metaphysic of truth by replacing it with equally convincing disguises. She substitutes her illusions for the science of the metaphysician. For, according to Nietzsche, the illusion of the artist, the Apollonian will to illusion, is more profound, complete, and effective than the will to truth. The castrating woman chooses appearance over reality, the "as-it-appears" over the "as-it-is." She learns that illusion is more effective then reality:

But after the inventive genius of the young female artists has run riot for some time in such indiscreet revelations of youth . . . then they at last discover, time and again, that they have not been good judges of their own interest; that if they wish to have power over men the game of hide-and-seek with the beautiful body is more likely to win than naked or half-naked honesty.[22]

Honesty is not as powerful as illusion; after all, honest science reaches its limit, while illusion can continue forever. As Nietzsche proclaims, "When the inquirer, having pushed to the circumference, realizes how logic in that place curls about itself and bites its own tail, he is struck with a new kind of perception; a tragic perception, which requires, to make it tolerable, the remedy of art."[23]

The castrating woman/artist rejects the limitations of logic and science. She harbors a secret scorn for science:

For what is rarer than a woman who really knows what science is? Indeed the best of them cherish in their breasts a secret scorn for science, as if they were somehow superior to it.[24]

. . . clever people frequently have an aversion to science, as have, for instance, almost all artists.[25]

Science worships the Truth and scoffs at the artist's illusions. Artists and actors create illusions which appear real; they tempt science. The castrating woman is the seducer, tempting the metaphysic of truth away from its foundation.

The castrating woman, the artist/actor, can, however, be seduced by her own illusion. She may begin to believe that the illusion she created is the source of her power; she forgets that she created the illusion. She clings fanatically to her illusion. This is the will to illusion as it serves descending life. Here the castrating woman holds fast to one perspective at the cost of all others—life is the price which must be paid. She is the actor as the hysterical little woman.[26] She mistakes the means, her illusion, for an end. The castrating woman becomes another version of the castrated woman.

When, however, the will to illusion is in the service of ascending life, that is, when it playfully affirms multiplicity, then the castrating woman is more powerful than the castrated woman. Her illusions undermine the stifling dogmatism of the will to truth yet they do not destroy truth alto-gether. Her illusions are Apollonian individuations which save us from the raw Dionysian force—the chaotic source of her power. Without her artistic creations we would be doomed to the limits of science. Nietzsche goes so far as to say that if we had not invented this cult of the untrue, art, the general untruth of science would lead to nausea and suicide.[27]

Art is a woman without which it is impossible to live. "In this supreme jeopardy of the will, art, the sorceress expert in healing, approaches us, only she can turn our fits of nausea into imaginations with which it is possible to live."[28] Art subjugates terror through the sublime and releases us from the tedium of absurdity through the comic. Art enables us to act—she overcomes becoming and thereby gives a reason to act; her illu-sions give life a foundation (although illusory) more stable than endless becoming, which enables us to act. No longer do we find value behind a bush, we create it. Artistic creation is the manifestation of the will to power as the will to illusion, as an Apollonian mask. "Those Apollonian masks—are necessary products of a deep look into the horror of nature: luminous spots, as it were, designed to cure an eye hurt by the ghastly night."[29]

Without masks nothing can be justified—only as an aesthetic phenom-enon can the world be justified. It cannot be justified by logic or science; for there is no justification independent of our interpretations.

The will to illusion, then, is a survival mechanism, an instinct which protects us from a deep look into the horror of nature (which, as we shall see, is the affirming woman—the will to power). The castrating woman is the survivor, the artist, the actor. She castrates the metaphysic of truth by creatively interpreting the world. She is the eternal dialectic of masks which perpetuates life. Nietzsche too is a dialectic of masks; he castrates the metaphysic of truth through his creative illusions and metaphors. The fact that he creates different faces leads to his ambiguity about truth and woman; he creates many different illusions about both. He was, He dreaded this castrating woman.

3. The Affirming Woman

Whereas objective truth de-sexed the castrated woman, and the castrat-ing woman, through illusion, de-authorized objective truth, the affirming woman is outside the discourse of truth. The affirming woman, says Nietzsche has no need for truth.

> Among woman.—Truth: Oh, you do not know truth! It is an outrage on all our pudeurs?—[30]

> DISGUST WITH TRUTH—Women are so constituted that all truth (in relation to men, love, children, society, aim of life) disgusts them—[31]

The affirming woman has no need for truth; she affirms herself without man and his logocentricism. She is the inarticulate "truth" which is more original than the metaphysic of truth or the illusion of art. Unlike the metaphysician who discovers a foundation for action and the artist who creates a foundation, the affirming woman is the self-perpetuating Dionysian force who has no need for a foundation. "A voice that rings authentic," says Nietzsche, through Dionysian art and its tragic symbolism cries out. "Be like me, the Original Mother, who, constantly creating, finds satisfction in the turbulent flux of appearances."[32] The affirming woman is the original mother, the unexhausted procreative will of life which is the will to power.[33] She is Dionysus, the desire for change, becoming: a desire which can manifest itself as destruction or creation, which can serve either declining or ascending life. This Dionysian force is an overfull power pregnant with the future.

Nietzsche repeatedly uses such biological metaphors—womb of being, mother eternally pregnant, procreative life—to describe the Dionysian force. The affirming woman is the eternally pregnant mother: she affirms herself continually by reproducing. This position of truth and woman, according to Nietzsche, is the most original, affirmative position which serves ascending life. The perfect woman, then, in Nietzsche's writings, is one who is always pregnant. Her pregnancy is presented as a type of immaculate conception, independent of man—clean, without the mess of the body.[34]

Nietzsche's use of the metaphor of procreation seems problematic. First, it seems inappropriate to speak of the affirming woman *reproducing*: she *produces*: she is original and creative. Reproduction connotes a re-creating, re-making something which is already made. The philosopher, for instance, tries to re-create reality. The affirming woman, however, is supposed to create reality anew, not out of already existing materials. She artistically produces, not reproduces, truth because she is independent of the metaphysic of truth.

Second, in passages where Nietzsche discusses the biological procreation of man, he refers to this instinct as a reactive force rather than an affirming force:

> Procreation . . . Only derived; originally, in those cases in which one will was unable to organise the collective mass it had appropriated, an *opposing* will came into power, which undertook to effect the separation and establish a new center of organization, after a struggle with the original will.[35]

Since the procreative force in human beings is not an original force, the use of the metaphor of procreation in order to describe an original force, the Dionysian force, seems inappropriate.

The Dionysian force—the will to power—is not a reactive force; rather, it is the origin of all force. Yet it is a myth, an origin which does not exist.[36] The will to power is layer after layer of masks with no face behind the costumes. The will to power is the affirming woman. She is layer upon layer of masks, a papier-mâché balloon.

> MASKS—There are women who, wherever one examines them, have no inside, but are mere masks.[37]

> Man thinks woman profound—why? Because he can never fathom her depths. Woman is not even shallow.[38]

She is hollow like a womb. She is the space, the womb, from which everything originates. This space is distance: the affirming woman is not an object in the distance: rather she is distance. Her power is distance. As distance, as space—pure womb—she does not exist. Just as there is no woman, there is no truth:

> That the value of the world lies in our interpretations: that previous interpretations have been perspective valuations by virtue of which we can survive in life, i.e., in the will to power, for growth of power: that every elevation of man brings with it the overcoming of narrower interpretations; that every strengthening and in-

crease of power opens up new perspectives and means believing in new horizons—this idea permeates my writings. The world with which we are concerned is false; it is "in flux" as something in a state of becoming, as a falsehood always changing but never getting nearer the truth; for there is no "truth."[39]

Truth, like woman, is an interpretation, not an objective reality. According to Nietzsche the power of truth and woman comes from their distance and ambiguity. "The enchantment and the most powerful effect of woman is, to use language of philosophers, an effect at a distance, an *actio in distans*: there belongs thereto, however, primarily and above all,—distance!"[40]

If this distance can never be closed, as Nietzsche suggests, then the goal Nietzsche assigns to us is ultimately unreachable. The Christian God and the Platonic Forms are replaced by another supersensible force: the will to power. Nietzsche, then, is always the castrated woman as well as the affirming woman. He is as sick as the metaphysicians who prescribe a frustratingly distant 'truth.'

Nietzsche, however, does not leave us at the precipice of our understanding looking longingly down at the distant ground. Although the distance between truth/woman and our understanding cannot be closed, it can be bridged by the artist/castrating woman. The protective instincts of the artist/castrating woman must disguise the power of the original Dionysian womb of being. The eternal torrent of the will to power/affirming woman is too horrible a sight unless masked: it is the hollow womb which needs a wall of tissue layers in order to procreate. "Man is a coward in the face of all that is eternally feminine," says Nietzsche.[41] Therefore this eternally feminine face, which is horrifying because it is hollow and must be masked.

If truth/woman existed as an object for scientific study, as a fact, as the philosopher/castrated woman would have us believe, it would be shallow and harmless; there would be no need for masks. Truth/woman would be stable, easy to fix before our eyes. It is the constant flux we cannot bear, the ambiguity. Truth/woman is not shallow: the aimless spiral of truth/woman is endless.

One possible way we theoretians (or artists) can interpret, create, truth/woman is the triad we have developed out of Nietzsche's writings: The Dionysian woman affirms herself outside of the metaphysic of truth. She is the will to power, the original mother, eternally pregnant. Yet this raw force of the womb of being is horrifying; we, therefore, require the masks created through the artist's will to illusion. The castrating woman disguises the Dionysian flux of the will to power through the masks of the artist and actor in order to provide some justification for our existence, no matter how illusory. She also destroys the authority of the metaphysic of truth by substituting a multitude of interpretations for the dogmatist's one, objective, reality. The dogmatist/feminist takes an illusion which began as a principle to preserve life, presents it as an apodictic principle, thereby subverting life. Following Derrida's suggestion, we have created a dialectic triad in order to interpret Nietzsche's philosophical ambiguity on the question of woman and truth; by unraveling one, we also unwind the other.

Notes

1. Friedrich Nietzsche, *Beyond Good and Evil*, trans. Helen Zimmern, in *The Complete Works of Nietzsche*, ed. Oscar Levy (New York: Russell & Russell, 1964), author's preface: see also *Human All Too Human*, v.ii, trans. Hellen Zimmern, p. 140; and *Twilight of the Idols*, trans. Anthony Ludovici, p. 3.

2. Jacques Derrida, *Spurs*, trans. Barbara Harlow (Chicago: University of Chicago Press, 1979), p. 101.

3. Friedrich Nietzsche, *The Birth of Tragedy*, trans. Francis Golffing (Garden City, N.Y.: Doubleday, 1956), section 18.

4. *Twilight*, p. 16.

5. Friedrich Nietzsche, *The Case of Wagner*, trans. A. Ludovici, in *The Complete Works*, p. 49.

6. Friedrich Nietzsche, *Ecce Homo*, trans. A. Ludovici, in *The Complete Works*, p. 9.

7. *Beyond*, p. 188; also *Human*, v.i., p. 301.

8. I think Nietzsche's opinion is unjustified because clearly not all feminists imitate men. There are multitudes of feminisms (as evidenced by the different essays in this volume).

9. *Twilight*, p. 24.

10. *Beyond*, p. 182.

11. Friedrich Nietzsche, *The Will to Power*, trans. W. Kaufman and R. J. Hollingdale (New York: Random House, 1962), p. 328, section 608.

12. *Twilight*, p. 27.

13. Friedrich Nietzsche, "On Truth and Falsity in the Ultramoral Sense," in *The Complete Works*, p. 183.

14. *Will*, p. 317, §585.

15. *Ecce*, p. 65.

16. *Will*, p. 194.

17. Ibid., p. 315, §385.

18. Ibid., p. 453, §853.

19. *Beyond*, p. 182, §232.

20. Friedrich Nietzsche, *Joyful Wisdom*, trans. T. Common in *The Complete Works*, pp. 319–20, §361.

21. *Spurs*, p. 97; my emphasis. Some people might argue that the castrating woman represents

Christian morality and the philosopher, not the will to illusion. Although this thesis could be defended with some passages from *Spurs*, these and other passages can be interpreted as arguments against this thesis (pp. 89, 97). Moreover, regardless of Derrida's interpretation of Nietzsche, Nietzsche's texts can be more neatly deciphered if the castrating woman is identified with the artist—the texts Derrida refers to do not suggest otherwise.

22. *Human*, v.ii, p. 305.
23. *Birth*, §15.
24. Nietzsche, *The Early Greeks*, trans. Maximillian Mugge, in *The Complete Works*, p. 25.
25. *Twilight*, p. 3.
26. *Joyful*, p. 71.
27. *Joyful*, §107.
28. *Birth*, §15.
29. Ibid., p. 60.
30. *Twilight*, p. 3.
31. *Human*, v.i., p. 140; see also p. 305.
32. *Birth*, p. 102.
33. Friedrich Nietzsche, *Thus Spake Zarathustra*, in *The Portable Nietzsche*, ed., and trans. W. Kaufman (New York: Viking Press, 1972), p. 226.
34. Given Nietzsche's concern with the body and senses, it seems inappropriate for him to present an image of a woman who creates independently of her world.
35. *Will*, p. 131, §657.
36. In *The Birth of Tragedy*, §18, Nietzsche calls the Dionysian vision a myth. However, in sections of the *Birth*, e.g., §16, Nietzsche suggests that music mirrors the thing-in-itself. He suggests that there is an original Nature which we can uncover.
37. *Human*, v.i, p. 300.
38. *Twilight*, p. 5.
39. *Will*, p. 330, §616.
40. *Joyful*, p. 99, §60; see also *Zarathustra*, p. 76.
41. *The Case of Wagner*, p. 7.

4

Veiled Lips

Luce Irigaray

Translated by Sara Speidel

Translator's Note: ". . . How, already, to speak (as a) woman? In passing back through the dominant discourse. In speaking to women. And among women. Can this speaking-woman be written? How? . . . "[1] Irigaray's writing is a response to these questions. All of her books are concerned with the problems of women in relation to language.[2] *Amante marine: de Friedrich Nietzsche,* in which the following portion of *Veiled Lips* appears, addresses these problems in and through the texts of Nietzsche— affirming the possibility of a feminine writing, in a style which diverges radically from traditional syntactical norms. Fragments of sentences exist side by side, without subordination—parts which are wholes, "and yet without unity." Punctuation seems to follow rhythmical patterns, empha- sizing intonation and phrasing (in a musical sense) rather than marking off discrete units of meaning. Subjects are frequently omitted or indicated by pronouns whose gender and antecedents are ambiguous. Words evoke multiple senses—simultaneously—setting in motion a continuous play in which no single, "proper" meaning can be identified. This plural, rhythmical, "non-unitary" mode of writing asks to be read "differently"—outside "the logic which dominates our most everyday statements,"[3] and beyond the models of discursive coherence and closure which, according to Irigaray, amount to a "death sentence" for woman (always defined negatively in the theoretical discourse of Western philosophy—as man's opposite, his "other," not-man). In disturbing the rules of discursive functioning, Irigaray's writing participates in her strategic re-questioning of woman's position in a system of representation which depends on the repression of her difference. At the same time, Irigaray's verbal style exemplifies—already—that other, feminine language, which "has nothing to do with the syntax which we have used for centuries, namely, that constructed according to the following organization: subject, predicate, or, subject, verb, object."[4]

Because "all theory of the 'subject' has always been appropriated by the masculine"[5]—because woman has traditionally been assigned the position of the object (of representation, of discourse)—the difficulty of "speaking (as a) woman," for Irigaray, involves the problem of how to "speak woman" without speaking about her, re-objectifying her—without speaking "like a man." Can woman's difference be articulated in language without redefining her as the "lack" in discourse, the silent "support for a proliferation of images" (of men)?[6] The strategy which Irigaray advances as a response to this dilemma is one that points to the sites of women's repression by focusing on the "blank" spaces of the (masculine) system of representation:

> The gaps between figures, actors. Spacings which organize the scene, 'blanks' which sub-tends its structuration and which nonetheless will not be read as such. Not read at all? Not seen at all? Indeed, never represented, nor representable, which is not to say inefficient in the present scenography. But fixed in oblivion, and waiting to become animated. Turning everything upside down . . ."[7]

Her interrogation of the master texts of philosophy and psychoanalysis—Plato, Freud, and most recently, Nietzsche—takes the form of a dialogue in which Irigaray "speaks woman" not by speaking "like a man," but by speaking to and with the writings of men.[8] In *Amante marine*, for example, she engages the question of woman in Nietzsche's texts by taking the position of Nietzsche's lover.[9] Assuming this intimacy, she moves in and out of Nietzsche's discourse, using his words—without always setting them off from her own—blurring the distinction between "Irigaray" and "Nietzsche." She avoids becoming fixed in one position. She criticizes, questions, invites, challenges . . . dissolving the fixity of Nietzsche's theoretical concepts by speaking them "differently"—mockingly, playfully, "lovingly":

> For too long the tie of compassion has held me back. I have wanted a better destiny for you—and me . . . To pass beyond/ disregard, isn't tht the way to go . . . ? And isn't this farewell still a sign of love? Reopening your horizon for a more distant one to come.[10]

In *Amante marine*, as in her other books, Irigaray's dialogue with male writers works to destroy the functioning of discourse with "nuptial tools":

> The tool is not a feminine attribute. But woman can re-utilize the marks made on her, in her, by the tool. Put another way: it remains for me to marry/make hay (*faire la noce*) with the philosophers. Which is not a simple undertaking . . . [11]

The undertaking she proposes and which she enacts in her dialogues depends on using the "tools" of masculine discourse. This strategy of mimeticism is not without risks, but it opens the possibility of a new relationship between the sexes—a relationship where woman is no longer reduced to an echo or mirror-image of man but speaks to/with him in a dialogue which recognizes her difference, which allows her to coexist, as other, without being subordinated in a process of imitation and reproduction.

Irigaray's refusal to represent woman, her practice of pointing to the "blanks" in philosophical discourse as potential spaces of difference/dialogue, involves the risk that this "woman" who resists representation may again serve as a silent support for the production of a male imaginary.[12] In response to the danger of reappropriation, Irigaray posits a specifically feminine imaginary, existing beyond the parameters of the masculine system of representation. From this perspective, woman would no longer experience her sexuality as a lack or empty space, but as multiple, diverse, mobile:

> Woman is neither closed nor open. Indefinite, in-finite, form is never completed in her. . . . This incompleteness of her form, of her morphology, permits her at every instant to become some-thing else, which isn't to say that she is ever unequivocally noth-ing. . . . No singular form, act, discourse, subject, masculine, feminine, can terminate the becoming of a woman's desire."[13]

Like Persephone in *Veiled Lips,* whose "affirmation already takes place this side of or beyond appearances,"[14] woman "diffuses herself . . . she comes and goes in herself and outside herself, without stopping."[15] The only one of the three mythological figures Irigaray discovers in Nietz-sche's text (Athena, Ariadne, Persephone) who retains her tie to the mother, Persephone is the only one whose becoming does not remain fixed in the production of a masculine imaginary. In Irigaray's rewriting of the myth, Persephone's passage back and forth—from the mother to the father—reveals the limits of the dominant system of representation, discloses the stakes in the masculine game (of castration). Her return to the mother affirms the possibility of a new relationship to the maternal body, which would no longer be repressed/denied as the scene of castra-tion. Irigaray's emphasis on the return to the maternal body in *Veiled Lips* points to the mother's power as a force of production—a force that has been appropriated for "man's" gain, "buried" by his "forgetting and ab-horrence of the body from which he was born."[16] The return to the body of woman/mother, the inscription of her desire—a "desire which most likely does not speak the same language as man's desire"[17]—continues Irigaray's dialogue with the discourse of philosophy, which "has not been merely an interpretation of the body [but] a misunderstanding of the body."[18]

As these prefatory remarks imply, Irigaray's writing in *Veiled Lips* unset-tles the notions of "meaning" at work in any simple approach to transla-tion. I have attempted to stay close to the body of the text, resisting, as much as possible, the temptation to normalize syntax and clarify by "reading in" the connections between words, phrases, and ideas which Irigaray's discourse leaves open. Connections between *Veiled Lips* and other texts are suggested in the notes which accompany the translation.

I would like to thank Don Eric Levine for his excellent advice and his good humor in struggling with difficult problems of translation.

Notes

1. Luce Irigaray, *Ce sexe qui n'en est pas un* (Paris, 1977), p. 119.

2. As well as *Ce sexe*, Irigaray's published works include: *Le langage des déments* (Paris, 1973); *Speculum, de l'autre femme* (Paris, 1974); *Et l'une ne bouge pas sans l'autre* (Paris, 1979); *Amante marine: de Friedrich Nietzsche* (Paris, 1980); *Passions élémentaires* (Paris, 1982); *L'oubli de l'air* (Paris, 1983).

3. "Women's Exile: Interview with Luce Irigaray." trans. Couze Venn, *Ideology and Consciousness*, I (1977), p. 64.

4. *Women's Exile*, p. 64.

5. Irigaray, *Speculum*, p. 165.

6. Irigaray, *Speculum*, p. 171.

7. Irigaray, *Speculum*, p. 171.

8. Irigaray's work may be seen as an ongoing dialogue with philosophical and psychoanalytic texts, *Speculum, de l'autre femme* presents itself as a "psychoanalytic" dialogue enacted in and around the theories of Plato and Freud. In *Ce sexe qui n'en est pas un*, Irigaray continues her interrogation of psychoanalytic theory from a number of different perspectives, including the transcription of an actual dialogue—in which she responds to questions from members of a seminar in philosophy—and an imaginary dialogue between herself and another woman (*When Our Lips Talk to Each Other/Quand nos lèvres se parlent*). Two recent books also take the form of imaginary dialogues: in *Et l'une ne bouge pas sans l'autre*, a daughter addresses her mother; in *Passions élémentaires*, a woman addresses her male lover. Within these dialogues *between* Irigaray and others—philosophers/women/mothers/lovers—another dialogue takes place, in which, without mentioning his name, Irigaray questions and answers Jacques Lacan.

9. Elizabeth Berg speaks of Irigaray's writing as a "lover's discourse" in *The Third Woman, Diacritics* 12 (1982), p. 16, where she discusses *Speculum* and *Amante marine* in relation to Sarah Kofman's *L'énigme de la femme: la femme dans les textes de Freud* (Paris, 1980).

10. Irigaray, *Amante marine*, p. 18

11. Irigaray, *Ce sexe*, p. 147.

12. See the selection on the *Imaginaire* in *Vocabulaire de la psychanalyse*, by J. Laplanche and J. B. Pontalis, trans. Peter Kussell and Jeffrey Mehlman in *French Freud, Yale French Studies* 48 (1972), pp. 191–93: the imaginary is one of the three essential registers which Lacan distinguishes in the psychoanalytic field: the imaginary, the symbolic, and the real. The imaginary register, which is "marked by a relation to the image of a similar being" (p. 191), involves the notion that during the period Lacan calls the "mirror stage" the child's ego is constituted through identification with his reflection in a mirror. The unified body image which the child sees in the mirror represents the ego and constitutes the child as ego through his identification with it. "This *Gestalt* symbolizes the mental permanence of the *I*, at the same time as it prefigures its alienating destination" (Jacques Lacan, *Ecrits*, trans. Alan Sheridan, New York and London, 1977, p. 2). In *Speculum*, Irigaray envisions the possibility of a concave mirror which (unlike Lacan's flat mirror) would not produce a faithful and unified image, but would distort and transform: "But perhaps, beyond this specular surface which supports discourse, what presents itself is not the void of nothingness but . . . a scintillating and incandescent concavity" (p. 178).

13. Irigaray, *Speculum*, p. 284.

14. Irigaray, *Amante marine*, p. 124.

15. Irigaray, *Amante marine*, p. 123.

16. Irigaray, *Passions élémentaires*, p. 107.

17. Irigaray, *This Sex which is not One*, trans. Claudia Reeder, in *New French Feminisms*, ed. Elaine Marks and Isabelle de Courtivron (Amherst, Mass., 1980), p. 101.

18. Friedrich Nietzsche, *The Gay Science*, trans. Walter Kaufmann (New York, 1974), p. 35.

It is to a woman—to the other—that the sanction of necessity for this/ her burial will be given. A woman, in truth: of divine reality. A deity conceived in the head of the God of gods. Well-born—without a mother.[1]

The ideal feminine, whose femininity serves to mediate between the bowels of the earth and the most celestial God: the father of the gods. Whose daughter she must be, a daughter born without ever having known the darkness of the maternal womb . . .

A woman engendered by the father alone—a process of reversal/trans-fer [re(n)versement][2] of values which takes place in the thought of man-the-father. Hidden in this process is woman—the secret of the idea's production. This conception, entirely spiritual in nature, represses and denies [(dé)nier] her, the woman who still remembers the blood. Feminin-ity will be the guarantee of this operation, insuring—even as a possible mediation—the breaking-off of relations between woman-the-mother and man-the-father.

Femininity—a splitting-in-two of God's thought which aids him in the totality of his work ("With regard to what I plan to do during the next ten years, I need them [women]," Letter from Nietzsche to Peter Gast, March 4, 1882). Remaining between: the gods above, and men, the gods below. Taking care of both places, arbitrating conflicts, watching over wars between those motivated by a violent love of fame. . . . Conciliatory, benevolent. . . . Seducing all and everyone with assuaging "justice": a middle-of-the-road idea. Neither anarchic nor despotic. A neutral space. At least in appearance. For, "I am all for the male, in all things but marriage . . . with all my heart I am my father's child" (Aeschylus, *The Eumenides*, 737–38).[3]

Femininity—an indispensable intermediary for the father in making his law prevail. The simulacrum which introduces the false into the true, effaces their difference, substituting for this difference an interval of pre-tense: the neutrality of femininity. Even God needs femininity in order to present himself as the only creator. In order to pass himself off for—what he is not. An operation which will be attributed to woman. And however little the woman may have forgotten that she owes her life to her mother also, this dissimulation will be her most divine reality. Life as femininity—the contrary. Everything is done to lead to this. And she will play (with) her part, make a mockery of it—the better because she isn't there.

Femininity—the secret of the production of sophism. Of the "lie" of the oracle, of the double dissimulation in the words of a god: Apollo testifying that the mother has no function in reproduction. The proof: the spiritual daughter of Olympian Zeus, offspring more perfect than any conceived by a goddess (*Eumenides*, 658–66).[4]

A phantasm, attributed to the father of the gods, will henceforth decide the rights of all. And since the most divine woman does not understand much about the discourse of truth, she acts her role perfectly: "No mother gave me birth, I am all for the male," etc. (*Eumenides*, 736f). Except for marriage [*l'hymen*].

"On the father's side," copulation no longer occurs. The woman remains a "stranger," who keeps and nourishes the "young shoot" unless "a god harms it" (*Eumenides*, 658–59). Man, product only of the male seed. "And I? Does mother's blood run in my veins?" (*Eumenides*, 606).[5] The same for woman. This genetic error draws the entire scene of truth into the realm of appearances: the reign of femininity. Reasonable, even speculative, somewhat warlike: fully armed, but a mediator nonetheless. Between high and low and all the extremes, but the sense is always projected from the same point. Which makes a circle?

With the patriarchal order, femininity forms a system. Dissimulation of woman in the thought of the father. Where she is created fully clothed and armed. Veiled, her beauty concealed. Nothing visible except her face. Therefore, not woman. She would no longer touch herself.[6] Only the face sees and is seen. And the voice clearly speaks the will of the father, which she translates into words audible to all—citizens. Femininity understands how to seduce, knows how to attract and captivate with the folds of her garments—a dissimulation which multiplies, multiplies her. She calculates her effects, times her blows . . .

But the incantation which moves, disturbs, sings—the impossibility of saying clearly, says all at once, everything together, one thing and the other without any articulable distinction—this "style" of evocation, *harmony*—is lacking in her. Only her father's daughter, she repeats his discourse without much understanding, carries out his law, spreading it everywhere, in the middle of everything, intermediary for all, to the point of intrigue, where her charm takes the place of violence. At least in appearance. Gives itself for . . .

A murder has taken place—femininity appeases anger, calls for the forgetting of bloodshed, lulls vengeance with her eloquence, promises tokens of esteem, honors, a cult, rites, sacrifices, a religious silence, if only the "[barren] children of fertile Night" withdraw to a "subterranean cavern," "loyal and propitious to the land" (*Eumenides*, 1034–40).

Femininity redoubles the burial of the mother with that of the chorus.[7] In order that Zeus, "the god of speech," prevail (*Eumenides*, 974).

This persuasion is necessary to subdue the wildness of a nature still resistant to the logic of truth. The growlings, the cries, the grumblings, the barkings, the abusive reproaches—and to the gods . . . —, the passion for blood. . . . The imprecations, the altercations, the exclamations, interrogations, . . . the laments, the moanings, the curses, . . . the songs, the hymns, the frenzies . . . All at once, all together, without anyone being identified. . . . And the dancing, the running, the leaping, . . . the movement . . . All at once and together. Up to the final silence. Mastering the chorus, driving back into a subterranean cavern.

The law of the father needed femininity—a semblance of woman—to get the better of the mother's passion, but also woman's pleasure.

Accordingly, what will arise will be all forms of music, no longer the chorus. Its rebirth will always be its reprise. Quite differently organized. The whole calculates itself, sums itself up, composes itself, suits itself to the "actors" and the "instruments," absent from the chorus. Which could not repeat itself. Beauty would occur there only once. That repetition takes place *in* the chorus signifies something entirely different: the impossibility of unity. Thus the same thing is sung again, a second time. But the "other" does not depart from the same: doesn't represent it, figure it, reproduce it. One and the other "say" the same, together. Without the one or without the other, but the same, and inseparable and non-identifiable in their exchange, and nevertheless at least two, *this* harmony no longer takes place.

In harmony, it (*ça*) touches itself again and this embrace, which corresponds closely to a state of nature, would allow the gaze to deploy itself further, since this visible, non-discriminable, natural contiguity will already have been excluded from its field. Having "overcome" it, the forms will doubtless be clearer, more elegant, "purer," but they will already be perverted into the semblance of "false" spectacles. Consoling in their beauty, seductive, appeasing. But drifting ever further from the Dionysian re-source.

Apollo, the seer, the always-already-speaking, who first ordered the murder of the mother. Effacing, disavowing, thus, the illegitimacy of his own birth? Blood spilled to confirm that he belongs to the one law, the law of the father.

A sacrifice which is necessary to maintain the order of the hearths. Apollo—the brother, in God, of Athena. The patriarchal right/the bonds of kinship. Orestes, who cut his mother's throat, finds refuge in the temple of this god, who is subject only to the will of Zeus. The women who cry out for revenge are driven back as bearers of corruption. Apollo no longer hears the chorus. He drives the "herd" of women away from his oracle.

> Out, I tell you, out of these halls—Fast,
> set the Prophet's chamber free!
> Or take the flash and stab of this, this flying viper
> shot from the longbow's golden chord strung taut!
>
> Heave in torment, black froth erupting from your lungs,
> vomit the clots of all the murders you have drained.
> But never touch my halls, you have no right.
>
> Go where heads are severed, eyes gouged out,
> where Justice and bloody slaughter are the same . . .
> castrations, wasted seed, young man's glories butchered,
> extremities maimed, and huge stones at the chest,
> and the victims wail for pity—
> spikes inching up the spine, torsos stuck on spikes.
>
> So, you hear your love feast, yearn to have it all?
> You revolt the gods. Your look,
> your whole regalia gives you away—your kind
> should infest a lion's cavern reeking blood.
> But never rub your filth on the Prophet's shrine.
> Out your flock without a herdsman—out!
> No god will ever shepherd you with love.
>
> (*Eumenides*, 179–97)

The wisdom of Apollo—his cruelty. The serenity of marriages blessed by the gods, the sweetest joys of mortals, the bed where fate joins man and woman—their cruelties. The father devouring his children, the departure of the married man for a war among men—the stakes: another woman, the sacrifice of the virgin daughter to gain the victory, the infidelity of the husband, his return accompanied by yet another woman—the anger of the woman, the mother.

The deafness of the god to the Furies. The voices of the goddesses of the earth reduced to silence by the goddess of heights: the daughter of the Father. The chorus of women/Athena. The mother/Athena. The daughter/Athena. The wife/Athena. All, all together—I-we, thou-you—wounded, humiliated, bleeding, beseeching, breathless, worn out from pursuit—and without wings—of the murderer who has the technique to fly and cross the seas. These women—thou or you, I or us—tired, heavy with sleep, dreaming—chilled by a painful shudder of anguish: "under the lash of a fierce executioner."

Justice which remembers blood/that of the immortal: the semblance, but cruel. The liquid spilled on the earth disappears forever. Earth drinks in the traces of the crime. Oblivion.

Remains—Hades, to whom mortals must render an account below the earth. Hades who sees all and records all in his memory. Contrary to the law of the gods above. Their truth, their beauty, their immortality. Between—Athena: the dissimulation of horror, masking the wound, covering up the difference of values. Pretense of the God of gods—standing in a long white robe which covers even her feet.

The ruse, in service to the master. Treachery which profits the father. Chaining women to housework, but for her, a public life. Preferring young men, but shunning marriage, her father's virgin. The inspiration and guardian of institutions. It should not be doubted that she is virile, if she drops her tunic. Armed: femininity. Playing with all the disguises. Childish, if necessary, without having known childhood; fraternal, the better to betray confidence; simulating friendship for women and leading them to retire willingly into cellars, underground caverns, private homes. Misleading, maddening, provoking the violation of oaths, murder, death . . . , without giving up her divine candor.

The ambivalence of God toward the mother, toward woman, incarnated in the person of the goddess. Which will be called, henceforth, women's imposture. Which is only a projection of the Father. Adorned, femininity—manifestation of the father's idea of feminine power. Appropriating the mother's power, swallowing it up, introjecting it, he engenders, produces this daughter who (only) gives herself for that which she is not: a simulacrum assumed by the God to help him in his work, to establish his empire. An empire of pretense which claims to do without

the body, an empire of death. The reign of seduction by appearances—
truth. Which also needs beauty, but as an illusion. Who thus no longer
touches, except for some objective—virile. Who no longer affects, is no
longer affected "in herself." Always already gauged, but only according
to the father's desire. Knowing only the pleasure of the master.

The recourse for the son who has cut his mother's throat: clasping the
stone effigy of an immortal goddess, kneeling and taking in his arms the
"statue" of Athena (*Eumenides*, 258–59). Asking her for mercy, giving
proof of his new innocence: as an act of purification he sacrificed a pig
(the mother/the pig), and the people he approached suffered no harm
(*Eumenides*, 282–85). Consequently, he is pure, a good citizen. Fit for
communal life among free men. Perhaps even to be king, to have power.

  The light of day annuls the crimes of night. Whoever argues judi-
ciously, thereby displays his innocence. The reasoning of a prudent man
washes the stains of murder from his hands. Zeus doesn't consider the
flock of women who are dripping with blood worthy of a hearing. Athena
demands a clear explanation.

  The tragedy of women will no longer be heard. All of them together—as a whole—at the same time, and yet without unity. One and
the other, and not reduced to the same, not subordinated to a single one,
this will no longer take place. Songs, hymns, cries, growlings, grumblings,
barkings . . . praises and reproaches . . . frenzies and sobriety . . . exclamations . . . affirmations . . . interrogations . . . laments, wailing, gaiety . . .
and dancing, running, leaping . . . all at once and together. Kept apart
from the order of the city, buried without sun, entombed below the town,
lulled beneath the appearance of serenity, of calm, of peace.

  The chorus reduced, enslaved, subdued, by the "persuasion" of Zeus's
daughter. Repeats what is spoken to it with a single voice: "Rejoice, rejoice in peace and abundance; rejoice, inhabitants of the city, seated next
to Zeus's altar, friends of the Virgin who loves you, and always devoted
to wisdom. Those who live beneath the wings of Pallas are respected by
her father" (*Eumenides*, 1014–20). The chorus beguiled, tamed, gives in
to her spell, marches toward its tomb in pious silence. The ancient rites
and sacrifices. "Peace, by the happiness of these hearths, is today secured
for the people of Pallas" (*Eumenides*, 1044–45).

  Pallas—her body veiled in white, in borrowed candor, the shroud over
the woman, the mortal adornment. The appeasing enchantment of the
god of speech.

"Do I still have ears? Am I all ears and nothing else? Here I stand in the flaming surf whose white tongues are licking at my feet; from all sides I hear howling, threats, screaming, roaring coming at me, while the old earth-shaker sings his aria in the lowest depths, deep as a bellowing bull, while pounding such an earth-shaking beat that the hearts of even these weather-beaten rocky monsters are trembling in their bodies. Then, suddenly, as if born out of nothing, there appears before the gate of this hellish labyrinth, only a few fathoms away—a large sailboat, gliding along as silently as a ghost. Oh, what a ghostly beauty! How magically it touches me! Has all the calm and taciturnity of the world embarked on it? Does my happiness itself sit in this quiet place—my happier ego, my second, departed self? Not to be dead and yet no longer alive? A spiritlike intermediate being: quietly observing, gliding, floating? As the boat that with its white sails moves like an immense butterfly over the dark sea. Yes! To move over existence! That's it! That would be something!

"It seems as if the noise here had led me into fantasies. All great noise leads us to move happiness into some quiet distance. When a man stands in the midst of his own noise, in the midst of his own surf of plans and projects, then he is apt also to see quiet, magical beings gliding past him and to long for their happiness and seclusion: *women*. He almost thinks that his better self dwells there among the women, and that in these quiet regions even the loudest surf turns into deathly quiet, and life itself into a dream about life. Yet! Yet! Noble enthusiast, even on the most beautiful sailboat there is a lot of noise, and unfortunately much small and petty noise. The magic and the most powerful effect of women is to produce feeling from a distance, in philosophical language, *actio in distans*, action at a distance, but this requires first of all and above all—*distance*" (*The Gay Science*, 60).[8]

From the pounding beat of the old earth-shaker appears, as if out of nothing and at a distance, a large sailboat gliding past, silently as a ghost.

This distant, magical calm, the happiness and folding-back-upon-itself, amounts to women. Near these creatures of dream where his better self dwells, the violence of his rhythm grows quiet—the secret of death and life become his own dream. A creation which spreads itself amid his throbbing beats, as if produced by their tumult.

So women would float in death. Always at a distance. Not exactly at hand, but well in sight. Allowing for an acceleration of rhythm without risk of losing the beat. From one beat to another, they remain there, tranquil. Giving and taking back again the dream of their compliantly offered sails.

Of distance, then. And as they are always together, in "themselves," of "themselves," it is necessary—always—to separate them. To violate. To steal. To veil. [*Violer. Voler. Voiler.*] The distancing of women, their absence—and from "themselves"—that is their "magic and most powerful effect." Not to be—if not for—dissimulation of nature. The operation which is lent to them, while they—threatening death—lend themselves to it, as if "by nature." By nature (a) woman would be at least double. Her "operation" would be to redouble or reduplicate. But, naturally, that which is nearest. That which is so near that the shape, the form, though visible, are blurred in the immediacy of the "act" of doubling. Without distinction between the model and the reproduction. Without a fitting interval between the one and the other. An indefinite increase, an ironic proliferation of the natural, which must be limited lest mastery collapse [*s'y abîme*]? Immersed in an always more.

How can one have an idea of this incessant and fertile coming and going, which undoes all opposition between here and there, of this endless intertwining, of this "in itself" at the same time and in the same place that it is in the other, and neither one nor the other, nor the same and its other? And this operation remains so foreign to him that, believing he must break this thing open, that he cannot appropriate it except by breaking in, forcing his way beyond present appearances, "man" arms himself with a pointed object—stylet, dagger, sometimes pen—to penetrate it. Bearing down with the weight of his entire being, to force her to fold. In order that she always remain open.[9]

But after he has thus separated her from herself, divided her in two, he doesn't know how to bring these/her edges back together. How to overcome the divergence thus created, to ignore what flows between. While she remains indefinitely the source of the retouching (of her lips), he must now jump from one bank to the other.

Ascribing his own project to her, he rises from the abyss—or the *abyme*.[10] The break between, the hardening of the edges, the forgotten river which now divides them.

Distance does not come from her, even if, for him, her seduction operates at a distance. Even if he lends her, at present, this element of her power. Not wishing to see the effect of his operation: the abyss between. Which averts and fascinates him with the attraction of a knife blow given to the other. In the belly/womb of the other. Whom he no longer simply approaches without risking death itself: by the dreadful return of his own action. The seizing for himself, the definitive incision between the lips which renders her silent and alluring as a tomb.

Out of this rending interval rise only phantoms and images. Dreams of life and death. Appeasing veils which mask the destruction constitutive of distance as such.

He has lost nothing except his consciousness. And if, for him, she engulfs everything, without end, this is because, if she retained an essence, he would read there the mark of his crime. It is better to forget it. Such is the foundation of his being, this annihilation upon which he erects himself. Which maintains his relationship to the non-truth of truth?

That he lends this operation to woman, and to a gesture of modesty which leads her to veil herself ceaselessly, can only make her laugh. The only thing that hides itself is that which appears-disappears. And, in truth, she has nothing to lose. Nothing to show or prove. She escapes, from this point of view, from castration.[11]

And his game, the game of castration, as far as she is concerned, is always that of the "man's woman." It always has to do with the veil or the sheath which she represents for him, with the envelope which she gives him to assist him, support him, affect him in her doubling operation.

To elude the threat of these potential dissimulations, the abduction of the daughter—still a virgin—to the domain of the father, of god.[12] The one, the daughter, removed from "herself," in artificial isolation, the other always searches for her(self), seeks to touch her(self) again. Thus she continues to become all that presents itself to her. Not distinguishing herself from what is nearest. Which could amount to what is most distant—and from "herself"—if this is what is imposed on her: the veils, the masks, where she is hidden. To what is most proper, if it is this which dominates. Appropriated by proximity.

This is what confuses—the distancing in proximity; or its opposite. That which does not return, simply, to its "operation." Rather, she is indifferent to what is nearest, through an excess of sym-pathy. Within/ between her/them, the barrier has been suspended which separates and deceives.

The ruse of the father, of god? To steal/violate one so that the other produces doubles for him indefinitely. Appropriate one so that the other, the others, distracted, continue the same operation, but to his advantage. Multiplying his own goods. Indefinitely.

Woman's exile from herself entails her inexhaustible mimesis/mimicry for the father's benefit.[13] The her/death—which she sustains, which she redoubles, but which is only the form of him who removes her from "herself"—which amounts to this, making her reproduce anything, to the point of confusing it/herself, losing it/herself; the *abyme*, the abyss. Making her pass through, in approximation, the entire horizon of space-time. The gap between—where her retouching is always hidden. All discourse: a repetition, but at a distance, of/from "nature." A reply which has already been mastered. She, gliding under, over, all along, against, across . . . these manifestations or appearances, empty of herself/them. Always wandering, distracted, floating, fugitive, lost—by nature.

By nature? So as not to forget the meaning, what is understood, has sense, here and there, such as: "When we love a woman, we easily conceive a hatred for nature on account of all the repulsive natural functions to which every woman is subject. We prefer to avert our thoughts from them, but when our soul touches on these matters for once, it shrugs as it were and looks contemptuously at nature: we feel insulted; nature seems to encroach on our possessions, and with the profanest hands at that. Then we close our ears to physiology and decree secretly: 'I want to hear nothing about the fact that a human being is something more than *soul and form*.' 'The human being under the skin' is for all lovers a horror and unthinkable, a blasphemy against love.

"Well, this kind of aversion that lovers still feel about the sordid aspects of nature, every worshiper of God and his 'holy omnipotence' formerly felt: everything said about nature by astronomers, geologists, physiologists, or physicians, struck him as an encroachment into his precious, personal domain, and thus as an aggression—and a shameless one at that. Even 'natural law' sounded to him like a slander against God; really he would have much preferred to see all mechanics derived from acts of a moral will or an arbitrary will. But since nobody was able to render this service, he concealed [*se dissimuler*] nature and mechanics from himself as best he could and lived in a dream. Oh, these men of former times knew how to dream and did not find it necessary to sleep first. And we others, men of today, we will master this art all too well, despite all of our good will toward the day and staying awake. It is quite enough to love, to hate, to desire, simply to feel—and right away the spirit and power of the dream overcome us, and with our eyes open, coldly contemptuous of all danger, we climb up on the most hazardous paths to scale the roofs and spires of fantasy—without any sense of dizziness, as if we had been born to climb, we somnambulists of the day! We artists! We who hide from nature. We who are moonstruck and God-struck. We wanderers, still as death, unwearied voyagers on heights that we do not see as heights but as plains, as our certainty" (*The Gay Science*, 59).

Nature can only love itself or be loved in dissimulation: as in a dream. Barely experiencing nature, resenting it, men of former times and of today scale the roofs and spires of fantasy. Born as they are to ascend—to raise themselves up/erect themselves. And without the least vertigo, if this ascent is hidden from them. If they see nothing but art, these somnambulists of the day, these seekers of God, these moonstruck men with open eyes.

   Their dream: to cover the natural with veils. To climb always higher, to remove themselves ever further, to abandon themselves to the certainty which, from the hazardous summits, they no longer even discern as an evasion—but as their plains, their plans. Averted from their thoughts, from all the repulsive things to which nature subjects every woman (?). Impatience, contempt, when their soul touches these matters which seem to encroach on their possessions: hands which profane their ideals. Deafness, horrified by what is no longer concealed by the skin, the ultimate artistic support, in which any slight gap or opening would be inadmissible for lovers—a sacrilege against love. Aversion toward the sordid aspects of nature: the blasphemous, aggressive aspects. Moral and esthetic faults in that which the lover intends to restore to the voluntary and the arbitrary.

   But since no one can render him this service, he conceals nature from himself and lives in a dream.

The lover's dreams, attributed to woman. Dreams which wish for: the dissimulation of nature. The remoteness of the heights which escape from the repugnant aspects of love.

   Remains: the abyss. And yet . . . if it comes about. If the unwearied travelers come close to the edge/the shore, the abrupt limit of the platforms of certainty. There is the risk that shallows may emerge, the danger of slippage[14] on an artistically concealed elevation—the fall of the die. A sense of dizziness once again threatens the tightrope-walkers of God: who

can avoid giving himself for. The horizon which collapses. The adornment which comes undone. The mask which falls.

If this happens, charge woman with a violent breach of propriety, an
inconceivable dis-tance. And envelop her/oneself in imperceptible veils.
Exalt her/climb up to the skies: in a fantastical search for God. "Beyond
the difference of the sexes, the ideal" which, sometimes, becomes incarnate.

"A deep and powerful alto voice of the kind one sometimes hears in the
theatre can suddenly raise the curtain upon possibilities in which we
usually do not believe. All at once we believe that somewhere in the
world there would be women with sublime, heroic, and royal souls, capable of and ready for grandiose responses, resolutions, and sacrifices, capable of and ready for rule over men because in them the best elements of
man apart from his sex have become an incarnate ideal. The intention of
the theatre, to be sure, is not at all that such voices should create this
notion of women; what they are supposed to represent is usually the ideal
male lover such as Romeo. But to judge by my experience, the theatre
regularly miscalculates at that point, as does the composer who expects
that kind of effect from such a voice. Such lovers are unconvincing: such
voices always retain the motherly coloration of the mistress of the
house—most of all when they make one think of love" (*The Gay Science*,
70).

The magic and most powerful effect of women: to echo the lofty souls of
men. To embody—without difference—their ideals. And since men are
the gods of language: to give voice to them, to provide material support
for their transcendent production.

The empire of the word/speech needs the ear and the voice in order to
reproduce itself. But let these modes be incarnated, once again, by
woman. Who, not understanding much about truth, faithfully duplicates
the investment, always returns the stakes.

The risk: in adapting themselves/in being appropriated (in appropriating for themselves), these organs can also depropriate.[15] Unless the
woman is sublime, a true artist. The perfect duplication, the faultless
mime, the game without loss. Perfect indifference which is faithful to the
lover. Ready for grandiose sacrifices, without the least lapse in execution.
Without any uncontrolled emotion? The music of Ariadne: finally on the
other side of immediate pleasure and pain.[16]

An exemplary echo chamber. An enclosure—sealed off, of course—admirably suited for resonance. A physical ensemble which enters into vibration with, amplifies, what it receives, and the more so as the exciting vibration approaches the level of a "natural frequency"—an ensemble evidently constructed in terms of a model—in terms of this system. A labyrinth whose internal cavities are always already limited, oriented, speculated for the faithful re-production of whatever enters there. A simulacrum without a hint of pretense. A theatre where all traces of scenery vanish. A machine which reveals nothing of its construction, allows nothing to be suspected of its technique, nothing to be guessed of its artifices. Nature remodeled, without apparent fabrication or ensnaring intervention. Without even a need to conceal, paint, tint, mask. Ariadne would finally have no underside, no inside, no depth, no cleft, no hole, no gulf, no abyss. Infinitely averted from herself.

Her secret: all in webs. She spins interminably, even at night. And without unravelling. The dream woman. Perfectly absent from "herself." Vertiginously engulfed in the nothingness of nature. The echo of the master's words or desires—but unique, solitary, untiringly repeated and reproduced in an enchanting voice, even at night. All in song. Giving herself for—for him—endlessly. Eternal—without body. Pure mechanism.

Hymen perpetually in play, in suspense of falling due. Always and never a virgin—without difference.[17] Beneath the veil subsists only the veil. Still too ignorant or already too sceptical for pleasure.

What men desire? What remains for them is the operation of attraction which confers power. To approach in order to redouble, distance, or exchange—himself. But, she, infinitely outside herself. Wonderfully averted.

The abyss, without reserve. Which the master ascribes to her, while this "elevation" amounts to his horror of nature. From now on, if he does not keep himself at a distance—and if he has not dressed her (prepared her), the vertigo of this bottomless depth seizes him: dis-tance without any possible return. Without lips, which, open or closed, also keep time, mark the rhythm of distancing taking place.

*   *   *

Woman, the idea, the one becoming the other—the other, the one—according to how they have been dressed (prepared)—(she/it) becomes transcendent, inaccessible, seductive. But if the void is her fullest measure, she drags everything along in her loss. "Of herself." She satisfies the desire for nothingness. Playing (with) the figure of death. If indeed she plays at all. But one ascribes so much to one who has nothing of her own. The risk: nothing will be left over. To abolish the game, in affirming that it was nothing but a game. Then—the raised stakes, the repetition, the return—perhaps not simply. Does she give herself? Or give herself for?

And in this *for*, who refrains from giving himself? Does he give himself? Or only for? And to what end?

Fallen, the phallic display, its reserve. To take up the question again and think it over. And to see, at this point, if the process of propriation would still dominate "the incessant war of the sexes," "the mortal hatred of the sexes" . . . For the affirmation or the abolition of difference?

Fallen, these envelopes of proper values. To reconsider how the giving-oneself could sub-sist—between the sexes. For the back and forth movement of exchange is perhaps only a simulacrum within the same, a passage from the same to the same. Whence the necessity for disguises: the break between the one and the other—but still within the same—which could not enter into relations except in disguise/fancy dress (except in drag). By a supplement of dissimulation: have them brought back to woman. Reduce the feminine to this.

Femininity lends itself to this: assumes everything one attributes to it, imposes on it. Is nothing other than a place of substitution between? Substitution, hiding place or blank canvas for productions and reproductions. Can simulate—chance. But comes back to a machine constructed by the iron hands of necessity.

"And not everything is purpose that is called purpose, and still less is everything will that is called will. And if you come to the conclusion, 'Then there is only one domain, that of stupidity and hazard?'—it must be added that, yes, perhaps there is only one domain, perhaps there is neither will nor aim, perhaps we have only imagined these things. Those iron hands of necessity that shake the dice-box of chance continue their game infinitely, hence, it *must* happen that certain throws perfectly resemble every degree of appropriateness and good sense. *Perhaps* our own voluntary acts and purposes are merely such throws, and we are too limited and vain to understand our extreme limitation: to know that we shake the dice-box with iron hands, and do nothing in our most deliber-

ate actions but play the game of necessity. Perhaps! In order to rise beyond this "perhaps" we would need already to have been guests in the
underworld, far beyond every surface, to have played dice and bet at the
table with Persephone herself" (*The Dawn*).[18]

In playing dice with Persephone, this "perhaps" would find—perhaps?—
that it falls due.[19] In venturing to bet with her, the goddess of the infernal
depths. Far beyond any surface.

The thread is lost. The voice? of life and death? loses itself here.

Persephone. The suspension of etymology. The rupture—in herself? in
itself?—of the name, without subjection to a source, an origin, an ancestry. Passage—undesignatable, in truth—unnamable, without doubt—
unequivocally indeterminable—of the daughter—from the mother to the
father. An operation of defloration?

Ambiguity must disguise this operation. Variously. Pretending to be
the brother. But of the mother or of the father? Of both: through a com-
plication characteristic of divine genealogies. But it will be as a member
of the father's side that he forces himself upon her. The goods are, in fact,
granted only to the males in the family. As goods, Persephone belongs to
them. But the distribution of the patrimony involved separate domains,
which divide the brothers, drive them apart, without any possibility of
relationship. Death and life have become their respective portions. Irrec-
oncilable. Insurmountable distance. Inasmuch as the attributes of the
brother below must be valued as subterranean realm and as abyss.

Ambivalence with regard to the possession of the earth, of the mother,
which redoubles itself in Hades. Invisible, henceforth, and with no possibility of meeting his brother above.

Man infinitely distanced from himself, in himself, by the impossible appropriation of the mother. To re-approach himself, between this one and
that one—the exchange of *Korè*. But this operation demands dissimulation: they can no longer see each other. The high and the low, the celestial and the infernal, the light and the dark, the truth and its reverse, the
reality and its shadow . . . no longer come together. Giving-receiving no
longer takes place between the one and the other. All ties between them
must be masked: relations must take place only in secret.

And doubly. The daughter stolen away from her mother, from herself,
by her father, the brother, the father's other, who takes her against/with-
out her consent. The *Korè* is given by the heavenly god to the infernal

god, who only takes possession of her in ravishing her. Stolen, violated, veiled [Volée, violée, voilée], a second time.

So it goes with exchange between man (men). Appropriation, its usage, its usury. The excess altering the object. The in-addition or surplus which devalues value: virginity. Which—between man (men)—amounts to the dissimulation of the product and its proof. Which is really taken away in nature: the daughter of the mother and the proximity of the two. Man approaches, but factitiously, thanks to this abduction and the gap between mother and daughter. He transforms the need or desire for proximity into a value-envelope of exchange.

Koré allows herself to be seduced, through ignorance, to be carried off to her ruin. Her attraction to the flower and the fruit, still "natural" for her, found itself confused by the power of resemblance—the end of the maiden, torn away from her mother-nature, carried away into death, by the contemplation of (a) narcissus and her taste for seeds. But without recognizing the appropriateness of these analogies. Carried away by surprise, secretly, for a lack of knowledge, of technique, of pretense.

Carried off into a world which is strange to her, she weeps. But no one hears her. And her mother, who does hear this anguished cry, cannot discover the place of her disappearance. No living person points it out to her.

Persephone—a voice caught up in death, without a trace of her abduction. From *Korè* to Persephone, the passage must be forgotten. To bring the one and the other together is impossible. Between the naturally virginal maiden and the stolen, violated woman/wife, fixed in her becoming by her fall into an abyss which is foreign to her—death, for men—the intervention of a giving-up-for/giving-oneself-up-for, of a pretense of femininity which would forbid her return. The one must never remember the other. Having entered that world, she must not come back from it. Must not cross again through that invisible veil which restrains her, that shadow which surrounds her, that death which encircles her. Which she sustains.

Her dissimulation? Her price among man (men). She must remain there, without tearing the hymen that conceals the falling due of the bloody blow, a blow which marks the horizon of ends/purposes: harmony, played (at), among necessity, will, arbitrariness.

Persephone doesn't remain there. Whence the risk of betting with her. The "perhaps" sometimes falls due/finds its expression. Sometimes the game unmasks itself—the limit of the game. For Persephone knows all the rolls of the dice. The highest and the lowest, the most beautiful and the most horrible, the feints and their realities. She passes, without stopping, from the ones to the others, but knows their differences.

Alone, a woman must go from the most obscure to the most sublime of the gods. Reascending, redescending the course, and without forgetting the operation which made her intimate with these depths. Transgressing—again and again—the rupture nonetheless consummated, between proximity and property. The "will" of the mother-nature and that of the father. To live in the increase of abundance, in its intoxication, and according to the law which divides the goods, determines their allocation—giving them meaning and names, immobilizing their "natural" becoming so that they are produced/produce themselves, reproduce, reproduce—always already measured. A controlled prosperity, and in its source. No longer left to the rhythm of the seasons, for example. Subject to an unchangeable measure, to a fixed value.

Knowing both worlds, Persephone—and without appearing to scorn this destiny—will spend twice as much time in "natural" rapture. Her springs and summers. This necessity, dictated by Demeter's refusal to produce while separated from her daughter, her other "self," leaves her only the winter with her husband: The cold season. Removed, distant, and from herself, ruined [abîmée]. Persephone becomes the frozen being. Truth of all production cut off from the natural. Subordinate from then on to a technique of mirage, which separates her from herself. Veiled, outside and in, the Korè is arrested in her becoming. Eternally and never again a virgin.

*　*　*

In art, this perspective will again be simulated, depicted, contrived according to an optics which is—perhaps?—not that of "physiology." The result of which is that she is—perhaps?—still absent. That she doesn't take place there.

To know this, to wager with Persephone. But this is—perhpas?—to risk seeing the end of the game. For she knows all the rules, and more. And can reopen what is believed to be the horizon of ends/purposes. Persephone, in effect, is not content with one. She can sub-sist in different ones.

Of woman, artistically stolen/concealed, she has experienced the power and the charm. But she knows what men owe to the passage through death. More than Athena, who was never a little girl. And more than Ariadne, who did not know Hades. Persephone has experienced the two veils, the two masks/hiding places, the two edges, the two faults in the invisible.[20] And the coming and going between the one and the other. Recrossing without stopping and without end the frontier of these abysses. From below and from above.

And if one would interpret her, "ambience," perhaps that would lead to another physiology of art? a "new plurality"? For which perspective would not inevitably be the "fundamental condition of all life" but that which, already, mortifies it.

Because, for one thing, Korè-Persephone escapes perspective. Her depth, in all its dimensions, never presents itself to the gaze, from any point of view. She disregards/goes beyond every horizon. Avoids becoming visible, even without Hades. Whence the veils with which she must cover herself in order to pass herself off for—what she is not.

She does not simply limit herself to this. Except as a mechanism—inorganic. If she deceives, it is because the phallic display does not amount to her, cannot show her. Would she wish to be completely assimilated, to resemble it totally?

But in the retouching of her lips—passive and active, experienced without resentment—she remains always intimate with the other, disposed to accept him again and again with/in her. And she doesn't take him *into* herself. The other is not, here or there, taken with/in the whole of her self. She doesn't "will" or "desire" herself except with the other. She takes endless pleasure in embracing the other. A movement always simultaneously internal and external: passing between the edges and extending itself to the thickness or depth of the flesh, as if outside, more or less distant from the universe. She comes and goes, in herself and outside herself, without stopping. In at least four dimensions: from left to right, from right to left, from front to back, from back to front, the threshold from the inside to the outside of the body.

In this way, the expansion of her "world" would be unceasingly produced, a "world" which does not unfold in any square or circle or . . . and remains without the limits of a horizon. What happens there embraces itself in the movement—if it remains other which touches it(self). This rhythm, barely perceptible, even to "small ears,"[21] sub-tends, nourishes, and goes along with the others, like a background of air and light which doesn't hear or see itself as such. Bathing and illuminating everything without becoming visible. A tactile substratum, dedicated to forgetfulness, when the eye and the ear alone wish to marry.[22]

Her affirmation already takes place this side of or beyond appearance, and without a veil. She diffuses herself, like a harmony which sub-tends, envelops, and subtly "fills" every spectacle, prior to the caesura of forms and according to a movement other than scansion into syncopes. A continuum to which even the veil will lend the material support of its fabric.

This affirmation, without subject or object, does not go as far as the abyss. Except for whoever cannot perceive it or think it, except as "the profound essence" of the Dionysian. But there is no essence without the will to bring it back or reduce it to a relationship with a unique mother-nature.

Harmony, in itself, in her, ceaselessly recrosses the limit from the outside to the inside of the one. It/she always brings together at least two. Not two unities, but a two which passes from the interior to the exterior, from the exterior to the interior of the ones, and without a break. Immediate mediation which never represents itself, never exposes itself as such. Not that it/she is covered by a veil, not even of appearance. When appearance manifests itself, she can still draw out enough to mark the folds, seams, and looseness of these coverings and dissimulations.

This duplicity of the veil has perhaps never received its interpretation. It/she remains for one who (re)covers, masks, defers the becoming visible. Who already lends herself in certain of her effects to a more discreet diffusion. Yet in some way is an envoy of the depths.

However, without that flesh, still in the flux of life, all forms and all things risk being fixed in the frozen stiffness of couples—juxtaposed, contrary, opposed, of similarities or differences—fertile perhaps in their relations, still productive, but without harmony.

For such music it is necessary that the passage between open differently, not onto a confrontation of limits, even interchangeable limits. Folded back upon appearances, each time, upon themselves. Men transgress their borders in order to appropriate some "thing" of the other, indeed to take (back) her property. A wedding ring thus encircles its prey, the other whom he doesn't manage to embrace/marry.

To marry requires a harmonious passage from the exterior to the interior, from the interior to the exterior of bodies. So that one arrives at the other without breaking into enclosures, without leaping over the river, without abduction into the abyss below or above. Let the two be here and there at the same time, which isn't to say that they are lost in each other.[23]

*   *   *

Ariadne? The perfectly resembling. Faithfully reproducing the perspectives which are proposed to her. Without fixing them in any truth, except the truth thus imposed? Without forces, except those with which she is inflated and which she doesn't keep. If it is not for? And again . . . in the instant, reduced to the deadly inertia of a double?

What remains is one who does not simply submit to any vision or question: her/the *voice*. Here, the in-addition/surplus which funds/resources all appearances. Because of this, her song always remains, beautiful as the first time: passage from life into the universe of resemblance.

This femininity, so perfectly accomplished, deceives. Multiply. Life gives itself—gives itself for—for an other, and according to his perspectives. Ariadne—double of the male. Reproduces only the masculine. That the masculine also desires the feminine perhaps redoubles the stakes. Doesn't change the game.

Unless to affirm that "physiology" is the same for the two sexes. Which covers certain natural horrors, hides them artistically. From whence the intoxication, the beyond-self, the in-addition-to-self, the surplus of life. But borrowed and arrested in the truth of (a) same. Bounded. And in its vertigo. The intoxication of being more, while remaining the same.

Which one by preference attributes to woman—double of the male. Whose operation is to redouble/increase herself "in herself" and without frame or limit. Increasing herself without bounds. Cheating at every game.

But this perspective will be deposited in or projected onto self-identity. So that she will be the privileged depository of the secret of truth—and of its non-truth—insofar as she serves to constitute the identity of the same. Yet this necessity unveils itself in her as a/her mechanistic destiny. Her passage through/into a matrix which determines life, figures the perceptible according to *one* perspective, subordinating them to a dominant value: the "ambience" of the masculine.

All chance, every so-called accidental meeting, taking place within the horizon of this will/desire: the permanence of the identical to itself. The completion of this quest? All being contrived to reproduce this end, without anarchy or manifest mastery.

All being? Thus woman. Who is not only one—the risk. Beneath all these/her appearances, beneath all these/her borrowings and artifices, this other still sub-sists. Beyond all these/her forms of life or death, still living. And as she is dis-tant—and in "herself"—she threatens all values with instability. In her they can always collapse: truth, appearances, will, power, eternal return. Miming them more or less adequately, this other never remains un(equ)ivocally. Who serves the master inasmuch as she hinders none of his impulses, espouses all his standards. Faithful to him in all her infidelities, she protects his "ambience"—permitting him to withdraw and to return—divergence between him and himself—according to the demands of his power.

So she who is always mobile renders him the possibility of movement in remaining, for him, the persistence of his being. Truth or appearances, according to his desire of the moment, his appetite of the instant. Truth and appearances and reality, power . . . she is—by virtue of her inexhaustible aptitude for mimicry—the living support of all the staging/production of the world. Variously veiled according to the epochs of history.

She mimes the whole, just as well. For her operation is to redouble. But in "herself" and without end. Pure increase, she becomes that which one proposes to her, imposes on her. But beneath all these/her masks, she sub-sists. Still. Each of these/her figures—and that of being—is already cheated as soon as she appears. Reserved and restrained there by that to which she gives herself, but already and only for, in her "natural" deployment/display.

If she collapses [*s'abîme*], she collapses because the envelope of air(s) with which one has covered her doesn't properly suit her. Thus, she deceives and deceives herself, separated between becoming "herself" and these mutations of form, these changes of perspectives, these revolutions of the sun, which she embraces without holding fast. At least simply.

And if the latest mode is that of phallic will (desire), she will prove to you that she is it, that you are right to believe it. Adding more, even to the point of bringing the phallus and the rest to their ruin.

For certainly, all perspectives already fixed, all forms already framed, every horizon already circumscribed, appear to her only as part of the game. Which will entertain her—perhaps? But for an instant. Time enough to experience the limit and begin her operation again.

Unless she is dead from birth. Immortal virgin, from never having been a young girl. Flower, hypostatized in truth, appearance, pretense . . . according to your will, the vicissitudes of your power, the moments of history. All at once, all together, to please you.

Arrest, and a sentence of death, without end.

Notes

1. Pallas Athena was born without her mother, emerging fully grown from the head of Zeus. In a passage from *Ecce Homo*, Nietzsche seems to allude to her birth (as Walter Kaufmann notes): "Considered in this way, my life is simply wonderful. For the task of a *revaluation of all values* more capacities have been needed than have ever dwelt together in a single individual—above all, even contrary capacities that had to be kept from disturbing, destroying one another. . . . Its *higher protection* manifested itself to such a high degree that I never even suspected what was growing in me—and one day all my capacities, suddenly ripe, *leaped forth* in their ultimate perfection" (Kaufmann translation, New York, 1967, pp. 254–55).

According to Hesiod, Athena was the child of Zeus and Metis (Wisdom, Cunning), but her birth presupposed the disappearance of her mother:

> Zeus, as King of the gods,
>   took as his first wife Metis,
> and she knew more than all the gods
>   or mortal people.
> But when she was about to be delivered
>   of the goddess, gray-eyed
> Athene, then Zeus, deceiving her perception
>   by treachery
> and by slippery speeches,
>   put her away inside his own belly.
> This was by the advice of Gaia,
>   and starry Ouranos,
> for so they counseled,
>   in order that no other everlasting
> god, beside Zeus, should ever be given
>   the kingly position.
> For it had been arranged, that, from her,
>   children surpassing in wisdom
> should be born, first the gray-eyed girl,
>   the Tritogeneia

Athene: and she is the equal of her father
  in wise counsel
and strength; but then a son to be King
  over gods and mortals
was to be born of her, and his heart
  would be overmastering:
but before this, Zeus put her away
  inside his own belly
so that this goddess should think for him,
  for good and for evil . . .
Then from his head, by himself,
He produced Athene of the gray eyes,
  great goddess . . .

(*Theogony*, lines 887–901, 923–25; trans. Richmond Latimore,
in *Hesiod*, Ann Arbor, 1959)

The father-gods who preceded Zeus—Ouranos and Kronos—both fell victim to sons who acted as embodiments of their mothers, of the mother's power to outwit and replace the father. Fearful of the children that Gaia, the Earth, would bear him, Ouranos, the Sky, tried to force her offspring back into her womb, but Gaia tricked him. To her son Kronos she gave a sickle, and when Ouranos entered her, Kronos—hiding in the Earth—castrated his father. Kronos, in turn, fearful of his children, ate each at birth, but Rheia, their mother—in league with Gaia—deceived him, feeding him a stone instead of Zeus. Zeus survived to overthrow Kronos. Faced with the cunning of Metis, Zeus evaded the destiny of his father and grandfather by devouring—not the children—but the mother herself. He ate Metis and, having made her his cunning, produced from his own head a child, Athena, the transformation of the mother's guile into an instrument of the father's policy and will. On Metis, see Marcel Dètienne and Jean-Pierre Vernant, *Cunning Intelligence in Greek Culture and Society*, trans. J. Lloyd (New York, 1978).

On the position of the mother as it is repeatedly envisioned in Western thought, cf., as well, Hélène Cixous, *Sorties*, a portion of *La jeune née* (Paris, 1975), translated by Ann Liddle in *New French Feminisms*, ed. Elaine Marks and Isabelle de Courtivron (Amherst, MA, 1980), pp. 90–98: "As soon as the ontological question is raised; as soon as you ask yourself what is meant by the question 'What is it?'; as soon as there is a will to say something. A will: desire, authority, you examine that, and you are led right back—to the father. You can even fail to notice that there's no place at all for women in the operation! In the extreme the world of 'being' can function to the exclusion of the mother. No need for the mother—provided that there is something of the maternal: and it is the father then who acts as—is—the mother." TRANS. and ED.

2. In *re(n)versement*, two words coexist, a word-play characteristic of a strategy of writing which Irigaray employs throughout *Amante marine*, an interplay of multiple (and, at times, quite different) meanings of words, "all at once, all together," with no meaning subordinate to another. Here, as in most cases where two or more possible meanings for a word are suggested by the text, both are indicated in the translation. In *re(n)versement*, *reversement* (pouring out again, pouring back [of a liquid], transfer [of funds, titles], shifting [of blame]), and *renversement* (reversal, overthrow, inversion, perhaps sublation in the Hegelian sense [*Aufhebung*]) indicate two distinct operations. TRANS.

3. Aeschylus, *The Oresteia*, trans. Robert Fagles (New York, 1975). All subsequent passages of the *Eumenides* are in the Fagles translation; at times that text has been modified to reflect more accurately the French translation which Irigaray employs. Line numbers refer to the Greek text.

In the *Eumenides*, Apollo—who has ordered Orestes to kill his mother Clytemnestra in revenge for the murder of his father Agamemnon—sends Orestes to Athena for judgment. The Furies, who form the chorus in the play, pursue him. Before coming to Athena's temple, Orestes performs a purifying ritual to which Irigaray will refer: he slaughters a pig. The fact that after the sacrifice he can mingle with the members of a community and cause no harm becomes evidence in his trial that he has been decontaminated and is "fit for a communal life among free men."

In the trial over which Athena presides, Apollo speaks for Orestes, asserting the priority of marital over blood ties and arguing that mothers function in reproduction only as receptacles for the child who is engendered by the father alone (see note 4). The Furies take the maternal side, insisting on revenge for Orestes' violent crime against the bond of kinship:

> Mother who bore me,
>   O dear Mother Night.
> to avenge the blinded dead
> and those who see by day,
>   now hear me! The whelp of Leto
> spurns my rights, he tears this trembling victim
>   from my grasp—the one to bleed,
> to atone away the mother-blood at last . . .
>
> This, this is our right,
>   spun for us by the Fates,
> the ones who bind the world,
> and none can shake our hold.
>   Show us the mortals overcome,
> insane to murder kin, we track them down
>   till they go beneath the earth,
> and the dead find little freedom in the end.
>   (321–36)

The trial ends with a compromise: Athena casts her lot for Orestes:

> My work is here, to render the final judgment.
> Orestes,
> I will cast my lot for you.
> No mother gave me birth. I am
> all for the male, in all things, but marriage.
> Yes, with all my heart I am my Father's child.
> I cannot set more store by the woman's death—
> She killed her husband, guardian of their house.
>   (729–41)

At the same time, Athena assuages the anger of the Furies, promising them a "cult, rites, sacrifices . . . " if they will retire to underground caverns, "bury" themselves beneath the town, subordinating their power to the good of Athens and remaining "loyal and propitious to the land."

Aeschylus's version of the Oresteia myth has often been read in terms of the psychological and political conflict between matriarchal and patriarchal orders, whose resolution marked a transcendence/transition—the triumph of the Olympian gods over the maternal, chthonic forces from which they emerged. See, for example, Hélène Cixous (Le jeune née, Paris, 1975, pp. 144–47) for whom Orestes' matricide—up to this point the worst of crimes—signals the "dawn of phallocentrism"— "the end of mothers," the inauguration of "the sublime era": "How to estimate the murder of the mother? What is the value of the blood? What is the value of the word? Contest between the Blood and the Word: the marriage contract, a bond accepted with the word and the will, is stronger, Apollo affirms, than the tie of kinship. The tie to the mother slackens. The tie to the word grows taut. . . . Henceforth, it will be necessary that the judicial come to the aid of the order of the father. That a new relationship be established between the body and justice" (p. 192).—TRANS.

4.

> *Apollo:* Here is the truth, I tell you—see how right I am.
> The woman you call the mother of the child
> is not the parent, just a nurse to the seed,
> the new-sown seed that grows and swells inside her.
> The *man* is the source of life—the one who mounts.
> She, like a stranger for a stranger, keeps
> the shoot alive unless god hurts the roots.
>
> I give you proof that all I say is true.
> The father can father forth without a mother.
> Here she stands, our living witness. Look—
> (*Exhibiting Athena*).
> Child sprung full-blown from Olympian Zeus
> never bred in the darkness of the womb
> but such a stock no goddess could conceive!
>
> —TRANS.

5. In Irigaray's text, this statement is attributed to Apollo. In Aeschylus's play, Orestes is the speaker.—TRANS.

6. Cf. *Women's Exile: Interview with Luce Irigaray,* trans. Couze Venn, *Ideology and Consciousness,* 1 (May 1977), pp. 62–76. The woman who no longer touches herself loses contact with the feminine since, for Irigaray, touch pervades the feminine imaginary—the configurations of desire that women can produce for themselves. Freud and Freudians like Lacan seem exclusively concerned with the male imaginary which depends on the possession of the phallus. In this connection, Irigaray writes, "The female sex is described as a lack, a 'hole.' Freud and psychoanalysts following him maintain that the only desire on the part of the woman, when she discovers she has 'no sex,' is to have a penis, i.e. *the only sexual organ which is recognized and valued*" (p. 62). Thus for Freud—as he himself suggests—"the repudiation of femininity must surely be a biological fact" (*Analysis Terminable and Interminable,* in *Therapy and Technique,* ed. Philip Rieff, New York, 1963), p. 27)—a "fact" which, as Irigaray notes, is not Freud's discovery but is a product of the "particular social and cultural economy, which has been maintained in the West at least since the Greeks" (p. 63). It is to evade this "fact," to posit a different "biology" that Irigaray writes. Since the biology is produced by a discourse that serves the male imaginary, Irigaray seeks a different discourse. "I think we must go back to the question not of the anatomy but of the morphology of female sex. In fact, it can be shown that all Western discourse presents a certain isomorphism with the masculine sex: the privilege of unity, form of the self, of the visible, of the specularisable, of the erection (which is the becoming in a form). Now this morpho-logic does not correspond to the female sex: there is not 'a' female sex. The 'no sex' that has been assigned to the woman can mean that she does not have a 'sex' and that her sex is not visible, or identifiable, or representable in a definite form . . . When one says, or believes that this sex is a 'hole,' it is a way of indicating that it cannot represent itself in either the dominant discourse or 'imaginary.' Thus I have tried to find what the specific modes of functioning of the female sex and 'imaginary' would be. Instead of, first of all, stopping at the 'parts' of this sex, such as they are defined in masculine parameters: the vagina or the home of the penis, the mechanism for producing children, or even, breasts (which can be willy-nilly, represented metaphorically as phallic), I'm trying to say that the female sex would be, above all, made up of '*two lips*.' These two lips of the female sex make it once and for all a return to unity, because they are always at least *two,* and that one can never determine of these two, which is one, which is the other: they are continually interchanging. They are neither identifiable nor separable one from the other. Besides, instead of that being the visible or the form which constitutes the dominant criteria, it is the *touch* which for the female sex seems to me primordial: *these 'two lips' are always joined in an embrace*" (pp. 64–65).

In a sense, the feminine imaginary is intrinsically auto-erotic since "woman . . . is always embracing herself within herself. . . . This continuity of feminine auto-eroticism is interrupted, however, by a kind of process which could be described as rape: by maintaining to women that they 'need' a penis, by instructing them that they are nothing by themselves, that they are not female without the penis" (p. 65). The rape which Irigaray describes can be seen as a pedagogical one: women are taught that Athena is the "feminine." TRANS.

   7. On the function of the chorus in Greek tragedy, cf. Nietzsche, *The Birth of Tragedy*, trans. Kaufmann (New York, 1967), pp. 64–65: "[W]e must understand Greek tragedy as the Dionysian chorus which ever anew discharges itself in an Apollinian world of images. Thus the choral parts with which tragedy is interlaced are, as it were, the womb that gave birth to the whole of the so-called dialogue, that is, the entire world of the stage, the real drama. In successive discharges this primal ground of tragedy radiates this vision of the drama which is by all means a dream apparition and to that extent epic in nature; but on the other hand, being the objectification of a Dionysian state, it represents not Apollinian redemption through mere appearance but, on the contrary, the shattering of the individual and his fusion with primal being." TRANS.

   8. Translations of passages from *The Gay Science* (*Women and their action at a distance* [60]; *We artists* [59]; *Women who master the masters* [70]) are taken with slight modifications from the Kaufmann translation (New York, 1974). Cf. the reading of 60 in Jacques Derrida's *Spurs: Nietzsche's Styles*, trans. Barbara Harlow (Chicago and London, 1979). Irigaray's response to Nietzsche responds to Derrida's text as well. In a sense (a traditional one), Derrida seems to become "woman" in *Veiled Lips*—his expression veiled, silenced and effaced, mediating between Irigaray and Nietzsche. Of course, Irigaray does not require such mediation. According to Derrida, "a woman seduces from a distance. In fact, distance is the very element of her power. Yet one must beware to keep one's own distance from her beguiling song of enchantment. A distance from distance must be maintained. Not only for protection (the most obvious advantage) against the spell of her fascination, but also as a way of succumbing to it, that distance (which is lacking) *is necessary* . . . It is necessary to keep one's distance . . . Such might also be the advice of one man to another: a sort of scheme for how to seduce without being seduced. If it is necessary to keep one's distance from the feminine operation, from the *actio in distans* . . . it is perhaps because the 'woman' is not a determinable identity. Perhaps woman is not some thing which announces itself from a distance, at a distance from some other thing. In that case it would not be a matter of retreat and approach. Perhaps woman—a non-identity, a non-figure, a simulacrum—is distance's very chasm, the out-distancing of distance, the interval's cadence, distance itself, if we could still say such a thing, distance *itself*. . . . There is no such thing as the essence of woman because woman averts, she is averted of herself. Out of the depths, endless and unfathomable, she engulfs and distorts all vestiges of essentiality, of identity, of property. And the philosophical discourse, blinded, founders on these shoals and is hurled down these depthless depths to its ruin. There is no such thing as the truth of woman, but it is because of that abyssal divergence of the truth, because that untruth is 'truth.' Woman is but one name for that untruth of truth. On the one hand . . . for him, Nietzsche, truth is like a woman. It resembles the veiled movement of feminine modesty . . . But, on the other hand, the credulous and dogmatic philosopher who *believes* in the truth that is woman, who believes in truth just as he believes in woman, this philosopher has understood nothing. He has understood nothing of truth, nor anything of woman. Because, indeed, if woman *is* truth, *she* at least knows that there is no truth, that truth has no place here and that no one has a place for truth. And she is woman precisely because she herself does not believe in truth itself, because she does not believe in what she is, in what she is believed to be, in what she thus is not . . . It rather is the 'man' who has decided to believe that his discourse on woman or truth might possibly be of any *concern* to her . . . For it is the man who believes in the truth of woman, in woman-truth" (pp. 49–53, 63–65).

   In Derrida's reading of Nietzsche, the question of woman becomes the question of an undecidable, of that which produces truth and which cannot—as a result—be produced by the truth. Elsewhere, Derrida writes that any logical system determines order by virtue of an element which it cannot in turn determine: "One of the elements of the systems . . . must also stand as the very possibility of systematicity," but this element "cannot be simply assigned a site within what it situates, cannot be subsumed under concepts whose contours it draws" (*Dissemination*, trans. Barbara Johnson, Chicago and London, 1981, p. 103). In Nietzsche, according to Derrida, "woman" is such an element, and the truth which woman situates and is—enables us to observe from a distance even as she separates herself from it—is the truth of castration. See note 11 below. TRANS.

9. Cf. Derrida, *Spurs*: "The title for this lecture was to have been *the question of style*. However—it is woman who will be my subject . . . In the question of style there is always the weight or *examen* of some pointed object. At times this object might only be a quill or a stylus. But it could just as easily be a stilleto, or even a rapier. Such objects might be used in a vicious attack against what philosophy appeals to in the name of matter or matrix, an attack whose thrust could not but leave its mark, could not but inscribe there some imprint or form. But they might also be used as protection against the threat of such an attack, in order to keep it at a distance, to repel it—as one bends or recoils before its force, in flight, behind veils and sails. . . . And as far as sails and veils are concerned, now that we have happened into them, Nietzsche must have been familiar with all genres. Thus the style would seem to advance in the manner of a *spur* of sorts (*épéron*). Like the prow, for example, of a sailing vessel, its *rostrum*, the projection of the ship which surges ahead to meet the sea's attack and cleave its hostile surface. Or yet again, and still in nautical terminology, the style might be compared to that rocky point, also called an *épéron*, on which the waves break at the harbor's entrance. So, it seems, style also uses its spurs as a means of protection against the terrifying, blinding, mortal threat (of that) which *presents* itself, which obstinately thrusts itself into view. And style thereby protects itself, meaning, truth—on the condition at least that it should not already be that gaping chasm which has been deflowered in the unveiling of the difference" (pp. 35–39). Derrida discusses writing as well as style. "Nietzsche's writing is an inscription of the truth. And such inscription, even if we do not venture to call it the feminine itself, is indeed the feminine 'operation.' Because woman is (her own) writing, style must return to her. In other words, it could be said that if style were a man (much as the penis, according to Freud is the 'normal prototype of fetishes'), then writing would be a woman" (p. 57). TRANS.

10. The word *abyss* translates the French *abîme*. Irigaray uses the archaic spelling *abyme*, not to denote *abyss* but to allude to the "abyss" in *mise en abyme*, a term originally from heraldry which Gide introduced into literary criticism in order to describe his own self-referential writing. Under Derrida's influence, *abyme* has gained currency as a name for the paradoxes attendant on textual self-referentiality.

In heraldry, a *mise en abyme* is an escutcheon which depicts a duplicate of itself, a duplicate which in turn depicts a duplicate, etc. Literally a "casting into the abyss," *mise an abyme* involves the illusion of an infinite regress which structures the representation of representation and, therefore, any form of self-consciousness: I think of myself thinking of myself thinking of myself and so on. Thus, the "abyss" which Irigaray uses *abyme* to name is the one which self-consciousness produces.

While here the text does not seem to establish a semantic distinction between abyss (*abîme*) and *abyme*, later Irigaray will use *abîme* not to denote the abyss of male self-representation but the position of woman who mimics the *abyme* but exceeds the illusion she mimes. See note 13. TRANS. and ED.

11. Cf. Derrida, *Spurs*: The "untruth of truth" for which "woman" is one name is the untruth of castration (p. 61). Freud posited as a general psychological fact our belief in this truth. Castration occurs or threatens: it has occurred in women and it threatens men. Women are the sign which represents its possibility for men. Inasmuch as castration can become a sign for any lack of power (or any lack of power can become a figuration of castration), inasmuch as truth involves a desire to assert power, it also involves a struggle against that which determines its logic; the (un)truth of truth, "woman," castration. But if "woman" signifies castration, woman also has the power to enact

that truth without being limited to it. Thus Nietzsche's reading of the feminine as Derrida presents it: "Unable to seduce or give vent to desire without it, 'woman' is in need of castration's effect. But evidently she does not believe in it. She who, unbelieving, still plays with castration, she is 'woman.' She takes aim and amuses herself *(en joue)* with it as she would with a new concept or structure of belief, but even as she plays she is gleefully anticipating her laughter, her mockery of man. With a knowledge that would outmeasure the most self-respecting dogmatic or credulous philosopher, woman knows that castration *does not take place*. This formula, however, must be manipulated with great prudence. Inasmuch as its undecidable mark, a non-mark even, indicates that area where castration is no longer determinable, it describes a margin whose very consequences are incalculable" (p. 61).

Cf., as well, Hélène Cixous, *The Laugh of the Medusa*, trans. Keith Cohen and Paula Cohen, in *New French Feminisms:* "Let the priests tremble, we're going to show them our sexts! Too bad for them if they fall apart upon discovering that women aren't men, or that the mother doesn't have one. But isn't this fear convenient for them? Wouldn't the worst be, isn't the worst, in truth, that women aren't castrated, that they have only to stop listening to the Sirens (for the Sirens were men) for history to change its meaning? You only have to look at Medusa straight on to see her. And she's not deadly. She's beautiful and she's laughing. . . . Castration? Let others toy with it. What's a desire originating from a lack? A pretty meager desire" (pp. 255, 262). TRANS.

12. The abduction of Persephone by Hades. See note 19. TRANS.

13. Although the commonly used definitions—"mimesis," "mimicry"—seem appropriate here, the French *mimétisme* might also be translated as *mimeticism*, particularly when it is used to describe a positive strategy for dealing with the problems of writing which the systematic coherence of philosophical discourse poses for women. In *Ce sexe qui n'en est pas un* (Paris: 1977), Irigaray speaks of the impossibility, for a woman, of articulating her sexual difference, of making statements like, "I am a woman," or, "I am a being of the feminine sex": . . . the articulation of the reality of my sex is impossible in discourse for a structural, eidetic reason. My sex is taken away, at all events, as the property of a subject, in the operation of predication which guarantees discursive coherence" (p. 145). Faced with the dilemma of speaking/writing "like a man" or remaining caught in the position which philosophical discourse assigns to "woman"—a position of powerlessness and in-coherence— Irigaray proposes that woman "rediscover the locus of her exploitation by discourse, without simply letting herself be reduced to that position." (p. 74). She suggests that mimeticism may be the only way for woman to reinscribe herself within the coherent systems of philosophy—"[the way], moreover, to which the feminine condition has assigned . . . But even this role is complex, for it implies lending oneself to anything, if not to everything. To *redouble* anything, anyone, to receive all imprints *without appropriating them* and *without adding to them*. That is to say, to be nothing but the possibility for the philosopher to (be) reflect(ed). Like the platonic *chora*, but also the mirror of the subject" (p. 147). TRANS.

14. *Slippage—dérapage*, a nautical term which describes the sliding of an anchor. For a discussion of the phenomenon of slippage in relation to discourse, see Jacques Lacan, *The insistence of the letter in the unconscious*, trans. Jan Miel, in *Structuralism*, ed. Jacques Ehrmann (Garden City, NY: Anchor Books, 1972), pp. 105f TRANS.

15. Cf. Derrida, *Spurs:* "The conceptual significations and values which would seem to decide the stakes or means in Nietzsche's analysis of the sexual difference, of the 'eternal war between the sexes,' and the 'mortal hatred of the sexes,' 'of love,' eroticism, etc., are all based on what might be called a process of *propriation* (appropriation, expropriation, taking, taking possession, gift and barter, mastery, servitude, etc.) . . . [T]he woman's appearance takes shape according to an already formalized law. Either, at times, woman is woman because she gives, *because she gives* herself, while the man for his part takes, possesses, indeed takes possession. Or else, at other times, she is woman because, in giving, she is in fact *giving herself for*, is simulating, and consequently assuring the possessive mastery for her own self. The *for* which appears in the 'to-give-oneself-for,' whatever its value,

whether it deceives by giving only an appearance of, or whether it actually introduces some destination, finality or twisted calculation, some return, redemption or gain, into the loss of proper-ty (*propre*), this *for* nonetheless continues to withhold the gift of a reserve. Henceforth all the signs of the sexual opposition are changed. Man and woman change places. They exchange masks *ad infinitum*. "Women have known how to secure for themselves by their subordination the greatest advantage, in fact the upper hand' *Human All Too Human*, (412) . . . As a result, the question, 'what *is* proper-ty (*propre*), what *is* appropriation, expropriation, mastery, servitude, etc.,' is no longer possible. Not only is propriation a sexual operation, but *before* it there was no sexuality . . . [P]ropriation is all the more powerful since it is its process that organized both the totality of language's process and symbolic exchange in general. By implication, then, it also organized all ontological statements. The history (of) truth (is) a process of propriation" (pp. 109–11). Cf., as well, Cixous in *La jeune née* where she identifies the history of propriation with the history of phallocentrism, with history and identity as dialectic (Paris, 1975, pp. 144–47). In *The Laugh of the Medusa*, Cixous writes of "the whole deceptive problematic of the gift": "Woman is obviously not that woman Nietzsche dreamed of who gives only in order to. Who could ever think of the gift as a gift-that-takes? Who else but man precisely the one who would like to take everything? If there is a 'propriety of woman,' it is paradoxically her capacity to depropriate unselfishly, body without end, without appendage, without principal 'parts.' If she is whole, it's a whole composed of parts that are wholes, not simple partial objects but a moving, limitlessly changing ensemble, a cosmos tirelessly traversed by Eros, an immense astral space not organized around any one sun that's any more of a star than the others" (*New French Feminisms*, p. 259). TRANS.

16. Ariadne—daughter of King Minos of Crete, proprietor of the Labyrinth where the Minotaur was confined—gave Theseus a spool of thread which he unwound as he entered the Labyrinth and followed to find his way safely out again. After he killed the Minotaur, Theseus escaped with Ariadne from Crete. He abandoned her on the island of Naxos—while she slept. Dionysus found Ariadne there and married her.

Nietzsche refers briefly to Ariadne in *Beyond Good and Evil* when he imagines a conversation between himself and Dionysus: "Thus once he [Dionysus] said: 'Under certain circumstances I love what is human'—and with this alluded to Ariadne, who was present—'man is to my mind an agreeable, courageous, inventive animal that has no equal on earth: it finds its way in any labyrinth" (Kaufmann translation, New York, 1966, p. 236). In *Ecce Homo* Nietzsche writes: "Who besides me knows what Ariadne is!—For all such riddles nobody so far had any solution; I doubt that anybody even saw any riddles here" (p. 308).

Among the *Dionysus Dithyrambs* that appear in an 1888 manuscript is a poem entitled *Ariadne's Lament*. The poem, which has been copied from *The Magician* chapter of *Zarathustra* (IV, 5), now concludes with the appearance of Dionysus to Ariadne:

> *Dionysus:* Be clever, Ariadne!
> You have small ears, you have my ears:
> Put a clever word into them!
> Must one not first hate each other
>   if one is to love each other?
> I am your labyrinth

(trans. Kaufmann, in *The Portable Nietzsche*, New York, 1968, p. 345).

An unpublished note from the same period reads: " 'Ariadne,' said Dionysus, 'You are a labyrinth: Theseus has lost his way in it, he has no more direction . . . Ariadne answered: 'I do not want to pity when I love; I am tired of pity. All heroes shall perish in me. That is my deepest love for Theseus: I destroy him' " (trans. Rose Pfeffer in *Disciple of Dionysus*, Lewisburg, PA, 1972, p. 121). A January 1889, letter to Cosima Wagner identifies her with Ariadne, Nietzsche with Dionysus. "Ariadne, I love you," Nietzsche writes—and signs the note, "Dionysus" (trans. Christopher Middleton, in *Selected Letters of Friedrich Nietzsche*, Chicago and London, 1969, p. 346).

In *Amante marine*, Irigaray echoes Nietzsche: "She is your labyrinth, you are her labyrinth. A passage from you to yourself loses itself in her, a passage from her to herself loses itself in you. And to seek there only a play of mirrors, isn't that to create the abyss *(abyme)?* . . . Without affirmation of difference, the inclusion of you in her, of her in you, is perpetuated in (the) labyrinthine mourning of desire or will in you and between you (p. 79). TRANS. and ED.

17. On *hymen*, cf. Derrida, *Dissemination*, pp. 209–13: *Hymen* "is first of all a sign of fusion, the consummation of a marriage, the identification of two beings, the confusion between two. *Between* the two, there is no longer difference but identity. Within this fusion, there is no longer any distance between desire (the awaiting of a full presence designed to fulfill it, to carry it out) and the fulfillment of presence, between distance and non-distance; there is no longer any difference between desire and satisfaction. . . . What counts here is the *between*, the in-between-ness of the hymen. The hymen "takes place" in the "inter-," in the spacing between desire and fulfillment, between perpetration and its recollection. . . . The hymen, the consummation of differences, the continuity and confusion of coitus, merges with what it seems to be derived from the hymen as protective screen, the jewel box of virginity, the vaginal partition, the fine, the invisible veil which, in front of the hystera, stands *between* the inside and the outside of a woman, and consequently between desire and fulfillment. It is neither desire nor pleasure but in between the two. . . . It is the hymen that desire dreams of piercing, of bursting, in an act of violence that is (at the same time or somewhere between) love and murder. If either one *did* take place, there would be no hymen. But neither would there simply be a hymen in (case events go) *no* place. With all the undecidability of its meaning, the hymen only takes place when it doesn't take place, when nothing *really* happens." TRANS.

18. Translation (slightly modified) from *The Complete Works of Friedrich Nietzsche*, ed. Dr. Oscar Levy (London, 1911), IX 137. TRANS.

19. Persephone is the daughter of Demeter and Zeus. Without her mother's knowledge, her father promised her to Hades, his brother. As Persephone was gathering flowers one day—as she reached out and picked a narcissus—the earth opened, and Hades appeared to carry her off to the Underworld. She remained there for nine days and nights while her mother roamed the earth, inconsolable, searching for her. When Demeter finally learned of Persephone's abduction, she refused to produce a harvest as long as she was separated from her daughter. Zeus agreed to bring Persephone back to her mother, but only on the condition that she had eaten nothing in the Underworld. Hades, hoping to keep Persephone, gave her some pomegranate seeds—which she ate—but he was forced to accept a compromise: Persephone would spend six months of every year with him and six months with Demeter.

The abduction of the daughter, Persephone, by Hades—her separation from her mother "by her father, the brother, the father's other, who takes her against/without her consent"—may figure the experience of women in relation to a system of representation which characterizes "woman" and her sex as unrepresentable, as a "lack" in the discourse. According to Irigaray, this discursive system is symptomatic of "a particular social and cultural economy which has been maintained in the West at least since the Greeks" (*Women's Exile*, p. 63) and which has censored the positive value of women's relationships to themselves and to other women: "I think that women are totally 'censored' in their carnal relationship with their mothers and other women. Indeed, Freud, in his own way, did see this. According to him, as soon as she realizes her castration, the little girl turns away from her mother, because the latter does not possess the valued sex which she thought she had. Then, Freud says, the little girl 'hates' her mother—and thus herself and all other women. According to him, she develops 'a penis envy': the only worthwhile value for her is that of the male sex. Freud describes this process in terms which can be criticized, and, importantly by describing it as normal and inevitable . . . But the fact remains: the relationship of women to their mothers and to other women—thus towards themselves—are subject to total narcissistic 'black-out'; these relationships are completely devalued. Indeed, I have never come across a woman who does not suffer from the problem of not being able to resolve in harmony, in the present system, her relationship with her mother and with other women. Psychoanalysis has totally mythologized and 'censored' the positive value of these relationships. . . . Everything happens as if there were a necessary break between the earliest investments, the earliest desires, the first narcissism of a little girl and those of a 'normal' adult woman. In the place of those who would be in a position of continuity with her 'pre-history,' she has, imposed on her, a language, fantasms, a desire which does not 'belong' to her and which establishes a break with her auto-eroticism. That kind of *schizo* which every woman experiences, in our socio-cultural system, only leaves her with nothing more than somatizations, corporal pains, mutism or mimetism with which to express herself: saying and doing 'like men' " (*Women's Exile*, p. 75).

Elsewhere, Irigaray speaks of the interruption of "the continuity of feminine auto-eroticism . . . by a kind of process which could be described as rape . . . " (see note 6). The "rape" of Persephone, "stolen away from her mother, herself," marks her (negative) entry into the symbolic order. In a "suspension of etymology," Persephone becomes *Korè*: she has no "proper" name, no autonomous symbolic representation, but changes her name as she is exchanged by men. "The subjectivity denied to woman is no doubt the mortgage-guarantee of the constitution of any object; object of representation, of discourse, of desire," Irigaray writes (*Speculum*, p. 165). As goods, as an object of exchange, Persephone belongs to the males in the family: "The trade that organizes patriarchal societies takes place exclusively among men. Women, signs, goods, currency, all pass from one man to another. . . . The work force, products, even those of mother-earth, would thus be the object of transactions among men only. This signifies that the *very possibility of the socio-cultural order would necessitate homosexuality*. Homosexuality is the law that regulates the socio-cultural order. Heterosexuality amounts to the assignment of roles in the economy: some are given the role of producing and exchanging subjects, while others are assigned the role of productive earth and goods. . . . All economic management would thus be homosexual. The management of desire, even the desire for woman, would also be homosexual. Woman exists only as the possibility of mediation, transaction, transition, transference—between man and his fellow-creatures, indeed between man and himself. If this strange status of the aforementioned heterosexuality has been able to pass unnoticed and can still do so, *how can one account for the relations between women in this system of trade?* Except by affirming that as soon as she desires (herself), as soon as she speaks (herself, to herself), the woman is a man. Within this system of trade, as soon as she relates to another woman, she is a *male* homosexual . . . *But what if the goods refused to go to market?* What if they maintained among themselves 'another' kind of trade? Exchange without identifiable terms of trade, without accounts, without end—without one plus one, without series, without number. Without a standard of value . . . Where use and exchange would mingle. Where the most valuable would also be the least held in reserve. Where nature would spend itself without exhaustion, trade without labor, give of itself—protected from masculine transactions—for nothing: there would be free enjoyment, well-being without suffering, pleasure without possession. How ironic calculations, savings, more or less ravishing appropriations, and arduous capitalizations would be! Utopia? Perhaps. Unless this mode of exchange has always undermined the order of trade and simply has not been recognized because the necessity of restricting incest to the realm of pure pretense has forbidden a certain economy of abundance." (Luce Irigaray, *When the Goods Get Together*, trans. Claudia Reeder, in *New French Feminisms*, pp. 107–10.) TRANS.

20. Irigaray uses the geological term "faults" (*failles*) to indicate the limits—the "physical" and metaphysical breaks or ruptures which Persephone continually crosses and recrosses. TRANS.

21. See note 16. TRANS.

22. In *The Birth of Tragedy*, Nietzsche identifies the Apollinian with the plastic arts, the Dionysian with music—thus in the reconciliation of these two forces in Greek tragedy, the marriage of the eye and ear. Nietzsche writes that "the continuous development of art is bound up with the *Apollinian* and *Dionysian* duality—just as procreation depends on the duality of the sexes, involving perpetual strife with only periodically intervening reconciliations" (p. 33).

On forgetting, Nietzsche writes that "in song and in dance man expresses himself as a member of a higher community; he has forgotten how to walk and speak and is on the way toward flying into the air, dancing . . . He is no longer an artist, he has become a work of art" (p. 37).

Cf., as well, Jean-François Lyotard on Nietzsche and Eternal Return: "Insist instead on *forgetting*. In representation and opposition there is memory: passing from one singularity to the other, both are held together (by channels of circulation, by devices, by libidinal fantasies or figures of invest-ment). An identity, the Same, is implicit in such memory. In Eternal Return, as desire of potential, there is precisely *no memory*. The *voyage* is a passage without a wake, a forgetting, exposures that are multiple only for discourse, not for themselves. That is why there is no *representation* for this voyage, for the nomadic of intensities" (*Notes sur le retour et le capital*, in *Des dispositifs pulsionnels*, Paris, 1973, p. 318). TRANS. and ED.

23. Cf. Derrida, *Spurs:* According to Derrida, there are three types of statements about women in Nietzsche's texts, "three fundamental propositions which represent three positions of value. . . . In the first of these propositions the woman, taken as a figure or potentate of falsehood, finds herself censured, debased and despised. In the name of truth and metaphysics she is accused here by the credulous man who, in support of his testimony, offers truth and his phallus as his own proper credentials. . . . Similarly, in the second proposition, the woman is censured, debased and despised, only in this case it is as the figure or potentate of truth . . . she either identifies with truth, or else she continues to play with it at a distance as if it were a fetish, manipulating it, even as she refuses to believe in it, to her advantage. . . . The woman, up to this point then, is twice castration: once as truth and once as non-truth. In the instance of the third proposition, however, beyond the double negation of the first two, woman is recognized and affirmed as an affirmative power, a dissimulatress, an artist, dionysiac. And no longer is it man who affirms her. She affirms herself, in and of herself, in man. Castration, here again, does not take place" (pp. 95–97). At the same time, Derrida suggests, if these three propositions occur in various forms throughout Nietzsche's texts, they are simultane-ously caught in the writing of those texts (the feminine operation) and as a result "Nietzsche too is a little lost there . . . might well be a little lost in the web of his text, lost much as a spider who finds he is unequal to the web he has spun . . . He was, he dreaded this castrated woman. He was, he dreaded this castrating woman. He was, he loved this affirming woman. At once, simultaneously or successively, depending on the positions of his body and the situation of his story, Nietzsche was all of these. Within himself, outside of himself, Nietzsche dealt with so many women" (p. 101). TRANS.

5

Nietzsche and Feminism: Transvaluing Women in *Thus Spoke Zarathustra*

Tamsin Lorraine

We all know that Nietzsche is no feminist. Despite suggestions that have been made regarding Nietzsche's identification with the feminine, we know what he has to say about actual women, and we know the lengths to which Nietzsche goes to make sure that when he enacts the feminine, he does so in a manly manner.[1]

So, what does Nietzsche have to do with feminism? Can a feminist go to Nietzsche's texts for nourishment and inspiration, or is she bound to be turned away by the passages that deliberately belittle and exclude her? Can and should she excise these passages as expendable in order to applaud Nietzsche's affirmations of the feminine, or does this present yet another appropriation of women, one that should be resisted?

In attempting to answer these questions, I hope not simply to affirm

Nietzsche's relevance for feminism, but also to suggest a feminist style of listening and speaking, reading and writing, drawn from Nietzsche's texts. It is my belief that we should neither ignore Nietzsche's misogyny nor fixate on it. The spirit of Nietzsche's thought demands that we both confront the "truths" he throws our way and also go beyond them. In addition, it seems to me that the process of confrontation and overcoming that his texts evoke has implications for effective engagement in the hotly contested debates of our own cultural scene. Zarathustra says more than once that he loves "him who wants to create over and beyond himself and thus perishes."[2] If we take seriously the feminist ideal of a non-oppressive society, and if the creation of such a future involves the destruction of old norms and patterns of being and relating, then we may still have something to learn from Zarathustra, who was also attempting to prepare the way for something better.

In what follows I will indicate four different positions in *Thus Spoke Zarathustra* with which a female reader might identify. I present these positions as options in subjectivity made available to the reader by the text. The first position is the one we might say most directly characterizes the female reader as woman—the woman Zarathustra speaks about to other men, the woman he says men want. The second position is the one that most directly characterizes the male reader—the brother or disciple whom Zarathustra exhorts to remain faithful to the earth and to whom Zarathustra devotes his gift-giving virtue. The third position provides an alternative conception of woman, perhaps more attractive to the female reader—woman as representative of life, the woman who fascinates, attracts, and ultimately eludes Zarathustra. Finally, there is the position occupied by Zarathustra himself as role-model and ideal.

Although, as I will argue, no one of these positions can be described as presenting a "feminist" option, the character of Zarathustra enacts a process that suggests how we might confront and overcome all the options presented in the text, even if Zarathustra himself does not do this. Thus, although it may be forever undecidable whether or not Nietzsche meant his texts for women's ears, we can learn from him how to read his texts against the grain of his own truths.

What does Zarathustra want from women? One response is that Zarathustra wants the same thing from a woman that he wants from a man—that is, that she should prepare the way for the overman, the future of humanity. In the section entitled "On the Friend," however, we get our first hint that woman's role is to be different from that of man. Woman, it turns out, is incapable of the kind of friendship Zarathustra advocates; she has too much of the slave and the tyrant concealed in her. She is only capable of love. It is perhaps because of her tendencies toward slavelike servitude and tyrannical blindness against everything she doesn't love that Zarathustra says in the section "On Little Old and Young Women" that happiness for men and women differs.:

> The happiness of man is: I will. The happiness of woman is: he wills . . . And woman must obey and find a depth of her surface. Surface is the disposition of woman . . . Man's disposition, however, is deep.[3]

Upon hearing these pronouncements, the little old woman who has invited Zarathustra to talk to her as he would to men about women asks him if he is right about women because nothing is impossible with woman. She then exclaims that if Zarathustra is going to women, he should not forget his whip.[4] This coda to this section undercuts Zarathustra's pronouncements somewhat, suggesting that his discussion of women is for men in the sense of indicating what men want and need from women, rather than what women actually are. It is Zarathustra's hope, apparently, that women remain faithful to man, not the earth. She is to attend to the nuances of her chosen man's body, not her own, in order to evoke the child and creative will within him.

In Zarathustra's ranking of rule and obedience, it would seem that women, simply by virtue of being women, are fit only for obeying. One could dismiss this aspect of Zarathustra's teaching as a cultural by-product; surely if Nietzsche had been writing now, Zarathustra would have taught something different. Surely Zarathustra would not have made a gender distinction between those who could and should attempt his path and those who shouldn't. Instead, men and women would sort themselves out through their own actions. Some would rise to become higher human beings, precursors of the overperson; some would serve the worthier leaders strong enough to command; others would sink back into the rabble unable to distinguish themselves.

On this reading, it may be discouraging that Zarathustra has so little to say directly to women, but women are used to finding their way into texts that would exclude them. Even if Zarathustra continually calls out, "O, my brothers!" many female readers have refused to put the book down as unsuitable for their sex. They have also refused to read the book as if they were eavesdropping on a conversation between men. Instead, they have attempted to read as active recipients of Zarathustra's words—participants in a dialogue from which they too might have something to learn. They have thus refused Zarathustra's exhortation to be educated for the recreation of the warrior and have instead identified with the warriors themselves.

In simply dismissing the option in subjectivity Zarathustra extends to women, however, we close off alternative possibilities that could be generated. In one sense, the role that Zarathustra would have woman play is analogous to that of Zarathustra, who also sees his brothers as his children, and hopes to evoke from them the birth of the overman. Zarathustra, too, is a dangerous plaything for man, looking for the child within him, waking up destructive as well as constructive instincts in hopes of something better. When Zarathustra says, "let woman be a plaything, pure and fine, like a gem, irradiated by the virtues of a world that has not yet arrived,"[5] we can recognize that waking others' hopes to an image of a future yet to come is in itself a creative act of will.

This analogy is sharply demarcated, however, at the point of substituting another's will for one's own. It is only by developing the capacity and strength to listen to one's own body that one can hope to get closer to the overperson. And it is to men, Zarathustra's brothers and potential warriors, that Zarathustra addresses his teachings on how to attain this development. What, then, might we learn by taking up the position of these warrior brothers?

Zarathustra calls out to those who can hear him for companions that will "write new values on new tablets."[6] Those who write new values are not those who merely react against the old values. They are highly disciplined warriors who have managed to create a law to which they subject themselves. The disciple is to listen with a delicate ear and find words and honors for the body and earth.[7] Zarathustra suggests that speaking or writing the body brings new virtues to light. The origin of one's virtue is to be found in those moments when the body is elevated and resurrected through speaking in parables.[8] It is in such moments that the origin of one's virtue is to be found.

We see this attitude enacted in *Zarathustra*. Nietzsche's aphoristic style, the loose narrative, the inconsistencies in Zarathustra's character, the contradictions in style and content, all point to various strategies enacted to create the language that will speak of the body.[9] Several times Zarathustra is overcome with despondency at becoming imprisoned in tombs, only to break through the prison-tombs of old words and ways of being with a life-affirming resolve of will, which provides impetus for further self-overcoming.[10] To remain faithful to the earth, one needs to continually remake oneself and one's speech. The old truths, the old values are never enough. New evaluations speak to one in strange and unfamiliar sounds, music of the soul that is heterogeneous to language. These moments require the attention a mother gives her child. It is thus that they can be nurtured into virtues. Without any thought of reward or revenge, the disciple is to love his virtues and allow them to grow.[11]

This feminine moment of receptiveness to the strange, the unfamiliar, the music beyond language, the body, is to be followed by a more masculine moment, necessary for guarding against nihilistic anarchy. In attending to what is heterogeneous to language, one runs the danger of running amok:

> You are not yet free, you still *search* for freedom. You are worn from your search and overawake. You aspire to the free heights, your soul thirsts for the stars. But your wicked instincts, too, thirst for freedom. Your wild dogs want freedom; they bark with joy in their cellar when your spirit plans to open all prisons.[12]

Thus, a battle among virtues is necessary. Each virtue will battle for the full strength of spirit to back it. In this battle, it is best if one or very few virtues come to the fore so that the individual can put as much force as possible behind the virtue(s) elevated into one's tablet of good.[13] This takes attentiveness, creative inventiveness in articulation, and rigorous discipline in execution. Thus, one's virtues are organized and written up in a new law or tablet of good, which channels one's will and guides one's actions.

Certainly, Zarathustra cares about his disciples, but although he calls them friends and brothers, they are continually in danger of sinking to the level of the rabble in his estimation. In the course of *Zarathustra*, Zarathustra often professes his ambivalence about spending time with other human beings. His first companions are jesters and corpses. When he decides to avoid the market place and the rabble and speak only to those who have ears to hear his teachings, things get a little better, but it is only in solitude that he can find true spiritual sustenance. It is in solitude that his wild wisdom becomes pregnant.[14] He then goes to his companions to relieve himself of the riches of his soul. It is his virtue to want to give to humanity its future—the overman.[15] It is his burden that the light he brings to humanity comes from within:

> But I live in my own light; I drink back into myself the flames that break out of me. I do not know the happiness of those who receive; and I have often dreamed that even stealing must be more blessed than receiving. This is my poverty, that my hand never rests from giving; this is my envy, that I see waiting eyes and the lit-up nights of longing.[16]

It is because Zarathustra loves humanity, because he perceives a future for humanity, that he perfects himself in order to return to his children and raise them to his heights,[17] by putting them to the test and evoking the creator within them.[18] But this is often a lonely task for Zarathustra; his children never seem to reach his level, and they are prone to distorting his teachings into hurdy-gurdy songs. Indeed, Zarathustra recognizes this latter danger in himself as well. It is not to his children, however, that he turns for fresh insight, but to life itself who, it just so happens, Zarathustra represents as a woman.

Thus, a third position we might try is that of the powerful woman that seems to fascinate Zarathustra so:

> Into your eyes I looked recently, O life! And into the unfathomable I then seemed to be sinking. But you pulled me out with a golden fishing rod, and you laughed mockingly when I called you unfathomable.[19]

Woman as life is "changeable and wild and a woman in every way, and not virtuous."[20] Out of all the characters in the book, Zarathustra seems to take Life and his Wild Wisdom (also characterized as a woman) most seriously. It is with Life that Zarathustra seems to be most anxious to have a relationship.

If Zarathustra despairs at various points that his children will ever love him well enough to become true companions with wills of their own, he also despairs of his own ability to keep up with Life:

> And now you are fleeing from me again, you sweet wildcat and ingrate!

I dance after you, I follow wherever your traces linger. Where are you? Give me your hand! Or only one finger![21]

And it is for the eternal recurrence of Life that Zarathustra forsakes all human women:

> Never yet have I found the woman from whom I wanted children, unless it be this woman whom I love: for I love you, O eternity.[22]

Life has no stake in virtues, values, or words. She mocks all of Zarathustra's truths—she is always somewhere else, somewhere beyond. She does not care for Zarathustra's discipline nor his command nor his rankings. Yet it is Life that Zarathustra would please, it is Life's love that he wants. Far from finding her honor in love for another, however, Life is unpredictable and shifty, impatient and elusive.

Precisely because she is so changeable, Life exerts a powerful effect on Zarathustra. She it is who cannot be pinned down, who always requires new words, new songs, new ways of being. To win her, one must always be trying something unprecedented, and letting the old perish in the attempt. She taunts and teases Zarathustra, never losing her appeal. She requires a dancer with his ear in his toes.[23] If Zarathustra does come into relationship with her from time to time, it is not because he is her ultimate satisfaction, but only because for a brief moment he has managed to keep up with her.

Here we can see the analogy between the human woman Zarathustra wants and Life as woman. Zarathustra wants both women to love him, and for this love to lead to the perfection of his own creative will. If he chooses to love Life rather than a woman, it is because Life is the most dangerous plaything of all and requires more of him than any human woman ever could.

We have already seen the cul-de-sac that the position of woman presents. The position of Life as woman presents a cul-de-sac as well. For even if Life is willful and scarcely faithful to man, she is still depicted here in relationship to him. What if Life is bored with all the attempts to win her favor and would much rather have a conversation? What if Life has other projects of her own, which have nothing to do with Zarathustra's perfection and which she'd like to share with him? What if Life involves, not merely dancing with one other, but dancing with a multitude of others to a complicated symphony of often dissonant notes?

If nothing is impossible for woman, what then, should the female reader do with the text of *Thus Spoke Zarathustra?* Should she listen to Zarathustra's statements about woman's happiness? But this would be to turn away from the truths of her own body. Should she attempt to become one of his disciples, loving Zarathustra, serving him by letting him command? But this would be to ignore his injunctions to aid him in nurturing the overman in others. Should she attempt to gain his favor by playing Life as the *femme fatale*, thus evoking others to be forever revising their articulations of virtue? But this would be to abandon her hope for humanity, the image that she sees in the stone.

Perhaps the best answer comes from Zarathustra himself. To redeem the past through the present in light of the future, one can neither deny that past, put something else in its place, nor let it determine one. Instead one can redeem it by affirming it in light of one's own vision for the future:

> I taught them all *my* creating and striving, to create and carry together into One what in man is fragment and riddle and dreadful accident; as creator, guesser of riddles, and redeemer of accidents, I taught them to work on the future and to redeem with their creation all that *has been*. To redeem what is past in man and to re-create all "it was" until the will says, "Thus I willed it! Thus I shall will it"—this I called redemption and this alone I taught them to call redemption.[24]

If I can read Nietzsche as a feminist and still feel affirmed, this is not because I can ignore the way in which Nietzsche's texts exclude or belittle women. Representing and valorizing life as the feminine undecidable, that which forever eludes us and incites us to creative self-overcoming, does nothing for women in their struggle for recognition and respect. If I can read Nietzsche as a feminist, it is because Nietzsche himself gives me some suggestions as to how to transform the often ugly and nauseating "truths" that are my cultural resource into something I can affirm in the present.

Zarathustra presents us some of his truths. These truths have implications for my future as a woman and as a human being. What I do with these truths, how I arrange or rearrange them, is up to me. Zarathustra suggests that when I break the old tablet of values, I should create a new one that speaks more honestly of the body. This suggests a listening and reading strategy that attends to nuances of feeling that are not immediately articulate. It suggests a patient and receptive waiting in the stillest hour for the perhaps unprecedented meaning that emerges. It suggests a resourceful flexibility in further developing that meaning, by giving it free play in a variety of forms and styles, letting various possibilities reverberate and following those possibilities where there is life and a quickening of feeling.

This attention to nuance also suggests the kind of destruction found in a process of digestion. Food is not useful to my body until I sort through it, reject what disgusts me, chew up the rest, break it down, assimilate it, expel the waste. What is true for you may not be to my taste, or I may assimilate it differently. I can't tell until I put it into my pot and cook it through.[25]

Going through the positions offered me in *Thus Spoke Zarathustra*, I don't have to reject any of them out of hand. Instead, I can affirm them all as providing material for my own future, material that I sort through, taking the flavors and aromas I need to conjure up the image dearest to me. I sniff out various aspects of each, distinguish different flavors, mix them up, using bits of one to spice up another. Thus, out of the dreadful fragments and accidents of this text I create a strong image of woman in keeping with my own taste for the future.

My Zarathustra would be an artist as well. She would dance with and after life, but she would also fall apart in order to dance with multiple partners. My Zarathustra would be a cook who flings the most nauseating as well as the more savory aspects of her culture into her pot to cook them through in keeping with her own tastes, but she would also let herself be dissolved and transformed in the pots of other cooks. Zarathustra as a woman would engage in the Dionysian process of creation, but she would also acknowledge herself as material formed through a process in which there is no longer any distinction to be made between creator and created. Such a woman would have the discriminating hardness to say no and the strength to break down old truths, but she would also have the receptive strength to disperse herself among others only to reemerge transfigured within her community of artists. To create such a position from this text—an image of whole woman that moves me, that represents my will to power—requires careful reading and a discriminating taste that is both destructive and disrespectful of old boundaries, and yet respectful to nuance and in hopeful flight after a living truth.

Perhaps Zarathustra is right to emphasize the image of the future one envisions in the shadow of the stone. I have been discouraged of late with the policing of borders practiced by feminists and anti-feminists alike. At times it seems to me that we have become more immersed in barricading and assaulting various already-laid-out positions than in ignoring old boundaries, in order to utilize creatively the full range of material available to us. If the feminist virtue is the hope for a non-oppressive society, then boundaries and categories, truths and goals, can and must be continually created and destroyed, only to be recreated again, in our attempts to keep step with the living truths that honor this hope.

Notes

1. For examples of feminist critiques of Nietzsche's masculinist bias see Jean Graybeal, *Language and "the Feminine" in Nietzsche and Heidegger* (Bloomington: Indiana University Press, 1990); Luce Irigaray, *Amante Marine: de Friedrich Nietzsche* (Paris: Les Editions de Minuit, 1980); N. S. Love, *Marx, Nietzsche, and Modernity* (New York: Columbia University Press, 1986); Tamsin Lorraine, *Gender, Identity, and the Production of Meaning* (Boulder, Colorado: Westview Press, 1990); Kelly Oliver, "Woman as Truth in Nietzsche's Writing," *Social Theory and Practice* 10 (Summer 1984): 185–199; and Kelly Oliver, "Nietzsche's Woman: The Post-structuralist Attempt to Do Away with Women," *Radical Philosophy* 48 (Spring 1988): 25–29.

2. Friedrich Nietzsche, *Thus Spoke Zarathustra*, trans. Walter Kaufmann (New York: Penguin, 1966), hereafter indicated as TSZ, p. 65.

3. TSZ, p. 67

4. A member of the audience at which this paper was initially read commented that in the infamous photograph of Nietzsche and a whip, the whip is in the hands of Lou Salomé, thus pointing out that this passage could be read ambiguously—perhaps the whip is meant to be used by woman and not man! This is an interesting suggestion, and I think indicates some of the tension in Nietzsche's characterization of women. Although Zarathustra is depicted as an artist who creates in keeping with his own will, the process of creation involves the strength to self-dissolve in responsiveness to others as well as the will to create. The question Nietzsche is never able to adequately answer is, how can one do this and still be "a warrior"?

5. TSZ, p. 66.

6. TSZ, p. 24.

7. "Indeed, this ego and the ego's contradiction and confusion still speak most honestly of its being—this creating, willing, valuing ego, which is the measure and value of things. And this most honest being, the ego, speaks of the body and still wants the body, even when it poetizes and raves and flutters with broken wings. It learns to speak ever more honestly, this ego: and the more it learns, the more words and honors it finds for body and earth" (TSZ, p. 32).

8. TSZ, p. 75.

9. Eric Blondel suggests that Nietzsche creates a fairly systematic set of metaphors that evoke the body in order to point us toward something beyond the text, something heterogeneous to language in general as well as to any words with which we might speak of the body itself. See Eric Blondel, *Nietzsche: The Body and Culture; Philosophy as a Philological Genealogy*, trans. Seán Hand (Stanford, California: Stanford University Press, 1991), pp. 28–31. I have considered this suggestion, in the reading I give here, in light of Kristeva's theory of the body, especially as it emerges in Julia Kris-

teva's, *Desire in Language: A Semiotic Approach to Literature and Art* (New York: Columbia University Press, 1980), and Irigaray's reading of Nietzsche in *Amante Marine*.

10. TSZ, p. 112.

11. "You are too *pure* for the filth of the words: revenge, punishment, reward, retribution. You love your virtue as a mother her child; but when has a mother ever wished to be paid for her love? Your virtue is what is dearest to you. The thirst of the ring lives in you: every ring strives and turns to reach itself again" (TSZ, p. 94).

12. TSZ, p. 43.

13. "My brother, are war and battle evil? But this evil is necessary; necessary are the envy and mistrust and calumny among your virtues. Behold how each of your virtues covets what is highest: each wants your whole spirit that it might become *her* herald; each wants your whole strength in wrath, hatred, and love" (TSZ, p. 37).

14. TSZ, p. 85.

15. "But my fervent will to create impels me ever again toward man; thus is the hammer impelled toward the stone. O men, in the stone there sleeps an image, the image of my images" (TSZ, p. 87).

16. TSZ, p. 106.

17. TSZ, p. 124.

18. TSZ, p. 161.

19. TSZ, p. 108.

20. TSZ, p. 108.

21. TSZ, p. 225.

22. TSZ, p. 231.

23. TSZ, p. 224.

24. TSZ, p. 198.

25. "I am Zarathustra the godless: I still cook every chance in my pot. And only when it has been cooked through there do I welcome it as my food" (TSZ, p. 171). Also see Lisa Heldke's article "Recipes for Theory Making" (*Hypatia* 3/2 [Summer 1988]: 15–29) for a helpful analogy between cooking and theory. Although Heldke cites Dewey rather than Nietzsche in developing this analogy, she also mentions attending to the nuance of flavor and aroma and the perhaps unprecedented varying of a given recipe in actual preparation. Zarathustra, however, would encourage more "disrespectful" tampering with recipes (indeed, a wholesale cacophony of experimentation and exploration) than Heldke would seem to suggest.

6

Gender in *The Gay Science*

Kathleen Marie Higgins

In his recent novel, *When Nietzsche Wept*, Irwin Yalom reiterates a common portrait of Nietzsche: a sexist *über alles*. Much as the quip "Isn't business ethics a contradiction in terms?" ubiquitously accosts philosophers involved in that subdiscipline, "What's a nice girl like you doing studying a misogynist like that?" has haunted my career in Nietzsche scholarship. I have never been entirely certain as to whether this *ad hominem* is more directed at me or at Nietzsche.

A sympathetic but jovial colleague played on this ambiguity by remarking, when he heard my topic for this essay, "Yes, that must be an interesting topic for someone who isn't even shallow." Yes, Nietzsche did say that women, far from deep, were not even shallow. But does this remark prove him a sexist? Are we even certain what it means?

I will attempt to complicate our appraisal of Nietzsche's alleged sexism by focusing on Book Two of *The Gay Science*. Considering his passages on women in that book, I will suggest along the way reasons why at least some readings of these as sexist should be rejected. More positively, I will show that these passages urge a reassessment of the relationship between men and women that can be seen as a contribution toward feminist theory (if an unwitting one), and that one of Nietzsche's intended impacts on his male readers is to initiate a radical revolution in their thinking about women.

I

The term "gender" is used advisedly in this context, for Nietzsche made the distinction, common in feminist discussion, between sex (the biological potential to play one role rather than another in reproduction) and gender (the contingently assigned roles that a society attaches to those who are biologically male or female). Nietzsche urged his readers to recognize the contingency of gender roles and to consider the desirability of changing them.

We can hardly begin to consider Nietzsche's suggestions in these regards, however, without confronting the allegation that Nietzsche was a paradigmatic sexist. Although many of the most important names in Western philosophy have been singled out for feminist censure, Nietzsche is often held up as an exemplar of all that is misogynistic, both in the philosophical tradition and within patriarchy generally. Nietzsche is identified as a misogynist for a variety of reasons. He is seen as an essentialist, an opponent of women's rights, an enthusiast of masculine virtue, and an advocate of male domination. While none of these attributions may be entirely apt, I agree with Nietzsche's feminist critics that he was, at least sometimes, too willing to rest content with truisms about women and to vent personal rage in the guise of philosophy.

That said, some of the attacks on Nietzsche are both unfair and unfortunate. I am not the only feminist to think so. Maudemarie Clark, Sarah Kofman, Maryanne Bertram, and Deborah Bergoffen have all suggested that certain of Nietzsche's views offer starting points for feminist theorizing. I will describe some attacks made on Nietzsche by certain other feminists, however, because they represent the popular perspective on

Nietzsche (if not that most typical of Nietzsche scholars) and because they indicate certain pitfalls that feminists would do best to avoid.

Carol Diethe's article "Nietzsche and the Woman Question," for example, criticizes Nietzsche in a number of unwarranted ways. Consider, for example, her complaint that Nietzsche's conception of the will to power entails an affirmation of the domination of women.

> If we take his key concept, the will to power, we find that it is so gender based that it practically comes to represent the archetypal phallic symbol. Bernstein describes it as a phenomenon which includes the "will to violate" so that the "feeling of power" (*Machtgefühl*) is generated, yet when he goes on to mention "Nietzsche's desire to avoid reducing the will to power to sexuality," he fails to realize that his own critique has relied heavily on the language of rape and the whole area of male dominance of women which stretches behind words such as "violation."[1]

Diethe simply accepts Bernstein's characterization of Nietzsche's view as accurate. She may be right in her claim that the will to power can be read as a phallic symbol, although I would want to know what assumptions are built into the latter notion. Even if so, it is not obvious why Nietzsche's employment of the concept is necessarily sexist. More generally, Diethe's passage involves a move that is far too prevalent in feminist writings on Nietzsche—the tendency to reduce Nietzsche's philosophy to a few obsessions and to yoke these inextricably to his views about women.

One common counterargument to feminist critiques of Nietzsche is that Nietzsche was simply blinded by the sexism of his era. Feminist critics rightly complain that a thinker should not be excused for common prejudice just because it *is* common prejudice. Nevertheless, the recognition that Nietzsche accepted some features of his society's sexist perspective on women does not warrant the judgment that he endorsed every one of his era's sexist sentiments. Diethe, for example, engages in this type of conflation when she equates Nietzsche's position with Schopenhauer's: "As Brann has pointed out, Nietzsche echoes Schopenhauer's ideas on women *wortgetreu* as the following passage demonstrates. Written by Schopenhauer, it could just as easily have been written by Nietzsche. . . ." Diethe goes on to cite Schopenhauer, beginning with "Because basically women are only there to propagate the race, and they fulfill themselves thereby, they live life more as a sexual partner than as an individual . . ." ("NWQ" pp. 870 and 874).

Ellen Kennedy, somewhat more fairly, insists in her article "Nietzsche: Women as *Untermensch*" that "Nietzsche really does have nothing more to offer . . . than the common prejudices of his age and sex."[2] Her conclusion, however, combines oversimplification of Nietzsche's philosophy with a worrisome insinuation that Nietzsche's work can only be appropriately read as a defense of the patriarchy.

> Both the ground for women's subordination in women's biology and Nietzsche's coherently masculine state of adventurers and warriors are founded on a Darwinistically derived master-sex. In light of this the preoccupation with Nietzsche as anti- or philo-Semitic seems rather antiquated; his ideal state is not "Teutonic," nor is Nietzsche a racialist in the earlier sense. But he is, in our sense of it, the founder of peculiarly modern patriarchy and the inventor of one of the crassest and most subtle misogynies: "The enormous expectation in sexual love and the sense of shame in this expectation spoils all perspective for women from the start." ("WU," pp. 197–98)

The passage from Nietzsche is not obviously sexist or crass. If one reads this as a psychological interpretation of the social pressures that constrain women's outlook on sexuality, one can see it as sympathetic—and a recognition of the social cultivation of certain attitudes in women. Nietzsche's remark is not so distant from more recent feminist descriptions of the internal obstacles to feminist liberation women confront. Isn't Nietzsche close to hinting that love is a sexist plot?

Aside from its questionable reading of Nietzsche's passage, Kennedy's comment is disturbing for its implication that, currently, sexism is a problem of vastly more importance than anti-Semitism. The insinuation that women and Jews are in competition for the status of most oppressed is philosophically, as well as morally, suspect. I find it hard to believe that the mechanisms that support prejudice are essentially different in one case than in another. Indeed, from a political standpoint, it is probable that competition among victims of prejudice only diverts energy that might more profitably be spent fighting it.

Kennedy's comment strikes me as symptomatic of a dangerous tendency sometimes evident within the Women's Movement—and probably also within any other movement aimed at overcoming oppression. I will term this tendency the Parrot News Syndrome, in reference to one of the skits presented on *Monty Python's Flying Circus.*[3] This skit was devoted to "Parrot News," a news broadcast that made mention of a number of events around the world and ended each report with the remark, "No parrots were involved." The target of satire here was the wide-ranging phenomenon of parochial news coverage, which in the United States typically involves concluding international reports with some mention of how many Americans were involved.

The Parrot News Syndrome in feminist discussion is the tendency to believe that women and responses to women should be emphasized whenever possible. My counterproposal accords with Freud's comment that sometimes a cigar is just a cigar. Sometimes, I contend, it is as inappropriate to foreground women and their concerns as it has traditionally been to push women consistently into the background.

The Parrot News Syndrome is evident in Diethe's account of Nietzsche's humor:

> Although Schopenhauer and Nietzsche are clearly wrong in their assumptions about women's natural instincts they can, to a certain extent, be respected for their views on the importance of childbearing, since so many women shared similar views (although, one must hasten to add, they often acted with a false consciousness of their own objective position in society). What is unforgivable in Nietzsche is his use of the sexist joke. ("NWQ" pp. 870–71)

Nietzsche has to use sexist jokes, according to Diethe, because "sexual discourse is vital to Nietzsche's canon; he constructs a virile male and must keep women servile. Sexist jokes are an efficient tool to use to that end. Even when he is talking about men, there is a hidden discourse on women beneath the text" ("NWQ" p. 871).

Diethe is appalled in particular by the images Nietzsche uses when he complains that "abortive women" use the feminist movement as an attack on "women who have turned out well." Certainly, Nietzsche's remark is not one that most feminists would admire: "By raising themselves higher, as 'woman in herself,' as the 'higher woman,' as a female 'idealist,' they want to lower the level of the general rank of woman; and there is no surer means for that than higher education, slacks, and political voting—cattle rights."[4]

Why does Diethe read this as a sexist joke? In the first place, why see it as a joke at all? Diethe obviously considers it "not funny"—but that surely does not entail that it is a joke. Second, why is this seen as a *sexist* joke? Diethe certainly interprets it as sexist humor: "Women's education is downgraded by being given equal importance with women's clothing, and women's votes are discounted by the reference to cattle. To be fair to Nietzsche, he had some uncomplimentary things to say about herd men and indeed about male scholars, but the sexual slur is reserved for women" ("NWQ" p. 870). But this simply ins't true. Nietzsche is no more referring to women when he speaks of cattle than the University of Pennsylvania student (allegedly) referred to blacks when he called his noisy neighbors "water buffaloes." Nietzsche fairly consistently refers to cattle, paradigmatic herd members, when he discusses voting, whether or not he is commenting on female suffrage. In *The Gay Science*, Section 174, for example, he describes the right to vote as a herd phenomenon:

> *Apart.*—Parliamentarianism—that is, public permission to choose between five basic political opinions—flatters and wins the favor of all those who would like to *seem* independent and individual, as if they fought for their opinions. Ultimately, how-ever, it is indifferent whether the herd is commanded to have one opinion or permitted to have five. Whoever deviates from the five public opinions and stands apart will always have the whole herd against him.[5]

Nietzsche's association of voting with cattle—presumably cattle of both sexes—is even more unmistakable in *The Gay Science*, Section 368.

> No one brings along the finest sense of his art to the theater, nor does the artist who works for the theater. There one is common people, audience, herd, female, pharisee, voting cattle, democrat, neighbor, fellow man; there even the most personal conscience is vanquished by the leveling magic of the great number; their stu-pidity has the effect of lasciviousness and contagion; the neighbor reigns, one becomes a mere neighbor. (p. 326)

Although Diethe is wrong in leaping to the conclusion that Nietzsche's humor is sexist, she is right to see Nietzsche's humor as an essential element of his rhetoric. In fact, Nietzsche's humor indicates a much more radical approach to gender consciousness than is evident in the thought of most of his philosophical contemporaries. Diethe's assumption that Nietzsche's "cattle" comment is sexist may reveal that she assumes that the right to vote is desirable (a view that I certainly share). On the assumption that Nietzsche is not disparaging the vote, she may reason, he must be disparaging women. Nietzsche, however, does disparage the vote. Men may vote by virtue of sexist privilege, but Nietzsche does not consider the vote's being desired to be evidence for its desirability.

Unfortunately, feminists sometimes move too quickly from the observation that men do something by virtue of male privilege to the view that the practice is necessarily desirable. I will continue the herd imagery by terming this strategy the Green Grass Syndrome. This syndrome is sometimes bolstered by the corollary that whatever women have traditionally done while excluded from male privilege is to be devalued.

Diethe's reading of another of Nietzsche's "sexist jokes," for example, at least borders on this perspective. She cites his comment about feminist attempts to "enlighten men" about the feminine essence in *Beyond Good and Evil*: "Unless a woman seeks a new adornment for herself in that way—I do not think adorning herself is part of the Eternal Feminine?—she surely wants to inspire fear of herself—perhaps she seeks mastery."[6] Diethe sees this passage as a joke referring to Goethe's "eternal feminine," but she does not find the parody elevating.

> This type of sexist joke, by which the mystique of Goethe's *ewig Weibliche* (sufficiently problematic in itself) is downgraded to include woman's love of finery, indictes Nietzsche's own lack of confidence. He is unable to construct a proper theory to justify *das Aufklären* as a male province and retreats behind a jibe which pulls the reader's attention in another direction (Gretchen). This provides a veneer of respectability whilst at the same time seriously distorting Goethe's intention. The final comment on *Herrschaft* is poles apart from Goethe's portrayal of woman's power. Nietzsche's attitude towards woman is in turns aggressive and defensive, and his only solution to this ambivalence is the philosophical construct of the masterly man. ("NWQ" p. 869)

Why is adornment degrading? Nietzsche suggests elsewhere that adornment is essential if human relationships are to achieve their potential. His Zarathustra announces, "You cannot groom yourself too beautifully for your friend: for you shall be to him an arrow and a longing for the overman."[7] Moreover, Nietzsche inserts a question mark at the end of his parenthetic remark, "I do think adorning herself is part of the Eternal Feminine?" a gesture that suggests that he is far from certain what to make of feminine adornment. And isn't Nietzsche's inquiry a legitimate question about the gesture some members of one sex are making toward the other? Nietzsche may be accused of being heterosexist in this passage, since he considers the possibility that the gesture might be used to gain some advantage in the game of sexual attraction; but he does not seem to assume, as does Diethe herself, that a woman's interests in adornment is necessarily trivial or, when used as an instrument of power, necessarily pathetic.

One assumption that Diethe and Kennedy share is that Nietzsche held a stable perspective on women; and perhaps this assumption is the root of their oversimplification of his views. Kennedy remarks, "In Nietzsche's case, it is not an unfair conclusion to say that on the question of women, his refusal of us was as radical and thorough-going as it was consistent with the inherited prejudice of centuries of philosophers before him" ("WU," p. 196). Diethe similarly comments, ". . . Nietzsche's ideas on women . . . might well be unfortunate, but they are not an aberration: . . . his views on female sexuality and gender division are crucial to his thesis and remain constant throughout his work" ("NWQ" p. 871). Significantly, neither pays much attention to *The Gay Science* in formulating this assessment. Kennedy does not refer to it at all; Diethe mentions only a fragment from the fifth book, added in 1887, five years after the central discussion of women was published.

I concur with Prudence Allen who, surveying the range of Nietzsche's comments on women, concludes that they exhibit a number of specifiable tensions. "The internal incoherency in Nietzsche's theory resulting from this judgment suggests that Nietzsche's tension about women of the *status quo* did not flow from a sustained thinking about the subject."[8] Allen notes in particular the openness evident in *The Gay Science*, and Nietzsche's far less flexible attitude after the "perceived betrayal" of Lou Salomé, one of the few women toward whom Nietzsche displayed romantic interest: "Who knows what different directions Nietzsche's thought might have taken if he and Lou Salomé had been able to form a long-lasting and deep relationship. His writing about women before and during their relationship opens the door to new possibilities in woman's identity; immediately after the break the door is slammed shut" ("NTW," pp. 57–58). Allen concludes, "The potential dialectic of contraries found in Nietzsche's various forms of tension about women never achieved its full potential" ("NTW," p. 66). Nietzsche's strategy in *The Gay Science* suggests how promising, if short-lived, that potential actually was.

II

The Gay Science presents an entrée into gender theory that is genuinely exciting. Nietzsche's remarks on women in that work, however, have rarely been seen as anything out of the ordinary. Indeed, when they have been considered in themselves, they have most often been dismissed as low points in the book. The first of these passages, Section 59, appears in keeping with the rather disgusted tone of Nietzsche's contemporaries:

> When we love a woman, we easily conceive a hatred for nature on account of all the repulsive natural functions to which every woman is subject. We prefer not to think of all this; but when our soul touches on these matters for once, it shrugs as it were and looks contemptuously at nature: we feel insulted; nature seems to encroach on our possessions, and with the profanest hands at that. Then we refuse to pay heed to physiology and decree secretly: "I want to hear nothing about the fact that a human being is something more than soul and form." "The human being under the skin" is for all lovers a horror and unthinkable, a blasphemy against God and love. (p. 122)

This passage is certainly dated, by contemporary standards. For instance, were the reaction that Nietzsche describes really as fundamental as his tone suggests, modern-day fathers would resist being present at the births of their children much more strenuously than many do. The passage would also be hard to square with the romanticism of American youth in the late 1960s, who simultaneously celebrated "love" and revamped the reigning dress and grooming code to acknowledge much more visibly the physical actualities of women's bodily experience. Nietzsche's squeamishness here recalls that of Ruskin, who reportedly abstained from intercourse throughout his life because he was so shocked to discover that his wife had pubic hair.

Does this passage represent Nietzsche's conception of women? Even reading no farther, we can see that Nietzsche is discussing the attitudes of men, not women. In particular, Nietzsche is describing the kind of idealized eyes of love that might lead a man to insist that his beloved is exempt from the physical conditions that a more scientific eye would unquestionably acknowledge. Nietzsche's point is that, when motivated by desire to see the world a certain way, an individual will deny the obvious.

Nietzsche goes on to describe the mental gyrations that the loving man will perform to keep his beloved unsullied in his imagination. He presents these gyrations, however, as an analogy. This situation is comparable, Nietzsche argues, to that of the theist who denies natural laws because they seem incompatible with the omnipotence of God. Following on Book One of *The Gay Science*, which dealt largely with the status of knowledge and belief, Book Two is still discussing epistemological topics.

Now, however, Nietzsche is confronting his reader more personally than before. By mentioning women in Section 59, he reminds each (presumably male) reader of his own unwillingness to consider his (presumably female) beloved from a purely scientific point of view. The woman who appears at the beginning of this section functions to arouse self-reflection in the male reader. The first book's claims about the dubiousness of human "knowledge" are now brought close to home. Indeed, by the end of Section 59, Nietzsche describes even the current "scientific" individual as "moonstruck and God-struck." "We somnambulists of the day! We artists!" he remarks (p. 123). Including himself among those ensconced in dreams more than realities, he appears to be describing the status of knowledge in his era.

The (implicitly male) reader is unlikely to muster much resistance to this assault, for the opening two sections of Book Two, which directly precede Section 59, have set him up. The first challenges philosophical realists, who "hint that the world really is the way it appears" to them. These realists are "far too similar to an artist in love," who endeavors to enhance what is loved by means of fantasy. "Subtract the phantasm . . . . If you can!" Nietzsche taunts (p. 121). Human beings, he insists, are incapable of eliminating their own fantastic contributions to the way that things appear.

Worse yet, Nietzsche argues in the section that follows, we all take appearances to be the essence.

> This has given me the greatest trouble and still does: to realize that what things are called is incomparably more important than what they are. The reputation, name, and appearance, the usual measure and weight of a thing,—what it counts for— . . . all this grows from generation unto generation, merely because people believe in it, until it gradually grows to be part of the thing and turns into its very body. What at first was appearance becomes in the end, almost invariably, the essence and is effective as such. (pp. 121–22)

In effect, Nietzsche argues, we are all practicing realists, imagining that we see the essence of things when we see how they look to ourselves. Moreover, mere awareness will not stop our fantasizing.

> How foolish it would be to suppose that one only needs to point out this origin and this misty shroud of delusion in order to destroy the world that counts for real, so-called "reality." We can destroy only as creators.—But let us not forget this either: it is enough to create new names and estimations and probabilities in order to create in the long run new "things." (p. 122)

To follow these two passages with several sections on women—indeed, several sections on the ways that women appear—is rhetorically provocative. Nietzsche has already brought his attack on realists to bear on the reader, thereby challenging the reader to self-examination. He also preempts the reader's first line of defense: merely admitting that one takes appearance for reality does not prevent one from being bamboozled. The reader thus is in the uncomfortable condition of being attacked without ready recourse when the discussions of women begin. Already steered into self-analysis by the previous sections, he is now given a specific example of the self-deception that has so far been described abstractly. Assuming a primarily male audience, Nietzsche anticipates that the reader will find the topic of male fantasies about women uncomfortably personal. Whatever else, Nietzsche expects a response.

Nietzsche continues this strategy in Section 60, which again discusses male fantasies about women. He slightly varies the image of the previous section, now describing the man who "stands in the midst of his own noise, in the midst of his own surf of plans and projects . . . then he is apt also to see quiet, magical beings gliding past him and to long for their happiness and seclusion: women. He almost thinks that his better self dwells there among the women. . . . " Again, Nietzsche describes the appearance of women to the man in question as a dream constructed by virtue of a particular motive, this time a desire to escape his own noise.

> Yet! Yet! Noble enthusiast, even on the most beautiful sailboat there is a lot of noise, and unfortunately much small and petty noise. The magic and the most powerful effect of women is, in philosophical language, action at a distance, *actio in distans;* but this requires first of all and above all—*distance.* (p. 124)

One might interpret the characterization of "beautiful sailboats" with "much small and petty noise" as a sexist jibe. The following section (Section 61), however, urges a double-take. Here Nietzsche criticizes the ancient view that friendship is higher than self-sufficiency. Following on the previous section, the effect is to qualify the suggestion that distance should be maintained, at least from the opposite sex. While Section 61 does not explicitly discuss women, the reader has reason to think that Nietzsche means to include them; for Book One includes a passage that calls for friendship as a sublimation of sexual love: "Here and there on earth we may encounter a kind of continuation of love in which this possessive craving of two people for each other gives way to a new desire and lust for possession—a *shared* higher thirst for an ideal above them. But who knows such love? Who has experienced it? Its right name is *friendship*" (p. 89).

Nietzsche does not describe the friendship emerging from love as an exclusively male affair, even if he did take the homosexual relationships of Athens as a primary model for friendship elsewhere. Indeed, his description seems entirely open-ended, deliberately including women as potential candidates for friendship.

In the sections that follow, Nietzsche offers a number of vignettes or generalizations from vignettes, largely involving relationships between the sexes, and making rather acute if surprising observations about the nature of various women's motivations. Section 62 proclaims that love forgives the lover even lust. Kaufmann translates this as "his lust," suggesting that a woman is forgiving a man his lust. However, the German is non-committal with respect to the sexes of lover and beloved. Moreover, the direction of the lust is unspecified.

Section 63 compares "a musical mood" to a woman's reveries concerning love and the religious congregation's gathering in churches. How are these comparable? Sultry winds inspire each. The section offers examples to bear out Nietzsche's repeated insistence that much human behavior follows physical stimulation. Although the woman's reveries are described more as physical response than as intellectual activity, she is treated no differently in this regard than the church member or the emotionally inspired artist, male or female.

Section 64 describes "old women" as taking a superficial stance toward experience as a matter of etiquette. While Nietzsche's preface did not appear until the second edition of *The Gay Science,* this passage is reminiscent of Nietzsche's characterization of himself therein as one who has become superficial out of profundity, thanks to the wear of his experiences. Section 65 analyzes the plight of "a noble type of woman" who expresses deep devotion by sacrificing her virtue to a man who feels no devotion in response. These two sections are especially striking in that they reinterpret in positive terms female behavior that is commonly denigrated by men. Nietzsche suggests motivations that his primarily male readers are likely to understand, even respect. The old woman is presented as no fool; the fallen woman as a heroine.

Section 66 describes a feminine maneuver attributed to *allen Frauen. Alle Frauen* can be rendered "all women," as Kaufmann translates it. Nietzsche's term for women in this, as in most of these psychological vignettes, is the relatively respectful *Frau,* which typically means a married woman. Section 66 is exceedingly general, but Nietzsche's comment seems most apt for women who are matrons in their homes. Nietzsche's claim is that all *Frauen* exaggerate their weakness as a ploy to make men feel "clumsy, and guilty on that score," a feeling that may be particularly pronounced in the domestic sphere. Nietzsche presents this as a manipulative move devised by genuine weakness; but he also sees it as a clever tactic. "Thus they defend themselves against the strong and 'the law of the jungle [*Faustrecht*]' " (p. 125).

Section 67 reports another vignette, this time about a woman who, although apparently high-strung during her courtship with her husband, feels relative inner calm now that the relationship is secure. Nietzsche suggests that to keep the man she loves captivated, she would best feign her earlier instability. The section is entitled "Simulating—oneself," and

Nietzsche seems to applaud such a possibility. "Wouldn't she do well to simulate her old character? To simulate lack of love? Is this not the counsel of—love? *Vivat comoedia* [Long live comedy!]" (pp. 125–26).

Granted, Nietzsche is not entirely complimentary to the women he describes. Cows are once again in evidence: he indicates the current confidence of the women described in section 67 as "like a cow" (p. 125). The women attempting to make men feel clumsy are portrayed as genuinely weak. The fallen woman who gives herself to the man she loves is described as "afflicted with a certain poverty of the spirit," although she is "noble." Nevertheless Nietzsche's remarks reveal a genuine concern for the psychological motivations both of women generally and of specific types of women. Indeed, by suggesting that this situation can be viewed as part of the comedy of life, Nietzsche is according women's situation a status comparable to that of men.

That Nietzsche is concerned with the psychological motivations of particular types of women is true as well in certain later sections of *The Gay Science*. In section 119, he describes the type of woman who becomes a function of her husband; and in section 227, he depicts the folly of the woman who thinks that a man with no self-control will be easy to control. This whole set of passages counters the more typical treatment of women in the literature of Nietzsche's era, which may extol the Eternal Feminine, but pays little attention to particular actual women. Nietzsche contends that the feminine is neither eternal nor a unified principle; and he offers an array of female motivations to indicate the complexity of the psychological terrain.

Nietzsche makes this even more obvious in the subsequent passages that describe the cultural conditioning of women. Section 68 reports of a confrontation between a sage and someone who brings a youth to him, claiming, "Look, he is being corrupted by women."

> "It is men," said he, "that corrupt women; and all the failings of women should be atoned by and improved in men. For it is man who creates for himself the image of woman, and woman forms herself according to this image. . . . Will is the manner of men; willingness that of women. That is the law of the sexes—truly a hard law for women. All of humanity is innocent of its existence; but women are doubly innocent. Who could have oil and kindness enough for them?"

144 Nietzsche's Use of Women

Someone from the crowd that is apparently present yells that, "women need to be educated better!" But the sage responds that "men need to be educated better." Although the sage beckons the youth to follow him, we are told that the youth does not. Presumably, the youth does not follow the advice of the person who brought him to the sage eiher. In all probability, he returns to his business—that of being "corrupted."

This passage might be read as an "essentialist" characterization of gender, or an effort to put women "in their place." The sage, however, speaks in a descriptive tone. And insofar as he describes the relative roles of men and women in heterosexual relations, he is probably not overstepping the facts to describe the style of nineteenth-century males as expressing will and that of their female counterparts as turning on "willingness."

Given that the entire *Gay Science* plays on the varying levels of changes that human beings encounter, it seems reasonable to assume Nietzsche considers change with regard to the relations between the sexes to be possible. Indeed, such change seems to be precisely what the sage advocates when he urges that men be educated better. While there is no evidence here that Nietzsche does not find the differences between male and female erotic styles to be biologically based, he does seem to think that the way men and women behave toward each other is malleable. Thus, while Nietzsche may be a biological foundationalist, he is not a biological determinist.

Moreover, Nietzsche suggests that women's education is important, although, admittedly, he does not appear to think it should be identical to that of men. He makes this even more evident, without the intermediary of the fictional sage, in section 71, entitled "On female chastity." There he marvels at the "amazing and monstrous . . . education of upper-class women." These women, he contends, are taught to be "as ignorant as possible of erotic matters" and to be so filled with shame at any hint of such topics as to respond with flight. Then they are "hurled, as by a gruesome lightning bolt, into reality and knowledge, by marriage—precisely by the man they love and esteem the most! . . . Thus a psychic knot has been tied that may have no equal" (pp. 127–28). Individual women deal with this problem in different ways, but Nietzsche doubts that anyone has offered a full account of an individual woman's accommodation.

This barbaric education, Nietzsche submits, results in a woman's deliberate assumption of a kind of blindness. "Afterward, the same deep silence as before. Often a silence directed at herself, too. She closes her eyes to herself." Probably, too, the woman will desire children "as an apology or atonement" for the "question mark" that her husband raises regarding her honor. Nietzsche concludes, "In sum, one cannot be too kind about women" (p. 128).

Besides revealing what appears to be genuine sympathy for women, Nietzsche prefigures contemporary feminist arguments that certain characteristics of women are "cultural constructions," and dubious constructions at that. Far from trivializing women by his references to art at the opening of Book Two, Nietzsche takes the falseness of men's fantasies about women to be paradigms of deceptions that are taken as true. Nietzsche insists that women's reality is quite different from traditional male fabrications, and he jars his readers into sensing the discrepancy between their habitual thinking and actual women's points of view.

Presupposing a male audience, the passages on women are bound to be startling. By introducing the theme of "women," a topic on which Nietzsche can be sure that his readers have thoughts as well as feelings, he ensures a double-take on the part of the reader. By continuing with a whole series of sections referring to women, he enhances the likelihood that further double-takes will deepen the processes of self-examination and reassessment of one's own responses to women. Perspective is not fixed, Nietzsche's strategy reminds us. Perspectivism is an activity, and one in which Nietzsche's readers are forced to participate. Merely to entertain Nietzsche's vignettes is to re-envision women along culturally nonstandard lines.

Nietzsche challenges his readers to consider how the women he describes might understand themselves from the inside. Admittedly, these readers have no "objective" court of appeal to judge the accuracy of their experimental projections; but to attempt such an experiment at all is pioneering in an era when the typical philosophical pronouncement about women took no interest in women's perspectives. That Oliver Stone's movie *The Doors* begins with Jim Morrison quoting Nietzsche is more than biographically apt. Nietzsche tries to stimulate his readers to break through the barrier of gendered consciousness, to imagine, at least, life on the other side.

III

I have suggested that Nietzsche is not fully consistent in his attitude toward the opposite sex. Certainly, he would contend that no one is fully consistent on these matters; and in this he is not unlike most major theorists in the psychoanalytic movement, which learned largely from Nietzsche how to analyze human motivations. He considers apparent consistency in such personal matters a mask, if not a symptom.

Nietzsche's inconsistency may itself attract feminist ire; and the aims of the feminist political activist oppose Nietzsche's in fundamental respects. Nevertheless, Nietzsche is a forebear of feminist philosophy. In the first place, like Nietzsche, feminist philosophers begin by embracing perspectivism, the view that philosophy can only do justice to human experience by taking perspectival differences into account. Insofar as Nietzsche both articulates and defends the importance of perspectivism, his work prepares the groundwork for feminist analyses of the gender-based foundation of certain perspectival differences. Moreover, his tactics for inducing his readers to engage in perspectival thought experiments is a valuable precedent for feminist practice, assuming that feminist aims include insight into both male and female motivations, and not only strategic advantage for women.

Second, at least some feminist philosophers are interested in the methods of revolutionary transformations of consciousness. In the Preface for the Second Edition of *The Gay Science*, Nietzsche describes philosophy as a chronicle and transfiguration of "the states of health" one has undergone (p. 35). His own chronicles include his confessions, much in the fashion of a participant in a male consciousness-raising group, of his own sexist habits of thinking. Nietzsche also seems interested, at least in *The Gay Science*, in inducing transformations of consciousness regarding gender in his readers. While his ultimate goal is presumably neither limited to nor focused on gender, he takes gender to be a noteworthy case in point.

Third, Nietzsche takes stances on issues of special concern to feminists. For example, he rejects unisex androgyny as a goal. He consistently disputes the value of any ethical ideal that proposes the same traits for everyone. On the other hand, he embraces the notion that, optimally, an individual will develop traits that do not conform to the stereotypes culturally prescribed for his or her sex. In fact, he seems closer to urging a proliferation of genders than to insisting upon fixed roles for anyone.[9] Even if he is still locked into the notion of a heterosexual binarism (a matter that itself is debatable), his suggestions that there are many types of women with different psychological takes on reality initiate an exploration of the possibilities.

Fourth, Nietzsche encourages a reconsideration of relationships between men and women. More than most of his contemporaries, he seems committed to the notion that the roles and relations possible for members of different sexes are subject to change and that change of this sort is desirable.

Fifth, in suggesting that changes should occur in these regards, and that individuals should ideally not be constricted by social stereotypes, Nietzsche problematizes gender. Gender may not have been his own central concern, or even a topic that sustained his interest over his career. Nevertheless, in *The Gay Science* at least, Nietzsche was a pioneer in gender theory.

IV

Let us conclude by returning to the sexist joke. Section 75, the final section on women in Book Two of *The Gay Science,* is what Kaufmann describes as an "absurd" aphorism:

> *The third sex.*—"A small man is a paradox but still a man; but small females seem to me to belong to another sex than tall women," said an old dancing master. A small woman is never beautiful—said old Aristotle. (p. 130)

Kaufmann reads this as a poor paraphrase of Aristotle:

> Aristotle actually says: "Greatness of soul implies greatness, as beauty implies a good-sized body, and small people may be neat and well-proportioned but cannot be beautiful." (*Nicomachean Ethics*, 1123b)

Kaufmann concludes, "With this absurd aphorism the pages on women . . . reach their nadir and end. The rest of Book II . . . deals with art" (GS, p. 130n).

What should we make of Section 75? Is it akin to Schopenhauer's calling women an "undersized, narrow-shouldered, broad-hipped, and short-legged race"?[10] Could the joke, perhaps, be *on* Schopenhauer, if at women's expense, with Nietzsche claiming that the female sex is not one undersized race, but two? When Aristotle discusses human beings, he takes the male to be the paradigm; does Nietzsche include women here only to make fun of them? Is the joke sexist?

I don't think we should assume so. If anyone appears absurd in Section 75, it is Aristotle. To cast Aristotle as a dancing master seems *prima facie* ridiculous, in light of the ploddingly methodical gait of the Aristotlean texts that survive. Nietzsche is also making light of Aristotle's Peripatetic school.[11] More important, Aristotle is cast here as someone who is screening potential dance partners, and demanding a partner who matches his own stature. As a "dancing master," Aristotle seems to find ludicrous the idea of dancing with someone of a vastly different size—and so he postulates a new essence, a third sex, a caste of women whose height is vastly dissimilar to that of a man, at least a "great-souled" man.

But what is more perspectival than height? Nietzsche suggests, by rather unsympathetically paraphrasing Aristotle, that Aristotle formulated his "objective" observations from the stance of his own perspective. Aristotle, the original proponent of "essences" in Western philosophy, is as dependent on the contingencies of his own physiological perspective as anyone else.

Nietzsche makes his mirth regarding Aristotle's pronouncement more obvious in a later passage in *The Gay Science:* "*Great man.*—From the fact that somebody is 'a big man' we cannot infer that he is a man; perhaps he is merely a boy, or a chameleon of all the ages of life, or a bewitched little female" (p. 208). In other words, the scale of body demanded by Aristotle is far from "essential" to the matter of having a great soul—or to one's "gender," if this is understood as conformity to socially imposed ideals. The big man's body that so impressed Aristotle might be that of precisely the tiny woman that the fictional Aristotle rejects as a dancing partner. The big man might be a child, or a woman, or perhaps a member of the third sex.

In matters of height, we all have perspectives; and Nietzsche's joke on the great man Aristotle raises questions about his own position in this matter. Some of Nietzsche's acquaintances do offer testimony on this topic, but their comments only fortify the view that height is a matter of perspective. Ida von Miaskowski, for example, claims that

> Nietzsche's external appearance at the beginning of the seventies of the past century still stands vividly in my memory. He was only of medium height, but of slender build, brisk and lively. His fea-

tures seemed ordinary to me, but the wonderful eyes and impressive forehead made one forget this, and on the whole one had the impression of a personality that towered above the average, even externally.[12]

Ludwig von Scheffler disputes Miaskowski's impression.

> . . . he was of short rather than medium height. His head deep in the shoulders of his stocky yet delicate body. And the gleaming horn-rimmed glasses and the long hanging mustache deprived the face of that intellectual expression which often gives even short men an impressive air.[13]

Adolf Ruthardt had a still different stance.

> Above middle height, slender, well-formed, with erect but not stiff stance, his gestures harmonious, calm and sparing; the almost black hair, the thick Vercingetorix mustache, his light-colored, but distinguished-looking suit of the best cut and fit, allowed him so little to resemble the type of a German scholar that he called to mind rather a Southern French nobleman or an Italian or Spanish higher officer in civilian clothes.[14]

We may be entitled to draw the conclusion that Nietzsche was not tall. I think that we should also conclude that Nietzsche's humor is not straightforward. Often, at least, Nietzsche's jokes are startling—and this is a *prima facie* reason to doubt that they are sexist. A joke bent on reinforcing prejudice is unlikely to prove startling. If sexist jokes are not funny, at least part of the reason is that their point is tedious.

At the same time, jokes are almost always unfair. They are pointillistically perspectival, without any concern to round out the picture. The medium is ill-suited to do justice to the texture of female experience—or to any other texture. Nevertheless, jokes can, I think, be liberating. The vision they convey can undercut complacent commonplaces that entrench inflexible attitudes.

Whatever one might think of any particular joke, I think that feminists should eschew "political correctness" on humor as a rigidly held ideal. This is a third pitfall that I think feminists should try to avoid. In keeping with the tenor of my labels for the other two syndromes that I have

mentioned, I will call this the Water buffalo Syndrome.[15] In urging feminists to avoid pedantic stances of political correctness, I do not mean to
endorse that tiresome and usually unjustified complaint that feminists
lack humor. "Being serious" is a respectable strategy in anyone aiming to
make serious points, feminists included. To say to someone engaged in
serious criticism, "You're just being serious!" strikes me as a foolish (de-
fensive) response.

Humor itself, however, should be recognized as a respectable strategy
of provocation, as well as a spontaneous product of imagination. Any
renovation of gender roles will require imagination and the willingness
to be startled. If jokes accomplish double-takes on gender, as Nietzsche's
do in *The Gay Science*, they may be of service to feminists. I think that
feminists would do well to include such tactics among their strategies.

Ultimately, Nietzsche does not require any particular conclusion from
the readers of *The Gay Science*. But he almost ensures, through his sections on women, that those who are honest with themselves will recognize their own perspectival stances as men or as women. Far from
proselytizing for the entrenchment of his culture's ideas about gender,
Nietzsche forces his readers to stop taking gender for granted. He does
not theorize the answers, but he poses gender as questionable. In this, he
is far ahead of his contemporaries. As he commends himself in another
context, he saw questions where his contemporaries did not.

Notes

1. Carol Diethe, "Nietzsche and the Woman Question," *History of European Ideas* 11 (1987):
866; hereinafter abbreviated "NWQ." Further references to this article will appear parenthetically
in the text.

2. Ellen Kennedy, "Nietzsche: Women as *Untermensch*," in Ellen Kennedy and Susan Mendus,
eds., *Women in Western Political Philosophy: Kant to Nietzsche* (New York: St. Martin's Press, 1987), p.
194; hereafter abbreviated "WU." Further references to this article will appear parenthetically in
the text.

3. Were this an article in a different philosophical style, I would term this syndrome "PNS."
Fortunately, this is not that kind of essay.

4. Friedrich Nietzsche, *Ecce Homo*, translated in Diethe, "Nietzsche and the Woman Question,"
p. 874.

5. Friedrich Nietzsche, *The Gay Science*, trans. Walter Kaufmann (New York: Random House,
1974), pp. 174, 202; hereafter abbreviated GS.

6. Friedrich Nietzsche, *Beyond Good and Evil*, trans. Walter Kaufmann (New York: Random
House, 1966), 232, p. 163.

7. Friedrich Nietzsche, *Thus Spoke Zarathustra*, in *The Portable Nietzsche*, trans. and ed. Walter
Kaufmann (New York: Viking, 1968), p. 168.

8. Sister Prudence Allen, RSM, "Nietzsche's Tension about Women," *Lonergan Review: A Multidisciplinary Journal*, "Special Theme: Nietzsche: An Interdisciplinary Approach," 2 (1993): 50; hereafter abbreviated as "NTW."

9. Friedrich Nietzsche, *Human, All Too Human: A Book for Free Spirits*, trans. R. J. Hollingdale (Cambridge: Cambridge University Press, 1986), I, 380, p. 150.

10. Arthur Schopenhauer, "On Women," in *Studies in Pessimism*, trans. Thomas Bailey Saunders (New York: Macmillan, 1908), p.113.

11. My thanks to Andrew Brien, who alerted me to this dimension of Nietzsche's pun.

12. Ida von Miaskowski, "Erinnerungen an den jungen Friedrich Nietzsche," in *Neue Freie Presse* (Vienna), September 12, 1907; quoted in *Conversations with Nietzsche: A Life in the Words of His Contemporaries*, ed. Sander L. Gilman, trans. David J. Parent (New York: Oxford University Press, 1987), p. 53.

13. Ludwig von Scheffler, "Wie ich Nietzsche kennen lernte," *Neue Freie Presse* (Vienna), August 6–7, 1907; in *Conversations with Nietzsche*, p. 65.

14. Adolf Ruthardt, "Friedrich Nietzsche und Robert Schummann," *Zeitschrift für Musik* 88 (1921), pp. 489–91; in *Conversations with Nietzsche*, p. 183. Earl Nitschke described to me an incident in which Nietzsche compared his height to that of Goethe on the basis of a wall-marking showing Goethe's stature. Nietzsche claimed that his own height matched the marking exactly. If this is accurate, Nitschke observes, Nietzsche would have been approximately 5′4″ or 5′5″ tall.

15. I refer here to the case of an Israeli student at the University of Pennsylvania who was censured for saying to some black students who were making noise outside his dormroom, "Be quiet, you water buffaloes." He claimed that "water buffalo" is a common Israeli expression for referring to noisy individuals. The black students claimed that he was making a racist slur.

7

Ecce Homo: Abjection and "the Feminine"

Jean Graybeal

> To you, the riddle-drunks . . . because you don't want to fumble with a timid
> hand for a thread; and, where you can *guess*, you hate to *deduce*.
> —*Nietzsche, Ecce Homo,* "Why I Write Such Good Books," Section 3

Nietzsche had just finished sending final corrections for *Ecce Homo* to his
publisher when he collapsed into madness on January 3, 1889. *Ecce Homo*
is subtitled "How One Becomes What One Is," and it is a kind of intellectual autobiography, though hardly a naturalistic document. The first
full chapter of *Ecce Homo,* entitled "Why I Am So Wise," opens with a
riddle, leading the reader to believe that the solution or interpretation of
this riddle is crucial to the meaning of the life story which follows: "The
happiness [*Glück*] of my existence, its uniqueness perhaps, lies in its fate
[*Verhängniss*]: I am, to express it in the form of a riddle, as my father
already dead, while as my mother I still live and grow old."[1]

This chapter will attempt to enter the "riddle" of Nietzsche's happiness, or good fortune, which is, he says, to be dead as his father and to live on and grow old as his mother. The prominent placement of this statement leads us to expect further hints, more information, some way to make sense of a conundrum so centrally positioned. We do indeed receive large amounts of additional information, both about the narrator's sense of his dual or split nature, inherited from his parents, and about his relation to his father. But when it comes so specific references to his mother, or how it is that "as his mother" he still lives and grows old, the only text available until recently gives us just a single hint: "My mother is, at any rate, something very German."[2]

The reader is thus left with two riddles: Nietzsche's mysterious formulation "as my father I am already dead, as my mother I still live and grow old"; and a new riddle posed by the lack of information about his mother. Why would Nietzsche, a careful writer and always conscious of form, begin his autobiography with a riddle which promised to illuminate the whole uniqueness of his existence, and then give us only half of what we need to interpret it? As a matter of fact, this particular riddle has a simple answer: Nietzsche *did* realize he had been remiss, and he did include further evidence in his final revision of *Ecce Homo*. A variant version of Section 3 of "Why I Am So Wise," discovered and published in 1969, a version sent by Nietzsche to his publisher only days before his final collapse into madness, is indispensable for reading *Ecce Homo*; as we shall see, it supplies heretofore missing information necessary for an interpretation of the riddle of Nietzsche's existence.[3]

Before moving on to the evidence provided by this variant text, let us follow the clues already available in the first-published, earlier version of *Ecce Homo* as far as they can take us. The path we shall follow has three parts: the vision of the father, the theme of doubleness, and the mother as "German." On a literal level, the riddle "as my father I am already dead, while as my mother I still live and grow old" might seem simply to point to the actual biographical facts at the time of this writing. Nietzsche's father had died when Nietzsche was four years old; his mother would live until 1897, nine years beyond the composition of *Ecce Homo*. Yet it is *as* his father and mother that he claims to be both dead and alive; in what sense does he see himself *as* his own parents?

References to Nietzsche's father in *Ecce Homo* are invariably positive, and imply a strong identification between father and son. In Section 1 of "Why I Am So Wise," Nietzsche describes his father as "delicate, kind, and morbid, as a being that is destined merely to pass by."[4] He notes that his father died at the age of thirty-six, and claims that his own life began to "go down" when he was the same age.

In Section 3 he states, "I consider it a great privilege to have had such a father. . . . it requires no resolve on my part, but merely biding my time, to enter quite involuntarily into a world of lofty and delicate things."[5] He considers himself, because of this bond and identification with his father, to have "one foot beyond life." In this section, Nietzsche also identifies his father as the source of his "Polish" blood: "My ancestors were Polish noblemen: I have many racial instincts in my body from that source."[6] Finally, in Section 5, Nietzsche compares his own forbearance and lack of instinct for revenge to qualities of his father:

> At another point as well, I am merely my father once more, and, as it were, his continued life after an all-too-early death. Like everyone who has never lived among his equals and who finds the concept of "retaliation" as inaccessible as, say, the concept of "equal rights," I forbid myself all countermeasures, all protective measures, and, as is only fair, also any defense, any "justification," in cases when some small or *very great* folly is perpetrated against me.[7]

Nietzsche thus identifies with his father: they are both above or "beyond life," existing in a "world of lofty and delicate things"; they are "noble," "Polish," non-German (at least in some vague past); they are uninterested in retaliation and cannot fathom ordinary motives of self-defense; in short, they are exalted, pure, and altogether above mundane human existence. What is most revealing here for our purposes is Nietzsche's repeated assertion that he is continuing a life which was prematurely interrupted. He sees himself almost as a reincarnation of his father and is immensely grateful for his inheritance from him. But how does this help us with the first part of Nietzsche's riddle, "as my father I am already dead," since he claims that his father, through himself, is actually still living? Perhaps if he and his father are *one*, Nietzsche too has died; and indeed those much-praised characteristics of detachment, superhuman tolerance, delicacy, and altitude are "angelic"; they suggest a distanced, privileged, perhaps transcendent perspective on life. Thus, to the extent that Nietzsche lives on as his father, he is already dead, dead to the ordinary mortal world of attachment, feeling, and even self-defense.

The second strand of evidence relevant to the riddle is the theme of doubleness. Immediately after posing the riddle, Nietzsche writes:

> This double origin, just as if from the highest and lowest rungs on the ladder of life, at the same time *decadent* and *beginning*—this, if anything, explains that neutrality, that freedom from bias in relation to the total problem of life, that perhaps distinguishes me. I have a better nose for the signs of ascent and decline than anyone has ever had, I am the teacher *par excellence* about this—I know both, I am both.[8]

In light of Nietzsche's explicit statements about his father and his almost complete silence concerning his mother, we may infer only that the "highest rung" and "lowest rung" on the ladder of life refer respectively to his father's and his mother's influence and heritage. From the high, lofty type of the father, he is a decadent, declining example; at the same time, evidently from his mother's side, he has the sense of ascent, climbing up out of what is low, weak, or sick. From the lowest rung on the ladder of life, he can be a beginning, a creator of himself, perhaps in some sense his own mother. In Section 3, he writes: "This double series of experiences, this access to apparently separate worlds, is repeated in my nature in every respect—I am a *Doppelgänger*, I have the second sight in addition to the first. *And* perhaps also the third. . . ."

How strange that after emphasizing this doubleness, and after specifying all that his father bequeathed to him, Nietzsche should leave the mother's influence so nearly completely untouched. As noted above, in the standard version of Section 3 of "Why I Am So Wise," there is only one direct mention of Nietzsche's mother: "When I consider how often I am addressed as a Pole when I travel, even by Poles themselves, and how rarely I am taken for a German, it might seem that I have been merely externally sprinkled with what is German. Yet my mother, Franziska Oehler, is at any rate something very German. . . ."

This brief mention is immediately followed by a barrage of biographical information relevant not to the mother's side of the family, but to the father's. His mother is *etwas sehr Deutsches;* more about her he will not say. The contrast with the extravagant praise of his father is extreme, and we might be forced merely to speculate on what "something very German" might mean to Nietzsche, if he hadn't spelled it out in great detail later in this book.

It is not until the second major division of *Ecce Homo*, entitled "Why I Am So Clever," that Nietzsche begins to specify what he means by the word "German." A sampling of statements immediately dispels any impression that Nietzsche was a Germanophile:

> The origin of the German spirit [is] from distressed intestines. The German spirit is an indigestion; it does not finish with anything.[9]

> The slightest sluggishness of the intestines is entirely sufficient, once it has become a bad habit, to turn a genius into something mediocre, something "German."[10]

> The few cases of high culture that I have encountered in Germany have all been of French origin.[11]

> As far as Germany extends, she *corrupts* culture.[12]

> [I am] so alien in my deepest instincts to everything German that the mere proximity of a German retards my digestion.[13]

> I was *condemned* to Germans.[14]

> I shall never admit that a German *could* know what music is.[15]

German-ness for Nietzsche is tied up with indigestion, constipation, corruption, and complete insensitivity to culture. It is all that he experiences as abject, all that reminds him of the "baseness" of his own maternal heritage. In the first division of the book, Nietzsche ventured only to say that his mother was at any rate "something very German." Whether consciously or not, he piously deferred his invective about Germany and Germans until the second and third divisions of the book, and distanced the mention of mother as "something very German" from the characteristics he associates with German-ness.

He writes, "To think German, to feel German—I can do anything, but *that* goes beyond my powers."[16] For Nietzsche to "think" or "feel" German is impossible; he claims that he cannot in any way identify with the people he so despises, or even believe that he is a German like his mother. He rejects and represses his maternal inheritance, and distances himself from the negative complex of German attributes with which he associates his mother. But the word "German" has yet another connotation in this book. It is in fact also the name of Nietzsche's greatest love, his mother tongue, his language, the medium within and through which he struggled throughout his life to "become what he was."[17] The young Nietzsche, abandoned by his "angelic" father at the age of four, left to a household of women, was certainly left with "something very German," was "condemned to Germans," but was left also to "German" itself. He became a philologist, a lover of language, and remained one all his life. The second part of the riddle went, "as my mother I still live and grow old." Perhaps as his own mother, his own creator, he struggles to give birth to himself, always in and through language, through "German," the mother tongue. This mother "lives and grows old." She is perpetually, or at any rate periodically, pregnant. She becomes *la mère qui jouit,* the great unfigurable figure behind all of Nietzsche's experimentation with language, his erotic, insatiable, overflowing attempts to achieve full expression, to let his "river of love plunge into the pathless places."[18]

Perhaps for Nietzsche "to think German, to feel German" is impossible; but to speak German, to write German is imperative! Nietzsche writes of his favorite poet, Heine: "And how he handles German! Someday it will be said that Heine and I were by far the first artists of the German language—at an incalculable distance from everything that mere Germans have done with it."[19] Of course, Nietzsche's work must be at a *distance* from what mere Germans do with their language! Nietzsche here again identifies himself as a Pole, and Heine was a Jew; thus, both escape the fate of being "mere Germans."

Again, he says, in reference to the multiplicity of his inward states and the plural styles required to communicate them: "That this was possible precisely in the German language remained to be shown: previously I myself would have rejected it most severely. It wasn't known, before me, what one can do with the German language—what one can do with language in general."[20] This sounds megalomaniacal; it may be inflated. Yet there is some truth in it too. The transmutation of abjection into the ecstasy of language, into jouissance, has rarely been demonstrated as powerfully as by Nietzsche.

The riddle at the beginning of *Ecce Homo* was a way of expressing the good fortune or happiness of Nietzsche's existence, its uniqueness, its fate. As his father, with whom he strongly identifies, he is dead, above life, detached and safe; as his mother, whom he sees as "something very German," he lives on, grows old, continues to give birth to himself, always through and in relation to language. These conditions of doubleness and split consciousness, the loss and absence of the father, the suffocating presence of the mother, have pressured the subject of this autobiography into a jouissance in language, a way of achieving satisfaction, release, pleasure, even joy in language itself. For Nietzsche, happiness, uniqueness, and fate are inextricably tied together. Without any one of the three, none of the others is possible. "My formula for greatness in a person is *amor fāti*. . . . Not merely to endure what is necessary . . . but to love it."[21]

Not merely to endure his parentage but to love it was Nietzsche's task, and his attempt to love it underlies his literary and stylistic accomplishments.

The Riddle of the Text

Important new clues for the interpretation of Nietzsche's riddle have been available since 1969, when a newly discovered, later revision of Section 3 of "Why I Am So Wise" was published. In most editions of *Ecce Homo,* as we have seen, there exists only one direct reference to Nietzsche's mother. The version of Section 3 that appears in the complete critical edition of Nietzsche's works edited by Giorgio Colli and Mazzino Montinari is radically different from the one we have been examining. Montinari tells how Nietzsche's late revision of Section 3, unlike his many other last-minute changes, was rejected by his editor and friend as unsuitable for publication, and has been suppressed ever since.[22]

Nietzsche collapsed in January of 1889, very shortly after sending final revisions to his publisher, so the editing of *Ecce Homo* fell to his friend Peter Gast, one of whose letters shows that he removed certain passages which disturbed him. He explained: "At least to me, [they] produce an impression of great self-intoxication or perhaps of contempt and injustice which goes too far."[23] *Ecce Homo* was not published until 1908, and by that time control of the manuscripts had passed into the hands of Nietzsche's sister, whose self-interested handling of the materials is well known. She perpetuated Gast's policy of ignoring this late revision of Section 3, for reasons which will become clear below.

More relevant to our purposes than this story is a stylistic comparison of the earlier (published) and later (suppressed) versions of Section 3, the only section in all of *Ecce Homo* which provides any clues directly pertinent to the mother side of the riddle. Close analysis of the two versions shows that neither is representative of Nietzsche's highest abilities as a stylist. Each is an attempt to confront the subject of his mother directly: the first ends up in pious reportage, effectively blocking any access to the mother; the other is a study in transgressive fury. On most subjects, Nietzsche had managed to mediate between these extremes; on the subject of his mother, however, he was incapable of achieving a point of balance.

The early Section 3, some of which we have already examined above, begins with a reference to Nietzsche's double nature. He calls himself a *Doppelgänger* and notes that he has "second sight": he has an ability to take multiple perspectives, especially in matters of nationality. In the second paragraph (as divided in Kaufmann's English translation) he calls himself the "last anti-political German," yet claims Polish ancestry.

The third and central paragraph of the section contains the single mention of his mother, a mention which is immediately followed by a striking shift in style. As we have seen, he imagines he himself might have been "merely externally sprinkled with what is German," but his mother is "at any rate something very German." Precisely at this point, the prose undergoes a metamorphosis, and becomes very uncharacteristic of Nietzsche's work. Suddenly, as soon as the topic of his mother is broached, the page is densely packed with proper names, place names, and biographical details bearing little relation to the matter at hand. The focus shifts rapidly away from Nietzsche's mother to his *paternal* grandmother, Weimar, Goethe, Königsberg, Herder, Nietzsche's great-grandmother, and Napoleon. This sequence of details seems to have been prompted by the thought that Nietzsche's father's mother was also "very German"; but on the context of the riddle aobut the mother, clues to which the reader is avidly seeking, the information seems strictly beside the point. Then the focus returns to Nietzsche's father, and we learn his years of birth and death, positions, names of his famous pupils, and other miscellaneous details.[24]

The entire passage is uncharacteristic of Nietzsche's works, cluttered and full of uninterpreted and unrelated data. It simply recites a series of facts, all of which seem to aspire to some meaningful impression, but which actually succeed only in stultifying the reader and obscuring the matter at hand. Such a style would have to be called a banishment of style, a repression of expression. If the "meaning of every style" is, as Nietzsche claims, "to communicate a state, an inward tension of pathos,"[25] this passage seems almost intentionally to prevent communication, a communication which in this case might give too much away.

The section draws toward its close with the statement "I consider it a great privilege to have had such a father: it even seems to me that this explains whatever else I have of privileges—not including life, the great Yes to life." Perhaps the father could not provide this last privilege, having died so young and bequeathed to Nietzsche his own angelic stance. Finally Nietzsche reminds us again that he himself is beyond life: "In order to understand anything at all of my *Zarathustra* one must perhaps be similarly conditioned as I am—with one foot *beyond* life."

Thus ends the earlier version of Section 3 of the first chapter of *Ecce Homo*, related at its beginning and end to the major themes of the book, but conspicuously stilted and pedantic in the middle, immediately after the mention of his mother. Nietzsche seems to have bitten his tongue, to have cut off style, and, as we have seen, to have deferred until later in the book any further clues as to what he means by calling his mother "something very German." The whole section serves only to intensify the reader's riddle, to insinuate through pious near-silence a story that awaits proper circumstances to be told.

Evidently Nietzsche himself also found this section inadequate. The later revised version of Section 3 of "Why I Am So Wise" is strikingly different from the earlier one. Gast was to suppress it because he found it "self-intoxicated," full of "contempt" and "injustice." Kaufmann says that it "smacks of madness," and "one simply does not speak that way."[26] In the context of this investigation, however, it is a riveting example of the precise opposite of biting the tongue. The new version is a study in transgressive discourse, an outpouring, for the first time for public consumption, of the horror, bitterness, and abjection Nietzsche was experiencing in relation to his mother.

The new Section 3 opens with the statement "I consider it a great privilege to have had such a father." This sentence is the only one in common with the earlier, constipated, "German" version. Nietzsche goes on to say a little more about his father, replacing the names and dates of the earlier version with the observation that "the peasants to whom he preached . . . said an angel must look like that." In this new version he calls himself "a Polish nobleman *pur sang*, in whom also not a drop of bad blood is mixed, least of all German." Instead of being merely *angesprenkelt*, or sprinkled with German blood, as he speculated he might be in the earlier version, he now denies having even a drop of it.

The next few sentences, which deal directly with Nietzsche's mother, here conflated with his sister, are the heart of this section, and provide the evidence so conspicuously lacking in the earlier version. Nietzsche writes: "Whenever I seek the deepest contrast to myself, the incalculable meanness [or commonness] of instincts, then I always find my mother and sister."[27] Set on a height, searching far beneath himself for common- ness and instinct, he finds his mother and sister. "To believe myself re- lated to such *canaille* would be a blasphemy against my godliness."

Appropriate characterizations for these two are not to be found in German. Nietzsche chooses the French word *canaille* to sum them up, thus situating himself in the place of the cultured French and sneering at this "rabble" or "riffraff." To believe himself related to such low types would be a "blasphemy" against his "godliness." He styles himself so pure, so much the "Polish nobleman *pur sang,*" identified all at once with France, Poland, nobility, blue blood, and pure blood, that the obvious fact that he *must* be related to his mother is denied. He is motherless; his "godliness," his highness, cannot allow the "blasphemy" of being related to the lowness of his mother. "The treatment that I suffer from my mother and sister, up to this moment, infuses me with an unspeakable horror. . . ."

What can two such low creatures have done to fill his "godliness" with horror? This treatment, whatever it might be, continues *bis auf diesen Augenblick,* right up to the present moment. To be subjected to any sort of *Behandlung,* or treatment, at the hands of these women is horrific to Nietzsche; it is degrading; it renders him speechless; it infuses him, pas- sive before the power of the mother, with something that cannot, perhaps must not, be said. "Here works a perfect hell-machine, with unfailing certainty about the moment when one can bloodily wound me—in my highest moments . . . for there all strength is lacking to defend oneself against poisonous vermin."

Here the imagery becomes even more intense and explicit. The mother and sister are a "hell-machine," suggesting not only inhumanity but a lack even of any *cold* blood. To be a machine is to be nothing but calcula- tion, predetermined action, an unstoppable, unreasoning, unfeeling force. The image of a machine *of hell,* diabolical, originating in the depths of the underworld, combines terror before the unliving with the horror of evil itself.

This hell-machine has unfailing (hence inhuman) certainty about the *Augenblick,* the precise instant "when one can bloodily wound me." When could this be but in his *highest Augenblicken?*[28] Association of erec- tion and castration are suggested by this entire fantasy. The hellish perfection of inhuman, unfailing certainty of this female machine, a machine that knows exactly when to attack, when the victim is at the height of his exaltation, in his highest moments . . . all suggest Nietzsche's attribution to his mother and sister of his deepest fears related to his ability to express himself, to perform, to remain at the heights. A castrating mother awaits him at the bottom of his ladder of life as the opposite of his divinized, angelic, noble, pure-blooded, dead father. She threatens bloodily to wound him, although he has just claimed to be a "Polish nobleman *pur sang*" (no mention of *Blut!*), "in whom not a drop of bad blood is mixed, least of all German." He has only *pur sang* like his father, and none of the mother's bad, German blood; yet she is capable of bloodily wounding him, reminding him all too painfully of his low, "bloody" German origins.

The hell-machine is capable of wounding him in his highest moments, "for there all strength is lacking to defend oneself against poisonous vermin." Here the constellation of images becomes almost too transparent to require explication. At his highest moments, in spite of his nobility, godliness, and *pur sang*, he lacks all strength to defend himself against *giftiges Gewürm*, poisonous vermin. Adam in his innocence, at his height, before the fall, lacks all strength to defend himself from the *Gewürm*, worms, serpents, which threaten him with poison, with downfall, with the fall itself. Here the evocation of the classic Western complex of images linking women, sexuality, serpent, hell, blood, death, and fall is complete, and Nietzsche knows himself powerless before it, perhaps especially when he attempts to stay at his highest *Augenblick*—his Olympian elevation above it all.

At this point is interjected a sentence which provides a moment's relief from the horror and fear suggested by the preceding passages. "The physiological contiguity brings about such a *disharmonia praestabilita*." Through a sudden shift to Greek- and Latin-based words, words which suggest a scientific and philosophical remove, away from the pithy, primal (and mother-identified) Germanic vocabulary, Nietzsche momentarily distances himself from his mother, naming in pseudo-scientific terms the disturbance which the bodily nearness of his female relatives causes in him.

Finally comes the last reference to mother and sister: "But I confess that the most profound objection to the 'eternal recurrence,' my truly *abysmal* thought, is always mother and sister." Here we recall that the 'abyss" of the thought of eternal recurrence consists in the requirement that it be willed: one must be able to will that one's life be repeated eternally, down to the smallest details. The thought of eternal recurrence is integrally linked to *amor fāti*, and thus to the necessity of loving one's destiny, even insofar as it is determined by one's parentage.

Perhaps "mother and sister" are the only elements of his own fate which Nietzsche cannot imagine himself willing to recur. This is a striking statement from a man whose life seems to include so many other sources of suffering and pain. Or is it simply again that the lowness, or baseness, he associates with these two in itself constitutes an objection or argument against the possibility of this paradoxically sublime and *abgründlich*, "bottomless" thought? In any case, the female family members stand for the opposite of all with which Nietzsche identifies.

The late revision of Section 3 ends with a relatively calm meditation on the idea of kinship. Nietzsche writes, "All prevailing notions of degrees of kinship are unsurpassable physiological nonsense" *(ein physiologischer Widersinn, der nicht überboten werden kann)*. At first reading, this seems to be mere hyperbole, asserting that the *Widersinn*, the "nonsense" or "absurdity," of the idea of kinship is a real nonsense, nonsense that can't be topped, or as Kaufmann translates it, "a physiological absurdity that cannot be excelled." But *überbieten* may also be translated literally as "to outbid," or "overbid"; to propose a higher value or price; figuratively, to outdo or surpass. At one level the idea of kinship may simply be a very high, very absurd absurdity, one that can't be beat for its absurdity. Might it not also be a nonsense which in the end cannot be outbid, or outrun? A nonsense so real, so powerful, that devising some means of understanding it, relating to it, even of loving it (as in *amor fāti*) is imperative for the survival of the self?

Piety, Transgression, and Style

On the verge of disintegration, writing his autobiography, Nietzsche confronted at last the unavoidable nonsense of his parentage, his undeniable yet deeply unlovable connection with his mother . . . and found this contradiction unsustainable. He tried twice to write for public consumption about his mother and his sense of himself *as* his own mother, and the two versions of Section 3 shows this "subject in process/on trial" at two extremes. Nietzsche's first attempt to look directly at the mother effectively paralyzed him. As if confronted by the Medusa's head, he stopped still and stammered a passage of pious reportage, cluttered with factual details to the point of the exclusion of meaning. In the second attempt, he took the opposite tack. Faced with a terrifying abyss, Nietzsche plunged into rhetorical excess and fantasy, attempting to express the abjection he experienced in relation to this mother and sister.

The alternation or oscillation between piety and transgression so transparently demonstrated in the two versions of Section 3 is a driving force behind the stylistic achievement of Nietzsche's corpus taken as a whole. Neither of the two extant passages achieves the brilliance of some of Nietzsche's best work, but I believe there is a clear and cogent reason why this is so.

Kaufmann thinks that if Nietzsche had not lost his sanity at this point, and had therefore been able to work on this section a little longer, he could have created a better version than either of the two we have been examining.[29] But my point here is that it was precisely the unprecedented pressure to speak directly about the mother, for public consumption, that produced the two radically different and equally "inappropriate" passages.

Perhaps Kaufmann's conjecture benefits from a reversal: "Had Nietzsche been able to rewrite this passage, to hold together for the first time in his life his contradictory feelings of piety toward his mother and his extreme horror and hatred of all that she represented to him, he might indeed have retained his sanity, and more than just a little longer."

Such a conjecture may seem bizarre, but in a life so dominated and shaped by writing itself, our ordinary understanding of cause and effect must be questioned.[30] The subject creates itself through language; Nietzsche always forged toward his ever-evolving sense of identity through his writing. One of the central problematics for every subject, and surely for Nietzsche, is the relation to the parents, to one's own sexuality, and to the contrasexual. As Nietzsche worked and reworked the riddle of his double inheritance, he circled closer and closer to the drive to speak directly of the ultimately unspeakable, the foundational relation to the mother.

Is it not just as reasonable to presume that the pressure to integrate the self-contradictory feelings about the mother into one coherent, "sane" section *precipitated* Nietzsche's final crisis, as to assume that his sanity deserted him just before he would have the chance to accomplish this formidable task?

Neither interpretation needs to be seen as correct. But if, as I am arguing, the confrontation with "the feminine" was pivotal for Nietzsche's development as a writer, then the two versions of the section where he attempts to be most direct and explicit about that relationship itself are *equally* indispensable in the task of interpreting his works.

Just what is it that this later version of Section 3 adds to our understanding of the riddle of Nietzsche's existence? How does it further illuminate the statement "as my mother I still live and grow old"? Nietzsche had written, in introducing this riddle, that the "good luck" of his existence consisted in its "fate," which was in turn expressed by the riddle. Therefore, his good luck is his fate, which is to be dead as his father, and live and grow old as his mother.

Fate is a crucial idea for Nietzsche. The content of one's particular fate is much less important than the way in which one approaches and appropriates it. Nietzsche's definition of "greatness" consists in loving one's fate: "My formula for greatness in a human being is *amor fāti*: that one wants nothing to be different, not forward, not backward, not in all eternity. Not merely bear what is necessary, still less conceal it . . . but *love* it."[31]

Certainly Nietzsche's mother is part of his own fate. Can he love her as such? He writes that "the most profound objection to the 'eternal recurrence,' my truly *abysmal* thought, is always mother and sister." Their existence as part of his fate challenges his own ability to will their recurrence. But he has claimed that his fate is his good fortune. Is it precisely the difficulty of loving what is so unlovable that contributes to his sense of his own achievement?

Or did his attempt to love his fate, and thus to achieve the greatness to which he aspired, break bown on the requirement to include the mother in his love? The passages about his mother in the later variant of Section 3 certainly seem to belie Nietzsche's claim to be like his father, above human feeling, beyond life, without instincts for revenge. They are full of horror and disgust . . . he goes so far as to deny being related to his mother. These passages alone undermine any impression that Nietzsche himself was fully capable of loving all that was in his fate.

Maybe it is a mistake to try completely or systematically to unravel a riddle such as this one. After all, Nietzsche himself mocked those who "fumble with a timid hand for a thread," and encouraged us to guess rather than to deduce. My own guess is that Nietzsche, in spite of the horror of his mother shown in the later text, would stand by his equation of the riddle with the good luck of his existence. For him, there is no virtue in being born into harmonious circumstances. In fact, there is less opportunity for greatness, for the love of fate which only a complex and tension-filled fate makes great. What may we "guess," then, that Nietzsche means by living and growing old as his mother? Perhaps he is admitting that in spite of his protests, this lowness, bloodiness, horror, and poison are indeed parts of himself. The tension between the bodily existence and abjection associated with his mother and the elevation and angelic purity ascribed to his father is integral to who Nietzsche is. His imagery invokes the classic Western split assigning spirit to male and body to female, but even in his late revision of *Ecce Homo* he lets the riddle stand, and continues to assert that "as my mother I live and grow old."

Second, we may guess that the riddle expressed Nietzsche's sense of creating or giving birth to himself. "As my father" can be read "as my own father"; and his father's work is already done. His perspective from beyond life has been effectively passed on. "As my mother," "as my own mother," I must continue to give birth to myself anew. The self is never complete, never fully born, so as one's own mother, one lives and grows old.

A third possibility, suggested above, is that Nietzsche's mother, who was "something very German," may in some sense be "German" itself, the German language, in which and through which Nietzsche constantly struggled to create and discover himself, to "become what he was."

But perhaps it is a mistake to try to read the riddle as two separate halves. We are tempted into that tactic by the separate and radically different treatments afforded to the topics of father and mother by both versions of Section 3. Perhaps the image to hold on to is that of the subject suspended between two equally important figures or forces, searching for his own way of being himself. As his father he is dead, beyond life, and as his mother he is abjectly implicated in the horrors of "human, all-too-human" existence. Is there an authentic middle ground, a point of balance between leaving life behind and finding it horrifying? Yes: that point of balance is *amor fāti*, loving one's life as it actually is and has been. Suspension between two untenable poles then becomes a gift, a piece of "good luck" that makes possible—no, necessary—the discovery of the way between: the great Yes to life.

Nietzsche wrote: "I consider it a great privilege to have had such a father: it even seems to me that this explains whatever else I have of privileges—*not* including life, the great Yes to life." Life itself, the great

Yes to life, the attempt to love one's fate and create oneself in relation to it, is not a gift from either father or mother, but a result of the suspension between the two parents, between the representatives for Nietzsche of holiness and abjection, between piety and transgression, between a deathlike spirituality and a common, instinctual vitality.

Nietzsche tried twice to express the riddle of his existence; each time he foundered on the need to clarify his relation to his mother. But each text provides the "riddle-drunks" with different clues, teaching us to be better readers of Nietzsche and thus of ourselves . . . and to guess rather than deduce.

Notes

1. Friedrich Nietzsche, *Ecce Homo*, in *Werke in Drei Bäden*, Zweiter Band, ed. Karl Schlechta (Munich: Carl Hansen Verlag, 1955), p. 1070. Translations from German editions cited in this chapter are mine.

2. *Ecce Homo*, ed. Schlechta, p. 1073.

3. This later version of the text is included as authoritative in the Colli-Montinari edition of Nietzsche's works: Friedrich Nietzsche, *Werke: Kritische Gesamtausgabe*, ed. Giorgio Colli and Mazzino Montinari (Berlin: Walter de Gruyter and Co., 1969), Vol. VI, 3, pp. 265–267.

4. Nietzsche, *Ecce Homo*, ed. and trans. Walter Kaufmann (New York: Random House, 1967), p. 222.

5. *Ecce Homo*, trans. Kaufmann, p. 226.

6. Hollingdale has pointed out that the source of this idea is a "family legend," and that the Polish connection is unsubstantiated. (R. J. Hollingdale, *Nietzsche: The Man and His Philosophy* [Baton Rouge: Louisiana State University Press, 1965], p. 7.) It does figure importantly, however, throughout the book, and becomes one of Nietzsche's favorite ways of identifying with his father and distancing himself from all that is "German."

7. *Ecce Homo*, trans. Kaufmann, p. 228.

8. *Ecce Homo*, ed. Colli and Montinari, p. 262.

9. *Ecce Homo*, trans. Kaufmann, p. 238.

10. *Ecce Homo*, trans. Kaufmann, p. 240.

11. *Ecce Homo*, trans. Kaufmann, p. 243.

12. *Ecce Homo*, trans. Kaufmann, p. 244.

13. *Ecce Homo*, trans. Kaufmann, p. 247.

14. *Ecce Homo*, trans. Kaufmann, p. 249.

15. *Ecce Homo*, trans. Kaufmann, p. 251.

16. *Ecce Homo*, ed. Schlechta, p. 1102.

17. See the subtitle of *Ecce Homo: How One Becomes What One Is*.

18. Nietzsche, *Also Sprach Zarathustra: Ein Buch für Alle und Keinen* (Munich: Insel Verlag, 1948), p. 86.

19. *Ecce Homo*, ed. Schlechta, p. 1089.

20. *Ecce Homo*, "Why I Write Such Good Books," Section 4, ed. Colli and Montinari, p. 302.

21. *Ecce Homo*, "Why I Am So Clever," Section 10, ed. Colli and Montinari, p. 295.

22. Mazzino Montinari, "Ein Neuer Abschnitt in Nietzsches *Ecce Homo*," in *Nietzsche Studien* I (1972), pp. 380–418.

23. ". . . welche selbst mir den Eindruck zu grosser Selbsterauschung oder gar zu weit gehender Verachtung und Ungerechtigkeit machen . . ." (Peter Gast's letter to Franz Overbeck, dated Feb. 27, 1889, quoted by Montinari, p. 401).

24. The relevant passage of Section 3 as it appears in earlier editions is reproduced here:

> When I consider how often I am addressed as a Pole when I travel, even by Poles themselves, and how rarely I am taken for a German, it might seem that I have been merely externally *sprinkled* with what is German. Yet my mother, Franziska Oehler, is at any rate something very German; ditto, my grandmother on my father's side, Erdmuthe Krause. The latter lived all her youth in the middle of good old Weimar, not without some connection with the circle of Goethe. Her brother, the professor of theology Krause in Königsberg, was called to Weimar as general superintendent after Herder's death. It is not impossible that my mother, my great-grandmother, is mentioned in the diary of the young Goethe under the name of "Muthgen." Her second marriage was with the superintendent Nietzsche in Eilenburg; and in the great war year of 1813, on the day that Napoleon entered Eilenburg with his general staff, on the tenth of October, she gave birth. As a Saxon, she was a great admirer of Napoleon; it could be that I still am, too. My father, born in 1813, died in 1849. Before he accepted the pastor's position in the parish of Röcken, not far from Lützen, he lived for a few years in the castle of Altenburg and taught the four princesses there. His pupils are now the Queen of Hanover, the Grand Duchess Constantine, the Grand Duchess of Altenburg, and the Princess Therese of Saxe-Altenburg. He was full of deep reverence for the Prussian king Frederick William IV, from whom he had also received his pastoral position; the events of 1848 grieved him beyond all measure. I myself, born on the birthday of the above named king, on the fifteenth of October, received, as fitting, the Hohenzollern name *Freidrich* Wilhelm. There was at least one advantage to the choice of this day: my birthday was a holiday throughout my childhood. (Nietzsche, *Ecce Homo*, trans. Kaufmann, pp. 225–226)

25. *Ecce Homo,* trans. Kaufmann, p. 265.

26. Walter Kaufmann, *Nietzsche: Philosopher, Psychologist, Antichrist,* 4th ed. (Princeton: Princeton University Press, 1974), p. 457. Kaufmann devotes three pages to this new Section 3 in the appendix of his book, but does not find it important for understanding Nietzsche's thought, and has not included it in the "Variant Texts" section of his translation of *Ecce Homo.*

27. *Ecce Homo,* ed. Colli and Montinari, p. 266. The German text of these few sentences directly referring to mother and sister is reproduced here:

> Wenn ich die tiefste Gegensatz zu mir suche, die unausrechenbare Gemeinheit der Instinkte, so finde ich immer meine Mutter und Schwester,—Mit solcher canaille mich verwandt zu glauben wäre eine Lästerung auf meine Göttlichkeit. Die Behandlung, die ich von Seiten meiner Mutter und Schwester erfahre, bis auf diesen Augenblick, flösst mir ein unsägliches Grauen ein: hier arbeitet eine vollkommene Höllenmaschine, mit unfehlbarer Sicherheit über den Auggenblick, wo man mich blutig verwunden kann—in meinen höchsten Augenblicken, . . . denn da fehlt jede Kraft, sich gegen giftiges Gewürm zu wehren. . . . Die physiologische Contiguität ermöglicht eine solche disharmonia praestabilita. . . . Aber ich bekenne, dass der tiefste Einwand gegen die "ewige Widerkunft," mein eigentlich *abgründlicher Gedanke, immer Mutter und Schwester sind.*

28. "Instant" or "moment" may be an inadequate translation in this case. The "Augenblick," the eye-glance evokes the image of the phallic eye, the God's eye, the controlling "I," and the further repetition of the word twice more in this same sentence underlines its significance here.

29. Kaufmann, p. 457. Kaufmann comments on the relative lack of value of the later version of Section 3: "The handwriting was 'normal' and showed no signs of insanity. Nevertheless the style strikes me as far less sane that that of any other passage of equal length in *Ecce Homo* or in any of

his other books, and it is arguable how much weight one should give to Nietzsche's momentary wish to substitute this page for a section that contains some splendid formulations and is clearly, I think, superior in style as well as content" (p. 455). It is to be hoped that future English editions of *Ecce Homo* will supplement the earlier version of Section 3 with this later variant, without which the "riddle" of Nietzsche's existence remains opaque.

30. Alexander Nehamas makes this point throughout his book *Nietzsche: Life as Literature* (Cambridge: Harvard University Press, 1985).

31. *Ecce Homo,* trans. Kaufmann, p. 258.

Part Two

Feminists' Use of Nietzsche

8

Nietzschean Mythologies: The Inversion of Value and the War Against Women

Linda Singer

Friedrich Nietzsche is widely recognized as the philosopher of self-transcendence, who told of the coming of the Overman, the autonomous human being who would refound culture in a decaying Europe. But even those only casually acquainted with Nietzsche's thought know that he held some very bad opinions of women. The reader of Zarathustra,[1] for example, cannot but be stunned by the fact that a philosopher with Nietzsche's acuity and radical power of insight offers, in the voice of Zarathustra the prophet, pregnancy as the only solution to women's problems. Not only is the cavalierness of this remark shocking, but the oversimplification it represents is in total contrast with the painstaking treatment he gives to the problems of "human existence."

The reaction of the philosophical community to this aspect of Nietzsche's thought is itself revealing. Many, like Danto and Wilcox, do not broach the subject at all. Others, like Kaufmann, justify this failure of attention by declaring outright that Nietzsche's position on women is "philosophically irrelevant"[2]—one of the "human all too human" aspects of his thought, a foible or prejudice that is not significant to us qua philosophical scholars. This apologetic stance has, in effect, become over the years a consistent strategy of Nietzsche scholars. *The Philosopher's Index* lists no American article on the topic of Nietzsche and women. Although there are many unexplored aspects of Nietzsche's thought, the absence of any discussion on this topic, "justified" by the assumption that what Nietzsche thought about women lacks philosophical import, suggests a phallocentrism that is unacceptable in a discipline which prides itself on the depth and breadth of its will to think. It is also unacceptable to women in philosophy—whom Kaufmann seems not to regard very highly, judging by his remark. Finally, such a silence, such a tacit agreement among men of reason not to take this part of Nietzsche's thought seriously, i.e., not to deal with it critically as they do with other aspects of his thought, is inappropriate to the spirit of philosophizing that Nietzsche himself mapped out. What, then, is the ground of this "contract of silence"?

Kaufmann himself suggests the answer.[3] To paraphrase, he admits that Nietzsche said some pretty terrible things about women, but hastens to add that this is no reason to reject his thought as a whole. With this I entirely agree. But it is precisely because Nietzsche was such a powerful and fecund thinker, and because he has so profoundly influenced thinking within the continental tradition, that the irresponsible things he said about women should be clearly disclosed as irresponsible. This is what I propose to do. I do so not in a mood of contempt or resentment, but out of a respect for a thinker who has shaped the course of my own thinking. This is a war I hope to wage in the Nietzschean spirit.

I am going to begin with a few general statements about Nietzsche's treatment of women. Women are not dealt with systematically or in any extended way by Nietzsche. The substance of his remarks is for the most part representative of views of women which were current in his age, views which he seems to have appropriated uncritically—the positions he takes are rarely supported by arguments or evidence. When referring to women he tends to favor the aphorism, and many of his statements take the form of passing asides, often invoking women for contrast. He relies heavily on pejorative insults and one-liners—likening women to cows, hyenas, and other animals[4] and citing them as paradigms of such undesirable qualities as shallowness and superficiality.[5]

The use of women in this way suggests that Nietzsche probably did not take the integrity of woman's situation very seriously. The conventionality of his attitude toward women stands in woman's inferiority is both natural and chosen, Nietzsche is led at this third stage to argue that any effort by women to transcend their situation is in fact only a retrogressive movement of resentment. Any effort toward emancipation by women is transformed by this analysis into a gesture of vengeance by "abortive women" against their fertile and well-adjusted sisters.

The scale of values has been reversed against women. Their actions have become their opposites. All their efforts work against them. Women in Nietzsche's world do not make themselves. They decorate or pollute a world in which their place has already been determined. The adventures of self-creation that Nietzsche glorifies are explicitly denied them. For woman, *Amor Fati* is a song of oppression, because Nietzsche has created a situation to which no woman can rightfully say yes. I will now show how this reversal takes place by adumbrating how Nietzsche works out each of the three strategies.

I. The Mythology of Nature

The term "Eternal Feminine" appears frequently in Nietzsche's writing.[6] There is no corresponding term "Eternal Masculine." This indicates that for Nietzsche it is only feminine destiny that is written in the timeless rhythms of nature. Man's destiny is created through will and force in history.

Nietzsche's respect for woman (and it is limited) lies with her powers of fertility. Woman is more natural than man because it is she who is biologically indispensable—man for her is only a means. The flip side of this attitude is that childbearing and rearing is woman's first and last profession. Here Nietzsche's view of women is remarkably close to the Christian view he so despised. Woman is resurrected not as mother of the savior, but as mother of the Overman.

The only other roles that Nietzsche feels are natural for woman are those connected with her primary biological function. This restricts her activities to the sexual and domestic spheres. Woman, according to

Nietzsche, is suited to live her life as a function.[7] Her function is to serve man—to feed and heal him, to raise his family, and to charm and divert him. Nietzsche grounds this division of labor in a natural female propensity toward passivity and subservience.

> Comparing men and women on the whole, one may say: woman would not have the genius for finery if she did not have an instinct for a *secondary* role. (BGE, sec. 145)

> Woman wants to be taken and accepted as a possession, wants to be absorbed into the concept of possession, possessed. Consequently she wants someone who *takes* . . . he is supposed to become richer in "himself" through the accretion of strength, happiness, and faith given him by the woman who gives herself. . . . I do not see how one can get around this natural opposition by means of social contracts or with the best will in the world to be just. (GS, sec. 363)

This natural division of power constitutes the ground of the conflict between the sexes that Nietzsche regards as an unquestionable feature of human existence. The battle between the sexes is not the war that Nietzsche recommends for his model warrior. That is a conflict of equals waged with mutual respect. The war between the sexes is debilitating because it can never be won. Men and women will always honor their own radically divergent ideals.[8] Woman will never "stand up and fight like a man," and so he will never have the satisfaction of beating her at her own game. Woman's weapons in the sexual war are devious ones. She cultivates the arts of seduction and masquerade. She charms, flatters, and runs roughshod over reason. She relies on the following natural attributes:

> . . . cunning, suppleness, naivete of egoism, and uneducability and inner wildness, possessing desires and virtues of incomprehensible scope and movement. (BGE, sec. 239)

For Nietzsche these features of female existence are testimony to her inferiority. She is preoccupied with her appearance because she is capable of no more substantive mode of self-expression. Her uncritical belief in love reveals a malleable and dependent spirit. She is sly because she lacks the capacity for directness. Social roles echo biological ones.

Nietzsche's claim that the qualities he attributes to women are natural is problematic, and not only because it could be argued that many women lack these qualities. It is a tactic that is questionable philosophically, for it gives Nietzsche license to present his cultural prejudices as though they were laws of nature. It is in this spirit that he declares that slacks are unnatural for women. By moving into the realm of nature, Nietzsche treats the socially conditioned modes of female behavior in response to the demands of patriarchal culture as though they were instinctual and could not be otherwise. At one stroke he absolves men from complicity in the formation of these structures. He fails to recognize that woman's passive posture is necessitated by a culture which values her only as a diverting object and aims to keep her pregnant and uneducated. In a world which precludes female access to the direct forms of social achievement, and keeps woman economically and psychologically dependent upon men, love becomes her only means of securing the bond that will give her the only status available to her. In taking the survival tactics she has designed for instincts, Nietzsche misconstrues her situation.

But the move to the natural is particularly malicious because in appealing to nonhuman forces, Nietzsche implies that woman's situation need not be examined or explored—there is no reason to question its genesis or the means by which it has been perpetuated. We are left with a portrait of female existence as something to be endured, preferably quietly; it is not a set of possibilities to be appropriated and transformed. Nietzsche has created a situation where women cannot help but fulfill men's negative anticipations of what can be expected from them. Both women and men are doomed to continual frustration and disappointment with each other.

II. Under the Harsh Light of Judgment

This phase of Nietzsche's discussion of women concerns not biology, but values. We have moved from the realm of predestination to a position of responsibility. With this move there is a corresponding shift in attitude. Women are held accountable for their values, and are taken severely to task. The argument underlying this viewpoint has the following form:

(1) Some values and qualities are inferior to others.
(2) People with inferior values and qualities are inferior.
(3) Women are people with inferior values and qualities.
(4) Women are inferior people.

In this context, woman's existence is construed as the negative face of the Nietzschean ideal. Those values which Nietzsche finds distasteful are seen as feminine values. What ultimately discredits women for Nietzsche is that he regards their behavior as motivated by three attitudes for which he has absolutely no sympathy. Woman's existence is characterized by resentment, self-hatred, and the will to untruth.

The vengefulness of woman is a frequent theme in Nietzsche's work.

> In revenge and in love, woman is more barbarous than man. (BGE, sec. 139)

> A little woman who pursues her revenge would run over fate itself. . . . Woman is indescribably more evil than man; also cleverer; good nature is in woman a form of denegation. (EC III, sec. 5)

Nietzsche's remarks about female vengefulness are all in the "Hell hath no fury like a woman scorned" spirit. This places Nietzsche within a long tradition of thought which caricatures woman's anger in order to delegitimate it. According to Nietzsche, woman's anger is motivated only by cruelty. Hostility toward men is seen as entirely unoccasioned, a purely negative moment which engenders contempt. On this basis, Nietzsche excluded women from the creation of their own values.

Female vengefulness often takes the form of self-hatred, expressed as contempt and hostility for other women. Nietzsche interprets this phenomenon as woman's implicit acknowledgment of her inferiority, her self-awareness of her inadequacies. It is a phenomenon which Nietzsche uses to great advantage. It allows him to suggest that women, rather than men, are the real despisers, the real oppressors of other women, and that women are responsible for their condition.[9] Women's contempt for each other gives further force to Nietzsche's claims that women ought to feel ashamed of their pettiness, viciousness, and cruelty.[10] This attitude reveals to Nietzsche the true weakness of the female spirit.

Nietzsche did not invent the phenomenon of female self-hatred, but he has misinterpreted it as a refusal of existence, rather than as a refusal of female existence as constituted. Woman's vengefulness does stem from her position of weakness. It is her way of refusing a nexus of structures which places her in a disadvantaged position. Her contempt is not directed at women per se, but at the situation they all share—an existence which is so precarious and circumscribed that women often do become rivals for the limited amount of benefits to be distributed. The structures of culture encourage female competition as a way of deflecting women's energy from their rivalry with men. The refusal of women to accept this situation is a sign of their strength. As long as women are kept secondary and inferior, they have no good reason not to resent their predicament. Nietzsche's demand that women abandon this attitude is an impossible and self-serving demand.

Nietzsche's final reason for discrediting the claims of women is their aversion to truth.

> . . . what is truth to woman? From the beginning nothing has been more alien, repugnant and hostile to woman than truth—her great art is the lie, her highest concern mere beauty and appearance. Let us men confess it: we honor and love precisely this art and this instinct in women—we who have a hard time and for relief like to associate with beings under whose hands, eyes and tender follies our seriousness, our gravity and profundity almost appear to us like folly. (BGE, sec. 232)

Woman is invoked by Nietzsche as the purveyor of deception and dissimulation. Starting right with *The Birth of Tragedy*, Nietzsche associated the female principle with the forces of passion, frenzy, and irrationality. Even in this early work women were portrayed as a respite from, and counterpart to, the male ideal of rigorous truthfulness. Their proper domain is the realm of enchantment and mystery—they lack the discipline and fortitude that the rational life demands. Women are satisfied with surface and appearance, devoid of the tenacity necessary for the pursuit of truth.

It is not surprising that Nietzsche counsels philosophers to avoid women,[11] or that he counsels Europe to become virile[12] in order to head off a feminization of culture. In Nietzsche's mind the feminine is associated with all that he finds loathsome in people in general—any accommodation to the female spirit can only result in a pollution of the masculine will. In the next section of this paper I will show how this mode of understanding is used to ground a further circumscription of women's activities.

III. Fear, Resentment, and the Inversion of Value

This section is concerned with the way Nietzsche turns the tables on women by inverting the scale of value used to interpret their behavior and then using this against them. It is a movement best characterized by Nietzsche's own concept of revenge, where the threatened class transforms the system of valuation so as to undermine the strength of its enemies. The inversion itself remains undefended. Its purpose is to turn strength into weakness, to make victims of those who are most feared.

What Nietzsche and the men for whom he speaks resent and fear in woman is, ironically, that which also binds them most deeply to her—her sexuality. It is this which constitutes the ground of the difference between men and women; furthermore, in the sexual sphere woman is believed to have a natural superiority by virtue of her capacity to bear children. It is also in the sphere of sexuality that man is most vulnerable. It was Sartre rather than Nietzsche who made this point explicitly, but it is already implicit in Nietzsche's position. Woman, according to Sartre, constitutes man as flesh.[13] In revealing him to himself as most radically embodied, she also reveals to him his finitude. Woman thus becomes a strange sort of threat. This nexus of fear and resentment underlies Nietzsche's treatment of women, and motivates the metamorphosis whereby woman's superior sexual capability becomes the basis for putting her down once more. Her strength has been turned into a condition of weakness. This inversion engenders a portrait of female existence in radical opposition to male existence. Woman's situation is a Catch-22, an enterprise doomed to failure.

Nietzsche complains that his is the age of the "borification of women."[14] It is a statement consistent with his claims about woman's superficiality and shallowness. At the same time that he makes these claims, however, he also attacks the idea of equal education for women as a "typical sign of shallowness."[15] Catch-22 again! Women writers, like George Sand, are comical.[16] Lady clerks are viewed as an unhappy social development.[17] Science is too "rigid" and "severe" for women.[18] Nietzsche regards any attempt by women to move beyond the domestic sphere as a misdirection of instincts. "When a woman has scholarly inclinations, there is something wrong with her sexually."[19] All of her strivings are viewed as ill-conceived and ill-fated.

It should be no surprise, therefore, to learn that Nietzsche finds women boring. Their interests have been restricted to the narrowest of realms; they have been excluded from all those activities which men deem important. Thus it is no wonder that Nietzsche finds women limited, petty, and uninteresting. Nonetheless, he remains firmly committed to maintaining a male monopoly over the knowledge process. Zarathustra asserts "One should speak of woman only to man." Women are to remain in a state of conditioned ignorance. Nietzsche views woman's increasing sexual knowledge with distaste. He would much prefer to keep sexuality within the province of male control, at least as far as the dissemination of information is concerned. His motive for this is clear. As long as woman is kept ignorant, she is preserved in her status as an ever-available, undemanding sexual object. Women are kept safe as nonchallenging and uncritical havens for men in an otherwise demanding world.

Nietzsche is well aware that women's knowledge of their situation is dangerous to the current balance of sexual power. He thus tries to dissuade women from pursuing their self-development by threatening them with a horrible caricature of the "enlightened" woman. The woman who pursues her rights loses her modesty and taste. The movement to grant equal rights to women is but another manifestation of the democratic spirit which threatens Europe with decay. Nietzsche views the agitation for the emancipation of women as a socially disruptive force, and in his most extreme formulations sees it as signaling the demise of civilization.

> "Emancipation of women"—that is the instinctive hatred of the abortive woman who is incapable of giving birth against the woman who has turned out well—the fight against the "man" is always a mere means, pretext, tactic. By raising themselves higher as "woman in herself," as the "higher woman," as a female "idealist" they want to lower the general rank of woman, and there is no surer way than higher education, slacks, and political cattle-voting rights. At bottom, the emancipated are anarchists in the world of the "eternally feminine," the underprivileged whose fundamental motive is revenge. (EC III, 5)

This statement (and there are many others like it) constitutes the final dimension of Nietzsche's inversion of value. The inversion has broadened so that it turns any assertive female activity into a hostile, angry, or empty gesture. Women's rebellions are undermined, reduced to a facade—all of which is a shield against male feelings of sexual inadequacy. Any efforts by women to develop themselves are transformed into retrogressive and negative moments.

The power of Nietzsche's strategy is testified to by the persistence right down to our day of his strategies and arguments. Some Freudians still try to claim that feminists are rebelling against their femininity. Many people employ Nietzsche's tactic of manipulating the aggressions of women so as to deflect them from their rightful target. It is still fashionable, in some circles, to consider feminists unwomanly. Nietzsche's arguments are taken up by those reactionary forces which seek to exempt men and the culture they have created from responsibility for women's situation, at the same time seeking to undermine women's battle with them by refusing to acknowledge its rightful grounds.

The eternal hostility that Nietzsche claims exists between the sexes must be given a new formulation. If woman's hostility for man is only a ruse, then the force perpetuating this timeless conflict can only be the eternal hostility felt by men toward women. It is this attitude which leads Nietzsche to interpret every effort by women to increase their influence and strength as an invasion which must be rebuffed. What Nietzsche characterizes as his "healthy suspicion" of woman's struggle for self-enlightenment is not healthy, but repressive—because it excludes even the possibility that woman will ever measure up to the demands of authentic existence. Women is relegated to a sphere which is alien, inferior, other, and where all the tables have been turned against her. Self-transcendence has become a violation of nature, and *Amor Fati* the banner of systematic oppression. Nietzsche has, indeed, created a situation to which no woman can say yes.

If I am right in maintaining that Nietzsche's sexism results in an intolerable and unjustified caricature of female existence, the question remains as to how this criticism ought to influence our reading and assessment of Nietzsche's thought as a whole. The position I have taken resists any attempt to dismiss this aspect of Nietzsche's work as a peripheral concern of psychological rather than philosophical import. The motive behind all such moves to so-dismiss Nietzsche's sexism is, I do believe, to preclude a line of questioning that might lead to more serious challenges to Nietzsche's overall position. But I believe the implicit question must be pursued—Given how wrong he is about women, how seriously can we take Nietzsche's remarks about human existence in general?

As someone who wants to continue to read and study Nietzsche, and to encourage others to do so, I nonetheless find any attempt to shield Nietzsche from the larger implications of his sexist views unacceptable on both political and philosophical grounds. Politically, this stance perpetuates the prejudice which devalues women and "women's issues" by leaving fundamental assumptions unexamined. Philosophically, the refusal to take Nietzsche seriously, by reading his discussions of femininity as exercises in irony, parody, or satire, results in a serious misunderstanding and evaluation of his work as a whole.

My reading of Nietzsche's sexual politics understands him to be committed to a normative theory of sexual difference in which masculinity is the privileged or dominant form of humanness. During the course of my paper I have discussed Nietzsche's arguments to the effect that the secondary status of the feminine is based on natural and moral grounds, and I have cast doubt on the quality of those arguments. But the serious matter at hand is that the conclusions of these arguments reappear throughout Nietzsche's work as cultural norms in general. Nietzsche's devaluation of the feminine thus finds expression not only in his contempt for women, but in his devaluation of the feminine as it finds expression in cultural and social terms. The theme of masculine supremacy reappears most dramatically as a "protomacho" motif permeating Nietzsche's positive value schema. I think this wider masculine bias goes unnoticed, at least in part, because Nietzsche inherits many of his prejudices from a Western philosophical tradition whose sexist assumptions are only beginning to be seriously examined and questioned.

The machismo strain in Nietzsche's thought is evident in the way that he correlates the feminine principle with negativity, dissimulation, passivity, and weakness. When Nietzsche warns against a feminization of culture, he is concerned that European culture is becoming soft, domesticated, decorous, and effete. Femininity operates as a negative value pole against which the triumphs of a dominant masculinity can be measured and assessed. Femininity is reproductive; masculinity is productive. Feminine reproduction is achieved by the subordination of will to the forces of nature; masculine productivity is achieved through an action of will to power which masters (rather than submits to) the circumstances in which it finds itself. Femininity represents resignation to circumstance; masculinity, its creative transformation.

As a consequence, Nietzsche's discussion of self-overcoming and self-creation are dominated by masculine metaphors and prescriptions. The dominant metaphor is that of the warrior, with its attendant combat prescription. Nietzsche's vision of the social conflict of values is a battle-field vision in which ideas and perspectives clash in a war for positions of advantage and dominance. History is read as a series of conquests of the weak by the strong; interpersonal relations are understood on the model of master and slave. Given the combative character of the human world, the good thinker will need the qualities that make for a good warrior. The good thinker, like the good warrior, must be strong mentally and physically, cunning, daring, and self-sufficient, i.e., capable of surviving alone in the "wilderness" without the comforts of civilization. The good thinker is one who can eschew the company of others, not needing their comfort or protection; is vigorous, tenacious, capable of using force when necessary, being hard, a creature of will without bourgeois sentiment; and has no need of the domesticated virtues of compassion, generosity, and nurture—these are at best havens returned to once the battle is won, pleasant, restorative interludes between campaigns.

It is thus no accident that Nietzsche's philosopher warrior, like Plato's philosopher king, is a male figure. If philosophy is understood as combat, women (and the feminine sphere) must be left behind as one goes forth to do battle. The philosopher is male because philosophical activity is conceived in prototypical male terms, by appeal to the most radical case of differentiation of function by gender. Such metaphors do more harm than good, because of both their erroneous assumptions about sexual essentialism and the positive practices they suggest to philosophers.

Our age inherits this metaphor, which dramatically affects, in my view, the way in which contemporary philosophers do their philosophizing. The task of philosophical analysis and criticism is often conceived of as the development of a line of attack on one's opponent's position. We take potshots, which aim at poking holes in the enemy argument, or blowing it apart all together. We come armed with a corps of experts to help enforce our position. In philosophy, as in battle, there is often strength in numbers. We hope that if our argument is well-mounted and well-supported, its force will move the audience to our position, further weakening our opponent and empowering us. There is no place for sympathy or compassion here. One's position must be protected from enemy incursions. One's guard must never drop, lest it be taken for weakness. In philosophy, as on the battlefield, winning becomes crucial, especially when failure to master one's opponents results in one's own subordination and defeat.

The questions raised by Nietzsche's proto-masculine ethic do, therefore, extend beyond his discussion of women to the very analysis of philosophy itself. The question is whether we, as philosophers, choose to be dominated by Nietzsche's metaphors and live our lives in the combat zone, or whether we choose to try and free ourselves from his prejudices so that we can reenvision philosophical activity in terms which do not embody indefensible assumptions about the essential or eternal feminine and its masculine opposite. Authentic thinking, I most sincerely believe, proceeds best when it has moved beyond such prejudices.

What is valuable about reading Nietzsche, however, is that he provides us with the means with which to surpass what is uncarefully thought and unjustified in his work. His emphasis on the power of individuals to create themselves through a process of commitment and will offers one road past an essentialist conception of masculinity and femininity, and its reproduction as an arbitrary system of privilege in both the social and philosophical spheres. I believe, in the end, that Nietzsche's sexual politics betray his best insights, as well as what is best in the Western tradition of which he and we are a part. But just as Nietzsche used rational thought to reevaluate the history of rational thinking, so we can use Nietzsche as an occasion for reexamining his own sexist assumptions. In so doing, we will be led to envision ourselves and our activity in ways which exceed the limits of Nietzsche's vision, and yet proceed in the spirit of his philosophy.

Notes

1. See "Of Old and Young Women" in *Thus Spoke Zarathustra* (Z), trans. R. J. Hollingdale (Baltimore: Penguin, 1969).

2. Walter Kaufmann, *Nietzsche: Philosopher, Psychologist and Anti-Christ*, (Princeton: Princeton University Press, 1974), p. 84.

3. Ibid.

4. For some examples see: *Beyond Good and Evil* (BGE), trans. Walter Kaufmann (New York: Vintage, 1966), secs. 84, 86, 115, 131. See also: *On the Genealogy of Morals* (GM), trans. Walter Kaufmann (New York: Vintage, 1967), III, secs. 1, 14; see also "Of Chastity," "Of the Friend," and "Of the Higher Men" in *Thus Spoke Zarathustra*; see also *The Gay Science* (GS), trans. Walter Kaufmann (New York: Random House, 1974), secs. 67, 69, 72, 312.

5. For some examples see: *The Gay Science*, secs. 64–66, 74, 203, 361; see also *Beyond Good and Evil*, secs. 232–39 and *Thus Spoke Zarathustra*, "On the Spirit of Gravity" and "Second Dance Song."

6. See *Ecce Homo (EC)*, trans. Walter Kaufmann (New York: Vintage, 1967), Part III; see also: *Beyond Good and Evil*, secs. 232–39.

7. *The Gay Science*, sec. 119.

8. *Beyond Good and Evil*, secs. 85, 131, 238; *The Gay Science*, sec. 363.

9. *Beyond Good and Evil*, secs. 85, 232, 239.

10. *The Gay Science*, sec. 65.

11. *On the Genealogy of Morals*, III, sec. 8.

12. *The Gay Science*, sec. 363.

13. See "Concrete Relations with Others" in *Being and Nothingness*, trans. Hazel Barnes (New York: Washington Square Press, 1969).

14. *Beyond Good and Evil*, sec. 232.

15. Ibid., sec. 238.

16. Ibid., sec. 233.

17. Ibid., sec. 239.

18. Ibid., secs. 127, and 239.

19. Ibid., sec. 144.

9

Nietzsche's Misogyny

Maudemarie Clark

I want to begin by saying something about how I came to write this paper. I originally agreed to write it for a session of the North American Nietzsche Society on Nietzsche and Feminism, not because I knew what I wanted to say on the topic, but because I thought I should have something to say. I have been thinking and writing very sympathetically about Nietzsche for many years, during all of which I have considered myself a feminist. Yet many other people seem to believe that a Nietzschean feminist is a contradiction in terms—or at least close to that. Surely, I thought, I should be able to say something about why I do not.

At that point, however, I think my Nietzschean unconscious took over and asked: but why defend yourself if you can attack instead? Or that at least is how one might be tempted to interpret the question that seized

me to begin exploring in this paper. It was not: how can I be a Nietzschean and a feminist? but rather: why hasn't a feminist form of Nietzsche's philosophy been developed in the Anglo-American academic, and
especially the philosophical, world?

The two thinkers of the last century who rival Nietzsche in importance
and scope—namely, Marx and Freud—have given rise to Anglo-American forms of Feminism. Why hasn't Nietzsche? It is hardly plausible that
Nietzsche offers feminists nothing on a par with Freud's account of gender or Marx's account of the role of economic factors. Surely power and
empowerment, of which Nietzsche is the great theorist, are extremely
important concerns to feminists. And his analysis of resentment should
be useful to feminists for understanding much of what has been said and
done against women.

I do not want to deny that individual feminists have shown an interest
in Nietzsche, sometimes even signs of his influence on them, nor that
Nietzschean forms of feminism have been developed by French feminists
and others working under the influence of French post-structuralism. But
among feminists working in the Anglo-American philosophical tradition,
there seems to be no widespread interest in Nietzsche's work, nothing
comparable, for instance, to the interest in Nietzsche one now finds
among those doing ethics in that tradition, and certainly no general recognition of Nietzsche as a resource for feminist analysis.

I had hoped to use this paper to run through a number of possible
explanations for this state of affairs until I arrived at the one I still consider most promising: that Nietzsche is a self-proclaimed immoralist
whereas feminism seems to be an essentially moral position. However, I
never got that far, for I was waylaid by the interesting material that
emerged when I began looking at the first explanation that occurred to
me, namely, that perhaps Anglo-American feminists have been too put
off by Nietzsche's misogyny to take his thought seriously. And that is
how I found myself writing a paper on Nietzsche's misogyny.

This came as somewhat of a surprise, for I have always taken Nietzsche's misogyny for granted, but never considered it very important or
interesting. After all, misogyny distinguishes Nietzsche from few other
male writers of his time, and in contrast to, for instance, Freud's phallocentric prejudices masquerading as science, Nietzsche's misogynistic comments have probably done little actual harm to women. His nasty
comments about women have always seemed to me a reflection not of his
basic ideas, but of his understandable, if human, all-too-human need for

revenge against Lou Salomé. And Nietzsche himself gives us the theoretical resources to understand them in this way.

On the other hand, some interpreters claim to find a connection between Nietzsche's misogyny and some of his other ideas—his celebration of the will to power, for instance—and I myself have always been bothered by his most vitriolic comments on women, the so-called "truths about woman as such" Nietzsche puts forward in the closing sections of *Beyond Good and Evil*'s Part VII. The "Seven Little Sayings on Woman" of BG 237[1] seem tastelessly, almost obscenely, nasty. These include: "How the longest boredom flees, when a man comes crawling on his knees." And "Science and old age at length give weak virtue, too, some strength." Even worse is the insult of section 238 that woman is to be conceived of as "a possession, as property that can be locked, as something predestined for service and achieving her perfection in that." Nietzsche also seems to express contempt for feminism throughout these sections on woman, and to present anti-feminism as central to his thought. So I decided to use this paper as an opportunity to finally look carefully at this material, to see how bad, and how connected to his other ideas, it really is.

What I discovered is that I had underestimated Nietzsche—certainly not for the first time—and that the misogyny of Part VII of BG is not the simple and straightforward matter it appears to be. I will not be able to examine here the range of passages I would have to consider to make a claim about Nietzsche's misogyny as such. Confining myself to *Beyond Good and Evil* VII, I shall argue that the misogyny exhibited there is on the level of sentiment, *not belief,* and that it is used by Nietzsche to illustrate points he is trying to make about philosophy and the will to truth. I also want to suggest—though I will not have time to present the full argument—that we interpret BG VII's comments on feminism not as a rejection of feminism, but as a challenge to feminists to exhibit virtues comparable to what Nietzsche exhibits in dealing with his misogyny.

Part VII of *Beyond Good and Evil* is titled "Our Virtues." "Our virtues?" it begins.

> It is probable that we, too, still have our virtues, although in all fairness they will not be the simpleminded and foursquare virtues for which we hold our grandfathers in honor—and at arm's length. We Europeans of the day after tomorrow, we first-born of the twentieth century—with all our dangerous curiosity, our

multiplicity and art of disguises, our mellow, and, as it were, sweetened cruelty in spirit and senses—*if* we should have virtues, we shall presumably have only virtues that have learned to get along best with our most secret and cordial inclinations, with our most ardent needs. Well, then, let us look for them in our labyrinths—where as is well known, all sorts of things lose themselves, all sorts of things are lost for good.

Part VII thus sets out to search for *our* virtues—Nietzsche's, of course, and the philosophers to whom the book is addressed—the same ones who are asked in its first section: "*What* is it in us that wants truth?"

This question—probably the leading question of *Beyond Good and Evil*—does not receive its full answer until the sections immediately preceding the statement of Nietzsche's "truths" about "woman as such" at the end of Part VII. If we wish to understand these so-called "truths" in their context, it should occur to us that their placement is very strange unless they are intimately connected to what Nietzsche is trying to tell us about both virtue and the will to truth, and that perhaps, as I want to suggest, his "truths" about woman constitute a labyrinth in which we are meant to find the threads of Nietzsche's own virtue.

Beyond Good and Evil 227 leaves little doubt as to what Nietzsche considers "our" main virtue. Honesty, he says, is the "virtue from which we cannot get away, we free spirits," and he calls upon us to "work on it with all our malice and love and not weary of 'perfecting' ourselves in *our* virtue, the only one left us," so that its splendor may "one day remain spread out like a gilded blue mocking evening light over this aging culture and its musty and gloomy seriousness."

So I began to wonder if Nietzsche's truths about "woman as such" could be designed to illustrate for us the virtue of honesty. He certainly seems to be attempting honesty when he prefaces them with the well-known warning that "these are after all only—*my* truths." However, it is unclear exactly what this is supposed to mean. If Nietzsche claims that his comments about woman are true, he can't sensibly claim that they are true only for him. So the warning that these are "only *my* truths" may be Nietzsche's way of disclaiming the belief that his mysogynistic comments are true. I think we find a great deal of evidence for this interpretive hypothesis if we look at the warning's immediate context. On the issue of man and woman, Nietzsche writes, a thinker cannot relearn but only finish learning, only discover ultimately how this is "settled in him." At times we find certain solutions of problems that inspire strong faith in *us;* some call them henceforth *their* "convictions." Later—we see them as only steps to self-knowledge, sign-posts to the problem we *are*—rather to the great stupidity we are, to our spiritual *fatum,* to what is *unteachable* very 'down deep.' (BG 231)

This is immediately followed by the warning in question:

After this abundant civility that I have just evidenced in relation to myself I shall perphaps be permitted more readily to state a few truths about "woman as such"—assuming that it is known from the outset how very much these are after all only —*my* truths.

In other words, that these are "only [his] truths" should already be clear to us from the comments that evidence Nietzsche's "abundant civility" in relation to himself. Those comments told us that what thinkers have to say about man and woman merely express their convictions, and that convictions express the great stupidity they are, and are only steps to self-knowledge, sign-posts to the problem they are. Nietzsche thus admits in effect that his so-called "truths" about woman as such are really expressions of the great stupidity he is, and are therefore more likely to produce self-knowledge—if understood and analyzed appropriately—than knowledge of the world (in this case, of women).

At the very least, Nietzsche is letting us know that he is not claiming that his comments on woman are true. Some interpreters may find nothing puzzling in this, for they think that Nietzsche denies that any beliefs are true. But I have argued at length elsewhere that Nietzsche overcame this kind of nihilism in his later works,[2] and I can find no other basis he would have for denying that making an assertion involves putting it forward as true. So I am left with the puzzle of what his point could be when he makes assertions about woman after letting us know that he does not consider them true.

I start with the observation that Nietzsche would be able to use these assertions to express his feelings toward woman—for instance, his anger and resentment—even if he does not consider them true. The use of assertions we do not believe in an attempt to hurt those we love or are dependent upon is hardly uncommon among human beings, especially when in particularly childish moods. This suggests a way to make sense of Nietzsche's "Seven Little Sayings on Woman," which seem so unlike anything else he wrote and have always reminded me of children calling each other names and sticking out their tongues at each other. That, I now see, suits them perfectly to play the role of easily recognized expressions of resentment.

Who could fail to recognize the resentment in, for instance: "How the longest boredom flees, when a man comes crawling on his knees." And since these "little sayings" do not even have the grammatical form of assertions about woman, it is clear that we cannot simply read them as Nietzsche's beliefs about woman. Instead, we must arrive at these beliefs through a process of interpretation which requires us to consider what his point is in reciting for us these sayings about woman. (It is not even clear whose "little sayings" they are; they might be simply common sayings that BG 237 in effect quotes.)[3] Nietzsche's "Little Sayings On Woman" can therefore serve to warn us that his "truths" about "woman as such," the ones that do have the form of assertions about woman, also require interpretation, and that they might also be expressions of resentment disguised as beliefs. Nietzsche's "truths" about woman might serve to exhibit for us (and to express) his misogynistic feelings, even though he is honest enough to admit that the assertions these feelings inspire are not really true.

I would find this strategy for interpreting Nietzsche's misogynistic comments problematic—because too open to abuse—if it required us to deny that Nietzsche means or believes what he actually says about woman. But I think the interpretation I have suggested can be reformulated so that it avoids this problem. It requires only that we read Nietzsche very carefully and distinguish what he actually asserts from what the reader is likely to conclude (erroneously) from his assertions.

When Nietzsche asserts that woman does not *want* truth, that "her great art is the lie, her highest concern is mere appearance and beauty" (232), for instance, most readers will assume he means that women do not want truth. In fact, however, he is writing not about women, but about "woman as such," which he also calls "the eternal feminine." He is referring to the feminine essence, a social construction that individual women need not exemplify. The German that Kaufmann translates as "woman as such" is "*das Weib an sich*" or woman in herself. Given BG's central claim that *das Ding an sich* (BG 16) is a contradiction in terms, Nietzsche's use of the phrase "*das Weib an sich*" cannot be accidental. He is probably suggesting that our idea of the "eternal feminine" also in-volves a contradiction in terms, and therefore that no woman could really exemplify it. But I must leave this consideration for another time. In any case, though we might want to disagree with Nietzsche about what the common understanding of femininity involves, once we see that his truths about woman as such are about this construction rather than about individual women—especially if he thinks it involves a contradiction in terms—it is difficult to read them as either misogynistic or anti-feminist.

BG 238's claim that woman must be conceived as a possession is a slightly more complicated matter. Nietzsche actually claims that this is how woman must always be thought of by any man who has depth in his spirit as well as his desires, "including that depth of benevolence that is capable of severity and hardness." It seems to me clear that he is talking about how such a man must think of individual women insofar as he thinks of them as exemplifications of *das Weib an sich*, of the eternal feminine. This has no implications for how Nietzsche must think of women given his skepticism about such essences.

But why does Nietzsche think that a man of depth and benevolence must think of woman as a possession? Contrary to some interpretations of this passage,[4] I find no evidence in it, nor in any section of BG VII, that Nietzsche thinks a patriarchal structure is necessary for the existence of higher culture.[5] He does say it is worth pondering how necessary and even humanly desirable it was that the Greeks became more severe against woman as "their culture increased along with the extent of their power" (*Kraft*). I think the emphasis here is on the increase in the ability of males to use force against women.

This passage begins by calling "shallow" those who deny "the most abysmal antagonism" between man and woman, and the necessity of an "eternally hostile tension." I take the claim to be that such eternal hostil-ity exists between men and women insofar as they see themselves as em-bodiments of the eternal masculine and feminine. So it makes sense for Nietzsche to say that a man of depth and benevolence must think of embodiments of the eternal feminine as property, if Nietzsche thinks, as I assume he does, that this would be the best protection available to those cast in the role of the eternal feminine against the worst abuses of male hostility and power. He may be wrong about this, of course, but he nei-ther says nor implies that women should accept for themselves the status of property. Therefore, I do not see his claim here as anti-feminist.

In fact, if we read Part VII carefully, we will see that nothing in it asserts or entails that women should not seek their own enlightenment and emancipation from traditional sex roles and power struggles. Nietzsche's most explicit claim against such attempts is that they involve a "corruption of the instincts" (233) and a loss of "the sense for the ground on which one is most certain of victory" (239). Readers can be expected to conclude from such claims that Nietzsche is against the emancipation of women, and that he thinks he has reason to be.

But careful readers of Part VII will find that its earlier sections give grounds for making exactly parallel arguments against those who seek truth, and that Nietzsche nevertheless encourages their search. I will consider his claims about the will to truth in some detail in order to exhibit the parallel I have suggested that Nietzsche sets up between truth-seekers and feminists, and to answer another question I am sure many will wish to pose. This question is why, if I am at all right about his actual assertions, did Nietzsche go out of his way to make his comments on woman in these passages appear misogynist and anti-feminist.

The two sections immediately preceding BG 231's warning that these are "only *my* truths" finally answer the book's initial question: *what* is it in us that wants truth? 229 tells us that "Almost everything we call 'higher culture' is based on the spiritualization of cruelty, on its becoming more profound: this is my proposition." When applied to those who seek knowledge, this proposition becomes the claim that "Any insistence on profundity and thoroughness" in matters of knowledge, i.e., any will to truth, "is a violation, a desire to hurt the basic will of the spirit which unceasingly strives for the apparent and superficial."

BG 230 seeks to clarify this claim. It presents the desire for theoretical knowledge as an expression of the will to power.[6] The theoretician originally wants not truth, but to "appropriate the foreign," to "assimilate the new to the old, to simplify the manifold and to overlook or repulse whatever is totally contradictory." What is wanted, Nietzsche summarizes, is growth, "or, more precisely, the feeling of growth, the feeling of increased power." While intellectual appropriation may happen upon truth, it is too easily satisfied with a sense of mastery to exhibit a will to truth, i.e., an "insistence on profundity and thoroughness" in matters of knowledge. So it should be no surprise that Nietzsche thinks the will that leads to theorizing is served by an apparently opposite drive, which produces "a suddenly erupting decision in favor of ignorance, a satisfaction with the dark, with the limiting horizons, a Yea and Amen to ignorance—all of which is necessary in proportion to a spirit's power to appropriate, its 'digestive capacity.'"

But, then, to repeat Nietzsche's original question: if philosophers can be so easily satisfied with the dark and the superficial, what in them wants truth? The answer, given in BG 231, is that it is their cruelty, their will to power turned against itself. To develop a will to truth, Nietzsche is claiming, the spirit has to deprive itself of what it most wants: a sense of power or mastery of the world. It has to discipline itself to give up what it wants to believe—because of the sense of power belief would give—for the sake of what it has reason to believe. In so disciplining itself, according to Nietzsche's theory, the spirit still gets a sense of mastery, but it is mastery of the self rather than of the world.

But if the basic will of the spirit aims at mastery of the world (which I take to be equivalent to the non-self), how can it give that up for the sake of mastery of itself? I think Nietzsche's answer is that it can do so only if it interprets its power over self as power over the world. He claims, most explicitly in his GM, that the will to truth is the latest expression of the ascetic ideal, that thinkers have been able to commit themselves to giving up what they want to believe for the sake of what they have reason to believe only under the auspices of the ascetic ideal.[7]

The ascetic ideal is a life-devaluing ideal, which gives priests and philosophers a sense of mastering the material and temporal world precisely because it devalues that world, by treating it as a mere instrument or expression of the spiritual and eternal world with which comptemplative types identify. According to Nietzsche's story, however, this same ideal finally forbids itself the "lie involved" in belief in God, in metaphysics and in any spiritual or eternal world, thus leaving us with what BG 230 calls the "strange and insane task" of translating human beings back into nature, of interpreting their activities, virtues, and value in completely naturalistic terms. Part VII carries out this task in its account of honesty as an expression of cruelty.

Nietzsche calls "insane" the task of understanding philosophers and their honesty in naturalistic terms, I think, because he believes that the will to power was able to became a will to truth only insofar as honesty or truthfulness was interpreted in ascetic terms, as the overcoming of nature. The naturalistic interpretation of honesty to which truthfulness itself leads therefore involves the "insane" task of undercutting its own psychological support or attacking the ground on which it has been standing.

Truthful philosophers are therefore in a position even worse than the one Nietzsche ascribes to feminists, that of abandoning the ground on which they are most sure of victory. Philosophers probably abandoned the ground on which they were most sure of victory, on Nietzsche's view, when they abandoned God and metaphysics. And now he expects them to admit that their truthfulness is just a matter of their willingness to be cruel to themselves. This surely involves at least as much corruption of the instincts that have protected and furthered the interest of contemplative types—whom Nietzsche describes in GM (III: 10) as originally living under a tremendous "*oppression* of valuation"—as feminism involves a corruption of the instincts that have protected and furthered the interests of those forced to play the role of the "eternal feminine."

Yet, far from encouraging us to abandon our truthfulness, Nietzsche calls on us to perfect it, in the passage on "our virtue" I quote earlier. But how can we perfect our honesty without the support of the ascetic ideal? I have elsewhere interpreted Nietzsche's *Genealogy* as claiming that we need a new ideal for our truthfulness to serve.[8] Some of the thinking behind Nietzsche's claim is revealed by BG 227, the passage on "our virtue." Here Nietzsche suggests that, to get the help we will need in maintaining and perfecting the virtue of honesty, we dispatch to the assistance of our honesty "whatever we have in us of devilry . . . our subtlest, most disguised, most spiritual will to power and overcoming of the world . . . let us come to the assistance of our 'gods' with our 'devils.' " In other words, honesty needs the support of a sense of power over the world, and perfecting it therefore requires new sources for the sense of power philosophers previously acquired from their acceptance of the ascetic ideal.

One way of achieving a sense of power discussed in BG 230 is the "by no means unproblematic readiness of the spirit to deceive other spirits and to dissimilate in front of them." In this, Nietzsche writes, "the spirit enjoys the multiplicity and craftiness of its masks, it also enjoys the feeling of its security behind them: after all, it is surely its Protean arts that defend and conceal it best." If the interpretation I have offered is on the right track, Nietzsche must think of himself as employing precisely this strategy when he conceals from us what he is actually asserting about women and feminism—while leaving it fully accessible to the careful reader. Nietzsche thus illustrates for us what it means to bring our "devils" to the support of our "gods," and thus the kind of support he thinks the will to truth will need once we completely abandon the ascetic ideal.

In playing this game of concealment, Nietzsche is not, or not only, having fun at the expense of women and feminists. Misogyny is a particularly good issue with which to illustrate BG's claim about the future of our honesty, our will to truth. By expressing misogynistic sentiments, Nietzsche shows us that he has an interest in believing things about women that would justify those sentiments. What would justify such sentiments is precisely his "truths" about "woman as such," if they were truths about women. We can therefore interpret Nietzsche's comments about "woman as such" in Part VII of BG as overcoming what he would like to believe about women, out of his commitment to truth.

If this interpretation is correct, Nietzsche's comments on "woman as such" *exhibit* his honesty at work more clearly than anything else in BG, because nothing else shows us so clearly the conflict between what he would like to believe and what he knows he has reason to believe. So Nietzsche can bring out here, more vividly than he could otherwise, the issue of what allows him to be honest, to overcome his desire to believe, given his rejection of the ascetic ideal, all moral posturing, and all ascetic conceptions of virtue. This is, I think, the major role of play in Nietzsche—not a substitute for truth, as post-modernists sometimes seem to think, but an activity that supports truthfulness in its non-ascetic reincarnation that Nietzsche here attempts to promote. Play can also function as a sublimation of resentment, which Nietzsche also exhibits here.

In conclusion, let me make clear that I am not saying that Nietzsche is a feminist, or denying that he had problems with nineteenth-century feminism and would have them with contemporary feminism. The issue for him would still be, as BG 232 suggests, whether women really want enlightenment about themselves, whether we can will it. This means: whether we are willing to understand ourselves and our virtues in completely naturalistic terms and to promote feminism without the help of the ascetic ideal and what Nietzsche calls "moral tinsel words" (BG 230). Whether or not Nietzsche is anti-feminist ultimately comes down to whether a feminism beyond good and evil can and will be developed.[9] This is an issue for the future. But feminists interested in this possibility could do worse than to look both seriously and with a sense of humor at Nietzsche's attempt to turn resentment into laughter in *Beyond Good and Evil* VII.

Notes

1. I use "BG" to refer to *Jenseits von Gut un Böse* and "GM" for *Zur Genealogie der Moral*. I follow Kaufmann's translations, but I have, however, made several changes based on the Colli-Montinari

Studienausgabe: Friedrich Nietzsche (Berlin: de Gruyter, 1980). The translation of *Sprüchlein* as "little saying" rather than "epigram" in this sentence is a case in point. See note 3 for more on this choice.

2. See Maudemarie Clark, *Nietzsche on Truth and Philosophy* (Cambridge: Cambridge University Press, 1990), especially chapters 3–6, pp. 63–125.

3. That Nietzsche is in effect quoting sayings about women is suggested by the fact that unlike other sections of the book, BG 237 is given a title (namely, "Seven Little Sayings on Woman"). I owe this observation to Peter Burgard, who also pointed out to me that Kaufmann's translation of *Sprüchlein* as "epigram" (rather than "little saying") does not adequately capture the diminutive form of the original. Because of the association of Nietzsche himself with "epigrams," Kaufmann's translation also makes it easier to assume that the point of these sayings is to express Nietzsche's own beliefs. I do not find it plausible, however, that Nietzsche is simply quoting these sayings from the surrounding culture without any suggestion that he accepts them too, because not making it clear that he is simply quoting such nasty sayings sets up a presumption that he accepts them. We can explain why Nietzsche would set up this presumption, while at the same time leaving clues that we cannot interpret his sayings as straightforward expressions of his own beliefs, if we interpret them instead as expressions of his feelings.

4. For instance, see Ofelia Schutte, *Beyond Nihilism. Nietzsche Without Masks* (Chicago: University of Chicago Press, 1984), pp. 162, 178–180.

5. In fact, he suggests early in Part VII (BG 223) that given our "historical sense" and consequent willingness to dissect history to study the "costumes" of culture—i.e., the "moralities, articles of faith, tastes in arts, and religion"—perhaps nothing today has any future except our laughter. Among the "articles of faith" which have been dissected by those with a "historical sense" and which Nietzsche here suggests may have no future must certainly be included the naturalness and justice of a patriarchal structure.

6. See Chapter 7 of *Nietzsche on Truth and Philosophy*, pp. 205–244, for my interpretation of Nietzsche's claims about the will to power.

7. See Chapter 6 of *Nietzsche on Truth and Philosophy*, pp. 159–203, for my account of Nietzsche's claims concerning the ascetic ideal.

8. See the end of Chapter 6 of *Nietzsche on Truth and Philosophy*, pp. 193–203.

9. One attempt in that direction is Wendy Brown, "Feminist Hesitations, Postmodern Exposures," *differences: A Journal of Feminist Cultural Studies* 3:1 (1990): 63–84. Others are surely possible, e.g., ones that do not depend on a post-modernist critique of truth.

10

Sexual Dualism and Women's Self-Creation: On the Advantages and Disadvantages of Reading Nietzsche for Feminists

Lynne Tirrell

There is much to hate in what Nietzsche says about women, particularly if one follows Nietzsche's own advice and approaches his writings like cold baths—"quickly into them and quickly out again" (KSA 3:634; GS §381, p. 343). When Nietzsche says that a woman's "first and last profession" is "to give birth to strong children" (KSA 5:177; BGE §239, p. 169), for example, he is bound to alienate those who do not think that any person is reducible to one biological function. As awful as some of what Nietzsche has said about women is (and that example is not the worst), this essay is neither a tirade about his inherent misogynism nor an apology for some of his more virulent remarks.[1] It has been well documented that Nietzsche's writings deliver an unhealthy dose of misogyny, but it has not been generally noticed that they also contain the seeds of a deconstruction of that misogyny.

This paper will expose one set of deconstructing elements of Nietzsche's works with respect to his views on women. I shall argue that the wider philosophical context of Nietzsche's thought provides grounds for taking seriously several passages of *The Gay Science* that reveal a more sympathetic understanding of women, since these passages take seriously Nietzsche's antidualism, his perspectivism, and his early existentialist notion of the self. Once we see the destabilizing force of these passages and understand Nietzsche's remarks about women within this philosophical context, we will see that Nietzsche's works promise more insight than many feminists have previously noted. In particular, his attack on dualisms in *Beyond Good and Evil*, the discussions of the power of discourse that run through *The Gay Science* and beyond, the discussions of the importance of power that run through all his texts, are but a few of the issues of shared concern for Nietzsche and for many feminists. As this paper will suggest, a feminist analysis of these issues promises to inform contemporary feminist concerns about the importance of women's articulating our lives.

While considering Nietzsche's ideas about women in light of his broader philosophical positions, particularly his existentialist notion of the self, I shall compare his view to that of Simone de Beauvoir, whose work I shall argue he might have anticipated had he been more concerned with the internal consistency of his work. I will not be arguing the silly thesis that Nietzsche fails us because he was not Beauvoir, but later in the paper I will highlight a few key similarities and differences between them in order to illuminate the potential that lies within Nietzsche's work for feminists. It is significant that both Nietzsche and Beauvoir were concerned with their own need to tell the stories of their lives, working on the borderland between philosophy and literature, and that both tried to recreate the self that was telling in the process of the articulation.[2]

There are two distinct interpretive issues to contend with in coming to terms with Nietzsche's conception of women. First, there is the issue of how Nietzsche takes the question of the nature of and relation between the sexes to be "settled in him" (KSA 5:170; BGE §231, p. 162), and second, there is the issue of what his writings suggest about what the nature of and relation between the sexes is. In Nietzsche's case, the answers to the first question are overtly misogynistic, hostile, and shallow.

Nietzsche's most overtly misogynist remarks miss the point of his more general philosophical attack on dualism and ignore his attempt to articulate an existentialist conception of the self. More important, the answers to the second question suggest a much more sympathetic conception of woman, which sees her as created by socialization and by her having been defined in contrast to man. Taken together, we see that the two aspects of Nietzsche's thought on women create a tension in his writing that defies any definitive classification of his view.

Nietzsche himself would probably have us focus on his explicit statements about women; as *Ecce Homo* shows, Nietzsche took great pride in his authorial control, and these remarks are, after all, purposefully included in his texts. Most of these statements show little or no respect for women, and some passages argue that this is a view for which he should be held accountable. Consider, for example, *Beyond Good and Evil* 238, where he writes, "to go wrong on the fundamental problem of 'man and woman,' to deny the most abysmal antagonism between them and the necessity of an eternally hostile tension, to dream perhaps of equal rights, equal education, equal claims and obligations—that is a *typical* sign of shallowness, and a thinker who has proved shallow in this dangerous place—shallow in his instinct—may be considered altogether suspicious, even more—betrayed, exposed: probably he will be too 'short' for all fundamental problems of life, of the life yet to come, too, and incapable of attaining *any* depth" (KSA 5:175; BGE §238, pp. 166–67). As Kaufmann has pointed out, it is a good thing for Nietzsche that he is wrong about this, for in this passage Nietzsche displays the very shallowness he so condemns.[3] If we agree with Nietzsche on this, we will dismiss him unfairly as a poor thinker, and we will miss the insights his texts would lend to our own projects.[4]

Nietzsche's works present a complex character who took himself to hold a very negative view of women but who was not philosophically entitled to hold this view. Add to that his remarks about the importance of dissimulation, and it becomes ever more difficult to discern what Nietzsche really thought. Although Nietzsche is preoccupied with the self that he is creating through writing his books, he also is aware that the books may outstrip even the character created there.[5] So, let us take seriously Nietzsche's claim that "one does best to separate an artist from his work, not taking him as seriously as his work" (KSA 5:343; GM—III §4, p. 100), but this still leaves us with the interpretive question about which elements of the work to emphasize. Since the preponderance of work done on Nietzsche's views on women has focused on its misogynist elements, I will develop the other, nonmisogynist, side of Nietzsche's view. I hope to give Nietzsche's texts the most sympathetic reading possible, by showing how what he usually says about women fails to fit some of his deeper philosophical views and by highlighting what he says, but rarely, which *does* fit with these deeper philosophical views. If this sympathetic reading is plausible, then perhaps other of Nietzsche's views will become more accessible to feminist readers.

Nietzsche's condemnations of women tend to fall into two categories. He condemns them sometimes for their *nature* and sometimes for allowing themselves to be slaves to men. The first sort of criticism suggests an essentialist conception of woman's nature. Some passages clearly support this essentialist reading; consider Nietzsche's claim that "woman is *essentially* unpeaceful, like a cat, however well she may have trained herself to seem peaceful" (KSA 5:96; BGE §131, p. 87). Invoking the distinction between nature and nurture, Nietzsche suggests that women, deep down, have an unchangeable nature.[6] Passages such as this notwithstanding, it would be hypocritical for Nietzsche to rely upon an essentialist conception of women's nature, since his philosophy is so thoroughly antiessentialist. Here we must look at Nietzsche's doctrine in *Beyond Good and Evil* and in *The Gay Science* that what a thing is called is immeasurably more important than what it is, a discussion that anticipates the Sapir-Whorf hypothesis and later feminist discussions of the power of naming.[7] Nietzsche's conception of the nature of a thing is existentialist, and understanding this conception will help us to see that these condemnatory remarks of the first kind actually collapse into the second category: Nietzsche reviles women for being slaves to men. Women have not taken enough control of their self-creation. To understand this position, we must look briefly at Nietzsche's discussion of master/slave relations and the creation of the self. In the end we will see that although Nietzsche engages in blaming the victim and does not come anywhere near to developing a positive feminist conception of women's situation, we can nevertheless see that his work anticipated important aspects of Beauvoir's discussion of man as Self and woman as Other and the problems inherent in women's accepting this status.

The first section of this paper offers a sketch of Nietzsche's attack on dualism, using his discussion of the distinction between conscious and unconscious thought as an example. In the second section, I apply Nietzsche's attack on dualism to the dualist opposition between the sexes.

These two sections show one aspect of Nietzsche's thought that is worth appropriation (with expansion) by feminists. In the third section I set out Nietzsche's nonmisogynist conception of woman. This conception, bearing the marks of early existentialism, is in many ways a precursor to today's social-constructivist conceptions of the self.[8] It is marked by a sensitivity to the sexual situation of the upper-class women of Nietzsche's day and it suggests that Nietzsche was aware of and did not condone the injustice of a society that creates such women and such situations. Amazingly, Nietzsche was able to draw the connection between destructive forms of heterosexuality and the silencing of women.

Nietzsche's Attack on Dualism

Nietzsche's first philosophical work was dualist and realist in its conception: *The Birth of Tragedy* is dualist in that Nietzsche maintains a distinction between appearance and reality; it is realist in that he maintains that the (real) world has a character independent of any description of it.[9] Nietzsche goes even further than this, however, for he does not merely echo the traditional claim that appearance is different from underlying reality—Nietzsche claims that appearance is the very contrary of reality. The character of the appearance was developed in direct opposition to the reality underlying it. The cheerfulness of the Greeks was, for example, a reaction to their underlying terror brought on by their deeper understanding of the "primordial contradiction and primordial pain in the heart of the primal unity" (KSA 1:51; BT §6, p. 55). Their extreme rationality was a reaction to nature's extreme irrationality. This early dualist metaphysic in *The Birth of Tragedy* is followed in Nietzsche's later writings by an increasingly powerful attack on dualism per se.

In an early section of a late work, Nietzsche writes that there are two sorts of doubts one should have about varieties of dualism: (1) "whether there are any opposites at all," and (2) whether the values placed on purported opposites are accurate or "merely foreground estimates, only provisional perspectives" (KSA 5:16; BGE §2, p. 10). He suggests that what constitutes the value of what is deemed good is that these things are related to their opposites, and "maybe even one with them in essence" (KSA 5:17; BGE §2, p. 10). Nietzsche is willing to explore this sort of possibility, this "dangerous 'maybe' " when it applies to the more standard philosophical oppositions such as good/evil, mind/body, truth/falsity, conscious/unconscious thought, but when it comes to man/woman, Nietzsche has more difficulty toeing his own philosophical line. In this section, we will see what that line is, so that we may see what consistency would require.

Nietzsche's challenge to our belief in the opposition between conscious and unconscious thought begins with the claim that most of conscious thought should still be considered instinctive, even "higher" forms such as philosophical thought (KSA 5:17; BGE §3, p. 11). In section 6 of *Beyond Good and Evil*, he claims that all philosophy to date has been an "unconscious memoir" of its author (KSA 5:19; BGE §6, p. 13), and in section 17 he points out that even our conscious thought, for which we presume to take responsibility, is beyond our control. (He says "a thought comes when 'it' wishes, and not when 'I' wish" [KSA 5:31; BGE §17, p. 24].) This does not mean that all conscious thought can be reduced to instinct. Such a view would make Nietzsche a reductive monist, and Nietzsche is trying to be more radical than this. The reductive monist accepts the legitimacy of the opposition and then reduces one of the two poles to the other. Nietzsche, on the other hand, attacks the very legitimacy of the opposition.[10]

The sort of dualist dogmatism that Nietzsche describes in part 1 of *Beyond Good and Evil* seeks to discredit monism by saying that monism would discredit or taint things of the highest value, on the grounds that it would be a discredit for these highly valued things to arise from the same origins as things of lesser value.[11] If we are to continue holding conscious thought, for which we take responsibility, in high esteem, then we must think of it as having an origin different from that of unconscious thought (which even animals have). Unconscious thought, or instinct, has been traditionally associated with the body, while conscious thought has been associated with the soul. (Notice how one duality involves another.) Nietzsche's nonreductive monism leads him to claim that the soul or mind is not a different kind of substance than the body; it is a *refinement* of the same stuff (no commitment to substances intended). Body is not Descartes's "extended substance" any more than mind is "unextended substance." Nietzsche also rejects the association of the unconscious with the body and the conscious with the soul, saying that "consciousness is the last and latest development of the organic" (KSA 3:382; GS §11, p. 84). In taking consciousness to be "the *kernel* of man," we stunt its growth (KSA 3:382; GS §11, p. 85). Conscious thought, Nietzsche writes, still awaits incorporation into the instinctual level.

This very brief sketch of Nietzsche's discussion of the distinction between conscious and unconscious thought reflects a typical Nietzschean strategy. Nietzsche not only suggests that we need not posit two substances to explain the duality of conscious/unconscious thought, but he also inverts the values of these. Traditionally, conscious thought is valued more highly than unconscious (hence its association with the soul), but Nietzsche associates it with error and treats it like the new kid on the block. Eventually, it will be incorporated. Nietzsche's strategy for disarming the dualist is to claim that the distinction in question is not a distinction in *kind*, but only in degree. One value is not the opposite of the other, but its *refinement*. Further, in taking one value to be primary we reveal our perspective, not something about the world as such, and we exercise our will to power, imposing ourselves on the world. We succumb to this *"faith in opposite values"* (KSA 5:16; BGE §2, p. 10) because it simplifies life (KSA 5:41–42; BGE §24, p. 35), and perhaps even more because it provides such a powerful and tidy vehicle for our exercise of the will to power. In exercising our will to power we create the world in our own image.

Dualism and the Sexes

A parallel treatment of the dualist opposition between man and woman would begin with a recognition of a purported duality between them. That duality would then be attacked. Nietzsche's sexual dualism is apparent even late in *Beyond Good and Evil*, where he says that man and woman are *necessarily* in "an eternally hostile tension" (KSA 5:175; BGE §238, p. 166).[12] It is ironic that this claim appears in a work which attempts a general undermining of dualism and which sets out clearly what is at stake for the philosopher who accepts dualistic metaphysics. Two years later Nietzsche still held fast to the idea of a battle of the sexes, for in *Ecce Homo* he writes: "Has my definition of love been heard? It is the only one worthy of a philosopher. Love—in its means, war; at bottom, the deadly hatred of the sexes" (KSA 6:306; EH p. 267).

Nietzsche recognizes the duality but not its purportedness. What is missing from his works is any direct attack on this variety of dualism. Such an attack would rely on the two questions Nietzsche raises generally about dualism: (1) whether there really is a pair in exclusive opposition, and (2) whether the values assigned to those "opposites" are accurate. Raising these questions with respect to the man/woman duality, it is important today to distinguish between sex, which is a biological category, and gender, which is a psychosocial category. Nietzsche did not articulate this more contemporary distinction between sex and gender, but he did recognize the difference between being female and being a woman, taking the latter to be a socially constructed way of being.

Whether we take "man" and "woman" to designate biologically based sexes or socially based genders, the answer to whether the pair forms an exclusive ontological opposition is no. Today we know that strict biological sexual dualism is false. Most humans are born either male or female, but some researchers estimate that perhaps 5 percent of the population are born with ambiguous genitalia, neither male nor female hormonal structures, etc.[13] A more conservative estimate is one in every 200 to 300 live births.[14] These anatomical "abnormalities" rarely pose any medical risk for the child; nevertheless, usually within seventy-two hours of birth, a sex of rearing is determined for babies born with ambiguous genitalia.[15] Doctors and parents rapidly and surgically impose a sex of rearing because we live in a society in which sexual dualism is the *norm*, and they recognize that living outside that norm would have serious and painful social consequences for the child. Biological sexual dualism is a statistical regularity that we work to make a universal fact. The claim that there are only two genders turns out to be normative as well. Much psychological research suggests that when "masculine" and "feminine" are distinctly defined, few of us fit either category.[16] If we use these categories to anchor the poles of a continuum, it turns out that most people are in the middle, displaying a mixture of masculine and feminine traits. So neither biologically based sexes nor socially based genders form an exclusive ontological opposition.[17]

It is clear that Nietzsche did not take sexual dualism to be an unalterable fact about the world. I say this in anticipation of the following discussion of his more positive view of women, and because in his lambasting the feminist efforts of his contemporaries, Nietzsche argues that they are trying to make men out of women.[18] On an essentialist picture of the sexes, this is not a worry because it cannot be done. Nietzsche's fear that it will be done is of a piece with his antiessentialism.

Women are created as such by interpretations, and the new interpretations offered by his feminist contemporaries were threatening to undermine a way of life to which Nietzsche saw no satisfying alternative (see KSA 3:610–12; GS §363, pp. 318–20). Nietzsche does not explicitly make the distinction between sex and gender, and most of his claims about women are about females whose gender-identity fits their sex. Put anachronistically, Nietzsche holds "woman" to be a socially constructed category. He sees sexual dualism as normative and usually tries to uphold the value of that norm.

In section 239 of *Beyond Good and Evil,* for example, Nietzsche argues that the women's rights movement in Europe will result in a net *decrease* in women's power. By giving up traditional feminine roles, women give up their (currently) greatest source of power. The mistake of the modern woman, he holds, is to "lose the sense for the ground on which one is most certain of victory; to neglect practice with one's proper weapons" (KSA 5:176; BGE §239, p. 168). He calls this "a crumbling of feminine instincts" and a "defeminization" (KSA 5:177; BGE §239, p. 169). This sounds very essentialist, but keeping in mind Nietzsche's thesis that instincts are that part of our thought and judgment which is no longer scrutinized, I would argue that here he is talking about women as a biological category with a socially established gender identity (in part dependent upon that biology) that gives them power. Compare this to Simone de Beauvoir's position in the introduction to *The Second Sex,* where she says that one reason that women really have not fought for our rights as full autonomous human beings is that the only power we have had is this sort of derivative power we get through accepting femininity.[19] If we give that up, we risk losing everything. What is missing in Nietzsche, but not later in Beauvoir, is a recognition of the significance of the other forms of power—real power—that women could attain if dualistic sex roles were eradicated.[20] So although Nietzsche is aware of the distinction between the biological category "human female" and the social category "woman," he does not think through all the complexities of the power issues associated with the sexual dualism that defines the category "woman."

Nietzsche's first challenge to dualism, then, denies that there is any real or substantial difference between the two categories posited as opposites. Men and women are created as such by social interpretations, which embody and reinforce our norms. Nietzsche's second challenge to dualism concerns the accuracy of the assigned valuation of the pair. Applied to this case, the issue is whether accurate values have been assigned to men and women (or to masculinity and femininity). Before we can say whether the values are accurate, we must determine what they are. Nietzsche's own views on the relative valuation of men and women are contradictory. It is important to note at the outset that Nietzsche is no great respecter of any person qua member of a group.

Nietzsche suggests that women are the more esteemed (estimable?) sex when he writes: "Woman is indescribably more evil than man; also cleverer; good nature is in a woman a form of degeneration. . . . Woman, the more she is a woman, resists rights in general hand and foot: after all, the state of nature, the eternal war between the sexes, gives her by far the first rank" (KSA 6:306; EH pp. 266–67). This picture of woman, as one who is of the first rank because she refuses the rights and privileges of full citizenship and social status, is obviously a troubled one. In contemporary feminist terms, it is a reversal. He may *say* that she is of the first rank, but he says it because she makes sure that it is not so.[21] Nietzsche's principal estimation of woman's value emerges in his claim that "comparing man and woman on the whole, one may say: woman would not have the genius for finery if she did not have an instinct for a *secondary* role" (KSA 5:98; BGE §145, p. 89). Nietzsche holds that human instincts are that part of our thought which we have ceased to scrutinize; they are the lessons we have learned too well. Instinct is not part of our immutable nature but rather something created; so Nietzsche's appeal to woman's (supposed) instinct for being secondary marks that secondary status as socially inculcated.

If there were an argument against sexual dualism that followed the basic antidualist account we have seen, it would go something like this: (1) men have traditionally been more highly esteemed than women; (2) men and women are not really different in kind but in fact share the same essence and origins; (3) men and women are not really opposites but one is the refinement of the other; (4) we (men and women) give in to the oversimplification wrought by dualistic sex roles and differential valuation of the sexes because (a) it simplifies life and (b) it provides a vehicle for the exercise of the will to power.

This argument against sexual dualism is not explicit in Nietzsche's writings, but it is clearly an argument Nietzsche should have made. It is an argument that can be supported using Nietzsche's more general argument against dualism, his analysis of the master/slave relation, plus those of his insights about women which I will present in the next section. My point here is not a simple appropriation of Nietzsche's form of argument, nor is it simply exposure of his more positive view of women; I also want to show that there are grounds for feminists to take Nietzsche's wider philosophical thought seriously. Rather than address each premise of this argument individually, I will now turn to Nietzsche's more sympathetic discussion of women. This discussion illustrates Nietzsche's support for the crucial third and fourth premises of the argument against sexual dualism. In addition, this more sensitive conception of women foreshadows many of Beauvoir's and later feminists' insights precisely because it depends upon a basic existentialist account of the self.

An Early Existentialist View of Women

Book 2 of *The Gay Science* presents an important bridge between Nietzsche's early acceptance of dualism in *The Birth of Tragedy* and his later rejection of dualism in *Beyond Good and Evil*. Here, in the second book, Nietzsche grapples with the question of realism, beginning with a somewhat scattered but surprisingly insightful discussion of women and ending with a discussion of the ontological power of language. I said earlier that although Nietzsche is aware that "woman" is a category created through social interpretation, he does not think through all the complexities of the power issues associated with the sexual dualism that defines that category. (He does, however, seem to react to them.)[22] Let's turn now to Nietzsche's two most sensitive discussions of women's situation, both found in book 2 of *The Gay Science*.

In section 68 of *The Gay Science* Nietzsche offers a parable that is similar in style to his later *Thus Spoke Zarathustra*. In this passage Nietzsche displays a recognition that sex roles are to the advantage of men and the disadvantage of women, a recognition of the invisibility of the coerciveness of sexual dualism, and offers a lament that others seem unable to recognize this situation. I quote it in its entirety:

> *Will and willingness.*—Someone took a youth to a sage and said: "Look, he is being corrupted by women." The sage shook his head and smiled. "It is men," said he, "that corrupt women; and all the failings of women should be atoned by and improved in men. For

210 Feminists' Use of Nietzsche

> it is man who creates for himself the image of woman, and woman forms herself according to this image."
>
> "You are too kindhearted about women," said one of those present; "you do not know them." The sage replied: "Will is the manner of men; willingness that of women. That is the law of the sexes—truly, a hard law for women. All of humanity is innocent of its existence; but women are doubly innocent. Who could have oil and kindness enough for them?"
>
> "Damn oil! Damn kindness!" someone else shouted out of the crowd; "women need to be educated better!"—"Men need to be educated better," said the sage and beckoned to the youth to follow him.—The youth, however, did not follow him. (KSA 3:427; GS §68, p. 126)

Nietzsche says that man "creates for himself the image of woman, and woman forms herself according to this image." In this one can see the roots of Beauvoir's claim that woman "is defined and differentiated with reference to man and not he with reference to her; she is the incidental, the inessential as opposed to the essential. He is the Subject, he is the Absolute—she is the Other" (*The Second Sex*, p. xix). Both Nietzsche and Beauvoir are claiming that the duality of man/woman is asymmetrical, that man is primary, woman secondary, and that this asymmetry disadvantages women. For Nietzsche, woman's goal is not to be absolute but to be in command of her own perspective; she fails at this in part because "her great art is the lie, her highest concern is mere appearance and beauty" (KSA 5:171; BGE §232, p. 163). Woman's role as Other (to use Beauvoir's term) makes her an actress who depends upon pretense and illusion to survive. Her mistake is to get caught up in her own illusions: she fails to see herself except through the eyes of others. Nietzsche asks: "Seducing one's neighbor to a good opinion and afterwards believing piously in this opinion—who could equal women in this art?" (KSA 5:99; BGE §148, pp. 89–90).[23] Acting is not inherently bad; Nietzsche may even think that it is a necessary part of everyone's life (KSA 3:595–97; GS §356, pp. 302–4). The problem here is that in acting a part that someone else has written, a part which eventually becomes their reality, women do not develop their own perspective.

At bottom, the distinction between Self and Other and the relation between men and women are, in Nietzsche's framework, a matter of differing perspectives and differing values. The relation between Self and

Other is typified by Nietzsche's characters of the master and the slave, offered as empirical generalizations, and presented in both *Beyond Good and Evil* and *The Genealogy of Morals* (KSA 5:208–12; BGE §260, pp. 204–8). In *Beyond Good and Evil*, Nietzsche uses the distinction between master morality and slave morality as yet another example of the "opposite values" he condemns. The distinction plays a different role in *The Genealogy of Morals*, where Nietzsche sets out to discuss both the origin and the value of the values we hold. Although most interpreters focus on Nietzsche's discussion of the origins of morality, Nietzsche stressed the question of value, saying *"the value of these values themselves must first be called in question"* (KSA 5:253; GM—P §6, p. 20).[24]

The basic difference between master morality and slave morality is perspective. This difference in perspective is illustrated by how each acquires values. Both take the master as the primary value: master morality looks at the aristocracy and says "Oh we good noble happy ones!" Slave morality looks with resentment and fear at the same aristocracy and calls it evil. Both are focused on the master. Because the master looks to himself for his own values, Nietzsche claims that the master is a creator of values (KSA 5:208–12; BGE §260, pp. 204–8). The slave, on the other hand, seeks values from outside himself or herself. Slave morality is the morality of the powerless. For master morality, "good" is primary and defined by the master's own way of being, while "bad" is secondary and applies to "those other than [less than] us." For slave morality, "evil" is primary and defined by the master's own way of being, while "good" is secondary and derivative, and means "other than *them.*"

Nietzsche asks what the value of these values is to those who hold them. Let us begin with the masters and say a little more about what their values are. Seeing themselves as powerful, with power over others as well as over themselves, their actions are spontaneous, not reactive. Seeing themselves as the meaning and justification of their society, the masters accept the sacrifice of members of lower social strata for their own sake (the masters') (KSA 5:206–7; BGE §258, p. 202). Nietzsche describes this phenomenon as the *"pathos of distance"*: the aristocracy takes itself to be the seat of all value and defines all else as lower (KSA 5:205–6; BGE §257, pp. 201–2; see also KSA 5:258–60; GM—I §2, pp. 25–26). This *pathos* is necessary, he adds, for "the continual 'self-overcoming of man' " (KSA 5:205; BGE §257, p. 201) both on the social and on the individual level, and so Nietzsche claims that "every enhancement of the type 'man' has so far been the work of an aristocratic society—and it will be so again and again" (KSA 5:205; BGE §257, p. 201). The utility of this perspective should be obvious. The master feels free to sacrifice those who are ranked lower than he is—because they are not like him, and so different (or no) rules apply to their interaction (see, for example, KSA 5:219–20; BGE §265, p. 215).

Now there are those who will say, "Men aren't like that; they don't sacrifice women. If anything, men are sacrificed for women." This is a reversal and turns on what counts as sacrificing. Taking the positive self-regarding values of the slave as primary would make such a claim true—if that were a legitimate privileging. Slave morality is essentially relative; because it reacts to master morality, it cannot be considered in itself. (Most of the slave's values are not positive self-regarding values but are simply self-preserving, with a minimalist construal of what the self is and what counts as its preservation.) Nietzsche explicitly calls slave morality "a morality of utility" (KSA 5:211; BGE §260, p. 207); it is the morality of the oppressed. He says that it promotes values that ease the lot of the sufferer, and the list looks like a short list of womanly virtues: pity, humility, kindness, altruism, and the like. In women, these traits provide a kind of psychological protection from the harmful effects of being those who serve.[25]

In the middle of book 5 of *The Gay Science,* Nietzsche explicitly invokes the language of the master and slave to talk about heterosexual love. He claims that for woman, love means "total devotion" *to* the loved one; for man, love means total devotion *from* the other. Men who want to be totally devoted to their lovers, Nietzsche says, "simply are—not men" (KSA 3.611; GS §363, p. 319). He captures the constraining normativity of the definition of woman as slave when he says: "A man who loves like a woman becomes a slave; while a woman who loves like a woman becomes *a more perfect woman*" (KSA 3:611; GS §363, p. 319). It sounds as if calling her a slave would be redundant.

It is important that Nietzsche does not trivialize the sacrifices that women make for men. Just three sections after "Will and willingness," Nietzsche addresses the heart of women's objectification and oppression. In "On female chastity," Nietzsche introduces the theme of articulation as he explains the perils of white European upper-class woman's accepting the sexual education dictated by the men of her class. With surprising empathy for women's sexual situation, he writes:

> There is something quite amazing and monstrous about the education of upper-class women. What could be more paradoxical?

All the world is agreed that they are to be brought up as ignorant as possible of erotic matters, and that one has to imbue their souls with a profound sense of shame in such matters. . . . here they are supposed to remain ignorant even in their hearts; they are supposed to have neither eyes nor ears nor words nor thoughts for this—their "evil." . . . And then to be hurled, as by a gruesome lightning bolt, into reality and knowledge, by marriage—precisely by the man they love and esteem most! To catch love and shame in a contradiction and to be forced to experience at the same time delight, surrender, duty, pity, terror, and who knows what else, in the face of the unexpected neighborliness of god and beast!

Thus a psychic knot has been tied that may have no equal. . . .

Afterward, the same deep silence as before. Often a silence directed at herself, too. She closes her eyes to herself. . . .

In sum, one cannot be too kind about women. (KSA 3:428–29; GS §71, pp. 127–28.)

This passage shows Nietzsche's understanding of the cruelty of a sexual morality that demands of women that they deny their own eroticism, that places a woman's sexuality at odds with her morality, that makes men sexual agents and women sexual objects. By denying her the psychological apparatus to be a sexual agent, man cripples woman's erotic life. Nietzsche recognizes that one's erotic life is central to one's very being; he writes that the "degree and kind of a person's sexuality reach up into the ultimate pinnacle of his spirit" (KSA 5:87; BGE §75, p. 81).[26] In accepting thorough sexual ignorance, a woman loses the potential for a healthy erotic life. The debilitating effects of this sexual system range over much more than the woman's erotic life, however, for as a result the woman "closes her eyes to herself." She loses the power of self-articulation.

The absolute positing of a perspective by the Self is not limited to morality. It infuses all representation, and so all human life. "On female chastity" shows one method by which man creates for himself an image of woman to which women then conform. The desirable woman, the woman he will marry and support, is a virgin in all respects. By defining her virtue (her value) this way, man establishes a norm that a woman rejects at her economic, social, and psychological peril. As is typical of the norms that define femininity, this norm carries with it a double bind: she is damned if she complies, damned if she doesn't. The perils of noncompliance are obvious. The surprise is that Nietzsche saw the perils of compliance.

More generally, man creates woman in the same way he creates his world. Nietzsche says that this is done through the power of naming. He says:

> What things *are called* is incomparably more important than what they are. The reputation, name, and appearance, the usual measure and weight of a thing, what it counts for—originally almost always wrong and arbitrary, thrown over things like a dress and altogether foreign to their nature and even to their skin—all this grows from generation unto generation, merely because people believe in it, until it gradually grows to be part of the thing and turns into its very body. What at first was appearance becomes in the end, almost invariably, the essence and is effective as such. . . . it is enough to create new names and estimations and probabilities in order to create in the long run new "things." (KSA 3:422; GS §58, pp. 121–22)

Contemporary feminists are working hard to understand the power of language to shape our ways of being in the world, fully aware that the canons of discourse and culture have always been in the control of men.[27] A contemporary feminist using Nietzsche's terms would claim that through the exercise of the power of naming, men exercise their will to power. This power extends not only over women, but also over the "very nature" of the world itself. Beauvoir recognizes this when she says, "Representation of the world, like the world itself, is the work of men; they describe it from their own point of view, which they confuse with absolute truth" (*The Second Sex*, p. 161). Notice that Beauvoir says "absolute truth"; she does not deny that the power of naming yields true stories about the world. She denies that these true stories are unrevisable stories of unchanging reality. The stories are true because they create or help to create the reality they describe.

Nietzsche describes the effect of the power of naming exercised by men on women in a passage of *The Gay Science* that anticipates his discussion of the *pathos of distance* in *Beyond Good and Evil*. He writes:

> When a man stands in the midst of his own noise, in the midst of his own surf of plans and projects, then he is apt also to see quiet,

magical beings gliding past him and to long for their happiness and seclusion: *women*. He almost thinks that his better self dwells there among the women, and that in these quiet regions even the loudest surf turns into deathly quiet, and life itself into a dream about life. Yet! Yet! Noble enthusiast, even on the most beautiful sailboat there is a lot of noise, and unfortunately much small and petty noise. The magic and the most powerful effect of women is, in philosophical language, action at a distance, *actio in distans*; but this requires first of all and above all—*distance*. (KSA 3:424–25; GS §60, p. 124)

In taking man's perspective as primary, this passage illustrates the third point in the argument I said Nietzsche should hve made against sexual dualism. That point was that men and women are not really opposites but that one is the refinement of the other. Which of these we take to be the refinement shows *our* perspective and not something about the world as such. It is not that women *are* quiet, peaceful, magical beings; it is that men and women have maintained a distance, in part in order to keep the illusion going.

The coerciveness of sexual dualism is achieved because it simplifies life and provides a vehicle for the exercise of the will to power. Consider the particular form of sexual dualism of the stereotypical 1950s white middle-class couple, such as depicted by the characters on *The Donna Reed Show* and *Leave It to Beaver*. One thing rigid sex roles have going for them is that people can abdicate making decisions as to how to maintain and display their gender-identity. If I accept as a fact that I ought to aspire to be like Donna Stone or June Cleaver (interesting names), this acceptance simplifies my life. I can get on with the business of being a wife-mother-homemaker. In those roles, I will find some avenues for the exercise of my will to power. I may even feel more satisfied than my twin who tries to have a life that does not fit standard sex roles, for she suffers the trials of a trailblazer. Similarly, a man who sets out to be like Dr. Stone or Ward Cleaver will find ready-made avenues for the exercise of his will to power. The important question is whose will to power is exercised by the instantiation of these rigid sex roles in the first place. To answer that we must find out who, by and large, benefits most from the system, by and large. To identify the group by way of but a few of their benefits, that half of the dichotomy held in higher esteem, who control much more than half of the society's resources, who have equal rights under the law, that is whose will to power is exercised by sexual dualism as we know it.

Nietzsche's position in "Will and willingness" is encouraging, for there we see an unexpected sensitivity to the situation of women under sexual dualism. His insights there are important. What is discouraging, however, is the undercurrent of pessimism that imbues the parable. Will and willingness, he says, "is the law of the sexes," and "all of humanity is innocent of its existence." The invocation of law there does not signal essentialism, for Nietzsche is not arguing that the relation between the sexes is immutable. This law is a constitutive law; it defines the created natures of the sexes. What we must wonder about is in what sense humanity is innocent of this. Are we innocent in the sense that we are not responsible? That would make sense of Nietzsche's saying that "women are doubly innocent," but such a general exoneration would undermine the sage's saying that men corrupt women, that men need better education, and that men need to atone. The language of sin is strong here and cannot be overlooked.

The second pessimistic aspect of this parable is that the youth and the others disbelieve the sage. This is not a truth that the masses can accept. This was true in Nietzsche's day, and it is still true, for the most part, today.

Those who do accept the sort of position sketched in these passages face a difficult interpretive issue: Does this position offer any positive guidelines for women? Nietzsche did not see how the situation could be changed. Since heterosexual love seemed to him to be the root of woman's oppression, that is where the change would have to come. But that is where he saw no acceptable way out. He considers the possibility that men should come to love like women, but says that there cannot be an "equal will to renunciation," for "we should then get—I do not know what; perhaps an empty space?" (KSA 3:611; GS §363, p. 319). Here we can see Nietzsche failing to think through the options using his own philosophical positions, for he goes on to say: "Woman gives herself away, man acquires more—I do not see how one can get around this natural opposition by means of social contracts or with the best will in the world to be just, desirable as it may be not to remind oneself constantly how harsh, terrible, enigmatic, and immoral this antagonism is" (KSA 3:611–12; GS §363, p. 319).

In "Will and willingness" the sage locates the problem squarely with men, saying that men need to be better educated. Does this show that

Nietzsche takes women to be completely passive? Not necessarily. He surely sees women as severely constrained by a situation in which they are defined by men. He also sees that the situation makes it very hard for women to gain more power. Beauvoir extends this analysis when she claims that women see acceptance of male definition as the best or easiest or surest route to power. Women have little power under patriarchy, and rejecting male-defined ways for women to be makes us lose what little power we already have. This need to cling to power keeps us complicit in our secondary status. The analysis itself suggests avenues for liberation.

Although Nietzsche fails to apply his general philosophical frameworks here, we need not. A feminist application of his discussion of master/slave morality can be of help. Often Nietzsche writes as if slaves cannot help but be slaves, masters cannot but be masters, and that's that. On the other hand, Nietzsche's discussion of a slave revolt, which begins when resentment "becomes creative and gives birth to values," suggests no such inevitability (KSA 5:270; GM—I §10,p. 36).[28] According to Nietzsche, it is because the common man even seeks his own value from outside that the common man has always *been* just what he is considered to be (KSA 5:212–14; BGE §261, pp. 208–9).[29] Tracy Strong argues that "the *direction* of willing seems to be the key difference" between masters and slaves, for it "is outward and expended in the masters, inward and 'imposing a form upon oneself' in the slaves" (*Politics of Transfiguration*, p. 240). The master exerts his will upon the world, the slave exerts her will upon herself. Pathetically, when enslavement is most successful, the slave makes herself over into what the master takes her to be. At bottom, what matters is taking responsibility for one's own values and taking actions to reshape the world accordingly. Nietzsche condemns the slave's ressentiment, for the slave revolt brings the triumph of "natures that are denied the true reaction, that of deeds, and compensate themselves with imaginary revenge. While every noble morality develops from a triumphant affirmation of itself, slave morality from the outset says No to what is 'outside,' what is 'different,' what is 'not itself'; and this No is its creative deed" (KSA 5:270; GM—I §10, p. 36).

To be a slave, in general, is to be totally accessible to the will of another person, one's master. In discussing the "aura of negativity about [feminist] separatism," Marilyn Frye argues that such negativity is built into the very logic of the situation. She writes, "When we start from a position of total accessibility there *must* be an aspect of no-saying (which is the beginning of control) in *every effective* act and strategy, the effective ones

being precisely those which *shift power,* i.e., ones which involve manipulation and control of access" (*The Politics of Reality,* p. 104). Frye points
out that once women have more control, the need to say no to what is
now a threat will diminish, and our having gained control will result in
and be the result of our being "pleasing active beings with momentum of
our own, with sufficient shape and structure—with sufficient integrity—to generate friction" (pp. 104–5).

This amalgam of Nietzschean and feminist considerations suggests that
the slave may cease to be a slave once she affirms what she is, treating as
peripheral both what others are and what they take her to be. Such an
affirmation requires deeds in the world and a momentum of her own, not
just thoughts and imaginary changes. The positive guidelines that emerge
from Nietzsche's more sensitive view of women suggest that we develop
our own perspectives and establish our own values through action. We
will do this by taking the power of naming into our own hands, and thus
we will cease to be silenced by the debilitating effects of the contradictions of sexual dualism.

Remember that in "On female chastity" Nietzsche explains how woman's sexual objectification leads to her silencing. The danger of silencing
is the danger of loss of being. A more Nietzschean way to put this might
be that it is through articulation that we become who we are, and if we
give up our means for developing our own perspective then we give up
everything. Silence is born of fear—fear of pain, fear of death—and,
Nietzsche suggests, in the case of women silence is born of her fear of
man (KSA 5:171; BGE §232, p. 163).

These themes of silencing, articulation, and the need to take control
of one's life run through much of today's feminist discourse. In "The
Transformation of Silence into Language and Action," Audre Lorde explicitly addresses these very themes. She says that she has "come to believe over and over again that what is most important to me must be
spoken, made verbal and shared, even at the risk of having it bruised or
misunderstood," and adds that the source of her silence has been fear.[30]
Mary Daly clearly identifies the difficulty of breaking silence, saying that
"overcoming the silence of women is an extreme act, a sequence of extreme acts. Breaking our silence means living in existential courage."[31]
For Lorde, it took facing the very real, very immediate possibility of her
own death to show her how deeply regrettable those silences are. Lorde
warns women: "My silences had not protected me. Your silence will not
protect you" (p. 41). She challenges us: "What are the words you do not

yet have? What do you need to say? What are the tyrannies you swallow day by day and attempt to make your own, until you will sicken and die from them, still in silence?" (p. 41). At stake here is self-revelation, self-definition, and creating a world hospitable to the selves women seek to be. Articulating one's experience in one's own voice is an arduous ongoing process, for the development of a perspective involves constant consideration and reconsideration. Despite the difficulty of speaking out, when Lorde did, she found that her words forged connections with other women that were mutually sustaining: "It was the concern and caring of all those women which gave me strength and enabled me to scrutinize the essentials of my living" (p. 41). At this point the feminist no longer keeps company with Nietzsche, for his project of self-creation is not the project of one who seeks or needs the company of others. His self-in-transformation is profoundly lonely and profoundly isolated.[32]

Conclusion

Nietzsche's misogyny is tempered by a surprising understanding of the situation of the (white, European, upper-class) women of his day. That more positive view has several significant features. It laments the impact on women of sexual dualism fueled by male control of the power of definition. It offers a positive framework for change, albeit one toward which Nietzsche has shown some ambivalence. That framework enjoins women, in contemporary feminist terms, to stop being male-defined and to actively engage in creating their own identities. This more positive view, when intermingled as it is with Nietzsche's misogynist claims with which we are all so familiar, radically destabilizes any straightforward attempt to classify his sexual politics.

Given this reading, why do I still call Nietzsche a misogynist? He shows sympathy for women and some understanding of sexual politics on occasion, but he also engages in and even glorifies blaming the victim. He does this in his discussion of slave morality, and he does it in his discussion of women. This is a species of the contempt that Nietzsche showed for anything he deemed "under." Further, Nietzsche's attack on dualisms pushed him in the direction suggested in this paper, yet *Beyond Good and Evil* takes precious little account of the analysis in *The Gay Science* that would advance that argument. He was not willing or perhaps able to take the sort of feminist stance that is nascent here. In addition, his sketch of an early existentialist conception of the self as constructed through perspective and valuation takes his thought directly to the sort of position developed by Beauvoir in *The Second Sex,* yet he did not make this position explicit. And finally, there are still all the apparently insensitive, philosophically and morally unjustified comments about women that are not easily overlooked.

There are two reasons not to brand Nietzsche simply as a misogynist, however. First, his views are mixed. A simple label oversimplifies. There are misogynist elements in his writings, and as we have seen here there are some remarkably nonmisogynist elements as well. (To go so far as calling them feminist would not be accurate.) My goal in highlighting these more positive passages in Nietzsche's works has been to suggest that we do the hard work of reevaluating his views on women and that we see where his philosophical views would take our own thought on the troubling social questions we face. Second, if we use such a simplistic label, then we run the risk of turning feminist scholars away from Nietzsche's texts unnecessarily. There is much in these texts worth studying, and not out of some kind of misguided philosophical hero-worship. The attack on dualisms in *Beyond Good and Evil,* the discussions of the power of discouse that run through *The Gay Science* and beyond, the discussions of the importance of power that run through all his texts, are but a few of the issues of shared concern for Nietzsche and for feminists.

The bottom line is that given the affinities and possibilities sketched in this paper, we should look at what works and what does not work in Nietzsche's metaphysics and epistemology—specifically in his views about what there is and how it came to be what it is, and in his views about the "nature" and politics of knowledge. Like many feminists, Nietzsche rejects many kinds of philosophical dogmatism in his attempts to articulate his conception of these issues. It will be useful to assess his achievements and his failures in light of *our* purposes, all the while recognizing how Nietzsche's purposes helped shape the positions we are examining. As the discussion here suggests, a feminist analysis of Nietzsche's perspectivism and discussion of the power of naming anticipates and can support contemporary feminist concerns about the importance of women's articulating our lives and reshaping our world.

Notes

1. For insightful discussions of the elements of Nietzsche's views that support his being labeled "misogynist," see Ofelia Schutte, *Beyond Nihilism: Nietzsche without Masks* (Chicago: University of

Chicago Press, 1984); Carol Diethe, "Nietzsche and the Woman Question," *History of European Ideas* 11 (1989): 865–75; and J. L. Thompson, "Nietzsche on Woman," *International Journal of Moral and Social Studies* 5 (1990): 207–20.

2. For an account of Nietzsche's self-creation through self-articulation through his work, see Alexander Nehamas, *Nietzsche: Life as Literature* (Cambridge: Harvard University Press, 1985). For an account of Beauvoir's project of self-articulation in a broader feminist context, see my "Definition and Power: Toward Authority without Privilege," *Hypatia* 9, no. 4 (1993): 1–34.

3. See Kaufmann's note 31 at BGE §238, p. 167.

4. To guard against oversimple readings of Nietzsche's apparently nasty remarks, see R. Hinton Thomas's complex and compelling reading of the notorious "do not forget your whip" remark in *Thus Spoke Zarathustra* (*Nietzsche in German Politics and Society, 1890–1918* [Manchester: Manchester University Press, 1983], pp. 132–40). Thomas argues that this passage "has no place in any discussion of Nietzsche's views on the treatment of women as such" (p. 140). See also Thomas's chapter "The Feminist Movement and Nietzsche" for some of the ways in which Nietzsche's views were appropriated by some of his feminist contemporaries.

5. This interpretation of Nietzsche is developed by Nehamas in *Nietzsche: Life as Literature*.

6. See also section 239 of *Beyond Good and Evil*, where Nietzsche says: "What inspires respect for woman, and often enough even fear, is her *nature*, which is more 'natural' than man's, the genuine, cunning suppleness of a beast of prey, the tiger's claw under the glove, the naïveté of her egoism, her uneducability and inner wildness, the incomprehensibility, scope, and movement of her desires and virtues" (KSA 5:178; BGE §239, p. 169). Despite the animalistic imagery here, it is important that Nietzsche uses a comparative.

7. See for example KSA 3:422; GS §58, pp. 121–22.

8. It is important to note that there is considerable debate amongst philosophers developing social constructivism as to the nature of the individual and the extent and duration of the social construction across the individual's lifetime. Some argue that individuals are largely if not completely determined by their social setting, while others leave room for individual self-determination and self-construction within a social context. It would take a paper in itself to explain this debate and where Nietzsche's views would fit in; my point is that there are overlapping issues for these philosophers and for Nietzsche. For an excellent discussion of a feminist social constructivist position, see Marilyn Friedman, "Feminism and Modern Friendship: Dislocating the Community," in *Feminism and Political Theory*, ed. Cass R. Sunstein (Chicago: University of Chicago Press, 1990), pp. 143–58. For a discussion of Nietzsche's conception of the self, see Tracy B. Strong, *Friedrich Nietzsche and the Politics of Transfiguration* (Berkeley and Los Angeles: University of California Press, 1975, 1988).

9. Philosophical realism is not quite the same as literary realism, and it is the philosophical variety that I attribute to Nietzsche here. The philosophical realist holds that there is a world independent of any description or perception of it, that (contrary to the idealist) the "external world" is not a creation of our mind(s). Philosophical realism is a very sensible position which most people—philosophers or not—hold most of the time. Unfortunately, it generates a host of problems concerning the possibility of knowledge (e.g., of the physical world, of other minds) which lead those who think about these issues into a variety of less obviously sensible positions, like idealism, nominalism, pragmatism, and so on. These other positions settle the epistemological issues, but abandon our everyday commonsense version of realism to do it.

10. I owe this understanding of Nietzsche to Alexander Nehamas.

11. This kind of dogmatism is obviously a throwback to Platonism.

12. Sexual dualism is the normative positing of two sex classes that are interdefined, taking one class as primary and the other as secondary. Our current heterosexist patriarchal sex class system is one form of sexual dualism. Sexual dualism is a normative system, but it purports to be descriptive; it is ideology parading as fact. As both Nietzsche and Beauvoir have pointed out, an effective system

of norms has significant descriptive consequences. When a society embraces a norm that says that women ought to live in certain ways, and women accept the norm and do live in those ways, then those practices that constitute the way of living can and do shape who those women are and who they can be. For example, a norm that dictates that the education of men is a necessity and that the education of women is a luxury has tremendous impact on the kinds of people women become within the societies that embrace that norm. We must be careful to understand that even well-entrenched descriptions that arise from such a normative base have the potential to be overturned.

13. This figure is reported by Marilyn Frye and attributed to Eileen Van Tassell; see Frye's "Sexism," in *The Politics of Reality: Essays in Feminist Theory* (Freedom, Calif.: Crossing Press, 1983), pp. 17–40. The actual incidence of sexual ambiguities is very hard to ascertain, because there are so many types of ambiguities and there is no general compilation of the data; see *Practice of Pediatrics*, ed. Vincent C. Kelley, 11 vols. (Hagerstown, Md.: Harper, 1984–), 7:chaps. 60–61.

14. This is the estimate of Stuart Kupfer, M.D., a pediatric endocrinologist at the University of North Carolina School of Medicine in Chapel Hill.

15. *Schaffer's Diseases of the Newborn*, 5th ed., ed. Mary Ellen Avery and H. William Taeusch, Jr. (Philadelphia: W. B. Saunders, 1984), pp. 511–12. As soon as it is medically feasible, these children are made into one sex or the other through surgery and medical treatment. In cases of ambiguous genitalia, genetic structure may be used to determine the child's future sex of rearing. Usually, the determination depends upon what the urologist, the endocrinologist, and the surgeon can do with the child's anatomy.

16. Interestingly, those who do fit these extreme categories also tend to be psychologically or socially dysfunctional. See, for example, Sandra L. Bem, "The Measurement of Psychological Androgyny," *Journal of Consulting and Clinical Psychology* 42 (1974): 155–62, and Sandra L. Bem and Daryl J. Bem, "Training the Woman to Know Her Place: The Power of a Nonconscious Ideology," in *Roles Women Play: Readings toward Women's Liberation*, ed. Michele Hoffnung Garskof (Belmont, Calif.: Brooks/Cole, 1971), pp. 84–96.

17. Nietzsche, I think, is more concerned with the psychosocial aspects of people and so would be more interested in the application to gender than in the application to sex.

18. Consider for example: "When a woman has scholarly inclinations there is usually something wrong with her sexually. Sterility itself disposes one toward a certain masculinity of taste; for man is, if I may say so, 'the sterile animal' " (KSA 5:98; BGE §144, p. 89; see also KSA 5:175–78; BGE §239, pp. 167–70).

19. Simone de Beauvoir, *The Second Sex*, trans. H. M. Parshley (New York: Vintage, 1974). See also Sarah L. Hoagland's "Femininity, Resistance, and Sabotage," in *Women and Values: Readings in Recent Feminist Philosophy*, 2d ed., ed. Marilyn Pearsall (Belmont, Calif.: Wadsworth, 1993), pp. 90–97, and chapters 1 and 2 of her *Lesbian Ethics: Toward New Value* (Palo Alto, Calif.: Institute of Lesbian Studies, 1988) for discussions that highlight some of the ways in which women have sought to resist male domination while apparently not giving up the limited but important privileges of femininity.

20. I say "eradicated" here because I think radical feminists and socialist feminists have shown that it is not enough for one woman (or several) to reject social sex-role stereotyping and live that rejection. Such heroism may be necessary to the liberation of all women, but it does not constitute that liberation.

21. Nietzsche is sensitive to the irony of romantic love for women; see, for example, KSA 3:511; GS §227, p. 211.

22. Ofelia Schutte writes that "there is a highly anti-critical streak in Nietzsche's *entire* theory of the 'order of rank' and the practical applications derived from it" (*Beyond Nihilism*, p. 182). Although I agree with Schutte on this, my point is the weaker claim that Nietzsche is uncritical here.

23. For an excellent contemporary discussion of the problem of feminine narcissism, see Sandra Lee Bartky's "Narcissism, Femininity, and Alienation," in *Femininity and Domination: Studies in the Phenomenology of Oppression* (New York: Routledge, 1990), pp. 33–44.

24. Similarly, feminists may care to learn about the origins of our current sex class system, but I would argue that the pressing question is the value of that system. It is only by undermining those values we reject and finding alternative ways to embody those we accept that we will be able to change the system (eradicate patriarchy). Nietzsche poses the question: What if morality is precisely what keeps us down, keeps us low and base, prevents us from attaining the *"highest power and splendor actually possible to the type man?"* (KSA 5:253; GM—P §6, p. 20). Good question for women too.

25. While many men will say that they do not see themselves in the description of the masters, for they do not see themselves (individually) as the meaning and justification of their society, when they are pressed to name such a normative base, often the answer will concern the work and goals of men. The service of women can be seen in much of our paid and unpaid labor, and it is under-scored by the fact that in our society nearly all domestic labor is done by women. Whatever their class status, as long as they do not have paid daily domestic help, it is common for the man in a cohabitating heterosexual couple to accept that the woman will stay up late after a hard day at work to finish cleaning the house, tending the needs of the children (if any), preparing food, doing laundry, and so on. Or, if she does not work outside the home, he will consider it a luxury that she "gets to stay home all day" and "not work," but just cleans the house, feeds and clothes and teaches the children, and so on. It is important to remember that often men's work generates recognition and rewards that women's work, traditionally construed, does not. She works in support of him, and although she may share in his rewards, the rewards are ultimately his. This is one sort of sacrifice, of self and interests, of economic, social, and psychological reward, that justifies the analogy developed here; see Arlie Hochschild, *The Second Shift: Working Parents and the Revolution at Home* (New York: Viking, 1989), for an intriguing discussion of how even among couples with explicit ideological commitments to shared domestic labor, the women still do more than half.

26. The German is more generic than the English in this case: "Grad und Art der Geschlechtlich-keit eines Menschen reicht bis in den letzten Gipfel seines Geistes hinauf."

27. This issue has been a concern of Mary Daly's at least since the time of *Beyond God the Father* (Boston: Beacon, 1973), where she says that "women have had the power of *naming* stolen from us" (p. 8). See also Maria Lugones, "Playfulness, 'World'-Travelling, and Loving Perception," in *Lesbian Philosophies and Cultures*, ed. Jeffner Allen (Albany: SUNY Press, 1990), pp. 159–80; Lugones and Elizabeth V. Spelman, "Have We Got a Theory for You! Feminist Theory, Cultural Imperialism, and the Demand for 'The Woman's Voice,' " *Hypatia: A Special Issue of Women's Studies International Forum* 6 (1983): 573–81; Alice Walker, "In Search of Our Mothers' Gardens," in *In Search of Our Mothers' Gardens: Womanist Prose* (San Diego: Harvest/HBJ, 1983), pp. 231–43; and Carolyn G. Heilbrun, *Writing a Woman's Life* (New York: Ballantine, 1988). For a helpful discussion of these issues with respect to philosophy of law, see Martha Minow, *Making All the Difference: Inclusion, Exclusion, and American Law* (Ithaca: Cornell University Press, 1990).

28. Slave morality is essentially "No-saying," for it says no to the world of the master, which it perceives as hostile. Nietzsche says that slave morality needs the hostile world created by master morality (which really directs no hostility toward the slaves). If it is to exist, it exists by inverting "the value-positing eye" (KSA 5:271; GM—I §10, p. 36). The analogies and disanalogies between this case and the case of the sexes should be obvious.

29. Compare with the following from Beauvoir's introduction: "As George Bernard Shaw puts it, in substance, 'The American white relegates the black to the rank of shoeshine boy; and he con-cludes from this that the black is good for nothing but shining shoes.' This vicious circle is met with in all analogous circumstances; when an individual (or a group of individuals) is kept in a situation of inferiority, the fact is that he *is* inferior. But the significance of the verb *to be* must be rightly understood here; it is in bad faith to give it a static value when it really has the dynamic Hegelian sense of 'to have become.' Yes, women on the whole *are* today inferior to men; that is, their situation affords them fewer possibilities. The question is: should that state of affairs continue?" (Beauvoir, *The Second Sex*, p. xxviii).

30. Audre Lorde, "The Transformation of Silence into Language and Action," in *Sister / Outsider: Essays and Speeches* (Freedom, Calif.: Crossing Press, 1984), p. 40.

31. Mary Daly, *Gyn/Ecology: The Metaethics of Radical Feminism* (Boston: Beacon, 1978, 1990), p. 21.

32. For a discussion of the importance of community to the project of self-articulation, see my "Definition and Power."

11

Nietzsche Was No Feminist . . .

Debra B. Bergoffen

What is flirtation? One might say that it is behavior leading another to believe that sexual intimacy is possible, while preventing that possibility from becoming a certainty. In other words, flirting is a promise of sexual intercourse without a guarantee. . . . [Tereza] disturbed the balance between promise and lack of guarantee (which when maintained is a sign of flirtistic virtuosity); she promised too ardently, and without making it clear that the promise involved no guarantee on her part. Which is another way of saying that she gave everyone the impression of being there for the taking. But when men responded by asking for what they felt they had been promised, they met with strong resistance, and their only explanation for it was that she was deceitful and malicious.

—*Milan Kundera, The Unbearable Lightness of Being*

Nietzsche was no feminist. The question of woman, however percolates his thought. He tells us to go to her with a whip, to suppose she is truth, to address her as life, to call her Baubô. He calls her Zarathustra's mistress and the stillest hour. Nietzsche always seems to be calling to, or telling us something about woman. Like almost everything else in Nietzsche's thought, however, this something he keeps telling us is less than perfectly clear.

I do not intend to make Nietzsche a feminist. Instead, I take as my point of reference the question that opens the preface to *Beyond Good and Evil*: "Supposing truth is a woman—what then?" I pursue the idea that Nietzsche is engaged with questions of the feminist field. With this in mind, I take up the following thought: Nietzsche, by entangling the questions of psychology, Zarathustra, the death of god, the ascetic ideal, and the eternal recurrence, with questions of the feminine, points to the ways in which the question of woman, far from being at the margins of philosophy, lies close to its heart. I think Nietzsche had some sense of this.

Why this aphorism on woman rather than another? Nothing in Nietzsche's thought demands it. When dealing with the un- (the anti) systematic thought called Nietzsche, there are no given points of departure. There are, however, questions of interpretation. Matters of textual response. And always risks. What follows then is an interpretive risk that claims that there are good reasons for privileging, "Supposing truth is a woman—what then?" and that argues that pursuing these good reasons gets us somewhere in understanding Nietzsche and feminist thought. The good reasons come down to this: the place of the thought; the what of the thought; the how of the thought. Given its place at the beginning of the genealogy of *Beyond Good and Evil*, "Supposing truth is a woman" links the question of woman to the issue of origins. Given that it raises the question of truth, it links the question of woman to the issue of philosophy. Given that it is expressed as a hypothetical, it links the question of woman to the issues of discourse and rhetoric.

"Supposing truth is a woman" is the first line of the first paragraph of the preface to *Beyond Good and Evil*. It places the question of woman at the beginning that is even before the beginning. The full paragraph reads:

> Supposing truth is a woman—what then? Are there not grounds for the suspicion that all philosophers, insofar as they were dogmatists have been very inexpert about women? That the gruesome seriousness, the clumsy obtrusiveness with which they have usually approached truth so far have been awkward and very improper methods for winning a woman's heart. What is certain is that she has not allowed herself to be won—and today every kind of dogmatism is left standing dispirited and discouraged. *If* it is left standing at all! For there are scoffers who claim that it has fallen, that all dogmatism lies on the ground—even more, that all dogmatism is dying.[1]

The next paragraph begins with the following:

> Speaking seriously, there are good reasons why all philosophical dogmatizing, however solemn and definitive its airs used to be,

may nevertheless have been no more than a noble childishness and tryonism.[2]

A typical Nietzschean conundrum. So he wasn't speaking seriously when he supposed that truth was a woman? Is this a clue to pay attention to the supposition or to dismiss it? In speaking seriously, is Nietzsche now joining the ranks of the dogmatic philosophers or using a rhetorical device to remind us that he is doing philosophy? In telling us that he is now speaking seriously, is Nietzsche telling us that the good reasons we are about to hear are clumsy approaches to truth or genealogical insights? In assuring us that only now is he speaking seriously, is Nietzsche assuring us that the supposition is a throwaway line? Something to get our attention—nothing more? Or is he signaling his understanding that this supposition, being something too dangerous for us to hear, can only be said if it repudiates itself in its speaking?

Not speaking seriously can be serious business when the philosopher is Nietzsche. With this in mind (and with a little help from Freud who, in *The Interpretation of Dreams* and in *Jokes and their Relation to the Unconsciousness*, taught us a few things about the seriousness of the not serious), I return to this first paragraph—this beginning before the beginning and take some time with this unserious thought, "Supposing truth is a woman—what then?"

To think of truth as a woman and of philosophers as inept, failed suitors is to make philosophy a matter between man and woman. A matter of desire. To think in this way turns the traditional question of philosophy, How shall man discover the truth? into the genealogical, Nietzschean question, Why does man want truth? It also seems to turn the facts on their heads. This supposing truth is a woman—doesn't it ignore the ways in which, within the Western tradition at least, truth has always been marked *man*? Doesn't it forget the Christian truth: God the Father as the ground of the sacred law?[3] The social contract truth: the *fraternal* law at the social and political roots of the modern state?[4] The scientific/psychoanalytic truth: the *paternal* metaphor as the condition of the possibility of the subject?[5]

Or does this supposing truth is a woman, as the first line of a work dedicated to overcoming the truth of morality tell the whole story? Does it, given the ways in which we find the masculine figure inscribed in the highest truths and grounding values of the Western tradition, sound as the echo of Nietzsche's announcement of the death of God? For if, in declaring the death of God, Nietzsche is pointing to the disappearance of the highest value, but not declaring the disappearance of values[6]—that is, if the death of God means the end of the reign of the hierarchy of values and the beginning of an economy of exchange values such that all values are infinitely transformable and convertible—then woman would seem to be an apt name for this economy. Woman, as Freud, Lévi-Strauss, and Irigaray have taught us, has always been the sign of exchange value. To date, her exchanges have been in the service of the highest values of man's desire: God, civilization, the incest taboo. But if there are no highest values and she is all that is left . . . ?

"Supposing truth is a woman." Supposing, with Irigaray, she is the sex which is not one. Supposing she is the one who can be exchanged for anything. Have we not then dissolved Being/Truth into language and the tradition constituted by the transmission and interpretation of messages?[7] Have we not then given up/overcome the question of origin?

Within the context of *Beyond Good and Evil* the answer to this question might be yes, but given the additional context of Nietzsche's genealogical methods, the answer must be no. And, perhaps more to the point, taken in itself the name *woman* cannot be used to elude the issue of origin. Woman is the name of our origin. We are all/each of woman born.

So there is this difference between announcing the death of God and supposing truth is a woman. The death of God suggests the end of the reign of the origin. Supposing truth is a woman recalls us to the question of origins. But being called back to the question of origins by the name *woman* shares this with the announcement of the death of God: we are called to confront the void and the desires of the imaginary.

The history of woman within the Western tradition is, as Nietzsche knows, quite complex. Though it can be said that she has never appeared as truth (if by truth we mean the highest value), it can also be said that she has repeatedly appeared as truth (if by truth we mean that which we desire and that which eludes us). For, within the Western tradition, we find woman, under the name of nature, appearing as the veiled truth that seduces us, that teases us, that must be forced to submit to our inquisitions.

Man believes that woman hides something from him—truth—that he wants. Nietzsche suggests that while woman may be truth, she may not be the truth man wants. He, knowing something that man does not, suggests that we might pause before punctuating woman's bashfulness. "Perhaps," he says, "truth is a woman who has reasons for not letting us see her reasons? Perhaps her name is—to speak Greek—Baubô."[8] The Greeks called her Baubô. The horror and obscenity of her sex. Freud names the horror for us: castration. Irigaray is more graphic. Woman is the hole that cannot be made whole. As origin she is not the ground of a teleological point of departure. As origin she is not a destiny. As origin she is the flow of the body. The overcomings that keep coming. As origin she threatens the stability of all values.[9]

No, this is not the origin of man's desire. No, man would rather play the games of seduction than be had. Better to recall the unforgettable origin as veiled woman in order to be able to figure her as man, than suppose that truth is a woman.

Freud spent the later years of his life fretting over the question of woman's desire. "What," he asked, "do women want?" He might have done better listening to Nietzsche who spent much of his creative life probing man's desire. Nietzsche knew that man wants to know woman. He knew that wanting to seduce her, man wants to know what she wants. But he also knew that this question of woman's desire, as a question posed by man, is a matter between men. Properly heard, the question of woman/truth sounds like this: What does man want the truth to be? Why does he want it this way? Why does he want it so badly? Hearing the question of woman/truth this way, Nietzsche discovered the dangers of man's desire. He discovered the ascetic ideal.

The task, as Nietzsche saw it, was not to probe woman's desire but to undo man's.[10] As human, man cannot forget the question of origins, as temporal man is the question of origin,[11] Nietzsche's formula of man's will, "an active desire . . . for the continuance of something desired once"[12] is repeated in Freud's formula for the resolved Oedipus complex: the finding of an object is always a refinding of the lost object. And Freud, when speaking of man, is specific regarding the lost desired object: she is the mother. The function of the resolution of the Oedipus complex, however, is to repress the desire for the mother. Refinding her is conditioned on man's not recognizing his desire. It is conditioned on his refiguring it according to the law of the father. Under this law, the lost mother is returned as the veiled bride.

Nietzsche's Zarathustra would undo the Oedipus complex. His memory of the will remembers the woman at the beginning. As the one who teaches the eternal recurrence of the *same*, he remembers that his desire returns upon itself. He remembers the once-desired woman as he pursues the object of his desire. He knows that all findings are refindings.

As the one who teaches the eternal recurrence after the death of God, however, Zarathustra knows that the original source of his desire was not a secure origin. As the one who stands securely for his own future according to the rule of the eternal recurrence, he does not pretend to stand on secure ground. He does not figure the image of the mother according to the law of the father. When he supposes that truth is a woman, he names her Baubô, the hole, the void, the nothingness.

If Zarathustra is the name of the man who remembers the woman at the beginning as the openness to overcoming rather than the castrated lack; if he is the one who refuses the not yet lack of the teleological origin for the once again overcoming of the eternal recurrence; then he may also be the one who enters the symbolic chain unanchored by the *paternal* metaphor. The Oedipal man's abyss is Zarathustra's Yes and Amen Song.

The truth that is woman, is also the woman that is life. As truth she is the ignorance, the chance, the fate that marks our origin. She is what Lyotard refers to as the unpresentable of the what is not.[13] As life she is the overcoming that is our origin and destiny. The eternal recurrence is the way in which Zarathustra remembers his desire for the truth and life that is woman. It is the way he repeats the desire which makes him what he is without forgetting the overcoming from whence he came and to whom his debts are due.

The eternal recurrence is the way Zarathustra, the man engaged in the overcoming of man, desires woman. Whether it is also the way the woman who speaks for herself, the woman who overcomes the way she is spoken by patriarchy, would desire woman cannot be presumed. Given that there are no assurances that woman's desire mirrors man's, there can be no assumption that the Übermensch and the self-spoken woman would reflect each other's image.

Discovering that she is the origin that her desire recalls her to, woman might be ready to take more risks. Her desire to return might disrupt the recurrence of the same without re-Oedipalizing it. Unlike Zarathustra who recognizes his finitude by refusing all metaphysical, ontological, or theological guarantees; who in the face of this abyss wills the eternal recurrence; who in this willing establishes himself as the finite guarantee of his self-overcoming; woman might figure her finitude, the lack of guarantees, within the structure of her will itself. She might flirt. That is, she might play more dangerously with the balance between the overcoming that undoes certainty and the continuity that constitutes us as human.

As flirt she might will without guarantee. Her will might be marked by the remembrance that there are no guarantees.

To those who are inept about women she will appear deceitful, malicious, fickle, incapable of standing for herself. To those more expert in the workings of desire, her commitment to flirt might appear as the antidote to the powers of the imaginary.

It comes down to something like this: for man the origin is always and necessarily other. To recognize his finitude is to recognize that he is not and cannot be either the origin or end of his being. The issue then becomes, according to Nietzsche, a question of being/becoming oneself. How can man become himself when he cannot anchor himself? How can he become himself if his origin and end are somewhere else? Patriarchy resorts to the veil. Cover the origin over. Recreate it in the image of man's desired end. Empower what was not there at the beginning by refiguring the overcoming as that which is overcome. Exit the finitude of otherness.

But God is dead. The masks are off. Zarathustra must express his desire to be his own origin while supposing that truth is a woman. God the father, the fraternal order, the paternal metaphor—all these strategies of undoing otherness are undone under the assumption of truth as woman. Supposing truth to be a woman, Zarathustra embraces the eternal recurrence. He wills himself to be himself, knowing that he is a player in a dice game where chance, not his will, prevails. In calling the origin chance or woman, Zarathustra refuses the demands of the imaginary. For whether he calls the origin chance or woman, he names the same thing: an other out of his control. As out of his control, this other cannot be appropriated. It can, however, be loved. Loving chance he desires her otherness eternally. He desires the return of and the return to the otherness of her overcoming. Desiring himself, he wills the return of the same.

For woman, the question of finitude is not entangled with the question of the origin as other. As origin she has no need to return. She is always, already there. But what does it mean, this being there, when the there, the origin that she is, is not a given point of departure but an overcoming? This is the question of finitude for woman. Standing for herself as the return of the same will not solve it. Where man's will confronts the otherness of the dice throw, her will must express it lest she repeat the imagos of patriarchy in another register. In her willing of herself she must mark herself as that which cannot be guaranteed/stabilized.

It is easy to see how her flirtatious willing might be/is misunderstood.

Recalling Nietzsche's reminder that "We no longer believe that truth remains truth when her veils have been stripped away,"[14] it is easy to see how the woman who configures finitude as flirtation might/does feed the imaginary desires of the dogmatic philosophers. It is easy to see how she might appear to justify those techniques of objectification and rape elicited by the philosopher's strategies of seduction. It is easy to see how as flirt she might secure her place as the object of the desires of the ascetic ideal; how she might become the anchor of the economy of lack.

It is not always so easy to see, however, that it is a matter of overcoming the ascetic ideal. Of not allowing it to determine the meaning of woman and her flirtations. It is not always easy to see that the flirt evokes the desires of seduction, objectification, and rape where the desires of the lack are already in play. It is not always easy to see how the flirtatious meanings of overcoming are cornered in the imagos of the desires of the ascetic ideal.

If, as has often been noted, woman has been man's accomplice in maintaining the structures of patriarchy,[15] it might not be inappropriate to suggest that in willing the eternal recurrence Zarathustra will need the complicity of the woman who speaks for herself. Without it the eternal recurrence runs the danger of becoming what Heidegger said it was: the last gasp of metaphysics. For in addition to the metaphysical dangers of the eternal recurrence noted by Heidegger, there is also the metaphysical lure of the idea of the origin as anchor. It is not enough for Zarathustra to recognize the otherness of his origin. To elude the metaphysical seduction, he must also recognize that the origin named woman is an origin of overcoming that overcomes the concept of origin as the beginning that sets things in order. The woman who speaks to him as other and origin must remind him that she is not the solution to the metaphysical questions of beginning, becoming, being and end. She must remind him that in returning to her he returns to the dice throw, to chance, to the overfullness that refuses boundaries. Refusing to become a mirror for the ascetic ideal's economy of lack, the woman who speaks herself, returns Zarathustra's desire to him. Her flirtations destabilize his desire for the return of the same with her refusal to be the same. They save his desire for the return of the same from degenerating into the compulsion to repeat. They do not, however, deny his desire. He is invited to come again. She is open to his return. And somewhere in this play of desire, they will both see that though it may be the promise of the same that keeps him returning, it is not the promise of the same, but the returning that marks the reciprocity of their desires. It is not the promise of the same, but the flirtatious refusal to fulfill the promise of sameness that keeps their desires in play.

Supposing the truth to be a woman, Western philosophy moved to contain her. It tolerated her flirtations only so long as they provided man the opportunity to display his skills of conquest. The metaphysicians who suppose truth to be a woman, who know that woman is a flirt, script her flirtations as a prologue to something other: the first moment in the teleological drama of marriage, motherhood and fidelity. Nietzsche supposes truth as woman differently. Instead of moving to stabilize her, he aligns her with chance. As the truth of the dice throw, woman as flirtation challenges the metaphysics of categories and limits. She names the abyss. She figures it as the unanchored field of the possibilities of the sensual. The metaphysicians recoil in terror. She laughs.

Bataille helps us to see this affinity between Nietzsche's truth as woman and games of chance when he writes:

> Chance as it turned out, corresponded to Nietzsche's intentions more accurately than power could. Only play gave me the possibility of exploring the far reaches of possibility and not prejudicing the results, of giving to the future alone and its free occurrence the power usually assigned to choosing sides (which is only a form of the past).[16]

If the danger of the spirit of revenge is the danger of choosing sides, then naming truth *woman* and signifying her as flirt is one way of putting the value of choosing sides into question. Truth as the game of flirtation is undone when sides are chosen; flirting is a free play where choosing sides stops the game by foreclosing further moves.

Recalling that Nietzsche's project is one of transvaluation, specifically that of the transvaluation of the Western tradition, and recalling the eternal recurrence, it seems fitting to note that Nietzsche is not the first Western thinker to name woman as truth, and not the first Western thinker to identify this truth as the laughter, sensuality, and seductiveness of life. Erasmus's *Praise of Folly* treads similar ground. Stop short of reading its final section and Nietzsche cannot be far behind. Popular as *Praise of Folly* was, however, its main character never found her way into the philosophical domain. Not at least until Nietzsche retrieved her and who in this retrieval may be seen as transvaluating the relationship between the myth of Iseult with its absolutes of love and fidelity and the myth of fickleness where "the notion of multiplicity replaces that of unity and is expressed in the reverse of the ideal: ribaldry."[17]

Nietzsche is neither Zarathustra nor the overman. He is the opening that names their possibility. He creates this opening by naming truth *woman*. The desires of the overcoming named Zarathustra are not, however, anchored in the supposition that truth is a woman. They are not anchored anywhere. And this is the point. The death of God means that there are no anchors. And if we can only make this point to those caught in the ascetic ideal by naming truth *woman*, so be it. But the name does not have to stick. Men no longer caught in the imaginary desires of the lack are under no compulsion to desire truth however it is named. Women, speaking their own voices, owe nothing to the name given them by others. They might insist that we recall Nietzsche's other words in *Beyond Good and Evil:*

[Woman] does not want truth: What is truth to woman? From the beginning, nothing has been more alien, repugnant and hostile to woman than truth.[18]

Notes

1. Friedrich Nietzsche, *Beyond Good and Evil*, trans. Walter Kaufmann (New York: Vintage Books, 1966), 2.
2. Ibid.
3. Mary Daly, *Beyond God the Father: Toward a Philosophy of Women's Liberation* (Boston: Beacon, 1973).
4. Carole Pateman, *The Disorder of Women* (Stanford: Stanford University Press, 1989); and Sigmund Freud, *Civilization and Its Discontents*, trans. James Strachey (New York: Norton, 1961).
5. Sigmund Freud, *Three Essays on the Theory of Sexuality*, trans. James Strachey (New York: Basic Books, 1962); and Jacques Lacan, *Ecrits*, trans. Alan Sheridan (New York: Norton, 1977), "On a Question Preliminary to any Possible Treatment of Psychosis" and "The Subversion of the Subject and the Dialectic of Desire in the Freudian Unconscious."
6. Gianni Vattimo, *The End of Modernity*, trans. Jon R. Snyder (Baltimore: Johns Hopkins University Press, 1988), "An Apology for Nihilism."
7. Ibid., 26.
8. Friedrich Nietzsche, *The Gay Science*, trans. Walter Kaufmann (New York: Vintage Books, 1974), Preface 4.
9. Luce Irigaray, *Marine Lover of Nietzsche*, trans. Gillian Gill (New York: Columbia University Press, 1991), 118.
10. For a discussion of Nietzsche's critique of the desires of patriarchy see Debra B. Bergoffen, "On the Advantage and Disadvantage of Nietzsche for Women," in *The Question of the Other*, ed. Arleen B. Dallery and Charles E. Scott (New York: State University of New York Press, 1989).

11. For an exploration of Nietzsche's analysis of humanity's temporality see Debra B. Bergoffen, "Seducing Historicism" *International Studies in Philosophy* 19, no. 2 (1987): 85–98.

12. Friedrich Nietzsche, *On The Genealogy of Morals*, trans. Walter Kaufmann and R. J. Hollingdale (New York: Vintage Books, 1967), Second Essay, 1.

13. Jean-François Lyotard, *The Postmodern Condition: A Report On Knowledge*, trans. Geoff Bennington and Brian Massumi (Minneapolis: University of Minnesota Press, 1984), 81.

14. Friedrich Nietzsche, *The Gay Science*, trans. Walter Kaufmann (New York: Vintage Books, 1974), Preface 4.

15. Simone de Beauvoir, *The Second Sex*, trans. H. M. Parshley (New York: Vintage Books, 1974).

16. Georges Bataille, *On Nietzsche*, trans. Bruce Boone (New York: Paragon House, 1992), xxv–vi.

17. Helene Peters, *The Existential Woman* (New York: Peter Lang, 1992), xiii.

18. Nietzsche, *Beyond Good and Evil*, "Our Virtues" 232.

12

Nietzsche's Women and Women's Nietzsche

Kathleen J. Wininger

Nietzsche and Some of His Female Contemporaries

Women's interest in Nietzsche has been denigrated by feminists and reactionaries alike. It has even been used as evidence of their lack of moral and intellectual seriousness. Otto Weininger in his celebrated book *Sex and Character* used women's appreciation of Nietzsche as a sign of their mental inferiority. He writes: "Women, indeed, have not the faculty of appreciating genius, although this is not the common view. Any extravagance that distinguishes a man from other men appeals to their sexual ambition. . . . For them the talented man is the man of genius, and Nietzsche is the type of what they consider genius."[1] According to Weininger, Nietzsche is merely talented. Women lack the refinement of thought which can distinguish genius from talent. Their deficiency is intellectual.

In spite of the criticism, many women have continued to find Nietzsche's philosophy useful. Some are feminists, others are not. There is a continuity of interest that dates back to Nietzsche's contemporaries. A great deal of his philosophy contains models that are meant to help understand changes. Those changes range from broad cultural shifts, ancient cultures to medieval, Christian to positivistic, to quite specific personal changes. For example, Nietzsche gives an illustration of how we learn to love a piece of music, explaining that our values regarding it change throughout an encounter over time.[2] The idea that values and truths change, intellectual fashions change, and that these ideas are culturally embedded have often appealed to women. The appeal is especially great to women who have as their own agenda social and intellectual transformation. Kathryn Addelson used his work on moral change to explicate the moral revolution involved in the nineteenth-century women's movement in this country.[3]

There were women in Nietzsche's own time who were interested in him and influenced by his ideas and who also influenced him. Most of these women were feminists of some type and involved in women-centered political action and intellectual activity. Lou Andreas-Salomé is the best known of these women but there are many other equally important. Among the most interesting is Hélène Stöcker who did work in aesthetics and intellectual history and was a research assistant to Dilthey. It is worth noting that these women's work is not generally known. Years ago we read how Nietzsche influenced a number of popular movements in his time, but that these people "failed to understand" him. It is interesting that some of these people were women and some of those movements were feminist.[4] Nietzsche's influence on working-class and socialist movements is also helpful in dispelling the idea that the man was merely an exponent of rugged, if not savage, individualism.

The women who worked on Nietzsche were called upon to defend their interest in his work. In 1884 Oscar Levy asked Helen Zimmern, a British writer and friend of Nietzsche's whom he asked to translate a number of his works, to explain her interest in Nietzsche and its compatibility with her feminism. She said in response, "I know what your question is aiming at; it has been asked often enough. I also know what Nietzsche wrote about women. . . . There are apparently men who have theories about women which they never put into practice. There are apparently others who can combine brutal practice with the most beautiful theories."[5] She told him that in her experience "Certainly he [Nietzsche] did not use the famous whip." Zimmern does not deny the misogyny in Nietzsche's writings. Instead she explains to Levy her perception of Nietzsche as a fellow intellectual and the way he treated her.

In fact, when we look at Nietzsche's interactions with real women (other than those in his family) we find a gentleness and respect. And we must remember that he eventually had contact with that new generation of European women many of whom were introduced to him by that well-known advocate of women's higher education, Malwida von Meysenbug.

Von Meysenbug did not ignore the misogyny in Nietzsche's early writings any more than did Zimmern. But she did recommend that he drop the subject of women. Von Meysenbug believed that he did not understand women. She attributes this to his not knowing many. This was in part due to the segregated nature of the educational institutions with which he was affiliated as a young man. She believed that with experience he would mature out of his facile generalizations. As she put it, "my faith in Nietzsche's high talent was too solid to regard this as more than a passing phase in his development."[6] Unfortunately it is possible to see Nietzsche as unable or unwilling to mature out of these views.

The difficulty of dealing with Nietzsche's misogyny goes back to his contemporaries. Present-day women have inherited a long and interesting tradition. These early thinkers are interesting writers and deserve to have their work taken seriously.[7] This essay will address the Nietzsche whom many woman have found compelling and appealing. Is it the "feminine" Nietzsche? It is certainly part of why he was accused of being "feminine," quixotic, immoral, and apolitical.

Nietzsche's Women: Nietzsche's Writings about Women

Nietzsche did not seem to understand women. The women in most of his writings are strange and remote creatures.[8] They certainly maintain the distance that both Nietzsche and Derrida think of as necessary for action or action. Women appear to be the one topic where Nietzsche accepts the cultural convention to dichotomize. Women are either seen as the object of erotic attraction (the coquette) or some version of the bearer of European religious morality and prudery.[9] The latter is sometimes seen in the form of the domestic disciplining mother, sometimes as the "intellectual" feminist.[10] They are ridiculed in any attempt to use reason or science.[11] The women are bound by convention, determined by biology or involved in an instinctual rebellion against the mother/feminist roles. When the women are coquettes they are still defined within a heterosexual context or contest where she is eluding capture but yet is a captive of masculine description.[12] This is the kind of women who chooses the role from among those available to her. It is not one who is instrumental in creating her own fate. Nietzsche does not give women that option. One can see these remarks as a hyperbolic challenge.

Nietzsche certainly employs stylistic techniques whose end is a call to action. The intentionally inflammatory is used with equal energy in his dealings with the history of philosophy, religion, or vegetarianism. He dares the reader to provide him with a defense. In the meantime there is the critical inquiry into values that he desires as part of the reevaluation of all values. The difference is the depth, subtlety, and seriousness with which he goes after the other objects of his critical energy and the insight we find in those critiques. We can oppose these to the relatively superficial remarks on women.

Women will find many of Nietzsche's writings about women problematic. One of the most troublesome things about these writings is their conventionality. Nietzsche was a startlingly original thinker in so many ways that one is disappointed in what looks like an unthinking reenactment in the long European tradition of misogyny. Many intelligent people have interpreted what Nietzsche says about women and some of them found interesting ways to read these passages. Some confirm a conventional misogyny while others find the use of certain feminine metaphors helpful or unconventional (or helpfully conventional in the case of Derrida, et al.).

The range of evaluation of Nietzsche's writings about women is very broad. Perhaps it shouldn't surprise us that the range of (post)modern writings by women, "feminist" men and others (for example, Derrida) is anticipated in the writings of his contemporaries. Sometimes his work has been said to be in praise of women. Ida von Miaskowski, a contemporary and friend, said "there are so many beautiful indeed, sublime words about women and marriage in his works."[13] He is praised as subtle (Derrida, John D. Caputo, David Farrell Krell, Keith Ausell-Pearson), yet decried as obvious and misogynist.[14] Some of these people saw symptoms of pathology in his writings. Ida von Miaskowski again, "The few hostile words he wrote about women—for I do not call a just castigation of certain weaknesses of the sex hostile—can, it seems to me, be attributed to his illness which sporadically showed its traces in his works quite early."[15] Georg Brandes considered him to be hostile to women. In a letter to Nietzsche he states, "There were also in the other work [BGE] some reflections on women in general which did not agree with my own line of thought."[16] And, "When you [Nietzsche] write about women you are very like him [August Strindberg]."[17] Strindberg's fanatic hatred of women is legendary. At other times Nietzsche's remarks were considered ironic or a result of poetic license. Resa von Schirnhofer, a student from Zurich who knew him through Malwida von Meysenbug, said, "Once he said that I should not take offense at the—later so notorious—whip-passage in *Zarathustra*. This had not occurred to me, since I did not read it as an indictment of women, but only as a poetic generalization of individual cases." Other commentators saw it as misguided. Malwida von Meysenbug, responding to a draft of *Human all to Human*, said, "I told him that, especially in regard to women, he ought to make no final pronouncements yet, since he still really knew far too few women."[18] Others saw him as merely typical of his time.

There have also been attempts to explain away his misogyny. There is something wrong with ignoring this aspect of his work.[19] Reading against the grain is one thing but failing to see the flaws in this man's work is especially problematic. Those issues that led to his personal elitism and the unfortunate use of his work by aesthetic elitists and fascists are unlikely to help us in our historical understanding or in our use of Nietzsche in present struggles. But it is important to acknowledge that they are there. Nietzsche makes many misogynist remarks. Nineteenth-century misogyny is complex: sexologists are defining heterosexual gender classifications; proto-psychoanalytic views of sexuality and gender are also emerging. As Zimmern pointed out, there is often a discrepancy between what these thinkers profess and what they do.[20]

What Nietzsche was concerned with was not women but a rather typical use of ideas of women in order to come up with a conception of masculinity. By doing this Nietzsche aligns himself with his masculine forbearers. Indeed many of his remarks are borrowed, like the recommendation that European women be kept in the manner of the Orientals. This suggestion comes right out of Schopenhauer's infamous essay. They are neither original nor profound. The passages on the whip are similar to those that can be found in Machiavelli. What they do is ally him with other men who construct their masculinity around contempt for women. This phenomenon has been analyzed by Klaus Theweleit in *Male Fantasies*[21] where he looks at the Freicorp, a group of mercenaries working after World War I, many of whom became involved with the National Socialist movement. We now understand conceptualizations of otherness be they cultural- or gender-specific to be about the construction of European masculinity, not about their "objects." This makes a detailed examination of such views on women of more limited interest to many feminists. Women are not the real subject of these writings.

The Feminine Nietzsche

In recent years a wide variety of commentators have taken Nietzsche's relation to women and to sexuality as key to understanding his entire philosophy.[22] Derrida, David Farrell Krell, Linda Singer, John Caputo, Jean McConnell Graybeal, are a few people who spring immediately to mind. Krell's book *Postponements*[23] begins with a quotation from Bachelard that asks, "who will discover the feminine Nietzsche for us?" The postponement to which the title refers is a project that Nietzsche continued to put off writing: a drama concerning women, sensual love, and tragic death.[24] Krell considers Derrida's well-known *Éperons/Spurs* to be concerned with the "feminine" Nietzsche. As he puts it: "*Spurs* brings the question of style, interpretation, and philosophical truth to converge on 'the woman question.' "[25] Krell goes on to use images of women: Ariadne, Corinna, Pana, Calina, to get at some of Nietzsche's styles. He also sees major ideas in Nietzsche's work, for example, "action at a distance" as best understood by appealing to an erotic attraction between a man and a woman "something attracts something else, something feels itself being drawn."[26] In Graybeal's book the questions that converge are those of women and art.[27]

Yet, the above interpretations, in which women and femininity are metaphorical images, belong in a slightly different category than the body of literature that has used Nietzsche's personal life with women as a determining feature of his work. Often these were not more subtle than the 1953 advertisement for *My Sister and I*. The copy reads: "The boy who grew up in a household of manless women—The strange relationship between Nietzsche and his sister Elizabeth—suppressed for fifty years—

revealed at last in the philosopher's own confession."[28] For a long time
the constitution of Nietzsche's childhood home served as the explanation
of both his "femininity" and his misogyny. People who have addressed
his relation to women from a narrowly psychological perspective have not
produced a very satisfactory account of his philosophy.[29] Their approach
is too reductive and dismissive of what he did accomplish. Yet in spite
of our resistance to this type of interpretation Nietzsche's philosophical
enterprise was, in a way, a psychological one. It was dominated by the
metaphor of health, which stood against the metaphysical, religious, and
positivist metaphors that had dominated philosophy. Integrating our sensuality, our physicality was seen as central to our health as individuals
and as a culture. We waver between finding his misogyny the most boring
thing about Nietzsche and the most fascinating. It is boring because it is
so typical and conventional. This is disappointing in an otherwise imaginative and daring thinker. It is the most fascinating issue because, like
the culture he was trying to heal, he suffered from his inability to make
peace with women and his own sexuality both metaphorically and literally.

Nietzsche uses the feminine as a term of contempt and abuse concerning other writers. Unfortunately this is not unconventional. With an
irony that seems to pervade his life, he has probably most often been
criticized as a feminine philosopher himself. One of the reasons he is not
taken seriously as a philosopher for a long time is his "unmanly" focus on
aesthetics, on values that change, and on cultural conventions. The
French Philosophes on whom he modeled some of his styles have themselves been long out of favor with an intellectual community more concerned with abstractions and technical accomplishments. Nietzsche
regarded this method of discrediting him as a mode of policing academic
boundaries. It is done in this case by suggesting that if a thinker conceives
of the discipline in a certain way (for example, not technical enough or
by engaging with popular culture) that person isn't a philosopher. Nietzsche believed that the extent of his methodological critiques were slow
to be taken seriously because of the very depth of the critiques. This
made it desirable for people remaining in the conventions and benefiting
by them to classify him outside of the discipline. Consequently his critiques did not even need to be addressed. These critiques are the most
interesting and exciting aspects of his work. The criticism of Nietzsche
as feminine is more profound than Nietzsche's criticism of other thinkers.

In both cases that charge was made to discredit. In his work there are new and different and valuable ideas.

In the late nineteenth century the description of Nietzsche as a feminine writer was tantamount to calling him bad. Sometimes the gradation in meaning of this charge is more complex and important.[30] But something more than this is surely meant by this description. Nietzsche is feminine because he plays. He doesn't come up with a dominating system. He is the quintessential enemy of control of that type which, as we shall see, he associates with fear. In his creation of a heroic human psychology, the issue of personal self-control should be considered in greater detail. But, in terms of external control by political or intellectual domination we find him unmoved.[31] Interestingly Emma Goldman agrees with this and considers him an early anarchist and an "aristocrat of the spirit." He uses these ideas as metaphors and looks at their place in Western cultural history, but they are not what moves him in his vision of a new philosophy.

This discussion of domination is not merely part of a feminist critique. Schopenhauer, in his well known essay "On Women," describes masculine activity as the desire for direct domination over things either by the exercise of power or by controlling them through knowledge. Nietzsche seems to reject both. Yet, he recognized the power behind the drive to mastery. Any one of our basic drives which "would be only too glad to present *itself* as the ultimate goal of existence and as the legitimate *master* of all other drives. For every drive is tyrannical [dominating]: and it is as *such* that it tries to philosophize."[32] He does not systematize. In part he does this to avoid this tyranny. In fact, he is trying to transform philosophy in such a way that this is no longer what constitutes legitimate philosophical activity. Yet, it is precisely avoiding these tendencies that has gotten him into so much trouble. I shall explore this further in the final section.

Nietzsche for Women

Nietzsche continues to operate within a construction of masculine supremacy. In fact, he reinstantiates it. Yet, he gives us a critique of patriarchical authority which is quite penetrating. While not denying his misogyny and assumptions regarding masculine supremacy, we can consider him an ally in many feminist endeavors. His philosophy was so critical of both the Western intellectual traditions and popular culture that it took a very long time for it to be taken seriously in established philosophical circles. There were a few early exceptions. The extremely popular lecturer in aesthetics, Georg Brandes gave lectures on Nietzsche's philosophy as early as 1888. Interestingly enough, Brandes was himself an outsider, a Jewish intellectual in a Protestant culture.

One of the reasons for the interest in Nietzsche by the first generation of women intellectuals in Europe is the freshness of his critique of patriarchal authority and the extent of it. There is not often the same investment in tradition by people who do not benefit by it. Many European intellectual traditions were dismissive or at least unflattering toward non-European cultures, people of lower classes, and women. Perhaps it is not surprising that Nietzsche's critiques found an immediate audience in European women, despite his overt misogyny and hostility to feminism. Even European women do not have the same stake in preserving culture. For them, the possibility of radical transformation represents optimism and hope. For many men, this is experienced as pessimism and loss. The discussion of Nietzsche's "nihilism" can be looked at in this way. He is a nihilist to those who want to hang on to absolute value systems whether Christian or rationalist. He is seen as optimistic to those who see those tendencies as dangerous or outmoded.

To say that Nietzsche engages in a critique of patriarchal authority needs to be explained. Patriarchy is an overused and underexamined word. Nietzsche criticized the law of the father and politics as they pertain to governmental institutions. But he was not particularly interested in either of these specific types of rule. He was, however, incredibly interested in and fascinated by the exercise of power and authority in nonpolitical spheres. This was coupled with his interest in distinctions and hierarchies in everyday life.

It is true that his end (in looking at these distinctions) was not egalitarian. In a way, this may make him more subtle. As a knower, he had a stake in these distinctions. They were what would make him different. He was interested in constructing a new mark of distinction, not in obliterating differences. Perhaps egalitarian thinkers are not the best explicators of class. Perhaps the aspirant, like Nietzsche, is in some ways better.

Nietzsche combined these perceptions of the workings of power and authority with a new vision of what philosophy actually was, and that was cultural criticism. Nietzsche believed that European cultures had come to a dead end. The values that unified the culture intellectually and popularly, had lost their power. Religious values, intellectual and moral, no longer dominated institutions or social practices. The alternative value that contemporary culture offered came in the form of democratic liberalisms and positivism. Nietzsche pointed out the spiritual poverty of these views at a time when they were still in ascendancy. We shall look first at one of his genealogies. These combine many aspects of his thought.

Most people at all familiar with Nietzsche are aware of his views of European history.[33] The Greek and Roman worlds (and other cultures) were dominated by a system of values constructed by people who had both political and cultural authority. This construct was built upon the existence of a slave class but was scarcely aware of that fact. The slaves were not an object of interest although they did provide the perception of distance and distinction that served to show the master classes elevation. Nietzsche sees the decline of this cultural system, and the rise of Christianity, not as a leveling of social values or a move toward and egalitarian order, but rather as a revolution that elevated the "slave" at the expense of the master. This reversal, which in some respects was a disaster for European culture, was ingenious and clever. It showed that the drive to experience oneself as powerful was present in all people, even the slaves. In this sense, slaves are proven to be slaves, not by constitution, but rather by circumstance. Unfortunately, when these slaves rebelled, they put into practice a set of social values that were not of their own making, but those that their social circumstances had imposed upon them. Meekness, industriousness, and ignorance were parts of their condition, which they then elevated to positive values. Morality under the master had involved the creation of values that constitute a self, individual, and community. Under Christianity, the common or mass participation continued to be based on obedience. The change was only in authority figure. The slaves who had hitherto been obedient to a master, now became obedient to God.

Nietzsche wants us to abandon the view of morality that gets its value from the fact that its value judgments are "higher" than those of one's culture or oneself. In the slave system the "moral value of our actions" was to be determined against a standard. The point of that standard and its worth were determined by the fact that they were judged by beings superior in some way: priests, gods, or philosophers. The emphasis on judgment in evaluation, rather than giving value, is what should disgust us. The preoccupation of some people with the moral values of others betrays their lack of security in their own values. They need communal conformity in their belief to make "their" values believable even to themselves. The idea that moralities should be policed comes from a culture that is preoccupied with passing judgment and insecure in its values.

Nietzsche does not believe that we live in a Christian culture. The patriarchal authority of a master morality has given way to the patriarchal authority of Christianity, but that has itself been given over to an acceptance of the authority of government. The turn to political authority and interest in nationalism that characterized Nietzsche's time, especially during the unification of Germany, is not a radical departure from previous values. It is a reinstatement of an authoritarian project with only a change in the names of the participants.

Nietzsche painted this picture with broad strokes. The history of European cultures evolves as large-scale tendencies to types of values that have certain effects. The changes that do take place happen for a purpose and are to a certain extent ordered by the participants. There is no progress, no larger order, but there is a pragmatic element to Nietzsche's evaluation of these historical values. We must answer questions not only about their origin but also about how they stand in relation to us. Can we live them? To this Nietzsche's answer was that the Christian values had outlived their usefulness. The revolution had been achieved, the master values overthrown, but conservatism within Christianity demands that values be unchanging. It also demands the enforcement of those values by the ultimate patriarchical authority: God the Father. These values were no longer what the culture needed nor were they things in which it could believe. At this point, as was suggested above, positive science is offered in place of God. There is a shift in authority to the inquirer. This shift was welcomed by many contemporary thinkers.

Nietzsche sees this model as a continuation of many of the intellectual values of previous philosophical methodologies. The continuity is to be found in claims to objectivity, where objectivity is based on reason divorced from emotion and in the more subtle "demand for certainty":

> Christianity, it seems to me, is still needed by most people in old Europe even today; therefore it still finds believers. . . . Metaphysics is still needed for some; but so is that impetuous *demand for certainty* that today discharges itself among large numbers of people in a scientific-positivistic form. The demand that one *wants*

by all means that something be firm (while on account of the ardor of this demand one is easier and more negligent about the demonstration of this certainty)—this, too, is still the demand for a support, a prop, in short that *instinct of weakness* which, to be sure, does not create religious, metaphysical systems, and convictions of all kinds but conserves them.[34]

These claims establish intellectual authority and become the values of the next (positivistic) age.

Values are more fundamental or necessary for knowledge than the criteria of our success because, without values, we cannot even begin the process:

> The question of values is more *fundamental* than the question of certainty: the latter becomes serious only by supposing that the value question has already been answered.[35]

In order to scrutinize a value one needs a viewpoint. One needs something in which one believes or has "faith":

> Strictly speaking there is no such thing as science "without any presuppositions"; this thought does not bear thinking through, it is paralogical: a philosophy, a "faith," must always be there first of all, so that science can acquire from it a direction, a meaning, a limit, a method, a *right* to exist.[36]

For Nietzsche, all activity, whether it be moral or epistemological is value-laden. The "values" are the presuppositions of our thought. Nietzsche is not just questioning Christianity; he is criticizing the way philosophy is done. He is interested in the overthrow of metaphysics, but his critique goes much further and includes all transcendental and even positivist philosophy.

His critiques of liberalism and egalitarianism have made him unpopular with a prior generation of American and British feminists who saw their goals as political and economic in a more limited sense. But Nietzsche's contemporaries were involved in a women's liberation movement that began as a movement to abolish state-sanctioned prostitution, provide respectable work as an alternative to prostitution for unwed mothers, and orphanages for children whose mothers could not care for them. Hélène

Stöcker's more radical wing of the movement suggested that the goals of the movement should change. The older movement demanded that men be held to the same sexually restrictive morality as are females. Instead Stöcker's group advocated that there be sexual freedom for men and women. This would entail the development of more liberal divorce laws and the ability of women to support themselves. Nietzsche's friendliness to ideas of sexuality and sensuality, the absence of dogmatism, and even the idea of an aristocracy of the spirit made him popular with women. Many of the women educated in that period were interested in art and wrote novels.[37] The aesthetic focus of his work struck them as helpful rather than irrelevant. An interest in meaning in an aesthetic context proved helpful to feminists liberating themselves from conceptualizations that were almost entirely based upon sensation, physical function, and beauty. Nietzsche's critique of asceticism helped to inspire Stöcker whose magazine *Die Neue Generation* tried "to make human sexuality a powerful instrument not only of reproduction, but of progressive evolution, and concurrently of a heightened and cultivated joy of life."[38]

Women have often used the liberalism associated with positivism. This and egalitarian humanism were also used by feminists in Nietzsche's time. His complaints about feminism to a certain extent follow his critiques of egalitarian social movements and ideologies. This is not the entirety of his complaint. He certainly makes remarks about the lack of femininity that goes along with this leveling of the sexes. But he gives us a critique of the cultural tendency to look for equality bolstered by totalizing impulses.

But liberalism has served women only so far. And, feminists have gotten into a lot of trouble with it. The assumptions about rational and general categories of fairness have been revealed as culturally specific, and the vary notions of abstract constructions of equality and fairness have been perceived as inhospitable and foreign to Jewish women, lesbians, and women of color, to name a few. These and other features of egalitarian theory and especially of the value-neutrality of positivism (that supposedly worked toward equality) presented problems that Nietzsche anticipated. There are always assumptions based on "faith," that is, based on presuppositions and we accept the assumption or convictions on which the discipline rests.

Having lived with a century of liberal values, we can see his points quite readily, especially the ideas that there are values behind all theories—even those that claim the value-neutrality of science, as the age of Positivism did. Nietzsche was very interested in exposing those values as values, and in seeing in them a perpetuation of the values found in Christianity, values he believed had already outlived their usefulness.

It is easy to see why some masculinist philosophers will dislike Nietzsche even though he conforms to their misogyny. While contempt for females is often expressed, Nietzsche has undermined many forms of patriarchal authority and privilege. He does this by exposing them as cultural phenomena that are the result of power and authority. They do not exist because they are right; rather, they exist because some people exercised their power and exerted authority. The view that Nietzsche offers is far too radical for thinkers who rarely account for value changes or changes in models of knowing because they think that values do not change. There are those whose only intellectual models of change come from an Hegelian unfolding of the world spirit. Because that model is rational and progressive it accounts for change without disturbing assumptions about the purity of intellect and existence of absolute values. What Marx and Nietzsche have in common is their view of the messy nature of social change. But even here, Marx is the more conservative thinker. Change is for him predictable and intelligible. For Nietzsche, the variety of ways in which power is proliferated are so complex and exist in so many forms[39] that prediction is not an easy task. Many interpreters who are interested in Nietzsche's individual ethic or the idea of the Übermensch fail to realize how important the social construction of value is for Nietzsche. They miss precisely this aspect of his work. The will to power is not only to be understood as merely a psychological drive. Nietzsche's interest in power is more complex. Social and cultural values are not the random and chaotic interactions of a number of self-governed individuals nor are they simply the product of the masses led in unthinking obedience.

Feminists are unlikely to be very positively disposed either toward the master or slave moralities. More often feminists are in sympathy with the liberalism associated with positivism. Yet, one can see why nineteenth- and early twentieth-century women intellectuals were positively disposed toward Nietzsche. There is present in his genealogical work a critique of specific patriarchical institutions and their attendant values. But perhaps more important to modern feminism is what he provides methodologically. He employs a method or methods that demand socially and historically contextual readings of intellectual values. He sees values as changing over time. Moral revolutions have happened in the past and they can continue in the present. As a philosopher he thinks it is his job to demand a social and cultural reform in the popular morality of his time.

Notes

1. Otto Weininger, *Sex and Character* (New York: AMS Press, 1975), 104.
2. *Die fröhliche Wissenschaft* (FW), §334.
3. Kathryn Addelson (then Kathryn Pyne Parsons), "Nietzsche and Moral Change," first published in Robert C. Solomon, *Nietzsche: A Collection of Critical Essays* (Garden City, N.Y.: Anchor Books, 1973).
4. See Richard Hinton Thomas, *Nietzsche in German Politics and Society, 1890–1918* (Manchester: Manchester University Press, 1983).
5. Sander Gilman, ed., *Conversations with Nietzsche: A Life in the Words of His Contemporaries* (New York: Oxford University Press, 1987), 168.
6. Ibid., 89.
7. My ultimate aim is to look at these women's intellectual work as independent thinkers. By doing so, one can counter the usual literature, which finds the question of whether or not Lou Andreas-Salomé slept with Nietzsche more important than what she thought.
8. This topic is the object of most essays on the subject. It is the feminine Nietzsche and Nietzsche's women that I shall discuss in this essay.
9. This section refers to the observations like those in *Jenseits von Gut und Böse* (*JGB*). These are fairly straightforward remarks taken literally. For a similar view, see Linda Singer, "Nietzschean Mythologies: The Inversion of Value and the War Against Women," *Soundings: An Interdisciplinary Journal* 66 (Fall 1983): 281–95.
10. *JGB*, §144.
11. Ibid., §232.
12. Ibid., preface.
13. "Erinnerungen an den jungen F. Nietzsche," *Neue Freie Presse* (Vienna), September 12, 1907. Gilman, *Conversations with Nietzsche*, 52.
14. Singer, "Nietzschean Mythologies."
15. "Erinnerungen an den jungen F. Nietzsche"; Gilman, *Conversations with Nietzsche*, 52.
16. Gilman, *Conversations with Nietzsche*, 63.
17. Ibid., 78.
18. "Der Erste Nietzsche," *Neue Freie Presse* (Vienna), September 18, 19, 21, 22, and 28, 1900.
19. Debra B. Bergoffen agrees with this view; "On Nietzsche's 'Supposing truth is a woman—what then?'" paper delivered at SPEP, 1992.
20. For this phenomenon in general, see Phyllis Rose, *Parallel Lives: Five Victorian Marriages* (New York: Alfred A. Knopf, 1984), and Ruth Brandon, *The New Women and the Old Men: Love, Sex, and the Woman Question* (New York: Norton, 1990).
21. Klaus Theweleit, *Male Fantasies*, trans. Stephen Conway, in collaboration with Erica Carter and Chris Turner (Minneapolis: University of Minnesota Press, 1987), 3–228.
22. This section will include ideas women commentators find in Nietzsche's female metaphors and his "feminine" style and psychologically reductionist readings.
23. David Farrell Krell, *Postponements: Woman, Sensuality, and Death in Nietzsche* (Bloomington: Indiana University Press, 1986).
24. Nietzsche referred to this project between 1870 and 1886.
25. Krell, *Postponements*, 3.
26. Ibid., 8.

27. Jean Graybeal, *Language and "the Feminine" in Nietzsche and Heidegger* (Bloomington: Indiana University Press, 1990).

28. *My Sister and I* (Los Angeles: Amok, 1990), lxvi.

29. Consider Alice Miller's "Friedrich Nietzsche: The Struggle Against the Truth," in Miller, *The Untouched Key: Tracing Childhood Trauma in Creativity and Destructiveness*, trans. Hildegarde and Hunter Hannum (New York: Doubleday, 1988). Miller's essay—the title itself is revealing—invites a view that can dismiss a great deal of what Nietzsche is saying as part of his pathology. In this case we have a diagnosis of arrested development due to childhood trauma that was never healed or properly addressed. The truth Nietzsche fails to realize is that his abuse as a child motivates his "mature work," and because that abuse is never healed, we never get a mature and vital Nietzsche. Miller ends her essay by asking, "And who knows what that vital Nietzsche would then have been able to give humanity?" (133). I find a more vital Nietzsche hard to imagine, although perhaps not a more mature one.

30. See, for example, the comments in Lou Andreas-Salomé, *Nietzsche*, ed., trans., and with an introd. by Siegfried Mandel (Redding Ridge, Conn.: Black Swan, 1988), 29–30.

31. In this I disagree with Ofelia Schutte, whose otherwise fine *Beyond Nihilism: Nietzsche Without Masks* (Chicago: University of Chicago Press, 1984) makes the opposite claim.

32. *JGB*, §6, trans. R. J. Hollingdale (New York: Penguin Books, 1972).

33. *JGB*, §§260–261, and *Zur Genealogie der Moral*, First Essay, §§1–17.

34. Friedrich Nietzsche, *The Gay Science* (*Die fröhliche Wissenschaft*), trans. Walter Kaufmann (New York: Random House, 1974), §347, "Believers and their need to believe."

35. Friedrich Nietzsche, *The Will to Power*, trans. Walter Kaufmann and R. J. Hollingdale (New York: Random House, 1967), §588.

36. Friedrich Nietzsche, *On the Genealogy of Morals*, trans. Walter Kaufmann (New York: Random House, 1969), III, §24.

37. Hélène Stöcker, Lou Andreas-Salomé, Lily Braun, Grete Meisel-Hess, and others.

38. Amy Hackett, "Hélène Stöcker: Left-Wing Intellectual and Sex Reformer," in *When Biology Became Destiny: Women in Weimar and Nazi Germany*, ed. Renate Bridenthal, Atina Grossmann, and Marion Kaplan (New York: Monthly Review Press, 1984), 115.

39. Including ones that Marx waved aside as insubstantial, like aesthetics.

13

The Slave Revolt in Epistemology

Daniel W. Conway

Philosophy reduced to "theory of knowledge" . . . that is philosophy in its last throes, an end, an agony, something inspiring pity. How could such a philosophy—*dominate*! (BGE 204)[1]

In his discussion of the ascetic ideal in *On the Genealogy of Morals*, Nietzsche warns us not to invest our redemptive hopes in science. Rather than provide or enable an alternative to the ascetic ideal, contemporary science in fact represents

> the *best* ally the ascetic ideal has at present, and precisely because it is the most unconscious, involuntary, hidden, and subterranean ally! (GM III:25)

Nietzsche exposes the "will to truth" that drives scientific inquiry as sheltering an unacknowledged *faith* in the redemptive capacity of truth, a faith that he proposes as complicit with the ascetic ideal. Rather than liberate us from the thrall of the ascetic ideal, the "will to truth" of contemporary science continues the millennia-long assault on the body and the affects: "*All* science . . . has at present the object of dissuading man from his former respect for himself, as if this had been nothing but a piece of bizarre conceit" (GM III:25).

Nietzsche's warning against the ascetic kernel of contemporary science provides an instructive backdrop against which we might assess the current debate among feminist theorists over the epistemic status of *objectivity*. Can the project of feminist epistemology accommodate a reconstituted notion of objectivity, and if so, how should this reconstituted notion be positively characterized? The two most currently authoritative parties to this debate are postmodern feminist epistemology, of which the work of Donna Haraway is representative, and feminist standpoint theory, as championed by Sandra Harding.

Nietzsche's perspectivism not only adumbrates the postmodern strategies of feminists like Donna Haraway but also issues a preemptive warning against the version of feminist standpoint theory espoused by Sandra Harding. Because Harding's epistemological project unwittingly serves the "will to truth" emblematic of contemporary science, her version of feminist standpoint theory ultimately discounts those immediate, embodied experiences of women that it presumes to subject to theoretical analysis. If the project of feminist epistemology is to incorporate the radically situated knowledges of women and other subjugated agents, then its practitioners must take the "postmodern" turn outlined by Nietzsche and implemented by Haraway.

Nietzsche's Perspectivism as a Model for Feminist Epistemology

Nietzsche's perspectivism, an epistemic thesis conveyed via a host of masculinist and residually misogynist images, might seem like an unlikely precursor of feminist epistemologies. But in fact Nietzsche provides an epistemic framework that both accommodates and prizes the radically situated experiences of women. In the following passage, which contains Nietzsche's most detailed and sustained discussion of the position now known as "perspectivism," he both warns us to beware of traditional epistemology and points us in a more promising direction:

let us be on guard against the dangerous old conceptual fiction that posited a "pure, will-less, painless, timeless knowing subject"; let us guard against the snares of such contradictory concepts as "pure reason," "absolute spirituality," "knowledge in itself"; these always demand that we should think of an eye that is completely unthinkable, an eye turned in no particular direction, in which the active and interpreting forces, through which alone seeing becomes seeing *something*, are supposed to be lacking. . . . There is *only* a perspectival seeing [*perspektivisches Sehen*], *only* a perspectival "knowing"; and the *more* affects we allow to speak [*zu Worte kommen*] about one thing, the *more* eyes, different eyes, we can use to observe one thing, the more complete will our "concept" of this thing, our "objectivity" be. (GM III:12)

In this brief passage, Nietzsche makes several points with which feminist theorists have expressed agreement. First of all, he warns us to beware of the traditional interpretation of objectivity as disinterested contemplation. The goal of disinterested contemplation presupposes "conceptual fictions" and "contradictory concepts," and furthermore requires us to posit a disembodied, disinterested knowing subject, "an eye turned in no particular direction." Nietzsche's perspectivism thus attempts to account for those affective components and determinants of knowledge that traditionally have been ignored or discounted by epistemology. His reconstituted notion of objectivity (consistently noted by his use of quotation marks) suggests that knowledge is a function of the embodied expression of our affective investment in the world. His perspectivism thus presupposes an account of subjects as radically situated, that is, as affectively invested, in the world and in their bodies.

Second, if we interpret these "eyes" as perspectives, whose "interpretive forces" are sustained by a suffusion of affect, then we see that for Nietzsche perspectives are not disembodied points of view that hover disinterestedly over the world. Indeed, Nietzsche's perspectivism is strategically designed to recuperate the metaphorics of vision that have dominated (and perverted) representational epistemology.[2] In order to appropriate the metaphorics of vision for his reconstituted notion of objectivity, Nietzsche glides effortlessly between the twin sensory images of "eyes" and "voices":

. . . the *more* affects we allow to speak about one thing, the *more* eyes, different eyes, we can use to observe one thing, the more complete will our "concept" of this thing, our "objectivity," be.

Eyes and affects, knowing and feeling, seeing and speaking, conception and perception, situation and expression: the pursuit of objectivity requires us to deconstruct these binary oppositions and integrate the supposedly antagonistic terms within each. Nietzsche's reconstituted notion of objectivity encourages a maximal expression of affective investment in the world—a chorus of radically situated "voices"—and thus stands 180 degrees removed from the traditional epistemological goal of disinterested, disaffected contemplation. In fact, he concludes his warning against disinterested contemplation by graphically likening the pursuit of objectivity to an act of self-directed castration: "to suspend each and every affect, supposing we were capable of this—what would that mean but to *castrate* the intellect?" (GM III:12).

"There is *only* a perspectival knowing" thus means that knowledge is possible only if one's affective engagement with the world is both recognized and expressed. If it is not, then one can at best lay claim to a desiccated, bloodless simulacrum of knowledge. Nietzsche's recuperation of the metaphorics of vision thus enables us to understand perspectives as *bodies*: suffused with affect, inextricably situated in the world, and inscribed with the pain and torment inflicted by normalizing mores and institutions. Nietzsche consequently reconstitutes the notion of objectivity as an aggregation of radically situated perspectives (or bodies)—none of which affords us an epistemically pure glimpse of the world. The task of the *Wissenschaftler* who aspires to objectivity is to compile as exhaustive an aggregation of radically situated perspectives (or bodies) as possible, to assemble an unprecedented chorus of affective voices.

Third, Nietzsche recommends his perspectivism not for its epistemic purity, but for the strategic advantage that accrues to his reconstituted notion of objectivity. His discussion of "perspectivism" appears within the context of his analysis of the ascetic ideal, with which he associates the traditional understanding of objectivity as disinterested contemplation. Nietzsche frequently contends that the pursuit of objectivity requires a concomitant assault on the affects, which in turn leads, paradoxically, to a diminution of our knowledge, to the subordination of situated knowledges to lifeless simulacra of knowledge. The strategic advantage of objectivity lies, he believes, in "the ability to *control* one's Pro and Con and to dispose of them, so that one knows how to employ a *variety* of perspectives and affective interpretations in the service of knowledge" (GM III:12).

Fourth, Nietzsche willingly accepts the self-referential implications of his endorsement of situated knowledges. He readily acknowledges that his own perspectivism too is situated, that it reflects the peculiar political interests of its author. "Perspectivism" is itself perspectival in nature, for it is the product of the partial perspective and embodied affect peculiar to Herr Nietzsche. Rather than stake an illicit claim to epistemic purity, Nietzsche quite openly voices the hostility and resentment that inform his own political campaign against the ascetic practices of traditional epistemology. It is no coincidence that Nietzsche's most illuminating articulation of his perspectivism appears in *On the Genealogy of Morals*, a book in which he enacts his own vested political interests in compiling a genealogy of morals.

Nietzsche's perspectivism thus provides a promising epistemological model for feminist theorists. But let us be clear about the opportunity cost of embracing his perspectivism: if we accept this reconstituted notion of objectivity, and seek a maximal aggregation of radically situated perspectives, then we must abandon the quest for a privileged, epistemically pure, God's-eye perspective on the world. We need not disavow our cultural, genealogical, or political preferences for certain perspectives, but we must be careful to situate these preferences within a discernible political agenda. The privilege of a particular perspective will derive entirely from its situation within the political agenda it expresses, and not from its internal coherence or privileged access to the real world.

The Legacy of Nietzsche's Perspectivism in Postmodern Feminist Epistemology

Virtually all feminists theorists, and at any rate those with whom I am primarily concerned here, follow Nietzsche in rejecting the traditional philosophical ideal of objectivity. Feminist theorists have long maintained that the achievement of objectivity would require agents to accede to a disembodied, trans-perspectival, patriarchal standpoint—a chimerical gambit that Donna Haraway calls "the God trick."[3] This "view from nowhere" acquires the privilege and cachet of a "view from everywhere," and it effectively devaluates the experiences of those agents whose knowledges of the world are most obviously and ineluctably situated. Some feminist theorists thus argue that this ideal of disinterested, detached objectivity is pursued at the expense and exclusion of the situated knowledges of women, especially women of color. Traditional (patriarchal) epistemology thus delivers only a simulacrum of objectivity, for its emphasis on disinterested detachment precisely discounts the partiality that accrues to a radically situated perspective.

At the same time, however, some feminist theorists are understandably reluctant to abandon the *notion* of objectively valid knowledge as the goal of philosophical inquiry. A reconstituted notion of objectivity would provide a standard whereby they might claim, for instance, that one scientific theory is better or more complete or more promising than another. In this light, we might think of the goal of feminist epistemology as the reconstitution of the notion of objectivity, such that feminist theorists might continue the critical enterprise of science without subscribing to its most pernicious concepts.

With respect to the positive content of this reconstituted notion of objectivity, a debate currently rages among feminist theorists. Donna Haraway, whose writing I will treat as representative of the project of postmodern feminist epistemology, contends that the objectivity of a perspective is a function of its *partiality*:

> The moral is simple: only partial perspective promises objective vision. . . . Feminist objectivity is about limited location and situated knowledge, not about transcendence and splitting of subject and object. In this way we might become answerable for what we learn and see.[4]

The partiality that Haraway prizes is achieved not through the disinterested detachment of subjects from the world, but through the radical situation of subjects in the world. Her suggested reconceptualization of "feminist objectivity" therefore devolves from her more fundamental reconceptualization of the world we seek to know in terms of the world in which we live. Haraway considers the pursuit of objectivity a feminist project because women have traditionally been excluded from the male fantasy of a detached, disinterested contemplation of disembodied truth. As a consequence, women have traditionally had no choice *but* to cultivate the objectivity that accrues to their situations. We might think of postmodern feminism as attempting to recover the situated knowledge involuntarily acquired by subjugated women, and subsequently turning it to their own political advantage. Postmodern feminism thus aims to assemble the epistemic resources of subjugated standpoints, so that the residents of these standpoints might eventually liberate themselves.

A perceived weakness of this reconstituted notion of objectivity is that postmodern feminists like Haraway cannot (and do not) assign a purely epistemic privilege to the subjugated standpoints of women and excluded others. More precisely, in accordance with her reconstitution of the notion of objectivity, Haraway appropriates the epistemic privilege traditionally assigned to the objectively valid perspective of detached, disembodied standpoints and relocates it in the partial perspective of radically situated standpoints:

> I would like a doctrine of embodied objectivity that accommodates paradoxical and critical feminist science projects: feminist objectivity means quite simply *situated knowledge*.[5]

Haraway's brand of feminism conveys a postmodern sensibility in large part because she has abandoned the quest for an epistemically pure, foundationally innocent standpoint. Indeed, a primary aim of her writing is to disabuse feminist theorists of the perceived need for an untainted, originary, epistemically pure standpoint from which to launch their various political campaigns. Partiality thus stands as the sole determinant of objectivity, and there exists no verifiable epistemic relation between objectivity and standpoints informed by positions of exclusion, oppression or victimage:

> A commitment to mobile positioning and to passionate detachment is dependent on the impossibility of innocent "identity" politics and epistemologies as strategies for seeing from the standpoints of the subjugated in order to see well.[6]

Postmodern feminists register a preference for the standpoints of excluded, subjugated women not because such standpoints are epistemically pure, but because "they seem to promise more adequate, sustained, objective, transforming accounts of the world."[7]

This preference is clearly political in nature, and Haraway makes no pretense of aspiring to epistemic purity or foundational innocence. For Haraway, any epistemic privilege necessarily implies a political (i.e., situated) preference. Her postmodern orientation elides the boundaries traditionally drawn between politics and epistemology, and it thus renders otiose the ideal of epistemic purity. All perspectives are partial, all standpoints situated—including those of feminist theorists. It is absolutely crucial to Haraway's postmodern feminist project that we acknowledge her claims *about* situated knowledge as *themselves* situated within the political agenda of postmodern feminism; postmodern feminists must therefore accept and accommodate the self-referential implications of their own epistemic claims.

The political agenda of postmodern feminism thus assigns to (some) subjugated standpoints a political preference or priority. Haraway, for example, believes that some subjugated standpoints may be more immediately revealing, especially since they have been discounted and excluded for so long. They may prove especially useful in coming to understand the political and psychological mechanisms whereby the patriarchy discounts the radically situated knowledges of others while claiming for its own (situated) knowledge an epistemic privilege that divorces objectivity from partiality:

> The standpoints of the subjugated . . . are savvy to modes of denial through repression, forgetting, and disappearing acts—ways of being nowhere while claiming to see comprehensively. The subjugated have a decent chance to be on to the god-trick and all its dazzling—and therefore blinding—illuminations.[8]

But these subjugated standpoints do not afford feminists an epistemically privileged view of the world independent of their political agenda. Feminist theorists who subscribe to Haraway's agenda must therefore resist the temptation to claim for subjugated standpoints the same type of privilege that patriarchy claims for itself. The epistemic "privilege" of subjugated standpoints must be understood in terms of the feminist reconceptualization of objectivity and revision of epistemology.

A subjugated standpoint may shed new light on the ways of an oppressor, but it in no way renders superfluous or redundant to science the standpoint of the oppressor. Because neither standpoint fully comprises the other, the aggregation of the two would move both parties (or a third party) closer to a more objective understanding of the world:

The science question in feminism is about objectivity as positioned rationality. Its images are not the products of escape and
transcendence of limits, i.e., the view from above, but the joining
of partial views and halting voices into a collective subject position that promises a vision of the means of ongoing finite embodiment, of living within limits and contradictions, i.e., of views
from somewhere.[9]

If some feminists have political reasons for disavowing this project of aggregation, or for adopting it selectively, then they must pursue their political agenda at the expense of the greater objectivity that they might
otherwise have gained. The decision to discount the situated knowledge
of another is always a political decision with political consequences, and
feminists should beware of appealing to epistemic purity to defend such
decisions.

Sandra Harding's Feminist Standpoint Theory

Sandra Harding articulates and defends what she calls the "feminist
standpoint epistemologies," which she presents as methodologically superior to the theory known as "feminist empiricism." The hallmark of feminist standpoint epistemologies is that they "direct us to start our research
and scholarship from the perspectives of women's lives."[10] The goal of the
standpoint epistemologies is to collect the immediate but "scientifically
inadequate" data from women's experiences, and to construct viable scientific theories based on—but not reducible to—these experiences.
    Feminist standpoint theory represents an attempt to incorporate into
epistemology the political insights delivered by a Hegelian-Marxist account of social relations.[11] Borrowing the familiar Hegelian categories of
"master" and "slave" to designate the polar perspectives occupied, respectively, by the patriarchy and its victims, standpoint theorists assign an
epistemic privilege to the standpoint of the "slave" within a gender-based
hierarchy. Forced by socially-inscribed gender relations to situate themselves (i.e., to work) in the world, women have gained, by dint of their
subjugation, an unparalleled understanding of the underlying logic that
governs social relations. Because women, and especially women of color,

have been relegated by the patriarchy to the position of "slaves," research in epistemology should begin from the lives of women.

While standpoint theorists variously construe the precise epistemic privilege that accrues to the standpoint of the "slave," they generally agree on its basic logical structure. As Sandra Harding explains:

> The logic of the standpoint epistemologies depends on the understanding that the "master's position" in any set of dominating social relations tends to produce distorted visions of the real regularities and underlying causal tendencies in social relations—including human interactions with nature. The feminist standpoint epistemologies argue that because men are in the master's position vis-à-vis women, women's social experience—conceptualized through the lenses of feminist theory—can provide the grounds for a less distorted understanding of the world around us.[12]

The "slave" not only sees the world differently, as the world-for-slave, but also sees "the world around us" more clearly and with a better understanding than the "master." As in the familiar Hegelian and Marxist narratives, an original experience of victimage and oppression equips the "slave" with the tools and knowledge to orchestrate a "revolution." While standpoint theorists occasionally describe their political *praxis* in Marxist terms, they usually characterize their "revolutions" in Hegelian terms, as revolutions in epistemology. Harding, for example, advertises her formulation of feminist standpoint theory as a prolegomenon to the development of a "successor science."

Harding's synopsis of the standpoint epistemologies not only reveals their underlying logic but also exposes the residual objectivism that tinctures many formulations of feminist standpoint theory. If the standpoint of the "master" "tends to produce distorted visions of the real regularities and underlying causal tendencies in social relations," then there *is* a real world, after all, which competing standpoints capture with varying degrees of distortion. Harding thus insists that

> [s]tarting off research from women's lives will generate less partial and distorted accounts not only of women's lives, but also of men's lives *and of the whole social order*.[13]

The residual objectivism that informs the standpoint epistemologies is no accident, for it lies embedded within the Hegelian-Marxist apparatus that standpoint theorists characteristically deploy. As we shall see below in more detail, this residual objectivism compromises the guiding insights of feminist standpoint theory.

In her own defense of the standpoint epistemologies, Sandra Harding attempts to furnish feminist standpoint theory with a more solid methodological grounding. Reacting not only to common misunderstandings of the standpoint epistemologies but also to the crude essentialism into which standpoint theorists occasionally lapse, Harding undertakes a more careful, and defensible, account of the epistemic privilege that accrues to the standpoint of the "slave."[14]

Like many feminist theorists, Harding rejects the traditional notion of objectivity, which she understands in terms of a misguided demand for value neutrality.[15] Traditional epistemology not only has failed to secure a disinterested "view from Nowhere" but also has discounted the experiences of those agents whose knowledges of the world are most obviously and ineluctably situated.[16] Despite her endorsement of feminist standpoint theory, Harding expresses a general agreement with the deconstructive designs of postmodern feminism, and she explicitly applauds Haraway's campaign to reconstitute objectivity in terms of situated knowledges.[17] Harding thus agrees that the pursuit of objectivity is a patriarchal exercise that systematically excludes the experiences of women. In a rhetorical question to which she implies that an affirmative response is in order, Harding asks:

> If it is the experience of subjugation that provides the grounding for the most desirable inquiries and knowledges, then should not the experience of . . . women who have suffered from racism provide the grounding for . . . feminist scientific and epistemological projects, not to mention ethics and politics?[18]

At the same time, however, Harding believes that *some* notion of objectivity is needed to head off the precipitous slide into relativism. For all of its flaws, the traditional notion of objectivity furnishes a critical context in which truth claims are publicly assessed according to established (if controversial) standards and criteria. The traditional notion of objectivity thus enables philosophers to rank competing theories and knowledge claims and to discredit those theories that are most obviously and

dangerously misguided. According to Harding, some such critical standard is crucial to the very project of feminist epistemology:

> What would be the point of a theory of knowledge that did not
> make prescriptions for how to go about getting knowledge or of a
> prescription for getting knowledge that did not arise from a theory
> about how knowledge can be and has been produced?[19]

In order to continue the enterprise of epistemology without subscribing
to its most pernicious concepts, Harding reconstitutes the notion of objectivity in terms of the "socially situated knowledges" that emerge from
partial perspectives, which, by definition, make no claim to value neutrality.[20] Harding's attention to "socially situated knowledge" reflects her
allegiance to what I take to be the signal insight of feminist standpoint
theory: every standpoint commands a limited measure of objectivity with
respect to the finite scope of its own perspective on the world. While no
single standpoint is so privileged that it yields a panoptic glimpse of the
world-in-itself, no standpoint is so impoverished that its occupants must
rely on (or defer to) others to determine the objective content of their
experiences. Indeed, if a limited measure of objectivity accrues to all partial perspectives, then no Promethean patriarch is entitled to determine
for others the content or the validity of the situated knowledge(s) they
derive from their respective standpoints.

Harding consequently proposes an alternative notion of objectivity,
called "strong objectivity," which represents the antithesis of value neutrality. "Strong objectivity" is a function not of some chimerical "god's-
eye perspective," but of the irrecuperably partial perspectives from which
"socially situated knowledges" emanate. According to Harding, then, objectively valid knowledge is gained not from some mythical "view from
Nowhere," floating untethered above the world, but from the partial
standpoints of agents situated in the world. The epistemologist who seeks
to acquire "strong objectivity" must therefore resign the comfortable detachment of the patriarchy and situate himself or herself "on the same
critical, causal plane as the object of his or her inquiry."[21]

In order to explain how standpoint theorists might secure the "strong
objectivity" she recommends, Harding draws a basic, guiding distinction
between "women's experiences" and "women's lives."[22] She associates
"women's experiences" with "what women say (and see)," and she describes "women's lives" as the observations and theories that arise from

careful, sober reflection on the nature of these experiences. Whereas "women's experiences . . . would not seem to be reliable grounds for deciding just which claims to knowledge are preferable,"[23] "women's lives" provide "an objective location . . . from which feminist research should begin."[24] The goal of the standpoint epistemologies is to collect the immediate, but "scientifically inadequate," data from women's experiences, and to construct viable scientific theories based on—but not reducible to—these experiences. It is important to note here that Harding's distinction sanctions the intercession of the standpoint epistemologist, who must decipher the raw data of "women's experiences" and translate them into the reliable, objective data of "women's lives."

Harding apparently believes, however, that "strong objectivity" is gained not (merely) through an aggregation of the partial perspective of radically situated standpoints, but also by privileging within this aggregate a cluster of standpoints distinguished by their experiences of oppression, exclusion and victimage:

> Epistemologically, the standpoint theories argue that it is an advantage to base thought in the everyday lives of people in oppressed and excluded groups.[25]

Subjugated standpoints are not merely important additions to the aggregate of perspectives that feminist epistemologists are assembling; they actually afford theorists a more accurate ("less distorted") glimpse of the world:

> The logic of the standpoint epistemologies depends on the understanding that the "master's position" in any set of dominating social relations tends to produce distorted visions of *the real regularities and underlying causal tendencies in social relations*—including human interactions with nature. The feminist standpoint epistemologies argue that because men are in the master's position vis-à-vis women, women's social experience—conceptualized throught the lenses of feminist theory—can provide the grounds for a less distorted understanding of the world around us.[26]

Harding apparently believes that the perspective of the "slave" is privileged insofar as the "slave" understands not only what it is like to be a "slave" but also what it must be like to be a "master." In order simply to survive, presumably, the "slave" has managed to discern and correct for the distortions imposed on the world by the perspective of the "master." So the "slave" not only sees the world differently but also sees the world more clearly and with a better understanding than the "master," whose own perspective is rendered redundant and superfluous by the epistemic privilege of the "slave."

In what is perhaps the most controversial element of her formulation of feminist standpoint theory, Harding explicitly links the objectivity of a critical standpoint to the political values and interests that inform it. A feminist standpoint, she claims, is not something one inherits simply by virtue of one's gendered situation in society, but something one *achieves* through protracted struggle in the political arena:

> This need for struggle emphasizes the fact that a feminist standpoint is not something that anyone can have simply by claiming it. It is an achievement. It differs in this respect from a perspective, which anyone can have simply by "opening one's eyes."[27]

Harding thus believes that the achievement of a feminist standpoint is a matter not of gender per se but of *praxis* in accordance with the appropriate political agenda. In fact, those who achieve a critical feminist standpoint through political activity are not necessarily those whose experiences are typically associated with the material conditions of oppression and domination. Men can achieve a feminist standpoint, Harding claims, and economically advantaged white women can begin their research, without apologies, from the lives of disadvantaged women of color.[28] The struggle required to command a genuinely feminist standpoint endows its ensuing knowledge claims with the "strong objectivity" that Harding designates as the starting point for epistemological research.

According to Harding, then, the achievement of an objective critical standpoint presupposes an allegiance to the guiding values and interests of feminist politics:

> Hence, feminist politics is not just a tolerable companion of feminist research but a necessary condition for generating less partial and perverse descriptions and explanations. In a socially stratified society the objectivity of the results of research is increased by political activism by and on behalf of oppressed, exploited, and dominated groups. Only through such struggles can we begin to

see beneath the appearances created by an unjust social order to the reality of how this social order is in fact constructed and maintained.[29]

Harding acknowledges the "apparent" circularity involved in grounding the objectivity of a feminist standpoint in feminist politics, but she insists that her argument "is at least not viciously circular."[30] As we shall see later on, however, Harding's circle is far more problematic than she realizes. If this circle escapes vitiation, it does so only by virtue of the residual objectivism upon which it trades.

Some Epistemic Questions About Feminist Standpoint Theory

Harding's account of her version of feminist standpoint theory raises several questions about the epistemic status of the standpoint epistemologies. In this section I shall rehearse eight Nietzschean objections to her attribution of an epistemic privilege to the standpoint of the "slave."

First of all, Harding's epistemological model would actually seem to preclude our direct access to the radically situated knowledges that she proposes as constitutive of "strong objectivity." Her guiding distinction between "women's experiences" and "women's lives" would appear to sanction the intercession of a competent epistemologist, who could convey better than these women the objective meaning of their "scientifically inadequate" experiences. This mediating epistemologist would presumably decipher the raw data of "women's experiences" and translate them into the reliable, objective data of "women's lives."

By legislating the intercession of the epistemologist, however, Harding actually compromises the immediacy of situation that characterizes "women's experiences," and which "women's lives" are supposed to convey in a theoretically adequate form. Instead of the "scientifically inadequate" experiences of disenfranchised women of color, we receive theorized interpretations of subjugated standpoints, filtered through the epistemically privileged, composite standpoint of the interceding epistemologist. Harding's epistemology thus renders inaccessible the radically situated knowledges that it proposes as constitutive of "strong objectivity." Rather than attain the "strong objectivity" she prizes, Harding instead secures a strongly edited objectivity: (ostensibly) based on the visceral experiences of women of color, but *interpreted by* the mediating epistemologist. Rather than convey the first-person, situated immediacy of "women's experiences," "strong objectivity" expresses the mediating epistemologist's second-person interpretation of these experiences.[31]

By virtue of its very charter, then, Harding's methodology compromises the partiality of perspective and situation of knowledge that it ostensibly seeks to attain. "Strong objectivity" may deliver important, illuminating insights into the experiences of subjugated agents, but the experiences it discloses are always mediated by the standpoint epistemologists, who appoint themselves to speak for those agents who cannot or will not speak for themselves in the "masterful" parlance of science.

Second, the epistemic privilege Harding celebrates does *not* accrue to those agents whose experiences directly reflect the material conditions of slavery, but to those agents whose political struggles empower them to translate the experiences of real slaves into "women's lives." As we have seen, the standpoint of the "slave" yields insights into the "real regularities" of "the world around us" *only* because it is achieved through political activity. This means, then, that the standpoint of the "slave" is achieved not by slaves per se, but only by those agents whose political bootstrapping has enabled them to transcend, to some degree, the material conditions of enslavement. This implicit division between those who *live* like slaves and those who command the privileged standpoint of the "slave" underlies Harding's explicit distinction between "women's experiences" and "women's lives." Indeed, the epistemic privilege that Harding assigns to the "slave" actually belongs to the standpoint occupied by her and the other epistemologists who translate "women's experiences" into "women's lives."

Harding's formulation of feminist standpoint theory thus introduces an ambiguous third term into the familiar Hegelian-Marxist narrative. The "masters" and the "slaves" are joined by a vanguard of *slave advocates*, whose political struggles have gained for them the critical standpoint from which genuinely liberatory strategies might eventually emerge. The term "slave advocate" is not Harding's, but my own. It is intended to capture those hybrids of mastery and enslavement who occupy the middle ground between the polar perspectives of "master" and "slave." This vanguard of slave advocates includes Harding's standpoint epistemologists, who construct "women's lives" from the data of "women's experiences."

These slave advocates are not themselves "slaves," for they enjoy suffi-cient critical distance from the material conditions of victimage and op-pression to subject these conditions to scientific scrutiny; nor are they "masters," for their political activism has effectively excluded them from the hierarchical social structure enforced by the patriarchy. Harding, for example, portrays herself as an outsider inside, insisting that her voice, too, is marginalized within "prefeminist" institutions.[32]

The problem with Harding's formulation, however, is that the Hege-lian-Marxist narrative she adopts cannot accommodate the *tertium quid* she attempts to inscribe into it. Hegel's phenomenological method brooks no deviation from the binary typology of master and slave, whose dialectical logic leads naturally to its own self-overcoming. Marx similarly scheduled the dialectical installation of communism to follow the unam-biguous polarization of the proletariat and the bourgeoisie; he conse-quently predicted the imminent assimilation of all third or hybrid social classes. Within the Hegelian-Marxist narrative, that is, the emergence of a distinct third term can be only apparent, only "dialectical." Harding's slave advocates must therefore constitute a disguised species of either "masters" or "slaves"—unless, of course, she intends now to revise the narrative she has uncritically adopted.

Third, if Harding's revision of the Hegelian-Marxist narrative is to succeed, then she must provide a compelling account of the *tertium quid* she introduces, such that these slave advocates defy classification as either "masters" *or* "slaves." While Harding adequately explains why she and her fellow epistemologists are not properly counted among the "slaves," her refusal of the mantle of the "master" is less convincing. In fact, she regularly attributes to herself and her fellow standpoint theorists the in-sights and privileges that are customarily associated with mastery. She may mean to promote the cause of the "slave," but she does so with the tools and language of the "master," which she has acquired in the course of her own fructifying political activities. Her proximity to the standpoint of the "master" is furthermore no accident, for the avowed goal of femi-nist politics, on her construal, is constituted by the achievement of rela-tive mastery. The danger here is that Harding's slave advocates may unwittingly reproduce the logic of the master/slave relationship, situating themselves in relation to the "slave" as the "master" stands to them.[33] The political struggles through which these theorists achieve a critical feminist standpoint may in fact transform them into proximate "masters," from whom, in the eyes of the "slave," ultimate "masters" are indistinguishable. Indeed, by what means could Harding possibly hope to escape or confound the intractable binary logic of the master/slave relationship?[34]

Fourth, Harding's reliance on an admittedly circular argument prevents her from offering an adequate account (or defense) of the future she confidently predicts for the "slave." Faced with the danger of a co-opted vanguard of slave advocates, we might inquire into the epistemic privilege that accrues to Harding's own standpoint: How is it, exactly, that *she* knows that the "slave" will inherit the future? Hegel, after all, validates his own preoccupation with the slave by staking a claim to the panoptic standpoint of Absolute Knowing. He can guide his readers through the dialectical labyrinth of history only because he has already deduced its logical outcome.[35] Marx claims a similar epistemic privilege for himself as a student of history and class struggles. He confidently prophesies the revolution of the proletariat and the installation of communism because he alone has divined the immutable, inexorable laws of history. The inevitable polarization of classes under advanced industrial capitalism guarantees the material conditions both of the revolution of the proletariat and of the eventual abolition of all social classes. Both Hegel and Marx claim to *know* that the victimage and oppression of the "slave" are only apparent, only temporary, only dialectical. In both cases, that is, a philosopher justifies an extravagant bet on a bedraggled underdog by claiming a "god's-eye" view of the eventual outcome.

In her endorsement of feminist standpoint theory, Harding casts a similar wager, foresaking traditional methods of epistemology in order to harvest the experiences of the victimized and dispossessed. While her formulation of feminist standpoint theory incorporates some fairly bold revisions, she accepts without question the Hegelian-Marxist theoretical apparatus upon which standpoint theorists characteristically rely. Although she distinguishes between the achievement of a standpoint through political struggle and the immediate experience of oppression and domination, she nevertheless assigns an epistemic privilege to the standpoint of the "slave." In fact, the primary advantage of beginning research from "women's lives" lies in the capacity of such standpoints to afford its occupants a more accurate glimpse of the world itself:

> Knowledge emerges for the oppressed through the struggles they wage against their oppressors. It is because women have struggled against male supremacy that research starting from their lives can

be made to yield up clearer and more nearly complete visions of social reality than are available only from the perspective of men's side of these struggles.[36]

Harding thus inherits the residual objectivism that informs feminist standpoint theory in general. There *is* a real world out there, of which subjugated standpoints deliver a clearer, "less distorted" view.[37] Like other standpoint theorists, she endorses the basic strategy of securing these foundational perspectives on the world: "feminist standpoint theory can direct the production of less partial and less distorted beliefs."[38]

Fifth, Harding's imputation of an epistemic privilege to the standpoint of the "slave" unwittingly reintroduces the recently retired notion of objectivity. If the "master" "tends to produce distorted visions of the real regularities and underlying causal tendencies in social relations," then the "master" fails even on the terms of traditional, patriarchal epistemology. Hence there *is* a privileged, "less distorted" standpoint (or cluster of standpoints), and the task of science is to gain command of these objective standpoints on the world. Rather than extricate epistemology from the snares of patriarchy, Harding thus delivers an inverted, matriarchal version of patriarchal objectivity, which enshrines the objectively valid perspective of *das Weib an sich*.[39]

Contrary to her own account, then, Harding appeals to a "divine" standpoint, from which she glimpses the eventual victory of the "slave." She can recommend the standpoint of the "slave," after all, only in the event that she too commands a similarly privileged standpoint, from which she can verify the epistemic achievement that she attributes to the "slave." As we have seen, she acknowledges the "apparent" circularity of her attempt to ground the "strong objectivity" of feminist standpoints in the fructifying struggles of feminist politics. She is confident that her circle escapes vitiation, but only because (or so I contend) it is not really a circle after all. The missing term, whose suppression engenders the appearance of circularity, is furnished by the residual objectivism to which she clings, but which she does not own. Feminist politics will succeed, in short, because feminist standpoints afford their occupants a privileged insight into the real relations that govern the world around us. Hence the epistemic "reward" of participating in the signature struggles of feminist politics: standpoint theorists gain, for themselves and their subjects, a foundational understanding of the objective regularities that inform gender-based hierarchies.

Having debunked the "view from above" prized by the patriarchy, Harding surreptitiously enshrines its antipode, the "view from below," as the new foundational standpoint. Because she replaces the "god's-eye" view of the world with a similarly privileged "victim's-eye" standpoint, she remains trapped within the epistemological paradigm she means to deconstruct. She exposes the "god-trick" favored by the patriarchy, only to supplant it with a "goddess-trick" of her own design.[40] Indeed, without some such anchorage in the residual objectivism that grounds the standpoint epistemologies, her decision to begin research from "women's lives" would otherwise appear arbitrary and capricious.

Sixth, while Harding would certainly deny that she appeals surreptitiously to a "god's-eye" point of view, the alternative is even less promising for her version of feminist standpoint theory. If her wager on the "slave" is *not* informed by a panoptic glimpse of the real relations and laws governing the historical development of hierarchical societies, then her formulation of feminist standpoint theory must rest on a wildly implausible hunch. To repudiate the philosophy and science of the "master," in favor of the unconfirmed, unarticulated insight of the "slave," is to forsake the only reliable instruments of liberation known to "masters" and "slaves" alike. Rather than urge the "slaves" to appropriate the tools of their own oppression, to learn the language and science of the "master," to beat the "master" at his own game, Harding encourages the "slaves" to plumb the depths of their victimage for the gnostic wisdom that supposedly lies hidden therein. Without the preternatural assurance confidently (if falsely) furnished by a Hegel or a Marx, the victory of the "slaves" could come to pass only as a miracle. Harding might just as well advise struggling students of "patriarchal" science and philosophy to entrust their dreams of liberation to the excluded alternative sciences of astrology and numerology.

Seventh, while Harding endorses the pursuit of "strong objectivity" via the aggregation of situated knowledges, she does not consistently situate *her own* (second-order) claims about situated knowledge. As a consequence, she occasionally conflates her own political preference for the subjugated standpoints of women of color with the epistemic purity of such standpoints. When speaking *about* these subjugated standpoints, Harding generally accounts for their privilege in terms of her situated political preference. When speaking *from* these standpoints, however, she tends to account for their privilege in terms of an epistemic purity that the distortions of the "master" compromise. Harding's *own* composite standpoint, which purports to integrate the visceral experiences of dispossessed women of color with the "masterful" theorizing of an educated, economically privileged, white college professor, is a detached, disembodied abstraction, a vestige (and perversion) of the antepostmodern patriarchal quest for objectivity. Whereas Haraway and other postmodern feminists have accepted the opportunity cost of a reconstituted notion of objectivity, Harding has not. Despite acknowledging the epistemological and political advantages of postmodern feminism, Harding clings to the idea that the standpoint of the "slave" affords us an epistemically pure(r) glimpse of the real world. Harding consequently breaks only incompletely and irresolutely with patriarchal epistemology, and thus declines Haraway's invitation to take the postmodern turn.

Harding's failure to situate politically her own claims about situated knowledges admits of potentially grave repercussions for feminist politics. Haraway warns of a "dream" that continues to haunt some feminists:

> The permanent partiality of feminist points of view has consequences for our expectations of forms of political organization and participation. We do not need a totality in order to work well. The feminist dream of a common language, like all dreams for a perfectly true language, of perfectly faithful naming of experience, is a totalizing and imperialist one.[41]

This "dream" of foundational innocence is not only epistemically bankrupt but also is politically disastrous, for it imposes upon feminist politics conditions of justification that are impossible to meet. Haraway's campaign to expose and debunk this "dream" effectively absolves feminists of any perceived responsibility for grounding or justifying a political agenda by appeal to epistemic criteria. Haraway regards both epistemology and politics as serious endeavors, but she does not require of the latter that it acquire its justificatory and motive force from the former—especially if the former retains its familiar patriarchal cast. The "privilege" of any postmodern feminist agenda must and will be purely political; the desire or need for a further, epistemic privilege will only frustrate feminist political activity.

Harding would appear to subscribe to this totalizing dream, for she attempts to ground her political agenda in the epistemic privilege of those subjugated standpoints that afford us a less distorted view of the real world. Her weakness for this "totalizing dream" thus betrays the degree of her complicity in the traditional patriarchal epistemology that she ostensibly seeks to dismantle. She has unwittingly embarked on a quest for epistemic purity, for the "totalizing and imperialist" standpoint demanded (but never achieved) by traditional, patriarchal epistemology.

Eighth, even if the standpoint of the "slave" *were* endowed with a privileged insight into the enduring structures of the real world, it is not clear that Harding ought to celebrate it as such. On Hegel's phenomenological account, for example, the slave progresses toward Absolute Knowing only because he consistently sees himself as a slave. Blinded to the dialectical progress that Hegel reveals behind his back, the slave remains a hapless underdog until his unanticipated epiphany of closure, at which time he is delivered to the standpoint of Absolute Knowing. If he were prematurely to fancy himself the master, he would promptly cease his transformative work on the world, thereby disabling the engine of dialectical progress. Marx similarly requires that the proletariat remain insecure in its ultimate destiny as the universal class. In order to achieve the class consciousness that will ensure the success of its bloody revolution, the proletariat must see itself as poised not on the threshold of communism, but on the brink of annihilation. Hence Marx's emmity for those "revisionists" who propose to reform capitalism from within: their "premature" awareness of their own restorative powers threatens to allay the discontents of the proletariat and to postpone the inevitable revolution. For both Hegel and Marx, self-conscious mastery signals a dead end; the future belongs only to those slaves who see themselves as slaves.

If Harding's standpoint "revolution" is to recapitulate the logic on which it is modeled, then the "slaves" who struggle to attain a critical standpoint must remain similarly unaware of the epistemic privilege they possess. If Harding's exhortations were to be widely circulated, then the dialectical incentive for further political struggles (and additional "strong objectivity") would immediately dissipate; her vanguard of slave advocates would settle comfortably into its role as the new (proximate) "masters." Harding's public endorsement of the standpoint of the "slave" would threaten to co-opt the fructifying struggles of feminist activists, prematurely halting their march toward "strong objectivity."

In the end, an end preordained by the Hegelian-Marxist narrative she uncritically adopts, Harding's only alternatives are equally unsatisfying. Whether she appeals surreptitiously to a "god's-eye" perspective, or wagers the future of feminism on the ultimate underdog, Harding offers no prospect of real liberation for those whom she casts as "slaves." In either event, she is playing goddess, and the ethical consequences for her human subjects are potentially disturbing.

The Slave Revolt in Epistemology

From a Nietzschean perspective, Harding's terminological predilections appear uncannily apposite, for her dubious investment of the standpoint of the "slave" with an epistemic privilege neatly recapitulates the strategies of slave morality, as documented in *On the Genealogy of Morals*. According to Nietzsche, the ascetic priest catalyzes the "slave revolt in morality" by supplying the slaves with metaphysical ammunition for use against the nobles—and ultimately against themselves. Under the tutelage of the ascetic priest, the slaves claim to *prefer* the punishment meted out to them, thus reinterpreting their suffering as a sign of their goodness. The slaves may eventually succeed in disarming the nobles, but only by consigning themselves to perpetual enslavement—herein lies their sole strategic advantage.

Harding valorizes the position of the "slave" precisely as Nietzsche's analysis of slave morality would lead us to expect: she essentially transforms victimage into virtue. Fomenting what amounts to a "slave revolt in epistemology," Harding decrees that certain disadvantaged and subjugated agents command a privileged standpoint *precisely because* they are victims. At first glance, Harding's strategy might appear to reprise Haraway's: both endeavor to turn the conditions of victimage to the advantage of the victims, to "seize the tools to mark the world that marked them as other."[42] But unlike Haraway, who openly situates her own epistemological inquiries in the political agenda of postmodern feminism, Harding fails to situate her own claims about (and upon) situated knowledges. Like its predecessor revolt in morality, then, the "slave revolt in epistemology" empowers the "slaves" only by displacing their agency and ensuring their continued enslavement.

Nietzsche's sketch of the ascetic priest instructively illuminates the political consequences of Harding's slave revolt in epistemology:

> He brings salves and balms with him, no doubt; but before he can act as physician, he first has to wound; when he then stills the pain of the wound *he at the same time infects the wound* . . . in [his]

presence everything necessarily grows sick, and everything sick tame. (GM III:15)

Like the ascetic priest, Harding presents herself—*qua* epistemologist—as the theoretical spokesperson for various subjugated standpoints, which she describes as instantiating the position of the "slave." Attempting to empower these disadvantaged agents *as* "slaves," Harding resorts to a quick fix. In order to alleviate the pain and alienation of their victimage, she promises these "slaves" the (illusory) epistemic privilege that derives from a "less distorted" perspective on the world. These subjugated standpoints, she insists, afford their otherwise dispossessed residents a more accurate glimpse of the world as it really is.

Harding's investment of the "slave" with an epistemic privilege not only is romantic, but furthermore trivializes the situation of victimage that gives rise to the "strong objectivity" she prizes. The standpoint of the "slave" is riddled with just as many unknown snares and prejudices as that of the "master"; the former standpoint may warrant Harding's political allegiance, but it is just as complicated (and problematic) epistemically as the latter standpoint.

Haraway alerts us to the precise error that Harding commits. Immediately after registering a preference for the partial perspective afforded by subjugated standpoints, Haraway reminds us of the need for feminists to situate politically their own claims about situated knowledge. In an admonition apposite to, though not explicitly directed toward, Harding's feminist standpoint theory, Haraway warns against

> the serious danger of romanticizing and/or appropriating the vision of the less powerful while claiming to see from their positions. To see from below is neither easily learned nor unproblematic, even if "we" "naturally" inhabit the great underground terrain of subjugated knowledges. The positionings of the subjugated are not exempt from critical re-examination, decoding, deconstruction, and interpretation; that is, from both semiological and hermeneutic modes of critical enquiry. The standpoints of the subjugated are not "innocent" positions.[43]

Postmodern feminists must consequently resist as misleading the unsituated claim that subjugated standpoints promise a better or clearer glimpse of the world. Residents of subjugated standpoints "see" the world differently, and their experiences of the world are currently of immense political value to feminist epistemology, if only by virtue of their systematic historical exclusion and devaluation.

Nietzsche's psychological profile of the ascetic priest indicates that Harding's version of feminist standpoint theory may treat only the "symptoms" of gender-based oppression, and not the underlying "illness" itself (GM III:17). If Nietzsche is right, then Harding's assurance of a privileged standpoint on the world is more likely eventually to alienate women further from their own experiences than to affirm and validate these experiences. The quick fix that Harding provides will consequently prove disastrous in the long run, for it ultimately prevents women from gaining the potentially liberatory insights that genuine objectivity might supply. If Nietzsche's analysis is applicable, then Harding's version of feminist standpoint theory not only empowers women *qua* victims but also empowers Harding herself *qua* slave advocate—much as the ascetic priest empowers the slaves *qua* sufferers and himself *qua* sufferers' advocate.

The Hegelian-Marxist narrative favored by standpoint theorists may essay an inspiring saga of pluck and perseverence, but it can also spin a romantic fantasy of victims as victors. Rather than validate the situated knowledges of women, Harding romanticizes, and thus distorts, the conditions of their oppression. Is it not likely that the world appears alien and inhospitable to the "slaves" in part because they do *not* understand the logic and motives emblematic of the patriarchy? To lead the "slaves" to believe otherwise, that they see the world more clearly than the "master," that their periscopic vision outstrips his Promethean science, verges upon cruelty. Were these "slaves" to attempt to implement the epistemic privilege that Harding assigns to them, they might unwittingly expose themselves to further victimage and oppression. Those women of color whose voices remain muffled, unheard, unarticulated—and *therefore* "scientifically inadequate"—would become further enslaved to the epistemologist who offers to derive theoretically the objective meaning of their experiences. Insofar as Harding discounts the situation of victimage that gives rise to the "strong objectivity" she prizes, she may eventually contribute to the further alienation of women from the objective content of their own experiences.[44]

The price Harding pays for her circle may therefore be prohibitively high, for her formulation of feminist standpoint theory potentially cultivates in these subjugated agents a dependency on the epistemologist to express in a "scientifically adequate" fashion their experiences of oppression. Those women of color, whose authentic voices remain muffled, un-heard, or unarticulated, would become further dependent upon the epistemologist who derives theoretically the objective meaning of their experiences. If such individuals were to object to their treatment at the hands of the epistemologist, would standpoint theorists be receptive to their objections? Here Harding may encounter some difficulty, for she is methodologically predisposed to treat "women's experiences" as "scien-tifically inadequate." How then would she "hear" the objections that her subjects might raise?[45]

Unwittingly reproducing the patriarchal logic she vows to derange, Harding may inadvertently establish herself as the new, proximate "mas-ter." The victims of oppression and domination would remain "slaves," dependent on their new "master" to speak for them. And while this new "master" may congratulate herself for her humane treatment of these "slaves," it is not clear that the "slaves" would necessarily prefer this new "master" to their old one, or that they would even distinguish between the two. Harding insists, as we have seen, that her voice, too, is marginal-ized within "prefeminist" institutions, but oppressed women of color may not reciprocate her robust sense of solidarity with them. On them, any distinction between ultimate and proximate "masters" may be utterly lost. To a disadvantaged woman of color who aspires to speak, and be heard, in her own authentic voice, the well-intentioned intercession of the standpoint epistemologist may be indistinguishable from the standard intrusions of the patriarchy.

Conclusion

As an antidote to the dream of foundational innocence, Donna Haraway proposes various imaginative exercises designed to liberate feminists from the perceived need for an originary, epistemically pure standpoint. As an enabling narrative for postmodern feminists, Haraway offers the myth of the cyborg, a composite, hybrid creature that embodies the irresolvable tensions and dualities that characterize late modernity.[46] The cyborg rep-resents the embodiment of purely prospective agency, an unhistorical mutant to which the past—along with the allure of innocence, origin, and redemption—is irretrievably lost. If feminists can imagine themselves in their political activity as cyborgs—which, in reality, women have always been—then they can perhaps exorcise the immobilizing specter of *das Weib an sich*, which continues to haunt their practices.

Here too Haraway follows Nietzsche. The prototype cyborg is none other than Zarathustra, the consummate micro-political agent of late modernity. The *Bildungsgang* of Zarathustra thus serves as something like a cyborg myth: operating in the shadow of the dead God, consigned by his crepuscular destiny to a belief in idols that he can neither respect nor reject, Zarathustra must somehow neutralize his romantic dreams of return and redemption. He eventually "becomes what he is" by turning that which oppresses him—his destiny, his fatality—to his own strategic advantage. He is ineluctably both free spirit and ascetic priest, and he implements both strands of this dual heritage to found a micro-community of higher men (Z IV:2-9). This community is unstable and ephemeral, lacking altogether in theoretical justifications, institutional reinforcements, and foundational myths. This community of higher men is exclusively prospective in its orientation; it has no laws, no history, and no goal above and beyond the survival of European nihilism.

Zarathustra founds this cyborg community, supplying it with a minimal micro-political infrastructure in the form of an inaugural "Ass Festival" (Z IV:17-18), but eventually withdraws from it. He comes to realize that his dual heritage renders him both life-giving and life-destroying. Although he has consecrated this micro-community in the twilight of the idols, he has also enslaved his companions and encouraged them to invest their redemptive hopes in him. Sensing that he has enslaved his companions and usurped the station of the dead God—having become someone for the sake of whom "living on earth is worthwhile" (Z IV:19)—he banishes the higher men and dissolves the micro-community he founded.

The final scene of *Zarathustra*, framed in cyclical imagery that suggests a closed system, captures the purely prospective agency that characterizes the cyborg. Restless in his sheltering solitude but chastened by the prospect of reprising the logic that doomed his previous political endeavors, Zarathustra rises nonetheless to greet the dawn. Bereft of hopes for ultimate success, armed solely with the will to survive the decadence of late modernity, Zarathustra "goes under" once again to found yet another, equally ephemeral, cyborg community.

Notes

1. With the exception of occasional emendations, I rely throughout this essay on Walter Kaufmann's editions/translations of Nietzsche's works for Random House and Viking Press. Numbers

refer to sections rather than to pages, and the following key explains the abbreviations for my citations. BGE: *Beyond Good and Evil*; GM: *On the Genealogy of Morals*; TI: *Twilight of the Idols*; Z: *Thus Spoke Zarathustra*.

2. Donna Haraway suggests a similar reclamation project: "I would like to proceed by placing metaphorical reliance on a much maligned sensory system in feminist discourse: vision. Vision can be good for avoiding binary oppositions. I would like to insist on the embodied nature of all vision, and so reclaim the sensory system that has been used to signify a leap out of the marked body and into a conquering gaze from nowhere." Donna J. Haraway, *Simians, Cyborgs, and Women* (London: Free Association Books, 1991), 188.

3. Haraway, 189.

4. Ibid., 190.

5. Ibid., 188.

6. Ibid., 192.

7. Ibid., 191.

8. Ibid., 191.

9. Ibid., 196.

10. Sandra Harding, *Whose Science? Whose Knowledge? Thinking From Women's Lives* (Ithaca: Cornell University Press, 1991), p. 249.

11. Classic statements of positions now collected under the umbrella of "feminist standpoint theory" include Nancy Hartsock, "The Feminist Standpoint: Developing the Ground for a Specifically Feminist Historical Materialism," in *Discovering Reality*, ed. Sandra Harding and Merrill Hintikka (Dordrecht: Reidel, 1983); Hilary Rose, "Hand, Brain, and Heart: A Feminist Epistemology for the Natural Sciences," in *Signs* 9:1 (1983); and Dorothy Smith, *The Everyday World as Problematic: A Feminist Sociology* (Boston: Northeastern University Press, 1987). Sandra Harding offers a sympathetic interpretation of the standpoint epistemologies in *The Science Question in Feminism*, especially chap. 7.

12. Harding (1986), 191.

13. Sandra Harding, "Rethinking Standpoint Epistemology: What Is 'Strong Objectivity'?" in *Feminist Epistemologies*, ed. Linda Alcoff and Elizabeth Potter (New York: Routledge, 1993), 56, emphasis added.

14. For a critical appraisal of Harding's defense of feminist standpoint theory, see Alan Soble's review of *Whose Science? Whose Knowledge? Thinking from Women's Lives*, in *International Studies in Philosophy of Science*, vol. 6, no. 2, 159–62.

15. Harding (1991), 188–91.

16. Ibid., 143–44.

17. Ibid., 11.

18. Harding (1986), 191.

19. Harding (1993), 72.

20. Harding (1991), 138–52.

21. Ibid., 161.

22. Ibid., 123.

23. Ibid., 123.

24. Ibid., 123.

25. Ibid., 271.

26. Harding (1986), 191, emphasis added. In her most recent book, Harding (1991) confirms her commitment to this residually objectivist model: " 'The winner tells the tale,' as historians point out, and so trying to construct the story from the perspective of the lives of those who resist oppression generates less partial and distorted accounts of nature and social relations" (126).

27. Harding (1991), 127.

28. Ibid., 127–28.

29. Ibid., 127. Here Harding follows the lead of Nancy Hartsock, who argues that "feminist theorists must demand that feminist theorizing be grounded in women's material activity and must as well be a part of the political struggle necessary to develop areas of social life modeled on this activity" (304).

30. Ibid., 142.

31. For a promising, if partial, solution to this difficult methodological question, see Lynn Hankinson Nelson, "Epistemological Communities," in Alcoff and Potter, Feminist Epistemologies, 121–59. Nelson recommends that epistemologists view the community, and not the individual, as the source and repository of all relevant knowledge claims. Although Nelson does not endorse the standpoint epistemologies, the methodological revision she recommends might succeed in tempering the potential intrusiveness of the standpoint theorist's research.

32. Harding (1991), 154–56.

33. Rosalind Edwards criticizes the standpoint epistemologies for failing to attend closely to the power relations embedded in their preferred methodology: "You cannot have feminist theories that explain differences without them actually being grounded in those differences. . . . How can we be sure our feminist methods are operating as we would wish from the point of view of the interviewee rather than our own unless we analyse what happens in interviews?" (478). "Connecting Method and Epistemology: A White Woman Interviewing Black Women," Women's Studies International Forum, Vol. 13, No. 5, 1990, pp. 477–490.

34. For a related criticism of the logic underlying the standpoint epistemologies, see Bat-Ami Bar On, "Marginality and Epistemic Privilege," in Alcoff and Potter, Feminist Epistemologies, 83–100. Bar On skillfully exposes the dangers involved in conceiving of "mastery" as emanating from a single, static center. In the complex societies of advanced industrial capitalism, virtually all agents simultaneously stand in relations of "mastery" to some and "enslavement" to others. As an alternative to the "single-center" theory of power preferred by standpoint epistemologists, Bar On proposes a "theorized dispersion of power among multiple centers" (94).

35. Harding apparently misses this crucial point of Hegelian epistemology. In defense of her unconventional methodology, she claims (1993) that "Hegel was not a slave, though he argued that the master/slave relationship could better be understood from the perspective of slaves' activities" (59). The "understanding" that Harding erroneously attributes to the slaves properly belongs to Hegel himself. He traces the development of history "from the perspective of slaves' activities" because he already knows (as the slaves do not) that the future belongs to the slaves.

36. Harding (1991), 126.

37. Cognizant, perhaps, of the problems generated by her objectivism, Harding (1991) occasionally substitutes "less distorted" for "clearer" (138), and "less false" for "true" (83), as if these substitutions might mitigate the residual objectivism of her claims.

38. Ibid., 138.

39. Discarded drafts of Beyond Good and Evil indicate that Nietzsche at one time intended to include a separate Part entitled Das Weib an sich. Vestiges of this intended Part are found in Sections 231–39 of Beyond Good and Evil. Because Nietzsche models das Weib an sich on the Kantian Ding an sich, we can assume with some confidence that the ridicule he heaps on the latter applies to the former as well. Nietzsche's point here is that both das Weib an sich and the Kantian Ding an sich are metaphysical inventions to which no human perspective or standpoint corresponds.

40. For this account of the complex logic of displacement and disembodiment, I am indebted to Susan Bordo's essay, "Feminism, Postmodernism, and Gender-Scepticism," in Feminism/Postmodernism, ed. Linda Nicholson (New York: Routledge, 1990), 133–56.

41. Haraway, 173.

42. Ibid., 175.

43. Ibid., 191.

44. For an expanded investigation of this line of criticism, see bell hooks, "Choosing the Margin

as a Space of Radical Openness," collected in *Yearning: Race, Gender, and Cultural Politics* (Boston: South End Press, 1990). hooks warns that the romanticization of "marginality" may actually dispossess oppressed agents of a fruitful "place of resistance" (150–51).

45. For a sympathetic treatment of this methodological problem, see Edwards, "Connecting Method and Epistemology," especially 485–89.

46. Haraway, chap. 8, "A Cyborg Manifesto."

14

Nietzsche's Politics

Ofelia Schutte

A critical understanding of Nietzsche's politics is necessary to a study of his theory of values. There is a twofold justification for this. First of all, on Nietzschean grounds, it is important to complement Nietzsche's critique of traditional values with an understanding of the political implications of his theory. In the *Genealogy* Nietzsche argues that all systems of values are inherently political. The values that ultimately triumph in any society do not necessarily reflect any philosophical truths, but rather the interests of those who can wield the most power.[1] This implies that one must always keep a critical attitude toward all posited values by raising such questions as: What are the political assumptions implicit in these values? By whose power have these values been posited? Who is to profit from the widespread acceptance of these values? These critical questions need not be raised only against opponents, but must also be directed toward oneself. In *Thus Spoke Zarathustra* and *Ecce Homo*, Nietzsche ties the process of self-criticism to the ongoing process of self-overcoming that characterizes the development of all life.[2] However, Nietzsche does not always carry out the mandate of self-criticism in practice. In pursuing the contradictions implicit in Nietzsche's position, I will be completing an aspect of his critical enterprise that is left unresolved in Nietzsche's late writings.

Secondly, an investigation of Nietzsche's politics is important because, once his political assumptions are made known, we need to raise questions as to how his political views apply to our present and future well-being. In keeping with this goal of the investigation, it is better to reject the assumption that Nietzsche is an undisputed authority on the political future of human beings. Nietzsche's suggestion in *Ecce Homo* that as the initiator of the "great politics" ("*grosse Politik*") he is speaking for humanity's destiny will be rejected.[3] The method I shall follow here is the demystification of Nietzsche's appeal to destiny as a justification for the force or truth of his ideas on politics and morality. Because I am skeptical of the validity of an appeal to destiny in the justification of any philosophical theory, I am especially interested in the use of such rhetoric by Nietzsche. This also calls for an investigation of the logical relationship between Nietzsche's politics and his critique of traditional morality. My aim is to arrive at a critical understanding of the interrelationship of some of Nietzsche's insights on human reality (metaphysical, psychological, ethical) rather than to offer an open or tacit justification for Nietzsche's ideas, regardless of what his ideas may turn out to be.

In the past there has been a tendency on the part of scholars to avoid uncovering some of the more politically controversial aspects of Nietzsche's theory of values. For example, while many texts from both his early and late writings show that Nietzsche repeatedly justified slavery and the exploitation of the disadvantaged for the sake of the development of a "higher culture," standard interpretations of Nietzsche proceed to discuss the meaning of a higher culture while bypassing the issue of slavery and exploitation. Against this approach it should be noted that Nietzsche did not sidestep. He defended the right of "superior" men to exploit the "inferior" as a necessary condition for the existence of a high culture. In this essay I will address, in particular, how Nietzsche defended the exploitation of the masses for the advantage of the "higher" individual as well as the exploitation of so-called "feminine" values for the sake of a "masculine" cultural ideal. Both of these themes are to be understood as interdependent applications of the idea that a worthy culture cannot exist without the exploitation of "lower" beings for the benefit of "higher" beings. In contrast to Nietzsche's direct statements on these matters, the tendency of criticism has been to de-thematize the interconnection between Nietzsche's defense of exploitation and his fairly traditional endorsement of a "strong" and "masculine" ideal for Western culture. As an illustration of how recent criticism has overlooked Nietzsche's defense of exploitation I shall briefly cite some representative examples from the work of Jaspers and Kaufmann.

In Jaspers' analysis of Nietzsche's politics it is openly acknowledged that Nietzsche regarded war to be as much a "necessity" for the state as the slave is for society. Having stated this, Jaspers proceeds to investigate the philosophical meaning of Nietzsche's remarks on war while at the same time no critical comment is made regarding Nietzsche's endorsement of slavery.[4] Jaspers' method is to defend Nietzsche's statements in the best way he can while bypassing anything that cannot be defended. Obviously, this type of analysis is highly unsatisfactory.

Kaufmann follows a similar strategy. On the issue of racial prejudice, for instance, Kaufmann has accomplished the difficult but legitimate task of clearing Nietzsche from charges of anti-Semitism.[5] And yet Kaufmann's analysis avoids raising the more radical question of whether Nietzsche's endorsement of the superiority of some races to others lends support to a *general* principle of ethnic or racial discrimination. Even a casual reading of *Beyond Good and Evil* will show that Nietzsche held strong views against the English.[6] While this might be dismissed as philosophically insignificant, a careful reading of Nietzsche's unpublished notes shows that on occasion Nietzsche suggested that entire races (judged decadent) ought to be exterminated and/or bred out of existence.[7] As an example Nietzsche suggests parenthetically the annihilation of the English. These statements which appear absurd to us may be said to be "playful" or "ironic," and, indeed, either of these conjectures may be correct. But it is also the case that Nietzsche's statements fit logically into a well-defined political ideology regarding what special groups and power structures ought to control the future of Europe. It is understandable that humanistic scholars should try to give the best possible reading of passages which carry an ambiguous meaning or which may seem to be superfluous to a philosopher's major theories on metaphysics, ethics or epistemology. However, the critical claim I wish to maintain is that Nietzsche's defense of exploitation cannot be entirely separated from his other theories. The nature of this connection needs to be investigated further.

As for the ambiguity of some of his statements, Nietzsche himself admits in his highly anti-democratic work, *Beyond Good and Evil,* that it is not in the interests of an anti-egalitarian "free spirit" (such as himself) "to betray in every particular [detail] *from what* a spirit can liberate himself and *to what* he may then be driven."[8] Still, he has said enough to convey to the reader the sense that as part of his intended transvaluation of all values he expects to see a rebirth in society's appreciation for a tyrannical type of government.[9]

There is also a more general philosophical issue at stake here. Jaspers and Kaufmann are correct in emphasizing the idea that Nietzsche was interested in laying down the conditions that would allow a regeneration of the human spirit and the quest for human fulfillment. Much of Nietzsche's work lends support to this hypothesis. But any philosophy that stresses the radical need for regeneration must also face the concrete problem of how that regeneration is to be achieved. The fact that the "rebirth" of the human spirit was the fundamental goal of Nietzsche's transvaluation of all values does not necessarily mean that Nietzsche was always correct in delineating how this goal would be attained. The critical reader must be able to hold Nietzsche accountable for the goals that Nietzsche himself proposed as well as insist that departures from this goal not be met with indifference by the scholarly community. The tension between the need for human fulfillment and the obstructions of decadence and various forms of prejudice is both a theoretical and practical problem for any theory of values that places an enormous stress on bringing about the possibilities of fulfillment. By confronting honestly how Nietzsche handled this tension—which may be broadly conceived as the tension between the affirmation and negation of human life—we can gain some extremely valuable insights about the strengths and weaknesses of Nietzsche's method as well as possibly keep from repeating in our own work some of the efforts to which Nietzsche may have been susceptible.

Rank, Aristocracy, Exploitation

Nietzsche had a set of political opinions which surface with almost predictable regularity in his aphoristic writings. But it is often thought that

Nietzsche was not interested in either the theory or practice of politics since he neither wrote nor intended to write a political treatise. His political opinions appear as tangential remarks in the context of a socio-cultural critique. Although the existence of a high culture is a very important concern for Nietzsche, this is not to say that Nietzsche was either uninterested in politics or that he considered politics unimportant. While he generally presented his political views as functions of the thesis that decadence is the primary characteristic of modern times, this approach is always supplemented by the judgment that decadence ought to be eliminated and that his entire philosophy is addressed to this crucial historical task. Nietzsche's logic therefore moves from the critique of contemporary culture to the advocacy of political and social change. The importance of articulating Nietzsche's political opinions is that they provide us with the most accessible yet not always evident information about the *direction* of Nietzsche's envisioned change. Everyone agrees that Nietzsche was a vehement critic of the political establishment of his time. The question remains, for what reasons did he criticize it, and to what ends?

The political changes envisioned by Nietzsche were intended by him to affect the course of modern history. For a base from which to criticize modern governmental policies and structures, Nietzsche turned to the distant past—to ancient Greece and Rome. For the realization of his political hopes he looked to the distant future. At the end of his career, however, he seemed to think that the time for change was imminent:

> For when truth enters into a fight with the lies of millenia, we shall have upheavals . . . the like of which has never been dreamed . . . all power structures of the old society will have exploded—all of them based on lies. . . . It is only beginning with me that the earth knows great politics [*grosse Politik*].[10]

In *Beyond Good and Evil* Nietzsche had expressed his hopes for the political future of Europe as follows:

> While the democratization of Europe leads to the production of a type that is prepared for *slavery* in the subtlest sense, in single, exceptional cases the *strong* human being will have to turn out stronger and richer than perhaps ever before. . . . I meant to say: the democratization of Europe is at the same time an involuntary

arrangement for the cultivation of *tyrants*—taking the word in every sense, including the most spiritual.[11]

While the tone of Nietzsche's statement is descriptive, Nietzsche was well aware that he was promoting an interpretation of history. Ultimately it is up to us to judge whether in exchange for a system of power structures based on "lies" (as Nietzsche took the political systems of his contemporaries to be) Nietzsche proposed anything fundamentally different. In the case noted here, Nietzsche's myth that the future of Europe belongs to the rule of select "tyrants" is no less false than the power structure of the old society that he takes to be based on lies. In spite of the overwhelming power structures that affect the lives of modern human beings, the future belongs to those who live in it, not necessarily to tyrants. Moreover, democratic institutions *may* cultivate in people the love of freedom rather than turn them into either slaves or tyrants. By making it appear that the rise to power of future tyrants is either historically inevitable or destined, Nietzsche avoids facing a much more important issue, *viz.*, how to view the human condition in a way that either corrects or transcends the master-slave dualism. Rather than look to history for possible alternatives to this dualism, Nietzsche used history to confirm his narrow perspective.

It is important to emphasize that Nietzsche was a strongly anti-democratic thinker. When Nietzsche turned to the past—to ancient Greece, for example—he did so for politically reactionary reasons. In ancient Greece and Rome he sought to find an alternative to the increasingly egalitarian trends of modern political movements. While other nineteenth-century thinkers looked to ancient Greece in order to celebrate the origins of democracy, Nietzsche used Greek society as a standard of excellence precisely for the opposite reason.[12] As early as 1871–72 Nietzsche praised the Greeks for their dependence on slavery, arguing that slavery is required for the flourishing of art and culture. "Slavery belongs to the essence of culture," he declares in "The Greek State," an unpublished essay written at the time of his intense association with the Wagners.[13] In this early piece Nietzsche argued in favor of increasing the misery of "toiling men" so as to facilitate for a small number of "olympic men" the production of the "*Kunstwelt.*" This view is not much different from that developed in *Beyond Good and Evil* and other late works (like *Twilight of the Idols*). The difference is that the "higher man" of Nietzsche's mature works is an initiate of Nietzsche's philosophy, rather than simply a genius. Nietzsche's higher man must have both known and overcome modern times. He must have overcome not only decadence (particularly the "herd" values characterized by modern petty bourgeois culture) but also the political ideals of the French Revolution, liberty, equality, fraternity for all. As far as Nietzsche was concerned, democracy, socialism, the labor movement, and the emancipation of women were all products of modern decadence. These were the political movements which his "transvaluation of all values" strongly opposed. It is also well known that Nietzsche opposed the cult of nationalism, particularly that of German nationalism. This is sometimes mistakenly taken as a sign of Nietzsche's anti-authoritarian posture. The truth, however, is that Nietzsche opposed nationalism primarily because a "nation" was to him still too small a unit of power in terms of its potential for making history.[14] Moreover, he opposed nationalism because he associated the development of a national consciousness with the proliferation of democratic and Christian ideals—ideals which he never ceased to portray to his readers as petty and "nauseous."

Together with the ethical theory of the "higher" man Nietzsche offers a strong defense of aristocracy—that is, aristocracy understood as government by the best men or "higher" men. Thus elitism is an *a priori* assumption of Nietzsche's political vision as well as of his moral theory. Nietzsche's doctrine of the overcoming of traditional morality by the "higher" individual, developed at great length in *Beyond Good and Evil*, directly reinforces his politics. In fact, Nietzsche's politics and his doctrine of the overcoming of morality by the superior person are inextricably connected with each other. The aim of Nietzsche's politics is to make the world correspond to an ethical view in which the control of all values is placed in the hands of a "superior type" of human being. But the very choice of this hierarchy of control indicates a radically politicized view of the universe. Nietzsche admits that the ethical theory of the "higher" human being is a political morality. In his own words, it is "a morality with the intention of training a ruling caste."[15] In *Beyond Good and Evil* he asserts: "I am beginning to touch on what is *serious* for me, the 'European problem' as I see it, the cultivation of a new caste that will rule Europe."[16] The ethical theory of the higher man, then, is invoked in support of various political positions which promote the concentration of power in the hands of these superior individuals. For example, Nietzsche uses the idea of the superior type to oppose the cause of nationalism, by relating the idea of a higher man to a "supra-national type."[17] He also uses the idea in a different context to support ethnic prejudice and racism, condemning some cultures or races (like the English) as unlikely to produce "higher men." In one case the idea of the higher man is used to destroy the ideological power of national boundaries; in the other, it is used to reinforce types of prejudice that may be nationally based. As stated earlier, Nietzsche can be defended specifically against charges of anti-Semitism, but not against the view, which he strongly held, that some "peoples" were inferior to others and therefore ought to be subjected to domination. His theory of the "worthy enemy" and, in general, his dissatisfaction with modern times kept him from declaring any one people to stand higher than all others. Still, he did not hesitate to name the English as worthy of disdain and even of total annihilation. The defense of a plurality of local customs and traditions offered by Nietzsche in *Thus Spoke Zarathustra* therefore cannot be taken as an unconditional defense of ethnic pluralism.[18] Rather it is subject to the qualification that only such "traditions" as are not corrupted by decadence ought to be allowed to develop and survive in a culture.

Nietzsche's critique of traditional morality—whether of the Christian, Kantian or utilitarian type—rests on his disagreement with the notions of human equality and of the universality of moral maxims. Kant's categorical imperative is reduced by Nietzsche to an expression of Kant's will to power, that is, to an expression of Kant's will to universalize the peculiarities of his moral outlook as if this were a maxim mandated to all human beings.[19] If Kant is to be dismissed so quickly, then what about Nietzsche's values? "To *me* justice speaks thus: 'Men are not equal.' Nor shall they become equal!"[20] These are the words of Nietzsche's Zarathustra, whose disparagement of "herd" values also serves to discredit the utilitarian's democratically oriented moral calculus. In *Beyond Good and Evil* Nietzsche explicitly replaces Christian, Kantian, and utilitarian ethical theories with the notion of an "order of rank" (*Rangordnung*) where superior and inferior types have a separate value and function within the whole:

> Every enhancement of the type "man" has so far been the work of an aristocratic society—and it will be so again and again—a society that believes in the long ladder of an order of rank and differences in value between man and man, and that needs slavery in some sense or other.[21]

In this way Nietzsche displaces the common bond that all human beings are capable of sharing as moral agents.

Once the egalitarian and universalist concerns of the Christian, Kantian and/or utilitarian ethics are discredited, the way is clear for a justification of slavery and exploitation. The idea that there must be "distance" among *types* of human beings translates politically and economically into the justification of castes or classes. Nietzsche's doctrine of an order of rank called for an aristocratic class who would not be ashamed of demanding the reinstitution of slavery. The practical problem of maintaining slaves—whether slavery is conceived literally or just in terms of the notion of cheap, available labor—also called for the exploitation of human beings. These two marks of a "healthy" society—slavery and exploitation—are discussed by Nietzsche in the concluding chapter to *Beyond Good and Evil*, significantly entitled "What Is Noble." I shall quote from these passages at length so that the full intent of Nietzsche's arguments can be appreciated:

> The essential characteristics of a good and healthy aristocracy . . . is that it experiences itself *not* as a function (whether of the monarchy or the commonwealth) but as their *meaning* and highest justification—that it accepts with a good conscience the sacrifice of untold human beings who, *for its sake,* must be reduced and lowered to incomplete human beings, to slaves, to instruments. Their fundamental faith simply has to be that society must *not* exist for society's sake but only as the foundation and scaffolding on which a choice type of being is able to raise itself to its higher task and to a higher state of being. . . .[20]

Here the exploitation of "untold human beings" is justified in quasi-metaphysical terms, although the net effect of the argument is strictly political. The implications are clear. A "good" and "healthy" aristocracy has been defined as one that can convince itself and all human beings under its rule that the "lower" must sacrifice itself to the "higher," while the ruling class has the power of defining what the "higher" shall be. The "noble" consciousness, then, is one that demands the sacrifice of other human beings and, convinced by its own elevated rhetoric, reduces them to slaves and instruments without the slightest feeling of guilt.

In the next aphorism the perspective shifts from a highly rhetorical defense of "sacrifice" and manipulation to a straightforward justification of violence and exploitation:

Refraining mutually from injury, violence and exploitation and placing one's will on a par with that of someone else—this may become, in a certain rough sense, good manners among individuals if the appropriate conditions are present. . . . But as soon as this principle is extended, and possibly accepted as the fundamental principle of society, it immediately proves to be what it really is—a will to the *denial* of life, a principle of disintegration and decay.[23]

Nietzsche was not speaking about exploitation in a figurative or isolated sense. He makes it clear in the same section that he is appealing to "life" to justify a methodical political and social practice:

. . . everywhere people are now raving, even under scientific disguises, about coming conditions of society in which "the exploitative aspect" will be removed—which sounds to me as if they promised to invent a way of life that would dispense with all organic functions. "Exploitation" does not belong to a corrupt or imperfect and primitive society; it belongs to the *essence* of what lives. . . .[24]

Here Nietzsche uses a different ploy than moral rhetoric to defend exploitation. The tactic, which characterizes every justification that he gives for his political ideas and principles, is that of appealing both to *necessity* and *destiny*. He declares that while exploitation is necessary ("to life"), it is the aristocracy's *destiny* to use it against the oppressed. The two arguments are combined to yield a justification for his political vision. That is, the "necessity" of violence is used only to justify aristocratic control over the masses. It is inconceivable to Nietzsche to use it in support of populist movements of emancipation from aristocratic controls. The context in which Nietzsche's justification of exploitation and violence is given is therefore quite clear. In the previous section Nietzsche had reflected that "when, for example, an aristocracy, like that of France at the beginning of the Revolution, throws away its privileges with a sublime disgust and sacrifices itself to an extravagance of its own moral feelings, that is corruption."[25] The implication, of course, is that while the Revolution may be said to have been fighting a "corrupt" aristocracy, the aristocracy's corruption lay not in its extravagant exploitation of the people but rather in the fact that it did not exploit the people sufficiently.

Surely, this was not Nietzsche's sole criticism of the French aristocracy and, surely, he is to some extent enjoying the flair of his rhetorical wit. But the fact that he makes this kind of statement shows just how far he is willing to go to defend the rights of a privileged class to exploit the non-privileged.

Through such a defense of exploitation Nietzsche intended to provide the new rulers of Europe that he envisioned with good conscience. He wanted to make them strong, hard, unsentimental, uncorrupt—in other words, unmodern. He was afraid that the placing of one's will "on a par" with that of other human beings meant corruption. But clearly if anything is corrupt, it is to propose that any human being should reduce another human being to the status of a slave or an instrument, no matter what elevated rhetoric is used to justify this reduction. How is Nietzsche's analysis of the meaning of corruption to be explained?

Certainly many different and possibly even complementary interpretations of Nietzsche's position may be given. Insofar as Nietzsche takes a strong critical stand against Christianity and democracy, his endorsement of an order of rank such as I have described may be taken as a negative consequence of his anti-Christian and anti-democratic position. In other words, one could say that since Nietzsche lacks belief in God and universal human rights, he is then "driven" to hold views on reducing some human beings to be the instrument of others, etc. However, this explanation is not fully satisfactory. Consider the reasons that Nietzsche gave for opposing Christianity and democracy. One of the important tenets Nietzsche rejected in Christianity was the dualism between good and evil. Moreover, his major opposition to universal human rights was the idea of reducing everyone to being the "same" as everyone else (i.e., "equal" to everyone else in a reductionist sense). And yet, Nietzsche's counterproposal of higher/lower, politically translated as the opposition between aristocrat and slave, involves a reduction of human beings to *sameness of type* within a *dualistic structure of inequality*.

Thus, in criticism of Nietzsche's politics it may be observed that the dualism of higher/lower is only a variation of the dualism between good and evil (positive and negative value). In spite of what Nietzsche says to the contrary in *Beyond Good and Evil* and the *Genealogy*, he has yet not overcome the dualism of good and evil because his analysis of decadence as an impurity that ought to be eliminated from society is much too reminiscent of the Manichean struggle between good and evil. Furthermore, his identification of Christians, democrats, socialists, feminists, etc., with decadent forces is completely oversimplified. Nietzsche's counterproposals to democracy do not take him any farther along the road to a non-alienated, non-fragmented conception of human reality than the dualistic and reductionist structures of value that he himself attacked.

Nor is it satisfactory to give a Sartrean explanation of Nietzsche's proposal of an elitist order of rank, in the sense that one could say that it is the project of every consciousness to wish to be God and, since God is dead, Nietzsche is simply putting himself in God's place by redefining the rank of all values according to his vision or his interests. One does not necessarily have to endorse violence and exploitation when one sets oneself up in God's place, even assuming that this is what Nietzsche was doing. Rather, one may just as well endorse principles such as the respect for all human beings and harmony as the ultimate goal of the moral life. In other words, it is not the lack of belief in God that accounts for Nietzsche's justification of exploitation of the many by the few.

It is more fruitful to look at patterns of contradiction internal to Nietzsche's theory of values. This discloses clues as to why a thinker as self-critical as Nietzsche makes extremely sharp critiques of the highest values of Western culture and at the same time exhibits a blatant suspension of the critical method when discussing certain political, ethical, and social values. We may discover how it is that a thinker who promoted the ultimate rebellion against absolute values—the death of God—as well as the end of human fragmentation and dualism (Zarathustra's *Übermensch*) also promotes dualism (aristocrat/slave) and the *deification of the superior person*. This contradiction shows that as far as Nietzsche's political views are concerned, the old God is not yet dead and the old dualism between good and evil has not been overcome. On the contrary, it has taken a most extreme and oppressive form. I believe it can be shown that where Nietzsche fails as a critical thinker is precisely where he suspends his critical project and openly promotes intolerance. Therefore, an important clue as to what keeps the great critic of Western civilization from living up to his intended goal of developing the moral and spiritual regeneration of humanity can be found by locating the set of values toward which Nietzsche prescribes intolerance.

Rank, Domination, and the Subordination of Women

Although Nietzsche questioned the validity of some authoritarian structures in Western culture such as the Christian church, there were several other authoritarian power structures with which he identified and which he did his best to safeguard from criticism. In other words, Nietzsche did not dispel all forms of authoritarianism when he sought to move beyond the dualism of good and evil. His failure to move behind blind authoritarianism mars his philosophical vision in just those places where Nietzsche defends intolerance. I will now complete the analysis of Nietzsche's defense of the right of the "higher" to exploit the "lower" by examining the nature of the power structures that Nietzsche saw fit to govern the relations between men and women.

Further on in his discussion of "What Is Noble" Nietzsche praises the aristocracy for its intolerance "in the education of youth, in their arrangements for women, in their marriage customs, in the relations of old and young" and he adds, "they consider intolerance itself a virtue, calling it 'justice.'"[26] Here we are not simply confronting the anti-egalitarian view of justice professed by Zarathustra that "men are not equal—nor shall they become equal." What is clear from this passage is that there appears to be a logical connection between Nietzsche's defense of intolerance, Nietzsche's defense of aristocratic privilege, and Nietzsche's defense of a sexist and authoritarian social and family structure. The master-slave dualism which Nietzsche proposed for society at large also operates *within* the ruling class in the form of a rigid structure of subordination in which the established men of the upper class control the younger men of that class and where, as we shall see, women and children can be legitimately viewed as man's property. The "intolerance" which Nietzsche commends is aimed at the preservation of this tradition. The implication is that it is a "higher" duty to preserve a "strong" patriarchal tradition than to question the justice of this tradition. Thus intolerance itself must call itself justice—otherwise in the name of justice one would question the validity of the tradition.

The major theme which surfaces from the series of practices whose intolerance is praised by Nietzsche is the theme of the domination of women by men. Several implications of this theme specifically affect the principles of Nietzsche's social philosophy. I should note parenthetically that Nietzsche's statements on women's social role may be distinguished from the recurring use of the term "woman" as a symbol for non-human abstractions in the course of Nietzsche's writings—e.g., "truth is a woman," "life is a woman," "wisdom is a woman," etc. When taken in the context of poetic or metaphorical discourse, Nietzsche's symbolic use of the term "woman" transcends the limits of his political and social concerns. Therefore, while the following observations do not exhaust the totality of Nietzsche's reflections on woman they are nevertheless fairly representative of Nietzsche's conception of the role that woman ought to assume in social life.

The authoritarian ideology that Nietzsche supported in the case of aristocratic government is not surprisingly replicated in Nietzsche's theory of the ideal family structure as presented in *Twilight of the Idols*. In this work Nietzsche confirms and develops his earlier pronouncements in *Beyond Good and Evil* by continuing to oppose democracy, the equal rights of women, and the rights of workers to organize. Because the family functions as the smallest and yet the most important social institution affecting all aspects of daily existence, the theory of *Rangordnung* must make its influence felt here just as much as in the political order at large. Again, Nietzsche used a critique of modern society from the political standpoint of the "far right" to destroy the relatively liberalizing trends in modern marriages and to introduce his own views on the principles that ought to guide the institution of marriage. As any other modern institution, marriage shares the weaknesses of the present age:

> *Critique of modernity.* Our institutions are no good any more: on that there is universal agreement. However, it is not their fault, but ours. . . . In order that there may be institutions, there must exist the kind of will, instinct, or imperative, which is anti-liberal to the point of malice: the will to tradition, to authority, to responsibility for centuries to come, to the solidarity of chains of generations, forward and backward *ad infinitum*. When this will is present, something like the *imperium romanum* is founded; or like Russia . . . the concept that suggests the opposite of the wretched European nervousness and system of small states. . . .[27]

Any departure from the will to tradition is held to be a sign of decadence.

Nietzsche claims that modern marriage has lost its meaning because it has lost its rationality. But in the same section he notes that the rationality (*Vernunft*) of an institution lies in its structure of domination:

> The rationality of marriage—that lay in the husband's sole juridical responsibility, which gave marriage a center of gravity, while today it limps on both legs. The rationality of marriage—that lay in its indissolubility in principle, which lent it an accent that

> could be heard above the accident of feeling, passion, and what is
> merely momentary. It also lay in the family's responsibility for the
> choice of a spouse. With the growing influence of love matches,
> the very foundation of marriage has been eliminated. . . .[28]

Nietzsche goes on to say that love is an idiosyncrasy upon which no
institution can be founded. Marriage must be founded not on a "feeling"
but on an instinct, viz., "on the sex drive, on the property drive (wife
and child as property), on the drive to dominate, which continually organizes for itself the smallest structure of domination, the family."[29] While
this may be an accurate description of some essential features of the patriarchal family structure, the claim does not follow that only where this
structure obtains can there be a marital relationship between men and
women. By reducing the nature of love to a mere accident or feeling
Nietzsche is able to argue that some of the most personal of human relationships (relationships between the sexes and between parents and children) should be founded on such impersonal (instinctual) characteristics
as the sex or property drive.

   Two main motifs of repression may be abstracted from Nietzsche's conception of a "rational" or uncorrupt marriage. These are the repression
of love and the domination of women and children. These themes, of
course, are closely interconnected. The outcome of Nietzsche's conception of marriage is the repression of individual feeling, especially the
feeling of love between the spouses. Nietzsche states that marriage
"ought" to be indissoluble, and further that the choice of a spouse ought
to be dictated by the familial authority structure. Nietzsche's idea of a
non-decadent marriage requires, along with the repression of feeling, the
domination of the wife and children by the husband-father figure. Both
types of repression are interconnected in that the woman and child also
symbolize the expression of emotion, the expression of love. Since the
"male" instincts stand for rationality and duty (moral self-righteousness)
while the "female" instincts stand for emotion and play, Nietzsche's preferences are quite clear when he states that the husband must be the
center of power in the marriage, that the marriage is decadent if it "limps
on both legs." Here Nietzsche has defended a master-slave hierarchy as
essential to the family as well as to society at large. The family, as the
smallest but most important social structure, consists of a master-slave
structure in which duty suppresses emotion, man suppresses woman, and
parents suppress the children (even after they grow up). The latter rela-

tionship—parents versus children—provides the form through which the structure of domination is passed from one generation to the next.

Given the extreme authoritarian statements Nietzsche makes about the family (nothing less than *total* domination of the feelings of the spouses is demanded), and also given Nietzsche's intelligence, his critical nature, and his acknowledged unhappiness with the authoritarian structure of his own limited family life, one may question whether Nietzsche really held these opinions about the institution of marriage seriously. Could he have voiced these opinions without caring much about them, to provoke some thinking and discussion of these issues? Or could this be one of several opinions he might have held? It must be admitted that in so unsystematic a writer as Nietzsche one cannot expect a single view on any topic, including marriage. However, one may note a logical pattern to his views, even when noticing several variations in his statements. For example, in an unpublished note from the same period as *Twilight of the Idols* Nietzsche cites the possibility of short-term marriages ("for years, for months, for days"), but these were envisioned primarily as an alternative to prostitution and as a way of allowing the birth of more children in the society.[30] In these arrangements sex is also unrelated to love and women were explicitly regarded as means to satisfy men's short-term sexual needs and society's need for children. Although Nietzsche's statements on the repression of feeling seem to be psychologically inconsistent with the unhappiness of his own family experience and although they are somewhat out of line with his defense of spontaneity and the affirmation of life, they are not inconsistent with his philosophical views on modernism, decadence, the order of rank, the "war" of the sexes, the psychology of domination—in short, all of the fundamental themes of the narrow psychology of the will to power. He himself states that the dissatisfaction that is felt with modern marriage should constitute "no objection to marriage but to modernity." Nietzsche's counterproposal to "modern ideas" is to reintroduce an extreme form of authoritarianism into the power structure of all social and economic institutions. Authoritarianism becomes the alternative to the "decadence" of modern life, while its censorship agent, intolerance, becomes the weapon of "justice" against the *threat* of criticism and (progressive) change.

The question still remains: why would anyone who suffered much unhappiness from a highly authoritarian family situation want to both intensify the structure of authority and prescribe this higher level of repression as a norm for future relationships? A psychological approach is needed to complete the investigation of Nietzsche's defense of authoritarianism since a philosophical method of argument is obstructed here by Nietzsche's uncritical recourse to the "virtue" of intolerance. In *The Mass Psychology of Fascism* Wilhelm Reich offers a possible explanation for the adherence of individuals to a blind psychological posture toward some forms of authority. Reich suggests that the authoritarian psychic structure can be so ingrained in an individual that even if other important needs conflict with it, the individual will hold fast to authoritarian values. In fact, he or she may find himself or herself especially drawn to authoritarian political leadership and to authoritarian social structures.[31] This general insight may be applied to Nietzsche's case by noting that Nietzsche's fascination with authority as well as his rebellion against authority are evident in his theories on sexuality, marriage, and the family structure just as they are evident in his rebellion against traditional morality and in his restructuring of morality through the idea of a destined "order of rank" among human "types." While Nietzsche fought some forms of authoritarianism very hard, apparently he was not able to measure the extent to which he himself remained dependent upon an authoritarian method of reasoning.

As suggested earlier, a major clue to why Nietzsche remains dependent upon blind authority can be taken from his statements on sexuality. For the purposes of this argument let us assume (with Freud and Reich) that the main repressive function of the family structure is the repression of spontaneous sexuality. Let us suppose, too, that religion is the main force that has been used traditionally to reinforce parental and social proscriptions of the enjoyment of sexual freedom. Immediately it will become clear that Nietzsche rebelled against the "castrating" effect of religion (especially Christianity) and that from a philosophical point of view he criticized all moralities of asceticism as anti-sexual and anti-natural ("anti-life"). However, still influenced by the male-dominated values of the Christian religion that he otherwise opposed, Nietzsche turned the psychic mechanism of repression not against the sex drive as such, but against the feeling of love associated with the sexuality of woman. In Nietzsche's proposed version of the authoritarian family, as well as in his theory of society at large, what is fundamentally repressed is not sexual activity as such but, on the one hand, the feeling of love for another human being and, on the other, the feeling of solidarity with other human beings as members of a common species with oneself. The members of the ruling class, as Nietzsche has envisioned them, cannot attain

full consciousness of their humanity because even the most intimate relationship they have with another human being (the sexual relationship)
is ruled by a master-slave power structure.[32]

Nietzsche's idea of an "order of rank" is an artificial and intellectually
unacceptable doctrine based on a rigorously oversimplified view of reality.
This rigid adherence to fixed categories is a special example of self-deception in a thinker whose primary metaphysical project was to show that
all being is in flux, that there is no "being," only "becoming." It represents an attempt to generate in society at large an ethical and political
structure which would simply duplicate the distorted experiences of a
highly isolated and socially alienated individual. Rather than being the
incarnation of natural justice, Nietzsche's order of rank is the attempted
institutionalization and objectification of a highly distanced and alienated view of human relations. A compulsive distance among individuals
(even among those of the highest rank) is mandated by the requirements
of *Rangordnung*. Even friends must obey the rules of distance dictated by
the order or rank. Nietzsche's Zarathustra teaches that the friend must
always be regarded as standing at a height. He counsels that one must
never reveal one's true nature to one's friend. The point of the disguise is
to cover up all of the weaknesses that make one human as well as to
exclude the possibility of love and compassion from the friendship. Men
who are incapable of pursuing Zarathustra's model of friendship are lik-
ened to women and animals.[33] Nietzsche's use of these images is inherently dualistic. The "higher" human being must draw the meaning of his
existence from the distance he perceives between himself and others
whom he calls the "herd," the "slave," the "wife," the "effeminate." The
distance insulates the "higher" person from the impurities of the "lower"
and helps to maintain the myth that the distant person is superhuman.
Thus the dualism between good and evil appears to plague Nietzsche's
theory of values from beginning to end—both in the doctrines that he
undertook to fight and in some of the principal alternatives that he set
up in their place.

Having said this much, however, my final project is to consider
whether Nietzsche can be said to be necessarily trapped in this dualistic
perspective or whether there are grounds to say that he could have tran-
scended it through the avenues in which he criticized dualism. This requires that, having noted the limitations of Nietzsche's theory of values,
we do not rest with too rigid a reading of the political implications of his
theory.

Conclusion

One of the more interesting political questions that can be directed at Nietzsche's politics is one he suggested himself when the object of his attack was the democrat or the Christian. When applied to Nietzsche, the question is: who is to profit from Nietzsche's proposed system of values? Who is to profit from the exploitation of the many by the few, of the "lower" by the "higher"? At once it is evident that it would be the "few" although not the "higher." Anyone whose height demanded the conscious exploitation and/or enslavement of others would be neither "high" nor "deep," as Nietzsche recurringly claimed. But that is another matter.

While Nietzsche's ideas are targeted against socialism and egalitarianism, I believe that it is a mistake to draw the inference from this alone that Nietzsche must be taken as a spokesman for capitalist and imperialist ideologies. Nietzsche's ideology was necessarily elitist, but he was not so crude as to perceive the elite as those who wield the most money or the most military power. The "imperialism" advocated by Nietzsche is of a much more subtle nature than this. It is an imperialism of "rank," of "moral authority," of "philosophic vision." Its elevated rhetoric and tone, however, do not match the blind and mediocre suggestions with which these phrases are associated as a matter of practical application. Nietzsche's rhetoric of rank is therefore highly misleading. Who would not want to see Europe led by men and women of the highest philosophical vision? But already we find in *Beyond Good and Evil* a major obstacle to the practical application of this ideal when we are told that the role of women is to be silent in politics and furthermore that woman is incapable of speaking truthfully.[34] Even so, *some* would say, who would not want to see Europe led by *men* of the highest philosophical vision, these "philosophers of the future" to whom Nietzsche dedicates his thoughts in *Beyond Good and Evil*? But when we inquire what these thoughts are in practical terms, we are led to unmask the elevated rhetoric as an empty effort to make a political and ethical myth out of a few banal and destructive attitudes, such as considering oneself a member of a highly select group or devaluing others so that, by contrast, one appears to be heroic.

Here I would call attention to the distinction between Nietzsche's "philosophical" and nonphilosophical thoughts which, given the nature of Nietzsche's aphoristic writings, has often been used to separate the essential from the nonessential elements in his writings. For example, Kaufmann has claimed that Nietzsche's views on women are inessential to his theory of values.[35] Danto has claimed that Nietzsche's references to slavery as a natural kind are a thoughtless error.[36] The distinction between what is essential to Nietzsche "as philosopher" and what is not has been used to either disclaim or deemphasize the connection between Nietzsche's high-sounding rhetoric (e.g., "order of rank," "higher man," "philosophers of the future") and the idiosyncratic opinions Nietzsche associated with these words (e.g., tyranny "in every sense," slavery in every sense, breeding in every sense).[37] I suggest, as a counterthesis, that the weeding out of the least attractive elements in Nietzsche's work amounts to either self-deceit or censorship, and that, in any case, this practice keeps us from understanding the whole of Nietzsche's vision. I have stressed that both the elevated rhetoric and the banal application of such terms as the "order of rank" and the "higher man" belong to Nietzsche's legacy. Nietzsche's work needs to be understood both where it is critical and where it is anti-critical. The issue my analysis raises is that there is a highly anti-critical streak in Nietzsche's *entire* theory of the "order of rank" and the practical applications drawn from it. By Nietzsche's own admission, the morality of *Rangordnung* upon which his political vision and his vision of "destiny" rest is highly uncritical. Here we encounter Nietzsche as Anti-Critic. In advocating the theory and practice of *Rangordnung,* Nietzsche becomes the Anti-Critic *par excellence.*

As long as one gives philosophical credibility to the rhetoric of the "superior type" or "higher" person and sets aside the political and practical implications of how this rhetoric is instantiated both by Nietzsche and by the historical patriarchal tradition in which we still live, we are defending what I shall call "the politics of unspecified prejudice." While the *logic* of unspecified prejudice calls for the higher/lower distinction without committing itself to any particulars to fill those categories, Nietzsche has made it quite clear what groups are by "nature" or "destiny" higher and what lower. Here are two statements regarding women and workers, two groups which Nietzsche has condemned to the "low." Reversing Goethe's statement that "the eternal feminine draws us higher," the author of *Beyond Good and Evil* wrote: "I do not doubt that every nobler woman will resist this faith, for she believes the same about the Eternal-Masculine."[38] The criterion for a woman's "nobility," then, is her "faith" that the male, as male, is more noble than herself. This insidious rhetoric is also applied to the slave, who is urged to believe that his exploitation is justified because the master/aristocrat is more noble than he. When one unmasks the realities of this rhetoric, one sees that the practical advantages do not go to "superior" persons—even assuming there were such types—but simply to the privileged classes of the established society. Nietzsche himself points this out in *Twilight of the Idols*:

> *The labor question.* The stupidity—at bottom, the degeneration of instinct, which is today the cause of *all* stupidities—is that there is a labor question at all. Certain things one does not question: that is the first imperative of instinct. . . . But what was done? . . . [T]he instincts by virtue of which the worker becomes possible as a class, possible in his own eyes, have been destroyed through and through with the most irresponsible thoughtlessness. The worker was qualified for military service, granted the right to organize and to vote: is it any wonder that the worker today experiences his own existence as distressing—morally speaking, as an injustice? But what is *wanted?* I ask once more. If one wants an end, one must also want the means: if one wants slaves, one is a fool if one educates them to be masters.[39]

Again, the theme of the "strength" of *not questioning* the structure of power that serves the interests of a privileged class is not simply antiliberal to the point of malice (as Nietzsche suggests in the aphorism that precedes this one). It is anti-critical to the point of malice. These statements on women, the working class, and the need of the privileged class for thoughtless and obedient "slaves" are not simply isolated opinions on Nietzsche's part, as sometimes they tend to be read. They are logically tied to other notions that Nietzsche is *commended* for holding—Such as the distinction between the "superior" person and the "herd," the belief in a "strong" culture, and even the love of one's fate. The fact that we ignore the concrete side of the issue while holding on to the more abstract side shows that in this case we are much less logical than Nietzsche, for we are the ones caught in a much larger type of contradiction even though his logic is tight with respect to the connection between elitism and oppression. This is the contradiction between his intended affirmation of life and his reactionary and nihilistic politics.

Still, the political implications of Nietzsche's thought can be turned around to some extent if we ask: was not Nietzsche correct in insisting upon a logical connection between a "strong" masculine ideal, a "strong" culture, and a blind system of political exploitation and psychological repression? Is it not true that if the goal of one's values is to implement a "strong" patriarchal system where a few will command and the rest will obey, it is then foolish to allow moral codes which favor the notions of the universal brotherhood and sisterhood of human beings? Does not the morality of universal human dignity entail in theory, if not also in practice, the elimination of all forms of elitism, domination, and oppression? In Nietzsche's idea of "greatness" one finds the logic of the extreme—of this he was well aware. But thanks to his uninhibited articulation of the extreme he has exposed the logic of patriarchal domination in its essence. While Nietzsche has outlined various incentives for overturning the democratic influences of modern times and for instituting a "purer" system of patriarchal domination under the banner of overcoming the "evils" of "effeminacy" and "decadence," it is up to us, not to him, to make the choice as to what we want our political future and our moral values to be. His appeals to destiny, intolerance, and the suspension of critical questioning of authoritarian political institutions are not convincing.

But Nietzsche was not simply a self-deceived spokesman for an extremely repressive system of patriarchal domination. There are also a series of important issues where he was able not only to expose but also to criticize substantially some of the most important (negative) effects of patriarchal culture. Nietzsche challenged the so-called "moral" system of rewards and punishments, the dualism between good and evil, the alienation of human consciousness from the earth, the nihilism inherent in many of our highest values, the false models of the individualism to which we have subscribed both philosophically and politically, and the inauthenticity of mass consciousness in our times. He has contributed to the development of metaphysics and epistemology by insisting upon an honest self-examination of the origins of our claims to knowledge and of our conception of being. On the positive side, his ontology gives tribute to what may be referred to metaphorically as the "innocence of becoming" or the dance of life. His unwillingness to reify such categories as substance and permanence and thereby to negate the vitality of the flux of becoming indicates that, at least in some areas of philosophical study, he denied some of the most basic principles of authoritarian world-conceptions inherited from the past. As we look into the future, these more promising issues may be given special attention to show the extent to which Nietzsche challenged the dualism of good and evil which he found to be so damaging to human fulfillment and the creative life."[40]

Notes

1. Nietzsche's critique of how Christianity acquired political power may be seen as an elaboration of this thesis. See *On the Genealogy of Morals*, trans. Walter Kaufmann and R. J. Hollingdale, in *On the Genealogy of Morals and Ecce Homo*, ed. Walter Kaufmann (New York: Vintage Books, 1967), part I, § 6 and passim.

2. See *Thus Spoke Zarathustra* [hereafter cited as Z], trans. Walter Kaufmann (New York: Viking Press, 1966), Part I, Prologue, § 4, pp. 14–16; Part II, "On the Famous Wise Men," pp. 103–105; "On Self-Overcoming," p. 116. See also *Ecce Homo* [hereafter cited as EH], trans. Walter Kaufmann, in *On the Genealogy of Morals and Ecce Homo*, op. cit., "Why I Am a Destiny," p. 326.

3. EH, pp. 326–35.

4. Karl Jaspers, *Nietzsche*, trans. C. R. Wallraff and R. J. Schmitz (Chicago: Henry Regnery, 1965), p. 256 ff.

5. Walter Kaufmann, *Nietzsche: Philosopher, Psychologist, Antichrist* (4th ed., Princeton: Princeton University Press, 1974), pp. 287–306.

6. *Beyond Good and Evil* [hereafter cited as J], trans. Walter Kaufmann (New York: Vintage Books, 1966). See especially § 252–253.

7. *Nietzsche Werke* [hereafter cited as NW], ed. Giorgio Colli and Mazzino Montinari (17 vols.; Berlin: De Gruyter, 1967–77), VII, 65, 25 [206–213]. The note dates from the spring of 1884; the particular reference to the English was omitted from *Der Wille zur Macht*, § 862.

8. J, § 44, p. 55.

9. J, § 242, pp. 176–77.

10. EH, p. 327.

11. J, § 242, p. 177.

12. See Georg Lukács' discussion of Nietzsche's philosophy in *Die Zerstörung der Vernunft* (3 vols.: Darmstadt und Neuwied: Hermann Luchterhand, 1974).

13. An English translation of this essay may be found in Volume II of *The Complete Works of Friedrich Nietzsche*, ed. Oscar Levy (18 vols.: New York: Russell and Russell, 1964).

14. See Nietzsche's "Critique of Modernity" in *Twilight of the Idols* [hereafter cited as G], trans. Walter Kaufmann, in *The Portable Nietzsche*, ed. Walter Kaufmann (New York: Viking Press, 1968), p. 543.

15. *The Will to Power*, trans. Walter Kaufmann and R. J. Hollingdale, ed. Walter Kaufmann (New York: Vintage Books, 1967), § 957, p. 502.

16. J, § 251, p. 189.

17. J, § 242, p. 176.

18. Z, I, "On the New Idol," pp. 48–51.

19. J, § 187, pp. 99–100.

20. Z, II, "On the Tarantulas," p. 101.

21. J, § 257, p. 201.

22. J, § 258, p. 202.

23. J, § 259, p. 203.

24. Ibid.

25. J, § 258, p. 202.

26. J, § 262, p. 210.

27. G, p. 543.

28. G, p. 544.

29. Ibid. For the idea of woman as property see also *J*, § 238, p. 167.

30. *NW*, VIII3, 291, 16 [35]. The statement also appears in *Der Wille zur Macht*, § 733, where the words "for days" are left out.

31. Reich, *The Mass Psychology of Fascism*, trans. V. R. Carfagno (New York: Touchstone, 1970), pp. 19–33.

32. As Marx noted, from the character of the relationship of man to woman one may assess the level of human development attained by man. This relationship reveals "how far man's *natural* relationship has become *human*" and "how far man's needs have become *human* needs." "Private Property and Communism," in *Early Writings*, trans. T. B. Bottomore (New York: McGraw-Hill, 1964), p. 154.

33. *Z*, I, "On the Friend," pp. 55–58.

34. *J*, § 232, 162–64.

35. Kaufmann, *Nietzsche*, p. 84.

36. Arthur Danto, *Nietzsche as Philosopher* (New York: Columbia University Press, 1965), p. 161.

37. Throughout most of *Beyond Good and Evil* Kaufmann translates *Zucht* and *Züchtung* as "cultivation." In his study of Nietzsche, however, Kaufmann admits that Nietzsche's use of these terms comes closer to "breeding" than to "cultivation." Still, he disclaims that Nietzsche meant "breeding" in the literal sense. See Kaufmann, *Nietzsche*, pp. 304–306.

38. *J*, § 236, p. 165.

39. G, "Skirmishes of an Untimely Man," § 40, p. 545.

40. I have developed these themes in *Beyond Nihilism* (Chicago: University of Chicago Press, 1984).

15

Nietzsche's Squandered Seductions: Feminism, the Body, and the Politics of Genealogy

David Owen

The unconscious disguise of physiological needs under the cloaks of the objective, ideal, purely spiritual goes to frightening lengths—and often I have asked myself whether, taken a large view, philosophy has not been merely an interpretation of the body and a *misunderstanding of the body*.

(Nietzsche, 1974, preface 2)

Having just paid myself such a deal of pretty compliments I may perhaps be more readily permitted to utter a few truths about 'woman as such': assuming it is now understood from the outset to how great an extent these are only—*my* truths.

(Nietzsche, 1973, 231)

The question of how to read Nietzsche's pronouncements on women presents a difficulty: on the one hand, one may read them as simply various aspects of a reactionary and contradictory essentialism; on the other hand, one may attempt to read them as masks manifesting an anti-essentialist pluralization and, indeed, dissolution of the category of 'woman'.[1] Both of these strategies of reading exhibit a certain ontological politics: the former manifests itself as a legislative determination of the order of meaning, while the latter discloses itself as poetic dissolution of the possibility of a determinate semantic order. The question of how to read the idea of 'woman' in Nietzsche's texts, places the philosopher within the opposition between the figures of the lawgiver and the poet. Confronted by this *either/or* of ontological politics, what is at stake is the status of philosophical reflection.[2]

Before going any further, however, and perhaps we have already gone too far, too fast, let's pause to ask the question of how this placing in question of the status of philosophy itself interacts with the question of 'woman' as an issue for feminist modes of thought.[3] The topic which appears to present itself within this reflective moment is that of the *either/or* of essentialism anti-essentialism with respect to the articulation of a feminist politics. To adopt an essentialist (i.e., metaphysical) conception of woman, is this not—paradoxically—to empower a feminist *politics* through an engagement in precisely that legislative exclusion of otherness which feminism attempts to overcome? While to displace 'woman' through an anti-essentialist poetics, is this not to exemplify an openness to otherness which, however, negates its own force through a surrendering of the identity of a *feminist* politics and, thereby, can only exhibit a capitulation to the *status quo*?[24] Perhaps and perhaps. The aim of this essay is to try to think through the interaction of the question of the status of philosophical reflection and the question of feminism through an engagement with Nietzsche's texts. We may then view the *either/or* structures which these questions confront us with not in terms of a demand for a decision but as an agonistic space in which thought becomes strategic.[5] I'll begin by sketching Nietzsche's perspective theory of affects and its relation to the idea of will to power and eternal recurrence, before taking up the implication of this philosophical stance for feminism. I'll then go on to consider the role of genealogy as both rational and rhetorical argumentation, before returning finally to the specific issue of Nietzsche's remarks on women.

A Perspective Theory of Affects

In a note from 1887 entitled *'Fundamental innovations'*, Nietzsche remarks, "In place of 'epistemology', a perspective theory of affects" (Nietzsche, 1968a: 255, §462); what is the character of this displacement? To clarify this we may address a fairly lengthy passage from the third essay of the *Genealogy* in which Nietzsche offers us both his understanding of epistemology and his alternative to it:

> Henceforth, my dear philosophers, let us be on guard against the dangerous old conceptual fiction that posited a 'pure, will-less, painless, timeless, knowing subject'; let us guard against the snares of such contradictory concepts as 'pure reason', 'absolute spirituality', 'knowledge in itself': these always demand that we should think of an eye that is completely unthinkable, an eye turned in no particular direction, in which the active and interpreting forces, through which alone seeing becomes seeing *something*, are supposed to be lacking; these always demand of the eye an absurdity and a nonsense. There is *only* a perspective seeing, *only* a perspective 'knowing'; and the *more* affects we allow to speak about one thing, the *more* eyes, different eyes, we can use to observe one thing, the more complete will our 'concept' of this thing, our 'objectivity' be. But to eliminate the will altogether, to suspend each and every affect, supposing we were capable of this—what would that mean but to *castrate* the intellect? (Nietzsche, 1969: 119, GM 111 §12)[6]

Within the metaphorical architecture Nietzsche deploys here two central themes emerge: a critique of epistemology as being grounded on illusory ideas of the noumenal subject and the thing-in-itself, and an anti-essentialist conception of 'knowledge' as *affective interpretation,* that is, a claim that our perspectives are grounded in the 'active and interpreting forces' of the body, namely, the affects.[7] In thinking about Nietzsche's account of knowledge, it may be worthwhile to focus briefly on each of these themes.

Nietzsche's critique of the idea of the noumenal subject is predicated on the claim that this idea represents the illegitimate assumption that the structure of grammar mirrors the structure of the world. The proposition 'I know', (like the proposition 'lightning flashes') doubles the event through a projection of the subject-predicate distinction onto the world (Nietzsche, 1969: 45, GM 1 §13). It is through this 'most rudimentary form of psychology' that there is created the belief 'in 'ego', in the ego as being, in the ego as substance, and which *projects* its belief in the ego-substance onto all things—only thus does it *create* the concept 'thing'. . . .' (Nietzsche, 1968b: 38, T1 *'Reason' in Philosophy* §5). The idea of the thing-in-itself is simply a product of the belief in a noumenal subject. For Nietzsche the idea of a thing-in-itself as an essence which is independent of all possible knowers is inherently contradictory (Nietzsche, 1973: 27–28, §16). He states his mature position on the appearance/reality distinction as follows:

> What is 'appearance' for me now? Certainly not the opposite of some essence: what could I say about any essence except to name the attributes of its appearance! Certainly not a dead mask that one could place on a unknown *x* or removed from it! (Nietzsche, 1974:116, §54).

This point is put rather more polemically in a note from 1888 when Nietzsche caustically comments: 'The perspective . . . decides the character of the 'appearance'! As if a world would still remain over after one deducted the perspective!' (Nietzsche, 1968a:305, §567).

The conclusions Nietzsche draws from this position are threefold: firstly, that the 'subject' may be considered as a multiplicity rather than as possessing some prefabricated unity (Nietzsche, 1973:25–26 §12 & 1968a:270–71, §490); secondly, that both the knowing subject and the known world are constituted through the activity of knowing;[8] and, thirdly, that the character of the knower and the known is governed by an affectually grounded perspective. The displacement of epistemology by a perspective theory of affects is grounded in these three claims.

In the section *"Our new infinite."* in *The Gay Science*, Nietzsche makes two points relevant to this discussion. Firstly, he notes that the question of whether all existence is engaged in interpretation, that is, whether or not there might be the possibility of a nonperspectival knowing, cannot be answered insofar as "the human intellect cannot avoid seeing itself in its own perspectives, and *only* in these"; and, secondly, he suggests that "the world has become 'infinite' for us all over again, inasmuch as we cannot reject the possibility that *it may include infinite interpretations*" (Nietzsche, 1974:336–37, §374). With the first of these claims, I take Nietzsche to be arguing that there are *ontological* limits to the kinds of perspectives through which we can constitute ourselves (we cannot experience time backwards, for example). However, with the second point, Nietzsche is suggesting that, even within these limits, an infinite number of interpretations may be possible. This latter claim becomes clear though only if we cease to think of the affectual forces which manifest themselves in perspectives as directly physiological in character (if they were the number of perspectives would surely be rather limited) and, rather, focus on them as physiological drives mediated through existential needs and cultural interests, where this process of mediation gives rise to what we may term 'practical interests'. This interpretation of the affects finds support in Nietzsche's genealogical interpretation of the ascetic ideal, where the physiological need of self-preservation is expressed as an existential interest which humans have in accounting for suffering (Nietzsche, 1969: GM III 23 & 28). Moreover, this interpretation suggests that, in referring to the embodied character of perspectives, Nietzsche is operating with a conception of the 'lived body' as the evaluating agency which is expressed in the activities of interpretation (we may note in passing that this dovetails with Nietzsche's contention that conscious thinking is only the smallest and most superficial part of the activity of thinking).[9] Consequently, we may summarize Nietzsche's position by stating that the perspective theory of affects entails the (anti-essentialist) claim that 'knowledge' is a product of interpretations anchored in the practical interests of the 'lived body.'[10]

What, then, are the implications of this theory? Generally, it operates as a critique of the claim that any perspective can claim an *a priori* position of privilege with respect to knowledge (and, thereby, as a critique of any perspective which makes such a claim). In this sense, Nietzsche is arguing that there are no theoretical grounds on which competing interpretations may be judged, however, this does not entail that there are *no* grounds on which such adjudication can be made.

On the contrary, by grounding the perspectives in the practical interests of the 'lived body', it would seem reasonable for Nietzsche to claim that the 'best' interpretation is that which expresses the dominant practical interests of the 'lived body' and is, thus, capable of ruling (i.e., imposing a structure on) the others. Actually we may go further than this, for insofar as we have no grounds on which to claim that distinct perspectives are necessarily incommensurable (though they may turn out to be so), it is quite possible to conceive of an oligarchy of ruling practical interests and, even, a democracy of practical interests.[11]

The significant points in need of examination here are twofold. Firstly, insofar as specific interpretations do turn out to be incommensurable, the very idea of judging between them requires a principle of intelligibility. We may also consider, secondly, that insofar as the idea of the 'lived body' discloses a conception of individuals as contingent cultural constructions, whose embodiedness entails the uniqueness of their experiences of the world, it follows that the specific content of their practical interests is also unique. This entails that what counts as the 'best' interpretation is not *necessarily* the same for all individuals and, therefore, that any possible universal principle of judgment must be strictly formal in character, in the sense of providing a rule which both applies to situations irrespective of their content and yet does not presuppose universality of content with respect to the outcome of its application (Kant's categorical imperative, for example, satisfies the first but not the second of these conditions). Such a principle of judgment is simultaneously a principle of rank in that judgment between conflicting interpretations is also a ranking of practical interests (or allied groups of practical interests).

Will to Power and Eternal Recurrence

The argument to be developed here is that the principle of intelligiblity that Nietzsche offers is the idea of the *will to power* and the principle of judgment he presents is the doctrine of *eternal recurrence*. The claim being made is that the idea of will to power denotes the formal architectonic interest of the 'lived body' in experiencing itself as a (organization) unity and that the doctrine of eternal recurrence articulates this interest as a ground of judgment.

Nietzsche requires a principle which renders intelligible the idea of adjudicating between incommensurable interpretations to avoid slipping into an absolute relativism, however, in the construction of his theory, Nietzsche has ruled out the possibility of appeal to any affect as possessing an *a priori* position of dominance (including the drive to self-preservation).[12] In this context, the purely formal architectonic interest of the 'lived body' in experiencing itself as a unity provides Nietzsche with a principle of intelligibility in that while incommensurable interpretations express the struggle of different affects (or alliances of affects), the goal of this struggle is the power to command (Nietzsche, 1968a:267, §481). The *telos* of all the practical interests is to become (i.e., give content to) the architectonic interest. The claim that this architectonic interest, operating as a principle of intelligibility, is denoted by the idea of will to power is based on Nietzsche's contention that all the effects are expressions of the will to power in a nominalist sense—you yourselves are also this will to power—and nothing besides!' (Nietzsche, 1968a:550, §1067)—and his identification of the will to power as the principle of intelligibility:

> The world seen from within, the world described and defined ac-
> cording to its "intelligible character"—it would be 'will to power'
> and nothing else. (Nietzsche, 1973:49 §36).

On this basis, it seems reasonable to construe the idea of will to power as
denoting the architectonic interest of the 'lived body'. Why though
should we consider the doctrine of eternal recurrence as articulating this
interest as a principle of judgment? This can, perhaps, be most clearly
illustrated by contrasting Nietzsche's position with that of Kant.

In a letter from 1978, Kant writes that it was the antinomies of pure
reason which awoke him from his dogmatic slumbers.[13] It is, perhaps, in
keeping this anti-dogmatic spirit awake that Nietzsche reveals his critical
relationship to Kant's thought. The specific site of Nietzsche's critique is
the dualist form that Kant's resolutions of the antinomies of pure reason
takes; namely, Kant's positing of two isomorphic realms of reason: the
realm of theoretical reason defined as a phenomenal realm of appearances
determined by the scientific laws of nature, and the realm of practical
reason identified as the noumenal realm of things in themselves governed
by the moral law of freedom. For Nietzsche, Kant's need for the idea of a
noumenal realm represents fundamentally "the same old sun, but shining
through mist and skepticism; the idea [of the real world] grown sublime,
pale, northerly, Königsbergian" (Nietzsche, 1968b:40, TI *How the 'Real
World' at last became a myth* §3). How is Nietzsche himself able to think
the relationship between freedom and necessity, if not as a metaphysical
relationship? An initial response would be to suggest that Nietzsche
thinks this relationship as a *temporal* relationship in which the past denotes the realm of necessity and the future that of freedom. The will
cannot will backwards, that is its most lonely affliction.[14] Within the
transformation that Nietzsche enacts here, however, the peculiar double
nature of man as both free and determined is preserved. This double
nature, however, exhibits itself not as phenomenal object and noumenal
subject, but as the 'lived body's' inscription within the temporal structure
of the *moment*—the gateway which marks the conjunction of past and
future[15]—as both becoming (freedom) and being (necessity). What are
the implications of Nietzsche's transformation of the thinking of the relationship of freedom and necessity for the question of autonomy? In Kant's
thought, the division between the sensible world and the intelligible
world yields a division between nature on the one hand and the free,
rational, moral will on the other. Kant presents autonomy in terms of

moral freedom, that is, an autonomous will is one whose determination has not been governed by heteronomous interests such as instinct, pleasure or desire. In other words, an empirical will manifests its autonomy insofar as the structure of this will exhibits an identity with the transcendental form of the moral law. By contrast, Nietzsche's thought offers us a division between past and future, a division between the 'lived body' as it was and the 'lived body' as it will be, which finds its site of confrontation in the structure of the moment. In this context, Nietzsche presents autonomy in terms of "the right to make promises" (Nietzsche, 1969:57–60, GM II §1–2), that is, an autonomous agency is one in which past agency affirms itself as future agency and future agency affirms itself as past agency, or, more precisely, an autonomous agency is one in which the moment of acting affirms both the acting and the momentariness of this acting. This contrast can be clarified further by comparing Kant's notion of the categorical imperative and Nietzsche's idea of the eternal return of the same.

The comparison can be illustrated by contrasting the Kantian maxim 'act always according to that maxim you can at the same time will as universal law' with the Nietzschean maxim 'act always according that that interpretation you can at the same time desire as eternally returning'. The crucial difference between these positions has been expressed well by Ansell-Pearson:

> Like the categorical imperative, the thought of eternal return has a universal character or form, but unlike the categorical imperative it does not posit a universal content. However, it might be argued in response that the categorical imperative too is a purely formal doctrine, for it has no determinate content. But the key point is that, although the categorical imperative is indeed formalistic, its willing does *presuppose* that the actions the autonomous will is to will are universal in content. . . . The eternal return, however, provides the form of universality only in the act of returning, whereas what returns (the actual content) and is willed to be returned cannot be universal, since each life (each becoming) is unique. (Ansell-Pearson, 1991:198)

What are the implications of this transformation? Kant's conception of autonomy is moral, for Nietzsche, precisely insofar as it presupposes universality with respect to content, whereas Nietzsche's own conception of autonomy is extra-moral insofar as it presupposes singularity relative to content. The crucial moment in this transformation is the movement from a probity which exhibits itself as universality to a probity which is singular.[16] The idea of eternal return, on this reading, denotes the structure of this singular probity, that is, the construction of a *pathos of distance*—"Do you desire this once more and innumerable times more?"—which *enables* the 'lived body' to reflect on itself *and* the construction of a formal imperative which *requires* the selection of the interpretation(s) and, therefore, the practical interest(s) which govern one's acting. The idea of eternal recurrence enables judgment at the same time as it demands judgment.[17] We should note here, moreover, that insofar as probity serves as the ground of one's own value and dignity as a human being, the idea of eternal recurrence entails a recognition of the dignity of others regardless of the 'content' which they give to their lives; this becomes apparent when we note that although probity is constituted as a relationship of self to self, this constitutive *activity* takes place within the space of intersubjective relationships with others. In considering this doctrine as a principle of judgment, we may also note that the force of this extra-moral imperative of probity (i.e., intellectual conscience) is dependent on its being experienced as a *bodily* thinking. This point is expressed by Nietzsche both in his presentation of Zarathustra's experience of his 'abysmal thought' as an affectual experience[18] and in the passage *"The greatest weight"* in *The Gay Science*, where he writes:

> If this thought gained possession of you, it would change you as you are or perhaps crush you. The question in each and everything, 'Do you desire this once more and innumerable times more?' would lie upon your actions as the greatest weight. Or how well would you have to become to yourself and to life *to crave nothing more fervently* than this ultimate eternal confirmation and seal? (Nietzsche, 1974:274, §341)

This comment should not surprise us, Nietzsche remarks in book five of *The Gay Science* that man "thinks continually without knowing it; the thinking that rises to *consciousness* is only the smallest part of all this— the most superficial and worst part" (Nietzsche, 1974:299, §354), but it does provide further support for the interpretation of the 'lived body' as agency in Nietzsche's philosophy.

At this juncture, having illustrated the theoretical apparatus which informs Nietzsche's anti-essentialist and non-relativist conception of philosophy, we can turn to the topic of the practical tasks of this philosophy. To explore this dimension of Nietzsche's project requires that we take up the notion of genealogy as a 'genre of reasoning' which operates as a practical deconstruction of the opposition between reason and the affects through the deployment of modes of argumentation which are simultaneously rational and rhetorical.[19] However, before attempting this task, it is necessary to explore briefly the implications that Nietzsche's conception of philosophy has for feminism.

Interlude: Philosophy, Feminism, and the Public Sphere

As the paradigmatic exemplar of public discourse, philosophy grounds its legislative authority in the identification of a public community whose needs and values it articulates. In this respect, reflection on the idea of the public sphere is intimately tied to the question of the authority of philosophy. Consequently, contemporary feminist critiques of the conceptions of the public which disclose themselves in the philosophical tradition bear directly on the topic of the legitimacy of philosophical authority. A central site for the articulation of such feminist critiques is the opposition of reason and affectivity. I shall briefly sketch the form of a feminist argument on this issue before turning to Nietzsche's significance for this question.

For feminism the ideal of an impartial normative rationality, which animates modern moral and political philosophy, expresses a logic of identity which "seeks to have everything under control, to idealize the bodily fact of sensuous immersion in a world that outruns the subject, to eliminate otherness" (Young, 1987:61). To achieve its 'desire' of a homogeneous unity, the ideal of impartiality as "the point of view of a solitary transcendent God" (Young, 1973:62) requires that normative reason expel from itself all that is particular, contingent, bodily. The structure of this movement may be summarized as follows:

> the construct of an impartial point of view is arrived at by abstracting from the concrete particularity of the person in situation. This requires abstracting from the particularity of bodily being, its needs and inclinations, and from the feelings that attach

to the experienced particularity of things and events. Normative reason is defined as impartial and reason defines the unity of the moral subject, both in the sense of knowing the universal principles of morality and in the sense of what all moral subjects have in common in the same way. This reason thus stands opposed to desire and affectivity as what differentiates and particularizes persons. (Young, 1987:62–63)

Two points attend the logic of this movement: firstly, a grounding of the authority of philosophy in its claim to impartiality and, secondly, the identification of the realm of reason with the public sphere and that of affectivity with the private sphere. Historically, this movement engenders an isomorphic relationship between the opposition of reason and affectivity, on the one hand, and man and woman, on the other hand. Now it should be noted at this juncture that feminist argumentation can develop in two distinct directions from this point: *either* it can seek to breach the historical isomorphism by retaining the opposition between (public) reason and (private) affectivity, yet divorcing this from sexual difference or, more radically, it can question the opposition between reason and affectivity which defines modern moral and political thought. How does Nietzsche's thought intersect with these modes of questioning?

To begin with, it would seem apparent that Nietzsche's perspective theory of affects offers a conception of philosophical activity which is not predicated on the opposition of reason and affectivity but, rather, through the idea of will to power articulates an understanding of 'affective reason' which does not abstract from the particularity of bodily desire. Moreover, by locating his thought as extra-moral—in the sense of deconstructing the ideal of an impartial normative rationality—Nietzsche opens up a space within which ethics is constructed as that probity whose structure is disclosed by eternal recurrence and which entails respect for otherness as a condition of one's own claim to respect. However, if Nietzsche's thought presents us with an attack on the metaphysical understanding of impartiality, with what is this to be replaced? To grasp this issue, we may argue, drawing on Nietzsche's understanding of 'objectivity' as viewing from multiple affectual perspectives,[20] that a concrete, non-metaphysical conception of 'impartiality' would entail evaluation from multiple affectual perspectives.[21]

With respect to feminist concerns, the implications of Nietzsche's thinking are twofold. Firstly, Nietzsche's perspective theory of affects and his idea of will to power presents a route for thinking beyond the opposition of reason and affectivity which opens up the possibility of rethinking the public/private distinction in a way that it does not engender the exclusion or repression of otherness. Secondly, the thought of eternal recurrence as a purely formal universal principle of judgment entails respect for otherness, while Nietzsche's notion of 'impartiality' registers a commitment to an understanding of justice in which judgment recognises its contingency and partiality. To explore the engaged character of this conception of philosophy, we may (re)turn to the topic of genealogy.

The Tasks of Genealogy

Genealogy as the practical engagement of philosophy with life may be read as a concern with elaborating how we have become what we are. This engagement discloses itself as a project of interpretative clarification which, firstly, traces the affectual bases of specific culturally entrenched interpretations through an account of emergence and development of the practical interests expressed in these interpretations; and, secondly, which examines the capacity of these interpretations to meet the architectonic interest of the 'lived body' in experiencing itself as a unity through an interpretation of the present; and, thirdly, elaborates the possibilities that its interpretation opens up to us. In this sense, genealogy is always a reading on a bias in that the condition of possibility of any genealogical investigation is that it expresses a particular practical interest.[22] We should also emphasize that, insofar as it is the 'lived body' which is the evaluating agency in Nietzsche's thought, genealogy must communicate to the 'lived body' as both conscious and unconscious thinking. Taking these points together we may note Nietzsche's conception of 'objectivity' and its stylistic correlate. The notion of 'objectivity' is set out in the third essay of the *Genealogy* where Nietzsche presents it as 'the ability *to control* one's Pro and Con and to dispose of them, so that one knows how to employ a variety of perspectives and affective interpretations in the service of knowledge. . . . the *more* affects we allow to speak about one thing, the more complete will our 'concept' of thing, our 'objectivity' be' (Nietzsche, 1969:119, GM III §12). The stylistic correlate to this multiplicity of interpretations is offered in *Ecce Homo*:

> To communicate a state, an inward tension of pathos, by means
> of signs, including the tempo of these signs—that is the meaning
> of every style; and considering that the multiplicity of inward
> states is exceptionally large in my case, I have many stylistic possi-
> bilities—the most multifarious art of style that has ever been at
> the disposal of one man. (Nietzsche, 1969:265, EH *Why I write*
> *such good books* §4)

The implication of this passage being, perhaps, that just as each practical
interest expresses itself consciously through language as interpretation, so
too it manifests itself unconsciously through language as style.[23] This, in
turn, entails that genealogical accounts must be capable of satisfying certain minimal criteria of, what we may term, rational-rhetorical accept-
ability, namely, adequacy at the level of interpretation (i.e., rational
coherence) and adequacy at the level of style (i.e., affectual correspondence).

In the context of this description of the project of genealogy as a mode
of rational and rhetorical argumentation, we may pose the question of
the politics of genealogy—the relation of this 'genre of reasoning' to the
either/or structure of essentialism and anti-essentialism posed with respect
to the status of philosophical reflection and the issue of feminist politics.
Let us use the example of Nietzsche's concept of 'modernity'. And let us
initially re-emphasize that the perspective theory of affects rules out any
idea of the concept of 'modernity; as referring to some essence of the
modern condition or 'modernity-in-itself', rather, the concept of 'modernity; is constituted by the appearance of the modern condition under
different interpretations. In the case of Nietzsche, the concept of 'modernity' is presented both as nihilism (the devaluation of all values)[24] and
collective degeneration (the diminution of man to the perfect herd animal).[25] In interpreting the modern condition as nihilism, Nietzsche is
expressing a practical interest in overcoming the will to truth; while in
viewing the modern condition as collective degeneration, he is expressing a practical interest in overcoming the will to equality. The implication of Nietzsche's interpretations of the modern condition in terms of
these practical interests is that he is making the claim that they are the
dominant practical interests of the age and, consequently, that the central concern of modern culture *must* be with constructing structures of
recognition which express these interests. Of course, to render this claim
credible Nietzsche has to generate both an account of how these practical

interests came to be the dominant interests and to elaborate the possibilities which the modern condition confronts us with. Now we may note
here that while the genealogical accounts and interpretations Nietzsche
offers with respect to these interests may be commensurable, they are
non-identical and as such constitute a constellation or force-field (to
borrow Adorno's metaphors) within which the semantic content of the
concept 'modernity' is constituted. The significant points disclosed by
this example are twofold.

Firstly, while Nietzsche rejects the idea of the concept of 'modernity'
as referring to any essence of the modern condition and may, *perhaps*,
admit that an infinite number of interpretations of the modern condition
are 'theoretically possible' (whatever this would mean), his grounding of
perspectives in the affects suggests that, in practice, concomitantly, there
are a limited number of possible interpretations of the modern condition.
Moreover, Nietzsche's position as expressed relative to the concept of
'modernity' is that it is the interpretations of the modern condition
which express the dominant practical interests of the age which rule the
constitution of the semantic content of this concept.[26] In this sense, we
can think of Nietzsche as operating a form of 'strategic essentialism',
that is, presenting the 'essence' of the modern condition as nihilism and
collective degeneration in order to strategically ground, as *legislation*, the
imperatives expressed by the practical interests of overcoming the will to
truth and the will to equality. At the same time, however, this 'strategic
essentialism' remains open, both in the sense that it is historically contingent and, therefore, that these particular practical interests may not (and,
indeed, are extremely unlikely to) remain culturally dominant, and, perhaps more importantly, in the sense that it cannot claim any *a priori*
university, the doctrine of eternal recurrence as a universal principle of
judgment rules out such a claim while entailing respect for otherness.

The second point which emerges from this example is that the force
of Nietzsche's claim that a dominant concern of modern culture *must*
be to construct structures of recognition which express the interests of
overcoming nihilism and collective degeneration is dependent on the
capacity of his genealogical accounts to constitute an affectually bound
'community of judgment' which acknowledges these interests as of primary concern.[27] In other words, it is dependent on, firstly, the adequacy
of Nietzsche's genealogical accounts in terms of rational coherence and
affectual correspondence, that is their capacity to communicate, to the
'lived body' of the reader (who has ears?),[28] the architectonic interest of

the 'lived body' in the rule of these particular practical interests and, secondly, the success of these practical interests in surviving the test of eternal recurrence.

The implications of this discussion for our questions concerning the status of philosophical reflection and the topic of a feminist politics are, it is hoped, apparent. With regard to the first of these, it seems that the philosopher as legislator and the philosopher as poet are mutually dependent in the sense that, substantively, it is the poetic construction of a community of judgment which grounds legislation, while, formally, it is the interest in legislation which grounds poetic expression. In considering the issue of a feminist politics, it appears that Nietzsche's genealogical practice offers a notion of 'strategic essentialism' which enables the construction of a specifically feminist politics around a concept of 'woman' constituted through particular practical interests, while remaining open to otherness in that this concept of 'woman' is a contingent construction.[29]

At this juncture, we may sum up this section by suggesting that what Nietzsche's conception of philosophy provides is an opening within which the question "Who are we?" is perpetually answered and yet remains perpetually open. However, in the light of this claim that Nietzsche's conception of philosophy is as such profoundly enabling for feminism, this may be an appropriate moment to turn to Nietzsche's remarks about women.

Nietzsche's Strategies: Varieties of "Woman"

In this discussion, rather than providing a comprehensive survey of Nietzsche's comments concerning the figure of woman, I will confine myself to only two of the types of remark that Nietzsche makes on this topic. Firstly, there are the comments attacking the idea of 'woman-as-such' or 'woman-in-herself' and the feminist movement of his time. Secondly, there are the remarks which re-evaluate the value of 'woman'. In considering these remarks, I'll restrict myself to Nietzsche's extended discussions of women in The Gay Science (§§60–75) and Beyond Good and Evil (Preface and §§231–239).

We may note initially that the first category of remark postulated, Nietzsche's attacks on the idea of 'woman-as-such' and the feminist

movement, may be rendered intelligible, without indulging in psychoanalytic speculation, as strategic interventions governed by Nietzsche's practical interests in overcoming the will-to-truth and the will-to-equality.
For example, these interests are addressed respectively in *Beyond Good
and Evil*, sections 232 and 239. In the former, Nietzsche writes:

> Woman wants to be independent: and to that end she is begin-
> ning to enlighten men about 'woman as such'—*this* is one of the
> worst developments in the general *uglification* of Europe. (Nietz-
> sche, 1973:144, §232)

The process of uglification being identified later in this section with the
scientific will to truth expressed in the Enlightenment; Nietzsche's concern manifests itself here as a critique of feminism as *bad taste* in the sense
that he regards feminism as exemplifying the desire for moral judgment
which requires precisely that metaphysical apparatus which engenders
nihilism.[30] In section 239, this critique is connected to Nietzsche's interest in attacking political Enlightenment as a will-to-equality.

> Since the French Revolution the influence of woman in Europe
> has grown *less* in the same proportion as her rights and claims
> have grown greater; and the 'emancipation of woman', in so far as
> it has been demanded by women themselves (and not merely by
> male shallow-plates), is thus revealed as a noteworthy symptom
> of the growing enfeeblement and blunting of the most feminine
> instincts. . . . To be sure, there are sufficient idiotic friends and
> corrupters of woman among the learned asses of the male sex who
> advise woman to defeminize herself in this fashion and to imitate
> all the stupidities with which 'man' in Europe, European 'manli-
> ness', is sick. . . . (Nietzsche, 1973: 148–49, §239)

The feminist movement, read on this bias, is a contribution to the "collective degeneration" of humans to the level of "the perfect herd animal"
in that it operates as a leveling movement which further undermines
the aristocratic ordering of society requisite to the production of "great
culture." [31] In articulating this critique of feminism both as a form of
metaphysical essentialism and as a political movement, Nietzsche is deploying a strategic identification of 'the feminine' which reproduces the
features ascribed to 'woman' by the metaphysical tradition. However, as

the second category of comments makes clear, this identification also involves a revaluation of 'woman' through a strategic reversal of the hierarchy of value constructed within the metaphysical tradition.

This strategy reveals itself, for example, in the opening of the preface to *Beyond Good and Evil* where Nietzsche remarks:

> Supposing truth to be woman-what? is the suspicion not well founded that all philosophers, when they have been dogmatists, have had little understanding of women? that the gruesome, the clumsy importunity with which they have hitherto been in the habit of approaching truth have been inept and improper means for winning a wench? Certainly she has not let herself be won— and today every dogmatism stands sad and discouraged. *If* it continues to stand at all! (BGE, *Preface*)

In identifying truth with woman, Nietzsche is inverting the Platonic understanding of truth as non-perspectival and, thereby, revaluing woman. This strategy is developed in various sections of *The Gay Science*, notably 60, 64, 339 and 361 in which the identification of woman with seduction, perspectivism, life, and art explores the different dimensions of this revaluation as a reclamation of the affects. However, in noting this inversion of metaphysical hierarchies, we should also note that, as in the first category of remark, Nietzsche inscribes the figure of 'woman' within an economy which reduplicates the metaphysical identification of 'woman' as "the other of the same."[32]

It is at this juncture that the purely *strategic* nature of Nietzsche's 'essentialism' becomes significant. The location of Nietzsche's comments in the context of his practical interests entails that their force is dependent on the capacity of Nietzsche's genealogies to constitute a community of judgment which recognizes the interests of overcoming the will-to-truth *and* the will-to-equality as dominant. Such a community being both contingent and open in the sense of recognizing its contingency. We may also note here that Nietzsche's two interests, while commensurable, are distinct, such that we can pose the question of the necessity of their relationship. If they are not *necessarily* related (and this is my own position), it follows that we may, for example, accept Nietzsche's criticisms of a metaphysical/essentialist feminism without endorsing his attack on the ideas of sexual equality and democracy. In other words, Nietzsche's remarks on women in no way vitiate the value of his general approach for contemporary feminist thought, while the value of his specific genealogies for feminism remains (as the value of genealogies should) perpetually contestable. Perhaps, too, this is an appropriate place at which to end this discussion—within a space of uncertainty in which the question "Who are we?" remains endlessly open to reflection.

References

Ansell-Pearson, K. (1991). *Nietzsche contra Rousseau*. Cambridge University Press, Cambridge.
Nietzsche, F. (1968a). *The Will to Power*. W. Kaufmann, and R. J. Hollingdale (trans.). Random House, New York.
Nietzsche, F. (1968b). *Twilight of the Idols & The Anti-Christ*. R.J. Hollingdale (trans.). Penguin, Middlesex.
Nietzsche, F. (1973). *Beyond Good and Evil*. R. J. Hollingdale (trans.). Penguin, Middlesex.
Nietzsche, F. (1974). *The Gay Science*. W. Kaufmann (trans.). Random House. New York.
Young, I. M. (1987). "Impartiality and the Civic Public." In *Feminism as Critique*. S. Benhabib, and D. Cornell (eds.). Polity Press, Cambridge.

Notes

1. Compare, for example, the readings offered by Ofelia Schutte in *Beyond Nihilism*, University of Chicago Press, Chicago (1984), with Jacques Derrida's in *Spurs: Nietzsche's Styles*, University of Chicago Press, Chicago (1987).

2. A text which addresses Nietzsche in terms of this aporia if interpretation and the question of the body (although not its relation to gender) is Eric Blondel's *Nietzsche: The Body and Culture*, Athlone Press, London (1991). See also my review in *History of the Human Sciences*, Vol. 5, No. 1 (1992).

3. I take feminism to refer to a concern with the interests, needs and desires of women. as such, feminism requires that the concept of 'woman' is given a certain substantive content in order to identify and articulate itself.

4. This point has been raised sharply by Kelly Oliver in her essay "Nietzsche's Woman: The Poststructuralist Attempt to do Away with Women," *Radical Philosophy* (Spring 1988).

5. It is perhaps one of the abiding problems, and seductions, of Rorty's thought that it remains within a rhetorical structure around the demand for decision presented by the formulation of *either/or*. I am grateful for Peter Lassman for pointing this out to me in his paper "Rorty's Rhetoric" (unpublished manuscript).

6. A fascinating and sophisticated reading of this passage is offered by Maudemarie Clark in chapter 5 of her book *Nietzsche on Truth and Philosophy*, Cambridge University Press, Cambridge (1990). However, by eluding the question of the affects, her reading remains rather disembodied; this is particularly apparent in her discussion of the idea of *will to power*.

7. This point has been forcefully made (as a critique of Rorty's voluntarism) by Daniel Conway in his essay "Disembodied Perspectives: Nietzsche contra Rorty," *Nietzsche Studien*, Vol. 21 (1992).

8. This point has been nicely argued by Tracy Strong in "Texts, Pretexts and the Subject" in his *Friedrich Nietzsche and the Politics of Transfiguration* (expanded edition), University of California Press, Berkeley and Los Angeles (1988).

9. Cf. Nietzsche 1974:298–99, §354.

10. Cf. Conway, ibid., p. 286, and Nietzsche, 1973:143–44, §231.

11. The political implications of the multitude of potential 'political forms' of the 'lived body' remain to be explored, although this topic has been touched on by Alexander Nehamas in *Nietzsche: Life as Literature*, Harvard University Press, Cambridge (1985). See in particular the chapter "How One Becomes What One Is."

12. Cf. Nietzsche, 1973:26, §13.

13. Kant to Garve, 26 September 1798, cited in M. A. Gillespie, *Hegel, Heidegger and the Ground of History*, University of Chicago Press, Chicago (1984), pp. 30–31.

14. Cf. Nietzsche *Thus Spoke Zarathustra*, R. J. Hollingdale (trans.). Penguin, Middlesex (1961), part II, "Of Redemption," p. 161.

15. Cf. Nietzsche, ibid., part III, "Of the Vision and the Riddle," pp. 178–79.

16. An interesting discussion of the issue of probity is developed by Jean-Luc Nancy in his essay "Our Probity!" On Truth in the Moral Sense in Nietzsche," in *Looking After Nietzsche*, L. A. Rickels (ed.). SUNY Press, Albany (1990).

17. For an excellent opposed reading of eternal recurrence and the theme of judgment, cf. Howard Caygill, "Affirmation and Eternal Return in the Free-Spirit Trilogy," in *Nietzsche and Modern German Thought*, K. Ansell-Pearson (ed.), Routledge, London (1991).

18. The nature of Zarathustra's "bodily experience" of the thought of eternal recurrence is particularly clear in Nietzsche, *Thus Spoke Zarathustra*, part III, "The Convalescent," pp. 232–38.

19. For example, one might note the recent collection edited by Michele Barrett and Ann Phillips, *Destabilizing Theory*, Routledge, London (1992), whose very title signals the stakes involved here.

20. Cf. Nietzsche, 1969:119, GM III §12.

21. Nietzsche gestures toward such a conception of 'impartial' judgment in Nietzsche, 1968a:149–50, §259.

22. One might suggest that Nietzsche's position here reveals a certain similarity to Max Weber's account of the construction of an ideal-type around particular evaluative interests; cf. " 'Objectivity' in Social Science and Social Policy," in *Methodology of the Social Sciences*, E. A. Shils, and H. A. Finch (trans.), The Free Press, New York, (1949). That Nietzsche's conception of genealogy views any investigation as operating on a bias, that is with a "system of injustice," is forcefully argued by Michel Foucault in his essay "Nietzsche, Genealogy, History," in *The Foucault Reader*, P. Rabinow (ed.), Penguin, Middlesex (1984).

23. One could develop this further through a deployment of the distinction between the symbolic and semiotic found in Julia Kristeva's *Revolution in Poetic Language*, Columbia University Press, New York (1984).

24. Cf. Nietzsche, 1968a:9, §2.

25. Cf. Nietzsche, 1973:108–9, §203.

26. Nietzsche may be read here as providing a site on which one could relate the essential contestability thesis developed from Wittgenstein's later philosophy of language to Max Weber's conception of methodology as governed by the "great cultural problems of the age" and his identification of the "scientific genius" as the figure whose "evaluative interests" define the dominant parameters of our self-understanding (a position Weber ascribed jointly to Nietzsche and Marx).

27. I'm deploying the idea of a "community of judgment" in the sense developed by Tracy Strong in his essay "Nietzsche's Political Aesthetics," in *Nietzsche's New Seas*, M. A. Gillespie, and T. A. Strong (eds.), University of Chicago Press, Chicago (1988).

28. The issue of reading has been acutely addressed by Kelly Oliver in her essay "The Ethics of

Reading: Nietzsche's *On the Genealogy of Morals*" (unpublished manuscript), in which she examines the ambivalences which attend Nietzsche's relationship to his audience through a focus on thematics of the body and desire which characterize Nietzsche's conceptions of writing and reading.

29. A similar position has been articulated by Samantha Ashenden in her essay "Foucault and Feminism" (unpublished manuscript) and relatedly by Kelly Oliver in her piece "Fractal Politics: How to Use 'The Subject,' " *Praxis International*, 11:2(July 1991).

30. Cf. Nietzsche, 1974:266, §335.

31. Cf. Nietzsche, 1973:173–74, §257.

32. The claim that Nietzsche's entire philosophy remains with this economy of identifying woman as the other of the same is elaborated by Luce Irigaray in her *Marine Lover of Frederich Nietzsche*, G. Gill (trans.), Columbia University Press, New York, (1991). It seems to me that, despite her sophistication, Irigaray's reading of Nietzsche as enchained within the *logos* of metaphysics fails to address the strategic nature of Nietzsche's thought. However, it may be that Irigaray's "love" seeps through into the notion of the body in ways I have failed to address here.

Select Bibliography

Ackermann, Robert John. *Nietzsche: A Frenzied Look*. Amherst: University of Massachusetts Press, 1990.

Addelson, Kathryn Pyne. "Nietzsche and Moral Change." In *Nietzsche: A Collection of Critical Essays*, edited by Robert Solomon. New York: Doubleday, 1973.

Ainley, Alison. " 'Ideal Selfishness': Nietzsche's Metaphor of Maternity." In *Exceedingly Nietzsche*, edited by David Farrell Krell and David Wood. London: Routledge, 1988.

Allen, Christine Garside. "Nietzsche's Ambivalence about Women." In *The Sexism of Social and Political Theory: Women and Reproduction from Plato to Nietzsche*, edited by Lorenne M. G. Clark and Lynda Lange. Toronto: University of Toronto Press, 1979.

Ansell-Pearson, Keith. "Who is the Übermensch? Time, Truth, and Woman in Nietzsche." *Journal of the History of Ideas* 53, no. 2 (1992): 309–31.

Babich, Babette E. *Nietzsche's Philosophy of Science: Reflecting Science on the Ground of Art and Life*. Albany: State University of New York Press, 1994.

Battersby, Christine. *Gender and Genius: Towards a Feminist Aesthetics*. Bloomington: Indiana University Press, 1989.

Behler, Diana. "Nietzsche and Postfeminism." In *Nietzsche-Studien: Internationales Jahrbuch für die Nietzsche-Forschung*, 1993.

Berg, Elizabeth L. "The Third Woman." *Diacritics* 12 (1982): 11–20.

Bergoffen, Debra B. "On the Advantages and Disadvantages of Nietzsche for Women." In *The Question of the Other: Essays in Contemporary Continental Philosophy*, edited by Arlene Dallery and Charles E. Scott. Albany: State University of New York Press, 1989.

Booth, David. "Nietzsche's 'Woman' Rhetoric: How Nietzsche's Misogyny Curtails the Implicit Feminism of His Critique of Metaphysics." *History of Philosophy Quarterly* 8, no. 3 (1991): 311–25.

Burney-Davis, Terri, and E. Stephen Krebbs. "The 'Vita Femina' and Truth." *History of European Ideas* 11 (1989): 841–47.

Butler, Judith. *Bodies that Matter: On the Discursive Limits of "Sex."* New York: Routledge, 1993.

Caputo, John D. "Supposing Truth To Be A Woman . . .": Heidegger, Nietzsche, Derrida." *Tulane Studies in Philosophy* 32 (1984): 15–21.

Clark, Maudemarie. *Nietzsche on Truth and Philosophy.* New York: Cambridge University Press, 1990.

Cocks, Joan. "Nietzsche and Contemporary Body Politics." *Differences* 3, no. 1 (1991): 144–58.

Cornell, Drucilla. *Transformations: Recollective Imagination and Sexual Difference.* New York: Routledge, 1993.

Crawford, Claudia. *To Nietzsche: Dionysus, I Love You! Ariadne.* Albany: State University of New York Press, 1995.

Del Caro, Adrian. "The Pseudoman in Nietzsche; or, The Threat of the Neuter." *New German Critique* 50 (1990): 135–56.

Deleuze, Gilles. *Nietzsche and Philosophy.* Translated by Hugh Tomlinson. New York: Columbia University Press, 1983.

Derrida, Jacques. "*Geschlecht*: Sexual Difference, Ontological Difference." In *A Derrida Reader: Between the Blinds,* edited by Peggy Kamuf. New York: Columbia University Press, 1991. (Originally published 1980.)

———. *Spurs/Eperons: Nietzsche's Styles/Les Styles de Nietzsche.* Translated by Barbara Harlow. Chicago: University of Chicago Press, 1979.

Diethe, Carol. "Nietzsche and the Woman Question." *History of European Ideas* 11 (1989): 865–75.

Diprose, Rosalyn. *The Bodies of Women: Ethics, Embodiment, and Sexual Difference.* New York: Routledge, 1994.

Doane, Mary Ann. "Veiling Over Desire: Close-ups of the Woman." In *Feminism and Psychoanalysis,* edited by Richard Feldstein and Judith Roof. Ithaca: Cornell University Press, 1989.

Draine, Betsy. "Writing, Deconstruction, and Other Unnatural Acts." *Why Nietzsche Now? A Boundary 2 Symposium* 9–10 (1981): 425–36.

Elam, Diane. *Feminism and Deconstruction.* New York: Routledge, 1994.

Foot, Philippa. "Nietzsche's Immoralism." *New York Review of Books* 13 (June 1991): 18–22.

Graybeal, Jean. *Language and "the Feminine" in Nietzsche and Heidegger.* Bloomington: Indiana University Press, 1990.

Grosz, Elizabeth. *Volatile Bodies: Toward a Corporeal Feminism.* Bloomington: Indiana University Press, 1994.

Higgins, Kathleen Marie. *Nietzsche's "Zarathustra."* Philadelphia: Temple University Press, 1987.

Irigaray, Luce. *An Ethics of Sexual Difference.* Translated by Carolyn Burke and Gillian C. Gill. Ithaca: Cornell University Press, 1993.

———. *Marine Lover of Friedrich Nietzsche.* Translated by Gillian C. Gill. New York: Columbia University Presses, 1991. (Originally published 1980.)

———. *Speculum of the Other Woman.* Translated by Gillian C. Gill. Ithaca: Cornell University Press, 1985.

Kennedy, Ellen. "Nietzsche: Women as Untermensch." In *Women in Western Political Philosophy: Kant to Nietzsche,* edited by Ellen Kennedy and Susan Mendus. New York: St. Martin's, 1987.

Kofman, Sarah. *The Enigma of Woman: Women in Freud's Writings*. Ithaca: Cornell University Press, 1985.

———. *Nietzsche and Metaphor*. Translated with an Introduction, Additional Notes, and a Bibliography by Duncan Large. Stanford: Stanford University Press, 1993. (Originally published 1983.)

Krell, David Farrell. *Postponements: Woman, Sensuality, and Death in Nietzsche*. Bloomington: Indiana University Press, 1986.

———. "To the Orange Grove at the Edge of the Sea: Remarks on Luce Irigaray's 'Amante Marine.'" In *Nietzsche and "The Feminine,"* edited by Peter J. Burgard. Charlottesville: University Press of Virginia, 1994.

Lorraine, Tamsin E. *Gender, Identity, and the Production of Meaning*. Boulder, Colo.: Westview, 1990.

Lungstrom, Janet. "Nietzsche Writing Woman/ Woman Writing Nietzsche: The Sexual Dialectic of Palingenesis." In *Nietzsche and "The Feminine,"* edited by Peter J. Burgard. Charlottesville: University Press of Virginia, 1994.

Magnus, Berndt, et al. *Nietzsche's Case: Philosophy As/And Literature*. New York: Routledge, 1993.

Martin, Biddy. *Woman and Modernity: The (Life)Styles of Lou-Andreas Salomé*. Ithaca: Cornell University Press, 1991.

Mortensen, Ellen. "Irigaray and Nietzsche: Echo and Narcissus Revisited?" In *The Fate of the New Nietzsche*, edited by Keith Ansell-Pearson and Howard Caygill. London: Aldgate, 1993.

Nash, Margaret. "Nietzschean Debris: Truth as Circe." In *Modern Engendering: Critical Feminist Readings in Modern Western Philosophy*, edited by Bat-Ami Bar On. Albany: State University of New York Press, 1994.

Nehemas, Alexander. *Nietzsche: Life as Literature*. Cambridge: Harvard University Press, 1985.

Oliver, Kelly. "Nietzsche's Woman: The Poststructuralist Attempt To Do Away With Women." *Radical Philosophy* 48 (1988): 25–29.

———. "The Plaint of Ariadne: Luce Irigaray's 'Amante Marine de Friedrich Nietzsche.'" In *The Fate of the New Nietzsche*, edited by Keith Ansell-Pearson and Howard Caygill. London: Aldgate, 1993.

———. *Womanizing Nietzsche: Philosophy's Relationship to the "Feminine."* New York: Routledge, 1995.

Oppel, Frances. "'Speaking of Immemorial Waters': Irigaray with Nietzsche." In *Nietzsche, Feminism, and Political Theory*, edited by Paul Patton. New York: Routledge, 1993.

Ormiston, Gayle. "Traces of Derrida: Nietzsche's Image of Woman." *Philosophy Today* (Summer 1984): 178–88.

Pautrat, Bernard. "Nietzsche Medused." In *Looking After Nietzsche*, edited by Laurence A. Rickels. Albany: State University of New York Press, 1990.

Schrift, Alan D. *Nietzsche and the Question of Interpretation: Between Hermeneutics and Deconstruction*. New York: Routledge, 1990.

———. *Nietzsche's French Legacy: A Genealogy of Poststructuralism*. New York: Routledge, 1995.

Schutte, Ofelia. *Beyond Nihilism: Nietzsche Without Masks*. Chicago: University of Chicago Press, 1984.

Sedgwick, Eve Kosofsky. *Epistemology of the Closet*. Berkeley and Los Angeles: University of California Press, 1990.

Shapiro, Gary. *Alcyone: Nietzsche on Gifts, Noise, and Women*. Albany: State University of New York Press, 1991.

Spivak, Gayatri Chakravorty. "Displacement and the Discourse of Woman." In *Displacement: Derrida and After*, edited by Mark Krupnik. Bloomington: Indiana University Press, 1983.

Starrett, Shari Neller. "Nietzsche: Women and Relationships of Strength." *Southwestern Philosophical Review* 6, no. 1 (1990): 73–79.

Thomas, R. Hinton. "Nietzsche, Women, and the Whip." In *Nietzsche in German Politics and Society, 1890–1918*. La Salle, Ill.: Open Court.

Thompson, J. L. "Nietzsche on Women." *International Journal of Moral and Social Studies* 5, no. 3 (1990): 207–20.

Tuana, Nancy. 1992. *Woman and the History of Philosophy*. New York: Paragon House, 1992.

West, Cornel. "Nietzsche's Prefiguration of Postmodern American Philosophy." *Why Nietzsche Now? A Boundary 2 Symposium* 9–10 (1981): 241–7.

Winders, James A. *Gender, Theory, and the Canon*. Madison: University of Wisconsin Press, 1991.

Contributors

DEBRA B. BERGOFFEN is professor of philosophy at George Mason University. She is the author of *The Philosophy of Simone de Beauvoir: Gendered Phenomenologies, Erotic Generosities* (State University of New York Press, 1997).

MAUDEMARIE CLARK is associate professor of philosophy at Colgate University. She is the author of *Nietzsche on Truth and Philosophy* (Cambridge University Press, 1990).

DANIEL W. CONWAY is associate professor of philosophy at the Pennsylvania State University. He is the author of *Nietzsche and the Political* (Routledge, 1996).

JACQUES DERRIDA is directeur d'études at the Ecole des Hautes Etudes en Sciences Sociales. His books include *Spurs: Nietzsche's Styles* (University of Chicago Press, 1979), *Dissemination* (University of Chicago Press, 1981), and *Margins of Philosophy* (University of Chicago Press, 1982).

JEAN GRAYBEAL is associate dean of the Gallatin School at New York University. She is the author of *Language and "the Feminine" in Nietzsche and Heidegger* (Indiana University Press, 1990).

KATHLEEN MARIE HIGGINS is professor of philosophy at the University of Texas, Austin. She is the author of *Nietzsche's Zarathustra* (Temple University Press, 1987) and *The Music of Our Lives* (Temple University Press, 1990).

LUCE IRIGARAY is a professor of philosophy and a psychoanalyst. She is director of research at the Centre National de la Recherche Scientifique, Paris. Her books include *An Ethics of Sexual Difference* (Cornell University Press, 1993), *Marine Lover of Friedrich Nietzsche* (Columbia University Press, 1991), *Speculum of the Other Woman* (Cornell University Press, 1985).

SARAH KOFMAN was professor of philosophy at the Sorbonne, Paris. Her publications include *Nietzsche and Metaphor* (Stanford University Press, 1993) and *The Enigma of Woman: Women in Freud's Writings* (Cornell University Press, 1985).

TAMSIN LORRAINE is associate professor of philosophy at Swarthmore College. She is the author of *Gender, Identity, and the Production of Meaning* (Westview, 1990).

KELLY OLIVER is associate professor of philosophy at the University of Texas, Austin. Her publications include *Reading Kristeva: Unraveling the Double-Bind* (Indiana University Press, 1993), *Womanizing Nietzsche: Philosophy's Relation to the "Feminine"* (Routledge, 1995), and *Family Values, Subjects Between Nature and Culture* (Routledge, 1997).

DAVID OWEN is lecturer in politics at the University of Southampton, England. His works include *Maturity and Modernity: Nietzsche, Weber, Foucault, and the Ambivalence of Reason* (Routledge, 1994) and *Nietzsche, Politics and Modernity: A Critique of Liberal Reason* (Sage Publications, 1995).

OFELIA SCHUTTE is professor of philosophy at the University of Florida, Gainesville. She is the author of *Beyond Nihilism: Nietzsche Without Masks* (University of Chicago Press, 1984) and *Cultural Identity and Social Liberation in Latin American Thought* (University of Chicago Press, 1986).

LINDA SINGER taught in the Department of Philosophy at Miami University, Ohio. her essays are collected in *Erotic Welfare: Sexual Theory and Politics in the Age of Epidemic* (ed. Judith Butler; Routledge, 1993).

LYNNE TIRRELL is associate professor in the Department of Philosophy at the University of Massachusetts, Boston. She has published articles in Continental philosophy.

KATHLEEN J. WININGER teaches in the Department of Philosophy at the University of Southern Maine.

Index

209–19; feminist theory and, 199–220,
221n.12; in Nietzsche, 12, 14–15, 16; Nietzsche's attack on, 203–5; Nietzsche's political
ideology and, 291–92, 300–304; sexes and,
205–9, 221n.12

Ecce Homo, 11, 64; abjection and feminine in,
152–67; genealogy in, 317–18; misogyny in,
201; self-realization and self-criticism in, 283;
sexes and dualism in, 205–6
education, Nietzsche on women and, 144–45,
180–81
Edwards, Rosalind, 280n.33
egalitarianism, Nietzsche's critique of, 247–49,
300–304
ego, in *Thus Spoke Zarathustra* and, 128n.7
Ehrenfels, Christian, 47–48
elitism, Nietzsche's embrace of, 287–89, 302–4
emancipation of women, Nietzsche on, 181–85
Enlightenment, Nietzsche's critique of, 321–22
Entfernung, Nietzsche's style and, 53
epistemology: feminist critique of Nietzsche
and, 15–16; feminist standpoint theory and,
260–74; in *The Gay Science*, 139–50; Nietzsche's slave revolt and, 252–79; perspective
theory of affects in, 307–11; perspectivism
and feminist theory of, 253–56; postmodern
feminist epistemology and perspectivism,
256–60; slave revolt and, 274–77
Erasmus, 233
error, motif of, in Nietzsche's work, 58–60
Eternal Feminine: in *Ecce Homo*, 153–67; misogyny of Nietzsche and, 193–97; mythology
of nature and, 175–77; Nietzsche's political
ideology and, 301
eternal recurrence: metaphysics and, 232–34;
will-to-power and, 311–15
Eumenides, 87–88, 92–93, 109n.3
European history, Nietzsche's critique of,
244–49
evil: master/slave morality and, 211–12; sexual
dualism and, 203–5, 208–9; in *Thus Spoke
Zarathustra*, 123–24, 129n.13; women linked
to, 2–3
existentialism: Nietzsche's concept of self and,
200, 202; Nietzsche's political ideology and,
293; sexual dualism and, 209–19
exploitation, political ideology of Nietzsche
and, 285–93

family, Nietzsche on institution of, 295–99
fate, in *Ecco Homo*, 165–67
faults, Irigaray's terminology of, 104, 117n.20
fear, fetishism and, 22–23; sexual dualism and,
218–19
feline imagery, in Nietzsche, 38, 48n.12; for
women, 38, 48nn.12–13
feminine narcissism, 210, 222n.23
femininity: existential view of women and,
213–19; feminine Nietzsche, 8–9, 241–43; Irigaray on, 87–107; as key to women's power,
207–8, 222nn.19–20; Nietzsche's suspicion
of, 182–85
feminist standpoint theory: epistemology and,
253, 260–74, 279n.16; Nietzsche and, 15–16;
slave revolt in morality and, 274–77,
279nn.11, 14, 280n.44
feminist theory: attacks on Nietzsche, 131–38;
castrated woman image, 68–72, 79n.8; castrating woman image, 72–75; existentialist
view of women and, 213–20; humor in Nietzsche and, 136–38, 148–50; on inconsistency
in Nietzsche, 146–47; language and women
and, 81–82; Nietzschean mythologies and,
173–85; Nietzsche's critique of, 321–23;
Nietzsche's critique of patriarchy and,
243–49; Nietzsche's female contemporaries,
236–38, 250n.7; perspectivism and epistemology, 253–56; politics of genealogy and,
306–23, 323n.3; postmodern feminist epistemology, 256–60; public discourse and,
315–17; sexual dualism in Nietzsche, 199–
220, 222nn.19–20; *Thus Spoke Zarathustra*
and, 119–28; truth of women and, 1–17;
Western canon and, ix–xi
fetishism: "coarse fetishism," 48n.1; Nietzsche's
theological perversions and, 21–48; *vs.* perversion, in Nietzsche, 23–27, 48n.16
flight imagery, reversal of values in Nietzsche
and, 34–35
food imagery, in *Thus Spoke Zarathustra*, 127–
28, 129n.25
Foucault, Michel, 324n.22
French Philosophes, Nietzsche and, 242
French Revolution, Nietzsche's political ideology and, 288–91
Freud, Sigmund: Baubô myth and, 49n.22; castration theory, 7, 48n.17; feminist theory and,
188; fetishism and, 22–23, 48n.16; Irigaray
on, 82, 111n.6; oneiric experiences and, 35;
on women and truth, 227–29